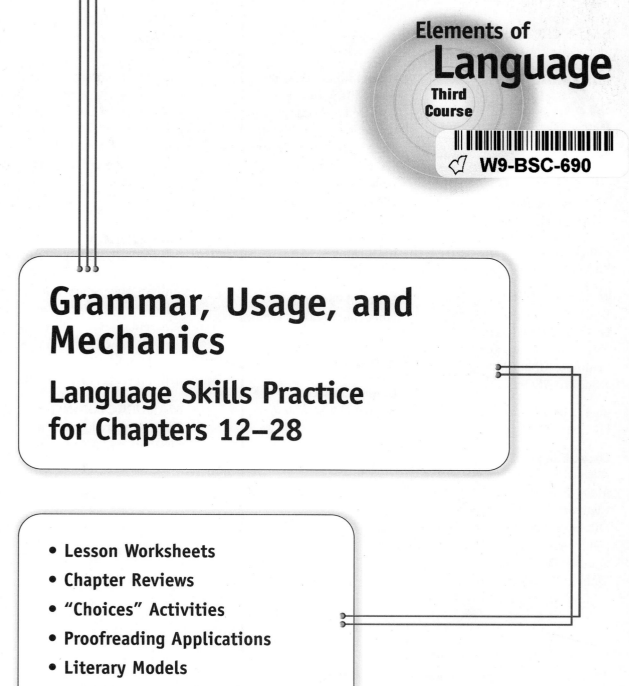

Elements of
Language
Third Course

W9-BSC-690

Grammar, Usage, and Mechanics

Language Skills Practice for Chapters 12–28

- Lesson Worksheets
- Chapter Reviews
- "Choices" Activities
- Proofreading Applications
- Literary Models
- Writing Applications

HOLT, RINEHART AND WINSTON

A Harcourt Classroom Education Company

Austin · New York · Orlando · Atlanta · San Francisco · Boston · Dallas · Toronto · London

STAFF CREDITS

EDITORIAL

Director
Mescal Evler

Manager of Editorial Operations
Bill Wahlgren

Executive Editor
Robert R. Hoyt

Project Editor
Kathryn Rogers

Writing and Editing
Eric Estlund, *Editor;* Randy Dickson, Annie Hartnett, Suzi A. Hunn, Jim Hynes, Kevin Lemoine, Amber M. Rigney, *Associate Editors*

Reviewer
Ed Vavra

Copyediting
Michael Neibergall, *Copyediting Manager;* Mary Malone, *Senior Copyeditor;* Joel Bourgeois, Elizabeth Dickson, Gabrielle Field, Jane Kominek, Millicent Ondras, Theresa Reding, Kathleen Scheiner, Laurie Schlesinger, *Copyeditors*

Project Administration
Marie Price, *Managing Editor;* Lori De La Garza, *Editorial Operations Coordinator;* Thomas Browne, Heather Cheyne, Diane Hardin, Mark Holland, Marcus Johnson, Jill O'Neal, Joyce Rector, Janet Riley, Kelly Tankersley, *Project Administration;* Gail Coupland, Ruth Hooker, Margaret Sanchez, *Word Processing*

Editorial Permissions
Janet Harrington, *Permissions Editor*

ART, DESIGN AND PHOTO

Graphic Services
Kristen Darby, *Manager*

Image Acquisitions
Joe London, *Director;* Tim Taylor, *Photo Research Supervisor;* Rick Benavides, *Assistant Photo Researcher;* Elaine Tate, *Supervisor;* Erin Cone, *Art Buyer*

Cover Design
Sunday Patterson

PRODUCTION

Belinda Barbosa Lopez, *Senior Production Coordinator*
Simira Davis, *Supervisor*
Nancy Hargis, *Media Production Supervisor*
Joan Lindsay, *Production Coordinator*
Beth Prevelige, *Prepress Manager*

MANUFACTURING

Shirley Cantrell, *Supervisor of Inventory and Manufacturing*

Printed in the United States of America

ISBN 0-03-056353-4

345–085–04030201

Contents

Contents

Chapter 15

THE CLAUSE:
INDEPENDENT AND SUBORDINATE CLAUSES

Chapter 16

AGREEMENT:
SUBJECT AND VERB, PRONOUN AND ANTECEDENT

Contents

Contents

Chapter 20

A GLOSSARY OF USAGE:
COMMON USAGE PROBLEMS

Chapter 21

CAPITAL LETTERS:
THE RULES FOR CAPITALIZATION

Chapter 22

PUNCTUATION:
END MARKS, ABBREVIATIONS, AND COMMAS

Contents

Contents

Using This Workbook

The worksheets in this workbook provide practice, reinforcement, and extension for Chapters 12–28 of *Elements of Language*.

Most of the worksheets you will find in this workbook are **traditional worksheets** providing practice and reinforcement activities on every rule and on all major instructional topics in the grammar, usage, and mechanics chapters in *Elements of Language*.

You will also find in the workbook several kinds of **Language in Context worksheets**, which have been developed to expand the exploration and study of grammar, usage, and mechanics. The Language in Context worksheets include Choices worksheets, Proofreading Applications, Literary Model Worksheets, and Writing Applications.

- **Choices** worksheets offer up to ten activities that provide new ways of approaching grammar, usage, and mechanics. Students can choose and complete one independent or group activity per worksheet. Choices activities stimulate learning through research, creative writing, nonfiction writing, discussion, drama, art, games, interviews, music, cross-curricular activities, technology, and other kinds of projects, including some designed entirely by students.

- **Proofreading Application** worksheets help students apply what they learn in class to contexts in the real world. Students use proofreading symbols like those found in the Writing section of the Quick Reference Handbook in *Elements of Language* to correct errors in grammar, usage, and mechanics in practical documents such as letters, applications, brochures, and reports.

- **Literary Model** worksheets provide literary models that demonstrate how published authors use various grammatical forms to create style or meaning. Students identify and analyze each author's linguistic choices and then use grammatical forms to create style or meaning in their own literary creations. Students are asked to reflect on their own linguistic choices and to draw connections between the choices they make and the style or meaning of their work.

- **Writing Application** worksheets are similar to the Writing Application activities in the grammar, usage, and mechanics chapters in *Elements of Language*. Following the writing process, students use specific grammatical forms as they create a publishable document such as a letter, report, script, or pamphlet.

The Teaching Resources include the **Answer Key** in a separate booklet titled *Grammar, Usage, and Mechanics: Language Skills Practice Answer Key*.

Choices: Exploring Parts of Speech

The following activities challenge you to find a connection between the parts of speech and the world around you. Do the activity below that suits your personality best, and then share your discoveries with your class.

TIME LINE

A First Time for Everything

What is the history of each part of speech? Make a time line showing when the terms *noun, pronoun, adjective, verb, adverb, preposition, conjunction,* and *interjection* were first used in English. (HINT: Look in the *Oxford English Dictionary*.) Then, with your teacher's approval, post your time line in the classroom.

RESEARCH

Deep Roots

Look up the etymologies of the parts of speech—*noun, pronoun, adjective, verb, adverb, preposition, conjunction,* and *interjection.* Name the root words of each term, and give your classmates a brief explanation of each.

VISUAL PRESENTATION

The Ins and Outs

Create a Venn diagram showing the relationships between transitive and intransitive verbs and action and linking verbs. Include example sentences for each section of the diagram. Explain the diagram so that everyone understands. Write several additional examples of verbs in sentences on the chalkboard, and help your classmates place them correctly in your diagram.

CREATIVE WRITING

Metamorphosing Metaphors

Write a poem composed mostly of words that can function as different parts of speech. Use each of these words as at least two parts of speech or even more, if you can!

ETYMOLOGY

Star Quality

Is grammar glamorous? Don't answer yet. First, look up the definition of the word *glamour,* and then decide. Next, write a short report detailing your findings and give copies to your classmates.

DRAMA

Shorthand

Compose a dialogue between two or more people. Here's the catch: Use only two parts of speech—any two you like. Tell your classmates to sit back and enjoy the show.

CREATIVE WRITING

A Household Word

Wouldn't it be great to have a word based on you or your name enter the English language? If there were a word based on your name, what would it be? What would its part of speech be? Write a story about how this word came into being.

CONTEST

Chameleon Conjunctions

Have a contest: Who can find a word that can function as the most parts of speech? The winner must present complete sentences appropriately using his or her word as each part of speech.

WORLD LANGUAGES

When in Rome

In today's world, many people speak more than one language. Ask around and find a few multilingual speakers. Ask them, "Do other languages use different parts of speech than English uses? If so, what are they?" Report your findings to the class.

ORIGINAL PROJECTS

None of the Above

If none of the projects above grab you, make up your own. Convert the parts of speech into colors, and color-code a paragraph. Translate the parts of speech into musical notes, code a paragraph, and play it. Identify some nouns, verbs, and adjectives that science has created in the last fifty years. Invent a new part of speech. Write a personality profile of a verb. Whatever you decide to do, get your teacher's approval first.

for **CHAPTER 12: THE PARTS OF SPEECH**   page 375

The Noun

12a. A *noun* is a word or word group that is used to name a person, a place, a thing, or an idea.

PERSONS	governor, children, Mr. Garcia, African Americans
PLACES	college, islands, rain forest, Kentucky
THINGS	computer, clouds, Ferris wheel, Lincoln Memorial
IDEAS	creativity, imagination, self-respect, Christianity

EXERCISE Underline each noun in the following sentences.

Example 1. The state of New Mexico is in the southwestern part of the United States.

1. New Mexico achieved statehood in the early twentieth century.

2. Santa Fe is the capital of this southwestern state.

3. It is the oldest and highest United States capital.

4. The city lies near the Sangre de Cristo Mountains, which is a range of the

Rocky Mountains.

5. The first European explorers here were Spanish.

6. Before Spanish colonists arrived, the Pueblo lived there peacefully.

7. The western end of the famous Santa Fe Trail was there.

8. The trail extended from Missouri to New Mexico.

9. It was a popular trade route for much of the nineteenth century.

10. Tourism is important to the economy of the state.

11. Santa Fe has many interesting attractions.

12. One popular attraction is the Palace of the Governors.

13. It is recognized as the oldest public building in the nation.

14. The palace is now a part of the Museum of New Mexico.

15. Santa Fe honors its Spanish and American Indian heritage at its many historical sites.

16. The city has one of the oldest churches in the United States.

17. Mission of San Miguel of Santa Fe is its name.

18. The Wheelwright Museum houses artwork created by Navajos.

19. In the center of the city are many shops and restaurants.

20. This bustling, historic area is named the Plaza.

Proper, Common, Concrete, and Abstract Nouns

A *proper noun* names a particular person, place, thing, or idea and is capitalized. A *common noun* names any one of a group of persons, places, things, or ideas and is generally not capitalized.

PROPER NOUNS	Sandra Cisneros, Houston, Statue of Liberty, Islam
COMMON NOUNS	author, city, monument, religion

A *concrete noun* names a person, place, or thing that can be perceived by one or more of the senses (sight, hearing, taste, touch, and smell). An *abstract noun* names an idea, feeling, quality, or characteristic.

CONCRETE NOUNS	violin, onions, word processor, Eiffel Tower
ABSTRACT NOUNS	peace, honor, self-control, Confucianism

EXERCISE A For each of the following sentences, draw one line under each common noun and two lines under each proper noun.

Example 1. Makenna, my friend, is a gifted violinist.

1. One of the fastest-growing sports in the United States is soccer.

2. *Moonrise, Hernandez, New Mexico* is one of the best-known photographs by Ansel Adams.

3. Climbers often speak of the mystical attraction they feel for Mount Everest.

4. Has Megan already invited you to her wedding?

5. His sister-in-law lives in Cedar Rapids.

6. Another name for Yom Kippur, which is a Jewish holiday, is Day of Atonement.

7. Bull sharks have been caught in the Mississippi River.

8. Enrico can play the trumpet, I believe.

9. Mount McKinley is also known as Denali.

10. The recipe calls for chopped jalapeños, doesn't it?

EXERCISE B On the line provided, identify each of the following nouns by writing *C* for *concrete noun* or *A* for *abstract noun*.

Example ___*A*___ **1.** beauty

_____**11.** peanuts

_____**12.** patriotism

_____**13.** totem pole

_____**14.** mountain

_____**15.** enthusiasm

_____**16.** truth

_____**17.** dragonfly

_____**18.** heritage

_____**19.** loyalty

_____**20.** Atlantic Ocean

Compound and Collective Nouns

A *compound noun* consists of two or more words used together as a single noun. The parts of a compound noun may be written as one word, as separate words, or as a hyphenated word.

ONE WORD	baseball, caregiver, willpower, Greenland
SEPARATE WORDS	guest of honor, school bus, North Forest High School
HYPHENATED WORD	self-confidence, president-elect, Stratford-on-Avon

A *collective noun* names a group.

EXAMPLES band, jury, class, swarm, group, herd

EXERCISE A Underline the compound nouns in the following sentences.

Example 1. We are planning a visit to our <u>grandparents</u> and other relatives in <u>San Francisco</u>.

1. This California city has perhaps the largest Chinese community in the United States.

2. Thousands of Chinese Americans live in Chinatown.

3. After the second new moon in winter, the Chinese New Year is celebrated by these and other Chinese people throughout the world.

4. My sister and brother-in-law sent me snapshots of last year's celebration.

5. The people say farewell to one year and welcome the next with great festivities.

6. Exploding firecrackers are part of the tradition.

7. Each year, my grandmother and I put up a new paper image of Tsao Shen, the Kitchen God.

8. Traditionally, many people eat seaweed for prosperity.

9. The celebration concludes with the Festival of Lanterns.

10. In 2000, the Chinese celebrated the Year of the Dragon.

EXERCISE B Underline the collective noun in each of the following pairs of nouns.

Example 1. <u>herd</u>   animals

11. children	family		**16.** Pep Club	cheerleaders
12. faculty	teachers		**17.** neighbors	community
13. committee	chairperson		**18.** orchestra	concert
14. Congress	Capitol		**19.** spectators	audience
15. football	team		**20.** flock	birds

Pronouns and Antecedents

12b. A *pronoun* is a word that is used in place of one or more nouns or pronouns.

The word that a pronoun stands for or refers to is called the *antecedent* of the pronoun. The pronoun may appear in the same sentence as its antecedent or in a nearby sentence.

EXAMPLES   The **children** gave **themselves** a big hand. [The antecedent of the pronoun *themselves* is *children*.]

Don and **Carla** finally solved the algebra **problem. They** had worked on **it** a long time. [The antecedents of the pronoun *They* are *Don* and *Carla*; the antecedent of the pronoun *it* is *problem*.]

EXERCISE A Underline the pronouns in the following sentences. Then, draw an arrow from each pronoun to its antecedent.

Example 1. Kendra searched for her ring, but she never found it.

1. Cesar invited his friends to go camping with him.

2. Erica said she had prepared the whole meal herself.

3. Why are the baseball players wearing their caps backward?

4. Jody and Michelle gathered things for a time capsule and buried it in their backyard.

5. Loni wore her suede boots in the snow. Now they are probably stained.

6. Juanita lent Dominic her calculator. He had left his in his locker.

7. Brian and Marla play golf whenever they can. It is their favorite sport.

8. Ahmal hopes to compete in the next Olympic games. Where will they be held?

9. Did Carolyn sprain her ankle while she was skating?

10. Carlos and Ann decided they could not stay indoors on such a beautiful day.

EXERCISE B Above the underlined words and word groups in the following sentences, write the pronouns that can correctly replace the underlined words and word groups.

Example 1. To many people, Jim Abbott is a hero. *They* Many people have found *his* Jim Abbott's courage and determination inspiring.

11. Baseball requires various talents and skills; the sport also demands great strength and stamina.

12. Jim Abbott played professional baseball despite the fact that Jim Abbott has only a thumb and no fingers on Jim Abbott's right hand.

13. Jim Abbott's disability did not stop Jim Abbott from succeeding as a major league pitcher.

14. Ed thought Ed had a baseball card showing Jim Abbott in Jim Abbott's New York Yankees uniform.

15. Perhaps the baseball card is in one of these other boxes. Let's look through these other boxes.

Personal, Reflexive, and Intensive Pronouns

A *personal pronoun* refers to the one speaking (first person), the one spoken to (second person), or the one spoken about (third person).

FIRST PERSON	I, me, my, mine, we, us, our, ours
SECOND PERSON	you, your, yours
THIRD PERSON	he, him, his, she, her, hers, it, its, they, them, their, theirs

A *reflexive pronoun* refers to the subject of a sentence and functions as a complement or as an object of a preposition. An *intensive pronoun* emphasizes its antecedent and has no grammatical function.

REFLEXIVE AND INTENSIVE PRONOUNS	myself, ourselves, yourself, yourselves, himself, herself, itself, themselves
EXAMPLES	**I** [personal] consider **myself** [reflexive] fortunate to have such good friends.
	They [personal] made the costumes **themselves** [intensive].

EXERCISE A   Underline the personal pronouns in the following sentences.

Example 1. She and I will meet you at the theater.

1. My teacher gave me another chance to answer the question correctly.

2. Did you see the painting that I did for the art fair at our school?

3. My mother reminded us that we had not fed the bird all day.

4. Cynthia and Julia took our books by mistake, and we picked up theirs.

5. Her father asked her to help him carry in the groceries from his car.

EXERCISE B   On the line in each of the following sentences, write a reflexive or an intensive pronoun that will correctly complete the sentence. Above the pronoun, write *REF* for *reflexive* or *INT* for *intensive*.

Example 1. The club members ____*themselves*____ prepared all of the food for their banquet.

6. What happened was an accident; you shouldn't blame _____.

7. Aunt Ling _____ made all of the decorations for the anniversary party.

8. Didn't Reginald paint a portrait of _____?

9. We could either buy the piñatas or make them _____.

10. I cut _____ when I was fixing the bicycle chain.

11. I am just not _____ today.

12. She raised the funds for the new equipment _____.

13. Tony is outside harvesting okra by _____.

14. Suzanne gave _____ a moment to catch her breath.

15. Did you two create that Web page _____?

Demonstrative, Interrogative, and Relative Pronouns

A *demonstrative pronoun* (*this, that, these, those*) is used to point out a specific person, place, thing, or idea.

EXAMPLE **This** is a snapshot of my pen pal from Quebec.

An *interrogative pronoun* (*who, whom, whose, which, what*) introduces a question.

EXAMPLE **What** is the capital of Canada?

A *relative pronoun* (*who, whom, whose, which, that*) introduces a subordinate clause.

EXAMPLE My brother works at the animal shelter **that** is located on Sycamore Street.

EXERCISE In each of the following sentences, identify the underlined pronoun by writing above it *DEM* for *demonstrative pronoun*, *INTER* for *interrogative pronoun*, or *REL* for *relative pronoun*.

Example 1. I applied for the job *that* I saw advertised in the school paper.

1. Who is your karate instructor?

2. Is that a picture of Charles Lindbergh's famous airplane?

3. The family that bought the house next door is moving in next week.

4. This is the song we sang in the talent show at school.

5. What will we do if it rains on the day of our picnic?

6. Who went to the movie with you yesterday?

7. Both actors who had lead roles in the play were somewhat nervous.

8. Those are the fans who sat near the back of the auditorium.

9. Of the planets Mars and Venus, which is closer to Earth?

10. Did you say that the girl who won the golf match is in the ninth grade?

11. Whom did Enrique invite to his Cinco de Mayo celebration?

12. This was the night for which the school orchestra had been preparing.

13. Which of the science exhibits is yours?

14. I enjoyed reading the short stories, especially those.

15. Who is the current secretary-general of the United Nations?

16. Oh, these are the tastiest empanadas I have ever eaten!

17. Marguerite, whose parents are doctors, knows a great deal about first aid.

18. Who is responsible for this?

19. Which of the puppies would you like to adopt?

20. Is that a direct quotation?

GRAMMAR

for **CHAPTER 12: THE PARTS OF SPEECH** *page 381*

Indefinite Pronouns

An *indefinite pronoun* refers to one or more persons, places, things, or ideas that may or may not be specifically named. Some common indefinite pronouns are *all, another, anybody, both, each, either, everyone, many, nothing, several,* and *some.*

EXAMPLES   A **few** of the students had already read **most** of the books on the list.

EXERCISE   Underline the indefinite pronouns in the following sentences.

Example 1. She knew the answers to <u>all</u> of the questions except <u>one</u>.

1. Everyone who went to the space camp had a wonderful experience.

2. Will you tell the others that the meeting has been canceled?

3. None of these keys will unlock either of those doors.

4. This peach is sweet. May I have another?

5. She can run faster than anyone on the school's track team.

6. I have read many of her short stories.

7. Is anything wrong? You act as if something is troubling you.

8. Ken and I spent much of July, August, September, and October working on a Kentucky horse farm.

9. Someone told me that the bald eagle is no longer on the list of endangered species.

10. The teacher asked, "Can anybody in the class name the capital of each of the states?"

11. A few of these baseball cards are extremely valuable.

12. Are you able to save any of your weekly allowance?

13. The performances by both of the comedians were hilarious!

14. Most of us have already seen that movie.

15. All but one of the club members voted to increase the membership dues.

16. Do we have everything we need for the picnic?

17. Neither of these flashlights works.

18. No one was absent from school today.

19. The principal requested that several of the art students paint a colorful mural on a wall of the school's lobby.

20. In their search for gold, some of the early prospectors found nothing but "fool's gold," or iron pyrite, which looks like gold.

ELEMENTS OF LANGUAGE I Third Course

Identifying Pronouns

12b. A *pronoun* is a word that is used in place of one or more nouns or pronouns.

EXAMPLES **She** bought **herself** a pair of skates like **those.** [*She* is a personal pronoun, *herself* is a reflexive pronoun, and *those* is a demonstrative pronoun.]
Who made **all** of the costumes **that** were on display? [*Who* is an interrogative pronoun, *all* is an indefinite pronoun, and *that* is a relative pronoun.]
Juanita finished the installation **herself.** [*Herself* is an intensive pronoun.]

EXERCISE In each of the following sentences, identify the underlined pronouns by writing above each one *PER* for *personal,* *REF* for *reflexive,* *INTEN* for *intensive,* *DEM* for *demonstrative,* *INTER* for *interrogative,* *REL* for *relative,* or *IND* for *indefinite.*

Example 1. Couldn't *we* develop the film *ourselves* in Dad's darkroom?

1. Those are the pilots whom the general himself chose for the mission.

2. She amused herself by reading a book by Erma Bombeck.

3. Oh, this is some of that delicious tuna salad.

4. What is the name of the senator who is speaking?

5. The cyclists took their water bottles with them on the trail.

6. We ourselves must decide the number of hours to study.

7. Shelley adopted two turtles, which she named Snapper and Swifty.

8. Whom did she invite to go to the movies with her?

9. In the woods, we spotted a doe that had a fawn.

10. Each of us had a good time on our trip to the aquarium.

11. Which of these are endangered species?

12. Someone told me that Erica had built the treehouse herself.

13. How badly did they hurt themselves when they fell?

14. This is one of the best computer games I have ever played!

15. Everyone tried to solve the riddle, but only a few were successful.

16. Who is the student who painted this beautiful seascape?

17. Have you ever read any of Nina Otero's works?

18. Unlike the others, Maria can read something once and recall almost every detail.

19. Is that the baseball that Mark McGwire autographed for your brother?

20. Saul likes to keep to himself whenever he studies for an exam.

The Adjective

12c. An *adjective* is a word that is used to modify a noun or a pronoun.

An adjective tells *what kind, which one,* or *how many.*

EXAMPLES **narrow** road, **helpful** teacher, **one-act** play

that person, **African American** holiday, **one-hundredth** anniversary

several chores, **fewer** errors, **twenty-five** minutes

The most frequently used adjectives are *a, an,* and *the.* These words are usually called *articles*.

EXERCISE Underline the adjectives in the following sentences. Then, circle the articles.

Example 1. Seven club members stayed for the entire meeting.

1. After the hot, humid summer, we welcomed the cool, crisp autumn days.

2. The driving test requires a thorough understanding of the various traffic signs.

3. The mayor surprised everyone at the winter carnival by arriving in a horse-drawn sleigh.

4. Completing these math projects took many hours.

5. The most important contest in professional football is the annual Super Bowl game.

6. Helena placed a bouquet of fresh flowers in a vase on the oak table.

7. The curious sightseers looked forward to exploring the mysterious cavern.

8. A young eagle soared swiftly beyond the billowy, snow-white clouds.

9. The new karate instructor is a skillful teacher.

10. In the nest were three tiny newborn robins.

11. I heard that they are remodeling this old barn to convert it into a spacious and

comfortable home.

12. Diana, a talented musician, plays cello in the local symphony.

13. Which of the species is the largest member of the vulture family?

14. Doesn't that movie contain vivid scenes of gratuitous violence?

15. Atop the snowcapped mountain peak were four weary but joyful climbers.

16. The swirling river wildly tossed the smaller empty boats.

17. *Jane Eyre,* a classic novel about enduring love, has been made into a movie several times.

18. The Mexican artist Rufino Tamayo created bold, colorful paintings.

19. One of the birthday gifts was a new remote-controlled car.

20. My best friend, Alicia, is an avid mystery reader.

for **CHAPTER 12: THE PARTS OF SPEECH**   `pages 382–83`

Pronoun or Adjective?

12b.   A *pronoun* is a word that is used in place of one or more nouns or pronouns.

12c.   An *adjective* is a word that is used to modify a noun or a pronoun.

Some words may be used as either pronouns or adjectives. For example, *this, that, these,* and *those* are called *demonstrative pronouns* when they take the place of nouns or other pronouns and are called *demonstrative adjectives* when they modify nouns or pronouns.

  PRONOUN   **That** is my sister's guitar.

  ADJECTIVE   **That** guitar belongs to my sister.

EXERCISE   In each of the following sentences, identify the part of speech of the underlined word by writing above the word *PRO* for *pronoun* or *ADJ* for *adjective.*

          ADJ

Example **1.** Danielle has <u>many</u> pets.

1. <u>These</u> fajitas certainly are spicy!

2. <u>These</u> are the spiciest fajitas I have ever tasted!

3. <u>Most</u> of the ninth-graders participated in the readathon.

4. <u>Most</u> ninth-graders participated in the readathon.

5. <u>Which</u> ice sculpture did you create?

6. <u>Which</u> of the ice sculptures did you create?

7. <u>This</u> is one of my favorite songs.

8. Do you like <u>this</u> song?

9. Aren't <u>those</u> wildflowers beautiful?

10. Yes, <u>those</u> are more colorful than the ones we saw earlier.

11. <u>What</u> are some languages you speak?

12. <u>What</u> other languages do you speak?

13. <u>That</u> skyscraper is the tallest one in the world.

14. <u>That</u> is the tallest skyscraper in the world.

15. <u>Either</u> answer is acceptable.

16. <u>Either</u> of the answers is acceptable.

17. <u>Some</u> animals hibernate during the winter.

18. Toads, turtles, and bats are <u>some</u> of the animals that hibernate during the winter.

19. <u>Whose</u> are these?

20. <u>Whose</u> skates are these?

Grammar, Usage, and Mechanics: Language Skills Practice   **11**

Noun or Adjective?

12a. A *noun* is a word or word group that is used to name a person, a place, a thing, or an idea.

12c. An *adjective* is a word that is used to modify a noun or a pronoun.

Many words can be used as nouns or as adjectives.

     NOUN Who was the first **American** to travel in space?

  ADJECTIVE Who made the first **American** flag?

EXERCISE In each of the following sentences, identify the part of speech of the underlined word or word group by writing above it *N* for *noun* or *ADJ* for *adjective*.

    Example 1. For dinner, Dad prepared a <u>chicken</u> casserole.

1. Geraldo is the <u>sports</u> reporter for the school newspaper.

2. Geraldo plays two <u>sports</u> at school: baseball and field hockey.

3. The students are busily working on their <u>science</u> projects.

4. Which course in <u>science</u> are you taking this year?

5. I took this snapshot of the <u>New York City</u> skyline.

6. Albany, not <u>New York City</u>, is the capital of New York.

7. For most of the <u>summer</u>, I worked at a local farmers' market.

8. Did you have a <u>summer</u> job?

9. The <u>library</u> stays open until 8:00 P.M.

10. I need to return these <u>library</u> books today.

11. That ocean liner is famous for its <u>winter</u> cruises.

12. Not every bird flies south for the <u>winter</u>.

13. According to the <u>bus</u> schedule, we should arrive by 3:15 P.M.

14. Do you want to travel by <u>bus</u>?

15. Mr. Morris served as <u>principal</u> of the school for twenty-three years.

16. I believe the <u>principal</u> crops of the Philippines include rice, corn, coconuts, bananas,

    and pineapples.

17. Our class read Joseph Bruchac's retelling of the <u>Seneca</u> tale titled "Sky Woman."

18. Long ago, the <u>Seneca</u> told this story to explain the creation of the earth.

19. Do you practice <u>soccer</u> after school every day?

20. Do you have <u>soccer</u> practice after school every day?

ELEMENTS OF LANGUAGE | Third Course

Adjectives in Sentences

12c.   An **_adjective_** is a word that is used to modify a noun or a pronoun.

An adjective usually comes before the noun or pronoun it modifies.
> **EXAMPLE**   *Dances with Wolves* portrays **Lakota Sioux** culture.

Sometimes, adjectives follow the words they modify.
> **EXAMPLES**   The protagonist, **alone** and **bored,** tries to befriend a wolf.
> This movie is **spectacular**!

EXERCISE   Underline the adjectives in the following sentences. Do not include *a, an,* and *the.* Then, draw an arrow from each underlined adjective to the word it modifies.

Example   **1.** For many reasons, I think that movie is great.

1. The movie is set in the West during the latter part of the nineteenth century.

2. John J. Dunbar, the main character, is a Civil War veteran.

3. Dunbar had been an army lieutenant.

4. The Lakota Sioux, cautious and apprehensive, eventually befriend Dunbar.

5. The friendly lieutenant maintains a peaceful relationship with the Lakota Sioux.

6. In the beginning some minor problems do arise.

7. A greater conflict occurs when other soldiers arrive.

8. Kevin Costner both starred in and directed this powerful film.

9. Costner is not only a talented actor but also a skilled director.

10. Costner was especially careful about presenting an accurate picture of the Lakota Sioux.

11. He hired a woman to teach the Lakota Sioux language to many actors in the film.

12. He also dispatched designers to find authentic clothing and jewelry.

13. Tending to so many details must have taken Costner and the film crew a long time.

14. Graham Greene and Floyd Red Crow Westerman were two of many American Indians

    selected for important parts in the movie.

15. The performances by these actors are certainly praiseworthy.

16. This movie was a box-office success.

17. Some Hollywood critics predicted that the three-hour movie would fail.

18. Numerous other movie critics, however, praised the film.

19. Did Costner receive any Oscar nominations for acting and directing?

20. This wonderful film received a number of nominations and won several awards.

GRAMMAR

The Verb

12d. A *verb* is a word that is used to express action or a state of being.

EXAMPLES   Both Mom and Dad **work** full time. [action]

My sister Amy and I **are** responsible for the care of the lawn. [state of being]

EXERCISE   Underline the verbs in the following sentences.

Examples 1. Every Saturday morning, Amy and I mow the yard and tend the flower garden.

2. I think the grass is taller.

1. Soon after breakfast, Amy and I go outside and begin our chores.

2. We start early because by noon the weather is usually too hot.

3. The minute the dew dries, Amy says to me, "Grab the lawn mower!"

4. While I cut the grass, Amy edges the lawn.

5. After we neatly clip the grass, we weed the flower garden.

6. I loosen the dirt around the flowers, and my sister pulls the weeds.

7. By noon both the lawn and the garden look decidedly better than they did earlier.

8. Tired and thirsty, we go inside, wash our hands, and eat lunch.

9. Nature, however, stands still for no one.

10. Almost at once, new weeds appear in the garden.

11. Within a few days the grass again creeps over the edges of the driveway.

12. Amy and I do the job all over again the next Saturday.

13. Fortunately, both of us like outdoor work and enjoy our jobs as "yardeners."

14. Every Saturday afternoon, we have another chore.

15. My sister and I clean our rooms.

16. Amy, who is neat, usually finishes before I do.

17. Consequently, she often helps me.

18. I certainly appreciate her assistance.

19. My sister and I work very well together.

20. We are not only sisters but also best friends.

Transitive and Intransitive Verbs

A *transitive verb* is a verb that expresses an action directed toward a person, place, or thing. The action expressed by a transitive verb passes from the doer (the *subject*) to the receiver (the *object*) of the action.

> **EXAMPLE**   Suddenly, we **spotted** a solitary eagle overhead. [The action of the verb *spotted* is directed toward the eagle.]

An *intransitive verb* expresses an action (or tells something about the subject) without the action passing to a receiver, or object.

> **EXAMPLE**   The eagle **soared** above. [The action of the verb *soared* does not pass to an object.]

EXERCISE   Underline the verb in each of the following sentences. Then, above each verb, write *T* if the verb is transitive or *I* if the verb is intransitive.

Example 1. Colonial America offered freedom to a variety of people.

1. In the 1600s, English taxes supported the Church of England.

2. Some people considered the taxes unfair.

3. For others, the Americas provided an opportunity for religious freedom.

4. Many people immigrated to the Colonies.

5. Victims of religious intolerance sought an escape from persecution.

6. The Puritans, for example, disagreed with many Church of England policies.

7. As a result, some Puritans left England.

8. This religious group founded settlements in Virginia and New England.

9. Indentured servants also traveled to American shores.

10. The poor of England desired economic opportunity.

11. They worked in America as payment for their passage.

12. Many remained in America after settlement of their debts.

13. Some indentured themselves for seven years.

14. Tenant farmers came, too.

15. They brought their dreams of prosperity with them.

16. These Colonial settlers arrived with hope.

17. From the American Indians, the immigrants learned a great deal.

18. New England colonists celebrated their first Thanksgiving Day in America in 1621.

19. They held the celebration after the harvest.

20. Many of their American Indian neighbors shared in the celebration.

Action Verbs

An *action verb* expresses either physical or mental action.

PHYSICAL ACTION   climb, sneeze, write, reply, pull

MENTAL ACTION   suppose, expect, consider, remember, ponder

Some verbs do not express action.

EXAMPLES   am, be, been, become, seem

EXERCISE A   On the line before each of the following verbs, write *P* if the verb expresses physical action, *M* if it expresses mental action, or *N* if it expresses no action.

Example ___ ᶯ ___ **1.** imagine

_____ **1.** seem   _____ **11.** speak

_____ **2.** dream   _____ **12.** know

_____ **3.** type   _____ **13.** skid

_____ **4.** stomp   _____ **14.** are

_____ **5.** is   _____ **15.** cherish

_____ **6.** regret   _____ **16.** yearn

_____ **7.** ski   _____ **17.** travel

_____ **8.** fly   _____ **18.** were

_____ **9.** was   _____ **19.** resent

_____ **10.** forget   _____ **20.** push

EXERCISE B   Underline only the action verbs in the following sentences.

Example 1. Although my mother very much enjoys her hobby, she sometimes thinks that it is too time-consuming.

21. In her spare time my mother designs and pieces quilts.

22. The first quilt she made is extremely special to me.

23. She used pieces of clothing that I wore when I was an infant.

24. Everyone we know admires her quilts and says they are incredibly beautiful.

25. My mother gets much joy and satisfaction from her hobby; in fact, she often calls her hobby a labor of love.

Linking Verbs

A *linking verb* connects the subject to a word or word group that identifies or describes the subject. The most commonly used linking verbs are the forms of the verb *be*. Other frequently used linking verbs are *appear, become, remain, seem, turn, smell, taste, feel, look,* and *sound*.

EXAMPLES Tyler **is** my best friend. [The verb *is* connects the subject *Tyler* to the noun *friend*, which identifies Tyler.]

The ice-covered branches **seem** fragile and glasslike. [The verb *seem* connects the subject *branches* to the adjectives *fragile* and *glasslike*, which describe the branches.]

EXERCISE In each of the following sentences, draw one line under the linking verb and two lines under the words that the verb connects.

Example 1. This yogurt smells sour.

1. Mother felt ill this morning.

2. Shirley is the secretary and the treasurer of the class.

3. The bread on the counter smelled delicious.

4. Connie grew bored and restless toward the end of the movie.

5. Affie seemed confused by the directions that you gave him.

6. Are we still friends?

7. The new student looks familiar to me.

8. Are all deserts hot and dry?

9. The scout leader was proud of her troop.

10. What is the problem?

11. During this time of year, the weather often becomes stormy in the late afternoon.

12. My voice sounds hoarse from all that cheering at the game.

13. The salesperson seemed annoyed by the shoppers who crowded the store.

14. The captain of the ship remained calm and optimistic.

15. This fabric turned white from exposure to the sun.

16. Do you know whether the library is open on Saturdays?

17. The lights grew dimmer in the theater.

18. The tourists were curious about the mysterious cave.

19. A few of the tomatoes on the vines are already ripe.

20. I absolutely have to say that I think the costume for my character in the play

looks ridiculous!

Verb Phrases

A *verb phrase* consists of at least one main verb and one or more helping verbs. A *helping verb* (or *auxiliary verb*) helps the main verb express action or a state of being. Besides forms of the verb *be*, common helping verbs include forms of the verbs *can, do, have, may, should,* and *will.*

EXAMPLE   I **have been researching** the Seven Wonders of the World.

EXERCISE Identify the verb phrases in the following sentences by drawing one line under each helping verb and two lines under each main verb.

Example **1.** Our class has been studying the Seven Wonders of the Ancient World.

1. Can you name the Seven Wonders of the Ancient World?

2. Some people may ask why these structures are called wonders.

3. Could it be that people have "wondered" how these monumental structures could have been built without the kinds of construction equipment that builders are using today?

4. The pyramids of Egypt were constructed around 2600 B.C.

5. The three pyramids are considered the oldest of the seven wonders.

6. The largest of the pyramids was commissioned by Khufu, an Egyptian king.

7. Of the seven wonders, this group of pyramids has survived in the best condition.

8. Are any of the pyramids being restored today?

9. The Hanging Gardens of Babylon were built by Nebuchadnezzar around 600 B.C.

10. These gardens were set on terraces high above a vaulted building.

11. Some historians have estimated the terraces' height at 75 feet to 300 feet.

12. The statue of Zeus at Olympia was made of ivory and gold.

13. The statue has not survived, but pictures of it do appear on coins.

14. Did Goths destroy the Temple of Artemis at Ephesus in the third century A.D.?

15. Some remains of the Mausoleum at Halicarnassus are housed in the British Museum.

16. The other two wonders—the Colossus of Rhodes and the Lighthouse of Alexandria—were completed in the third century B.C.

17. Did earthquakes destroy both of these wonders?

18. You should always look in several sources for information about the seven wonders.

19. You will find that some historians do not agree with this list of wonders.

20. For example, some historians have identified the Walls of Babylon, instead of the Hanging Gardens, as a wonder.

The Adverb

12e.   An **adverb** modifies a verb, an adjective, or another adverb.

An adverb tells *where, when, how,* or *to what extent (how long* or *how much).*

Where?	Please set the package **here.**
When?	**Yesterday** we went on a picnic.
How?	The audience responded **enthusiastically.**
To what extent?	Your advice was **quite** helpful.

EXERCISE   Underline each adverb in the following sentences. Above each adverb, write whether it tells *where, when, how,* or *to what extent.*

     where   when
Example   **1.** May we go there tomorrow?

1. During summer vacations I usually go to camp.

2. The swirling river tossed the boat wildly.

3. We will meet you later at the library.

4. Dangerously strong winds threatened the coastal villages.

5. Hurry! Our bus is already here!

6. Where do you go to school?

7. I try to avoid horror movies, for they frighten me badly.

8. The actor would not wear the silly costume chosen by the director.

9. "If you want a chance to win the tickets, call now!" cried the announcer.

10. The concert artist Yo-Yo Ma's performance was exceedingly polished.

11. Although I practice daily, I am a clumsy piano player.

12. The children held hands and crossed the street cautiously.

13. The weather in April was unusually warm.

14. Ricardo and I arrived earlier than the other guests.

15. The audience waited restlessly for the concert to begin.

16. Is this garden soil too sandy, Manuel?

17. Skateboarding is still a very popular form of recreation.

18. An elderly woman walked over and offered to help us.

19. The young street artist drew a caricature that was quite good.

20. On the first day at camp, we arose early and went fishing.

GRAMMAR

Adverbs and the Words They Modify

12e.   An **adverb** modifies a verb, an adjective, or another adverb.

An adverb tells *where, when, how,* or *to what extent (how long* or *how much).*

   EXAMPLES   Mia, who is **incredibly** athletic, plays basketball **exceptionally well.** [*Incredibly* modifies the adjective *athletic,* telling *to what extent; exceptionally* modifies the adverb *well,* telling *to what extent; well* modifies the verb *plays,* telling *how.*]

EXERCISE   Underline the adverbs in the following sentences. Draw an arrow from each adverb to the word or words it modifies. On the line provided, identify the part of speech of the word or words that each adverb modifies by writing *V* for *verb, ADJ* for *adjective,* or *ADV* for *adverb.*

Example ____*V, V*____ **1.** Usually, I do not have any fear of flying in airplanes.

_____ **1.** Yesterday, my family and I boarded a small plane.

_____ **2.** White, billowy clouds drifted rather calmly past my window.

_____ **3.** Earlier the weather service had predicted unseasonably stormy conditions.

_____ **4.** The flight attendants insisted most politely that we fasten our seat belts.

_____ **5.** We neared our destination, and the airplane suddenly plunged.

_____ **6.** Almost immediately, I checked my seat belt and braced myself.

_____ **7.** Soon, the pilot skillfully leveled the airplane.

_____ **8.** Seeing the runway, we relaxed, and the airplane landed safely.

_____ **9.** I was extremely happy to touch the ground.

_____ **10.** We rented a car and drove away slowly.

_____ **11.** We greatly enjoyed our road trip, for our route was very scenic.

_____ **12.** We reached our hotel fairly late.

_____ **13.** We eventually went to Venice, which sits on small Adriatic islands.

_____ **14.** Cars are not used there.

_____ **15.** Today, motorboats are more common than gondolas.

_____ **16.** The main water route is appropriately named the Grand Canal.

_____ **17.** Numerous bridges span the canals, connecting somewhat narrow streets.

_____ **18.** Saint Mark's Square is often quite crowded.

_____ **19.** Many remarkably beautiful buildings, including the Doges' Palace, rest nearby.

_____ **20.** The tall bell tower of Saint Mark is the most conspicuous structure in the square.

Noun or Adverb?

| **12a.** | A *noun* is a word or word group that is used to name a person, a place, a thing, or an idea. |
| **12e.** | An *adverb* modifies a verb, an adjective, or another adverb. |

An adverb tells *where, when, how,* or *to what extent (how long* or *how much).* Some words that can be used as adverbs can also be used as nouns.

> EXAMPLES   **Tomorrow** my sister begins her part-time job at the animal hospital. [*Tomorrow, telling when,* is an adverb that modifies the verb *begins.*]
>
> **Tomorrow** will be a special day. [*Tomorrow* is a noun that names the day.]

EXERCISE   For the following sentences, identify each underlined word by writing above it *N* for *noun* or *ADV* for *adverb.*

Example 1. Do you have a club meeting <u>tonight</u>?   *ADV*

1. Shouldn't we transplant these seedlings <u>now</u>?

2. Yes, <u>now</u> is a good time to transplant these seedlings.

3. <u>Here</u> is the place where you should stand.

4. Please stand <u>here</u>.

5. Ernesto crossed the finish line <u>first</u>.

6. The <u>first</u> to cross the finish line was Ernesto.

7. Are the essays for the writing contest due <u>Friday</u>?

8. Yes, the deadline for the essays is <u>Friday</u>.

9. Have you seen Emily <u>today</u>?

10. Isn't <u>today</u> the first day of winter?

11. Who used this computer <u>last</u>?

12. I think Sara was the <u>last</u> to use this computer.

13. Please be <u>home</u> by 9:00 P.M.

14. Her <u>home</u> is about a mile from here.

15. We painted the <u>outside</u> of the shed.

16. The children are playing <u>outside</u>.

17. I am looking forward to <u>then</u>.

18. I will be fifteen years old <u>then</u>.

19. Are you leaving <u>tonight</u> or early in the morning?

20. <u>Tonight</u> is opening night for our school play.

for **CHAPTER 12: THE PARTS OF SPEECH** | pages 400–401

The Preposition

| **12f.** | A **preposition** is a word that shows the relationship of a noun or pronoun to another word. |

The noun or pronoun that a preposition relates another word to is called the *object of the preposition*.

EXAMPLES I went **to** the new card shop **in** the mall. [The preposition *to* relates its object, *shop*, to the verb *went*. The preposition *in* relates its object, *mall*, to the noun *shop*.]

The card shop is located **next to** the bookstore. [The compound preposition *next to* shows the relationship of its object, *bookstore*, to the verb phrase *is located*.]

EXERCISE In the following sentences, underline each preposition and draw an arrow from the preposition to its object.

Example 1. I recently read about the origin of greeting cards.

1. In 1840, the British issued the first postage stamps.

2. Prior to this innovation, the recipient usually was responsible for the postage.

3. Thus, mail service was used mainly by the wealthy.

4. However, the new "penny post" made mail delivery affordable for most people.

5. Soon, people throughout Britain were sending each other greeting cards.

6. Greeting cards became popular in the United States also.

7. People bought Christmas cards and valentines from individual designers.

8. Joyce Hall, who earned a living with his picture postcards, founded a card company.

9. Over the years, Hall's company has grown into a successful business.

10. Today, in addition to Hall's company, many other card companies sell greeting cards.

11. Seemingly, there is a card for every occasion.

12. As I look through card racks, I am usually drawn to the humor section.

13. When I read the cover of a humorous card, I enjoy guessing what the funny verse inside the card will say.

14. At Christmas last year, my parents gave me a computer.

15. Along with the computer came software that enables me to create greeting cards.

16. I sent the first birthday card I created to my pen pal in the Philippines.

17. Across the card's cover, I wrote *HAPPY BIRTHDAY!*

18. I replaced the *I* in *BIRTHDAY* with a picture of a candle.

19. Then I placed a cake under the words so that they all looked like decorations on it.

20. Inside the card was a funny verse amid small pictures of wrapped gifts.

The Conjunction

| **12g.** | A *conjunction* is a word that joins words or word groups. |

COORDINATING CONJUNCTIONS	vitamins **and** minerals
	in the oven **or** on the grill
	Sara was born in Chicago, **but** she grew up in Dallas.
CORRELATIVE CONJUNCTIONS	**Both** Enrique **and** Saul
	not only in the morning **but also** at night
	Either my brother will drive me there **or** I will ride the bus.

EXERCISE A   Identify the conjunctions in the following sentences. Draw one line under the coordinating conjunctions and two lines under the correlative conjunctions.

Example 1. Both Tessa and I are taking dance lessons.

1. Neither Tessa nor I have ever seen a professional dance company perform live.

2. Today I bought tickets to an Alvin Ailey production, so I am quite excited.

3. Alvin Ailey was born in Texas in 1931, but he eventually moved to New York.

4. As a young man he danced in many shows, and in 1958, he formed the Alvin Ailey American Dance Theater.

5. Not only as a dancer but also as the choreographer of the dance company, Ailey was very much admired.

EXERCISE B   Use coordinating or correlative conjunctions to join each of the following pairs of words or word groups in a complete sentence. Write your sentences on the lines provided.

Example 1. I win/he wins   *Whether I win or he wins, we will remain friends.* _____

6. winter/summer _____

_____

7. Chico/Matt _____

_____

8. under the bed/behind the desk _____

_____

9. Jolene worked/she rested _____

_____

10. swiftly/quietly _____

_____

for **CHAPTER 12: THE PARTS OF SPEECH**   *pages 405–406*

The Interjection

12h. An *interjection* is a word that expresses emotion. An interjection has no grammatical relation to the rest of the sentence.

> **EXAMPLES**   **Wow!** What an incredible storm that was!
>
> I would like to go, but**,** **yikes,** I have too much work to do.

EXERCISE A   Underline the interjections in the following sentences.

Example 1. <u>Uh-oh</u>, has anyone seen my pet snake?

1. Yikes! There's a snake under the table!

2. Oops! I must have forgotten to cover the terrarium.

3. I like snakes, but, whoa, not when I'm eating dinner.

4. I tend to scream when snakes crawl over my feet, ugh!

5. Goodness! I've never seen such a long snake.

6. Oh, it's really harmless.

7. Wow! That's a relief!

8. Do you think that, well, you might want to put the snake back in its terrarium?

9. The snake, alas, seems to have disappeared.

10. Aha! There it is, hanging from the chandelier.

EXERCISE B   Rewrite each sentence, adding an interjection and appropriate punctuation.

Example 1. The island of Tobago has a variety of snakes. *Boy-oh-boy! What a variety of* _____

snakes the island of Tobago has! _____

11. Mom told us that not all of the snakes are dangerous, of course. _____

_____

12. A man named Snakeman was their guide in Trinidad. _____

_____

13. Snakeman held the world record for capturing bushmasters. _____

_____

14. Isn't the bushmaster a large, poisonous snake? _____

_____

15. The Asa Wright Nature Center in Trinidad encompasses close to five hundred acres. _____

_____

Determining Parts of Speech

12i. The way a word is used in a sentence determines what part of speech it is.

NOUN	Are these soft pillows filled with **down**?
ADVERB	If you write things **down,** you may recall them more easily.
PREPOSITION	The two squirrels scurried up and **down** the tree.

EXERCISE In the following sentences, identify the part of speech of each underlined word by writing above it one of these abbreviations:

N for *noun*	*PRO* for *pronoun*	*ADJ* for *adjective*	*V* for *verb*
ADV for *adverb*	*PREP* for *preposition*	*CONJ* for *conjunction*	*INTER* for *interjection*

Examples **1.** Would you like to have another enchilada? *N*

2. Is that enchilada sauce hot or mild? *ADJ*

1. Marianne exhibited her model spacecraft at the science fair.

2. How long did it take Marianne to build the model?

3. We stopped by your house, but you weren't home.

4. At what time did you stop by?

5. These are extremely tasty pears.

6. Substitute these new art supplies for your old ones.

7. Doesn't Ms. Napoli coach the girls' basketball team?

8. She is also the coach of the school's swim team.

9. Everyone but Bethany was at the meeting.

10. Actually, Bethany came to the meeting but left early.

11. Are you a member of the student council?

12. The council members meet twice a month.

13. All of the volunteers at the fund-raiser were a big help.

14. Selena always volunteers to help.

15. I left my books inside on the table.

16. I left my books inside my locker.

17. That painting must be extremely valuable.

18. That must be an extremely valuable painting.

19. Well, that seems like a good idea.

20. Don't you think that everyone on the team played well?

for **CHAPTER 12: THE PARTS OF SPEECH**   *pages 375–407*

Review A: **Parts of Speech**

EXERCISE In the following sentences, identify the part of speech of each underlined word or word group by writing above it one of these abbreviations:

N for *noun*   *PRO* for *pronoun*   *ADJ* for *adjective*   *V* for *verb*
ADV for *adverb*   *PREP* for *preposition*   *CONJ* for *conjunction*   *INTER* for *interjection*

Example 1. Every night, my <u>family</u> and I have what <u>we</u> call "talk time."

1. <u>This</u> is an <u>important</u> time for all of us.

2. We <u>discuss</u> what we have done <u>during</u> the day.

3. It is <u>usually</u> hard for <u>my</u> little brother to recall what he has done.

4. Then Mom <u>or</u> Dad asks him some <u>questions</u>.

5. "<u>Oh</u>, I remember <u>now</u>," my brother eventually says.

6. Then he begins telling <u>about</u> his <u>morning</u> adventures.

7. He <u>often</u> becomes quite <u>lively</u> when he talks about them.

8. <u>Some</u> of my brother's stories <u>sound</u> silly to me.

9. I <u>sometimes</u> become impatient because I want to talk about my day at <u>school</u>.

10. I start with tales about the ride on the <u>school bus</u> in the <u>morning</u>.

11. Then I tell about <u>all</u> of the classes I <u>have</u>.

12. My best friend, <u>Cheryl</u>, and I have <u>every</u> class together.

13. My favorite subjects are history and science, <u>so</u> I usually tell my family a great deal about <u>those</u> classes.

14. I especially have a lot to say when my history class has gone on a <u>field trip</u> or my science class <u>has performed</u> an experiment.

15. My brother <u>generally</u> shouts, "No more stories about fossils <u>and</u> explosions!"

16. My mother often has said to my brother, "<u>Let</u> your sister finish <u>her</u> story."

17. <u>In addition to</u> telling about my classes and extracurricular activities, I tell <u>about</u> what my friends and I do at lunch.

18. Frequently, <u>one</u> story leads to the next <u>one</u> and then to the next and the next.

19. As I keep going from one story to <u>another</u>, big grins appear <u>on</u> my parents' faces.

20. When I ask why they are grinning, they reply, "<u>Well</u>, wouldn't you <u>like</u> to hear a little about our day?"

for **CHAPTER 12: THE PARTS OF SPEECH** pages 375–407

Review B: **Parts of Speech**

EXERCISE In the following sentences, identify the part of speech of each underlined word or word group by writing above it one of these abbreviations:

N for *noun*   PRO for *pronoun*   ADJ for *adjective*   V for *verb*
ADV for *adverb*   PREP for *preposition*   CONJ for *conjunction*   INTER for *interjection*

Example 1. We always have a good time when we visit our grandparents in Texas.

1. My grandfather, a Texas rancher, loves dogs.

2. The porch of his ranch house ordinarily is full of dogs of all shapes and sizes.

3. My grandmother, who is fond of cats, has several big Persian cats.

4. They generally feel happiest inside the house because, outside, the dogs will chase them up the nearest tree.

5. Some of the smaller cats cannot climb back down, and a ranch hand must rescue them with a ladder.

6. "Whew, those dogs can be such a bother!" my grandmother exclaims.

7. Needless to say, the quiet cats and the playful dogs do not mix well.

8. Grandfather keeps the mischievous dogs away from the cattle.

9. Many of the steers angrily charge all dogs.

10. Grandfather's dogs usually stay inside the wooden fence, but occasionally they leave this safe place.

11. If they do wander near the cattle, the dogs are soon forced to retreat.

12. The dogs then return to their comparatively dull life inside the yard.

13. Frequent visits from us always delight them.

14. When the dogs see us, they wag their tails enthusiastically.

15. Generally, the excited dogs crowd around us.

16. My little brother's favorite dogs, naturally, are the puppies.

17. The roly-poly puppies frequently stumble and fall.

18. The puppies ordinarily stay near the kennels throughout their first year of life.

19. The oldest dog that lives at the ranch is a German shepherd named Rascal.

20. Rascal seems to act as protector of all of the other dogs on the ranch.

Review C: **Parts of Speech**

EXERCISE In the following sentences, identify the part of speech of each underlined word or word group by writing above it one of these abbreviations:

N for *noun*	*PRO* for *pronoun*	*ADJ* for *adjective*	*V* for *verb*
ADV for *adverb*	*PREP* for *preposition*	*CONJ* for *conjunction*	*INTER* for *interjection*

Example 1. Australia is home <u>to</u> *[PREP]* many unique species of plants <u>and</u> *[CONJ]* animals.

1. <u>Thousands</u> of wildflowers are <u>native</u> to Australia.

2. Among <u>those</u> species is a red-and-green wildflower called the <u>kangaroo paw</u>.

3. <u>Its</u> shape resembles <u>that</u> of a kangaroo's hind foot.

4. Other plants found in Australia include the <u>especially</u> fragrant <u>honeyflower</u> and the beautiful fuchsia.

5. <u>With</u> bright red blooms the spear lily <u>commonly</u> grows twelve feet tall.

6. Many different <u>varieties</u> of orchid <u>thrive</u> on the continent.

7. <u>Oh</u>, how <u>delicate</u> the lovely orchids are!

8. <u>Across</u> the continent grows the acacia, which is <u>often</u> called the wattle tree.

9. Early European settlers in Australia discovered that they <u>could build</u> walls and roofs by intertwining, <u>or</u> wattling, the flexible branches of the acacia.

10. Also growing <u>throughout</u> Australia is the <u>eucalyptus</u>, or the gum tree.

11. <u>Eucalyptus</u> leaves are the <u>principal</u> source of food for the koala.

12. The koala is a marsupial, an animal <u>that</u> has an external abdominal pouch for carrying and nursing its <u>young</u>.

13. <u>In addition to</u> the koala, more than forty kinds of kangaroo <u>live</u> in Australia.

14. One of the tallest species is the <u>red kangaroo</u>; <u>much</u> smaller are the wallaby and the rat kangaroo.

15. <u>Among</u> other Australian marsupials are the wombat, <u>which</u> resembles a small bear, and the bandicoot, which looks like a rat.

16. One of the <u>most</u> unusual mammals on the continent is the platypus.

17. The platypus is unlike most <u>other</u> mammals in that <u>it</u> lays eggs.

18. Australia also <u>has</u> many special birds, including the emu <u>and</u> the black swan.

19. Unlike most other birds, the emu cannot fly, <u>but</u> it <u>can run</u> very swiftly.

20. <u>Wow</u>! The black swan certainly looks <u>powerful</u> in flight!

Literary Model: Using Nouns to Create Setting

> Pressing herself flat against the rear wall of Señor Aguilar's hotel near the Avenida Ruiz, Lupita Torres bided her time. When she heard the doors of the big green *yanqui* car shut and the tourist start the engine, she slid forward, scraping her back on the rough white stucco.
>
> —from *Lupita Mañana* by Patricia Beatty

EXERCISE A

1. On the lines below, write each noun that appears in the above paragraph. Then, circle the proper nouns. (Note: One noun is in the possessive case; it ends with an apostrophe and an *s*.)

   _____

   _____

2. The nouns work together to create the sense of a particular cultural setting. What specific information do they give about the setting?

   _____

   _____

   _____

   _____

EXERCISE B   Rewrite the paragraph, replacing most of the nouns with nouns of your own choosing. Use nouns that create a different cultural setting. You may also change an adjective or two.

   _____

   _____

   _____

   _____

   _____

   _____

   _____

Literary Model (continued)

EXERCISE C   Write a paragraph describing two people walking up to the front door of your dream house. Use common and proper nouns to communicate a clear setting. For example, the house may be on a busy street in Paris, France, or it may be nestled among the sand dunes of a remote beach in North Carolina. Underline each noun.

_____

_____

_____

_____

_____

_____

_____

_____

_____

_____

_____

_____

_____

_____

_____

_____

EXERCISE D   If you replaced all the proper nouns in your paragraph with common nouns, would the paragraph create the same specific setting and tone? Explain why or why not.

_____

_____

_____

_____

_____

_____

_____

_____

Writing Application: Description

A word of advice that all writers learn is "Show—don't tell." Using well-chosen adjectives and adverbs, writers bring their subjects into sharp focus, giving concrete edges to their ideas and adding interest to their writing, just as a painter uses detail to create a lifelike portrait.

LESS INTERESTING   The batter ran the bases after hitting the home run.

MORE INTERESTING   The sweat-soaked batter triumphantly ran the bases after hitting the home run.

Think of other adjectives and adverbs that you could use to help readers "see" the action described in the sentence above.

WRITING ACTIVITY

You've probably heard of Leonardo da Vinci's famous *Mona Lisa,* which he finished painting in 1506. Find a picture of this painting, and write a paragraph describing the painting. Mona Lisa's smile has been called mysterious and playful—how will you describe it? Finish your description with your thoughts on what Leonardo's subject might have been thinking as she smiled. Include in your writing at least three carefully chosen adjectives and at least three interesting adverbs.

PREWRITING   Observe the painting carefully, jotting down whatever descriptive words come to mind as you look at it. You might even hold an imaginary conversation with Mona Lisa, asking her what she is thinking and writing what she might reply.

WRITING   Decide how you will arrange your descriptive details. Will you describe the whole painting and then focus on details, or start in the center of the painting and work outward? Focus on helping readers "see" the painting through your eyes.

REVISING   Share your description with a friend, and read someone else's. Discuss which details are most vivid and why. Can you replace any unclear words with specific words that clarify your view of the *Mona Lisa*? You may wish to consult a thesaurus to look for new ways to express an idea, but be sure to use a dictionary to check any word you want to use—you need to understand its meaning fully!

PUBLISHING   Check your paragraph for errors in grammar, usage, spelling, and punctuation. If you have used any proper adjectives, be sure that you have capitalized them. Then, create an advertisement for the *Mona Lisa,* using your description as the text. Design a brochure or poster that would sell this painting to a museum or art collector.

EXTENDING YOUR WRITING

You may wish to develop this writing exercise into a longer essay. You could write a review of the *Mona Lisa* (or of another work of art) for a school or community newspaper, or an evaluation of the painting for a class in art or history. As you develop your thoughts, you may want to use the library or the Internet to learn more about Leonardo da Vinci's creation of the painting.

Choices: Exploring the Parts of a Sentence

The following activities challenge you to find a connection between the parts of sentences and the world around you. Do the activity below that suits your personality best, and then share your discoveries with your class.

ORGANIZING INFORMATION

In a Nutshell

Compile a one-page listing of the rules in this chapter. Include at least one example for each rule. Then, distribute copies to each of your classmates. Make sure that your page design is easy to use and interesting.

MATHEMATICS

X + Y = Z

Start with ten mathematical equations. Then, translate these equations into sentences and label each subject, verb, and complement. Include examples showing compound subjects, compound verbs, and compound complements.

DEFINING

Where Is Webster When We Need Him?

What do you think of the definition of *sentence*? Try making up a better one! Working with a team, compose several alternative definitions for *sentence*. Then, put your ideas to the test. Present them to your classmates for discussion, and choose the best one.

DIALECT

The Force Is with Him

Hey, *Star Wars* fans, have you ever noticed that Yoda talks rather strangely? Why is that? Check out a *Star Wars* saga book or watch a video of one of the movies that Yoda is in, and write down some of Yoda's speeches. What makes his speech distinctive? What elements of the standard subject-verb-object order does Yoda invert, or reverse? Begin by identifying each subject, verb, and complement (if there is one) of Yoda's sentences. Then, identify the modifiers. Pay special attention to the way he uses *not*. Present your findings to the class.

VISUAL LEARNING

I Did It My Way

Turn to the Diagramming Appendix in your textbook. Do sentence diagrams like the ones there confuse you? No problem—design a new way of visually representing sentence structure. You might use color, shape, position, and even texture if you want. Then, present your new system to your classmates.

VISUAL DEMONSTRATION

Move It!

Help your classmates see how the elements of a sentence can move around. Get a group of five to ten people together, and create a sentence. Begin with a subject, a verb, and a complement. Make giant cards with the simple subject on one card, the verb on another, and the complement on yet another. Then, add other words or word groups—adjectives, adverbs, prepositional phrases, and so on; make cards for those, too. Next, each person should hold up a card and stand in sentence order in front of the class. Then, have some fun! Try different sentence orders—questions, commands, whatever you want. Add and subtract elements. Just move it!

FOREIGN LANGUAGES

Order of the Day

In what order do other languages usually present subjects, verbs, and objects? What differences and similarities can you find between the sentence structures of English and those of, for instance, Spanish? Write a few paragraphs detailing several of these points, or give a demonstration for the class.

Sentences and Sentence Fragments A

| **13a.** | A *sentence* is a word or word group that contains a subject and a verb and that expresses a complete thought. |

A *sentence fragment* is a word or word group that is capitalized and punctuated as a sentence but that does not contain both a subject and a verb or does not express a complete thought.

FRAGMENT   Bears extremely protective of their young. [no verb]

FRAGMENT   According to the film we saw. [incomplete thought]

SENTENCE   According to the film we saw, bears are extremely protective of their young.

EXERCISE   Identify each of the following groups of words as a sentence or a sentence fragment. On the line provided, write *S* for *sentence* or *F* for *fragment*.

Example ___F___ **1.** Once frightened by a bear.

_____ **1.** Bears are classified as carnivores, or meat eaters.

_____ **2.** Also enjoy feeding on plants and honey.

_____ **3.** Because they are myopic, or nearsighted.

_____ **4.** Bears have difficulty seeing objects that are far away.

_____ **5.** Their keen sense of hearing, which makes up for their limited vision.

_____ **6.** Bears can identify sounds at a great distance.

_____ **7.** Their most acute sense is that of smell.

_____ **8.** The tracks left by the bear's prey.

_____ **9.** The small prey unable to escape.

_____ **10.** Bears are powerful predators.

_____ **11.** The muscles in the upper part of a large bear's front legs.

_____ **12.** Bears are native to four continents.

_____ **13.** North America, South America, Europe, and Asia.

_____ **14.** In North America, which includes the United States.

_____ **15.** In North America live the brown bear, the grizzly bear, and the American black bear.

_____ **16.** Alaska is the home of the largest brown bear, the kodiak bear.

_____ **17.** The kodiak bear, which may reach a weight of about 1,700 pounds (780 kilograms) and a length of about 10 feet (3 meters).

_____ **18.** Native to Asia is the Malayan sun bear.

_____ **19.** The Malayan sun bear, smaller than any other species of bear.

_____ **20.** Inhabiting the mountain forests of South America is the spectacled bear.

Grammar, Usage, and Mechanics: Language Skills Practice

Sentences and Sentence Fragments B

13a. A *sentence* is a word or word group that contains a subject and a verb and that expresses a complete thought.

A *sentence fragment* is a word or word group that is capitalized and punctuated as a sentence but that does not contain both a subject and a verb or does not express a complete thought.

FRAGMENT   Described ancient cities of Mexico. [no subject]

FRAGMENT   Which we had found in this magazine. [incomplete thought]

SENTENCE   The articles, which we had found in this magazine, described ancient cities of Mexico.

EXERCISE A   Decide whether each group of words is a sentence or a sentence fragment. On the line provided, write *S* for *sentence* or *F* for *fragment*.

Example _____F_____ **1.** Gardens where Emperor Maximilian and Empress Carlota strolled.

_____ **1.** Cuernavaca, a city in Mexico.

_____ **2.** The famous Spanish explorer Cortés lived in a palace there.

_____ **3.** The Spaniards arrived in 1521.

_____ **4.** The resort with its tropical climate and hot springs.

_____ **5.** From the dining room at Las Mañanitas.

EXERCISE B   Each item below shows a sentence fragment. On the lines provided, rewrite the fragment to make it into a sentence.

Example 1. *Fragment:* Enjoyed seeing the sights and meeting the people. ___My cousins and I___
___enjoyed seeing the sights and meeting the people.___

6. *Fragment:* Our driver Cesar, who was a guide at the ruins. _____

_____

7. *Fragment:* Made our way back. _____

_____

8. *Fragment:* Waiting at the hotel. _____

_____

9. *Fragment:* Our cameras, which we took with us. _____

_____

10. *Fragment:* A pair of binoculars. _____

_____

Subjects and Predicates

| **13b.** | The *subject* tells whom or what the sentence is about, and the *predicate* says something about the subject. |

The *complete subject* and the *complete predicate* may be only one word each, or they may be more than one word.

COMPLETE SUBJECT **South Africa** produces much of the world's gold.

COMPLETE PREDICATE South Africa **produces much of the world's gold.**

EXERCISE A Decide whether the subject or the predicate is underlined in each of the following sentences. On the line provided, write *S* for *subject* or *P* for *predicate*.

Example ___*P*___ **1.** At a temperature of 2808 degrees Celsius, gold boils.

_____ **1.** Gold melts at 1064 degrees Celsius.

_____ **2.** A leaf of gold is less than one millimeter thick.

_____ **3.** Early craftworkers found ways to heat gold, pound it, and shape it to make

jewelry.

_____ **4.** Gold items over four thousand years old have been found on the coast of the Black Sea.

_____ **5.** Currently, South Africa is the leading producer of gold in the world.

_____ **6.** Silver may be combined with gold to make jewelry.

_____ **7.** In the early 1960s, the largest discovery of gold in the United States in the twentieth

century was made in Nevada.

_____ **8.** The first gold rush in the United States was in Georgia in 1828.

_____ **9.** In 1849 came the famous California gold rush.

_____ **10.** Was El Dorado, the legendary kingdom of gold, ever discovered?

EXERCISE B In each of the following sentences, draw one line under the complete subject and two lines under the complete predicate.

Example 1. Located in the northern part of Kentucky is Fort Knox.

11. The word *bullion* refers to bars or ingots of gold or silver.

12. Within steel and concrete vaults at Fort Knox lie bars of pure gold.

13. Since 1936, most of the gold in the United States has been kept at Fort Knox.

14. When did the United States stop minting gold coins?

15. Which country has the largest gold reserve?

for **CHAPTER 13: THE PARTS OF A SENTENCE** page 416

Simple and Complete Subjects

13c. The main word or word group that tells whom or what the sentence is about is called the *simple subject.*

The *complete subject* consists of the simple subject and any words, phrases, or clauses that modify the simple subject.

SENTENCE	Bicycle racing requires skill and stamina.
SIMPLE SUBJECT	racing
COMPLETE SUBJECT	Bicycle racing

EXERCISE A The complete subject is underlined in each of the following sentences. Circle each simple subject.

Example 1. The first African American world (champion) in bicycle racing was Marshall Taylor.

1. At age thirteen, Marshall Taylor won his first amateur bicycle race.

2. The owner of a bicycle factory hired him and encouraged him to race.

3. From 1896 to 1910, this famous and extremely popular cyclist raced in the United States, Europe, and Canada.

4. During those years, international and American championship titles were awarded to Taylor.

5. Taylor's induction into the bicycling hall of fame came after 117 wins in 168 races.

EXERCISE B In each of the following sentences, underline the complete subject and circle the simple subject.

Example 1. (One) of the most famous bicycle races is the Tour de France.

6. This well-known race was first held in 1903.

7. The course for the race extends about 2,500 miles through France and five other countries.

8. This famous cycling event lasts about three weeks.

9. The leader in the race wears a yellow jersey.

10. Some cyclists have won the race more than once.

11. Among the winners is Greg LeMond.

12. In 1986, this U.S. cyclist became the first non-European winner of the Tour de France.

13. In 1989 and in 1990, LeMond again placed first in international cycling's best-known event.

14. Another famous winner had to overcome grave difficulties.

15. In 1999, Lance Armstrong, having successfully struggled with cancer, made an incredible comeback and won the race.

Simple and Complete Predicates

13d. The *simple predicate,* or *verb,* is the main word or word group that tells something about the subject.

The simple predicate may be a one-word verb or a *verb phrase* (a verb with one or more helping verbs). The *complete predicate* consists of a verb and all the words that describe the verb and complete its meaning.

SENTENCE	I have been reading a collection of her stories.
SIMPLE PREDICATE	have been reading [verb phrase]
COMPLETE PREDICATE	have been reading a collection of her stories

EXERCISE A   The complete predicate is underlined in each of the following sentences. Circle the simple predicate.

Example 1. Leslie Marmon Silko's poetry (has) long (been) my favorite reading.

1. Silko has written many poems, short stories, and novels.

2. The author was raised at Laguna Pueblo in New Mexico.

3. In the 1960s, she attended high school in Albuquerque.

4. Many of Silko's stories have been inspired by American Indian folk tales.

5. In her youth she heard these stories from other family members.

6. The Laguna Pueblos' reverence for nature is traditional.

7. One of Silko's poems is based on the Pueblos' respect for the bear.

8. In 1974, Silko published her first collection of poems, *Laguna Woman*.

9. I have read many of the poems in that collection.

10. Do you have a copy of her story "The Man to Send Rain Clouds"?

EXERCISE B   In each of the following sentences, underline the complete predicate and circle the simple predicate.

Example 1. American Indians (have given) the world many foods.

11. Popcorn, one of the oldest forms of corn, may be native to Central America.

12. American Indians were growing popcorn more than one thousand years ago.

13. Popcorn was used for decorations and for food.

14. Popcorn without oil or butter is low in calories.

15. Almost all of the world's popcorn is grown in the United States.

NAME   CLASS   DATE

GRAMMAR

Complete and Simple Subjects and Predicates

13c. The main word or word group that tells whom or what the sentence is about is called the *simple subject.*

13d. The *simple predicate,* or *verb,* is the main word or word group that tells something about the subject.

The *complete subject* consists of the simple subject and any words, phrases, or clauses that modify the simple subject. The *complete predicate* consists of a verb and all the words that describe the verb and complete its meaning.

EXERCISE In each of the following sentences, underline the complete subject once and the complete predicate twice. Then, circle each simple subject and verb.

Example 1. Traditional Chinese painting is characterized by meticulous brush strokes.

1. Among the most famous Chinese artists is Chang Dai-chien.

2. I have seen several of the paintings by Chang Dai-chien.

3. Many art experts consider Chang a genius.

4. Dozens of Chang's paintings are in an exhibit at the museum.

5. Across the marble floor came the tour guide.

6. The tour guide pointed to the collection of paintings.

7. She directed our attention to an unusual painting.

8. On the bushy branches of a pine tree sits the artist.

9. Chang exhibited one hundred paintings at his first show in 1926.

10. Beside one painting hangs a gorgeous fan.

11. My sister had read the description of *Musical Performance.*

12. A digital picture of this painting appears on the Internet.

13. In the next gallery was artwork by Zhu Qizhan.

14. At the age of ninety, he accepted an invitation to lecture in the United States.

15. Did the group see all of his paintings with flowers and still lifes?

16. Included among the images is a picture of grapes.

17. A colorful landscape painting hangs nearby.

18. His landscapes are renowned for their technical achievement.

19. The mountains in this painting are beautiful.

20. Zhu Qizhan used impressionist techniques in his work.

Finding the Subject

13e. The subject of a sentence is never in a prepositional phrase.

> **EXAMPLE**   **Three** of the animals are at the watering hole. [*Three* is the subject. *Animals* is the object of the preposition *of.*]

Questions often begin with a verb, a helping verb, or a word such as *what, when, where, which, how,* or *why.* The subject of a question may follow the verb or may come between the helping verb and the main verb.

> **EXAMPLE**   In which country does the largest **herd** live? [The subject *herd* comes between the helping verb *does* and the main verb *live.*]

The word *there* or *here* is almost never the subject of a sentence. To find the subject, ask "Who?" or "What?" before the verb.

> **EXAMPLE**   There are two **species** of African rhinoceroses. [What are? *Species* are.]

EXERCISE A   In each of the following sentences, circle the subject of the underlined verb.

Example 1. How many (kinds) of rhinoceroses exist in the world?

1. There are five types of rhinoceroses.

2. What are the two species of African rhinoceroses called?

3. Here are some pictures of the black rhinoceros.

4. Where did the name for the black rhinoceros originate?

5. Can these rhinoceroses really uproot bushes and small trees?

EXERCISE B   For each of the following sentences, underline the subject once and the verb twice.

Example 1. How can we save this rhinoceros?

6. For what reasons are these African rhinoceroses in need of protection?

7. There is much interest in the black rhinoceros of Africa.

8. Is poaching affecting the survival rate of the black rhinoceros?

9. How have people like Kenneth Manyangadze helped the black rhinoceros?

10. Will Save Valley Wildlife Conservancy provide a safe home for African rhinoceroses?

11. In the preserve, there is a special area for the black rhinoceroses.

12. Where did Manyangadze see that two-ton female black rhinoceros?

13. How have volunteers saved some black rhinoceroses from poachers?

14. Here is a helpful tracking device.

15. In what ways can a tracking collar pinpoint the location of a rhinoceros in the wild?

The Understood Subject

In a request or command, the subject of a sentence is usually not stated. *You* is the *understood subject,* even when the request or command includes a *noun of direct address,* a name that identifies the person spoken to or addressed.

> **EXAMPLE** Please read the first question aloud, Tony. [Who is to read? *You* is the understood subject; *Tony* is a noun of direct address.]

EXERCISE Rewrite each of the following sentences as a request or a command with an understood subject. Use the underlined words in the first five sentences as nouns of direct address.

Example 1. <u>Amy</u> will show us a copy of the survey. _____

Show us a copy of the survey, Amy. _____

1. For tomorrow, the <u>class</u> will read the chapter. _____

_____

2. <u>Sherise</u> plans to tell us about the career of a highway patrol officer. _____

_____

3. <u>José</u> will explain the reasons for the popularity of those jobs. _____

_____

4. <u>Karen</u> will describe some careers in medicine. _____

_____

5. <u>Eduardo</u> will list the requirements for a career as a travel agent. _____

_____

6. You should respond to each survey question with only *yes* or *no.* _____

_____

7. You should take notes as you read the chapter. _____

_____

8. You should review these articles about computers. _____

_____

9. You can report your findings to the rest of the class. _____

_____

10. For additional information, you can search the Internet. _____

_____

for **CHAPTER 13: THE PARTS OF A SENTENCE** | page 424

Compound Subjects

| **13f.** | A *compound subject* consists of two or more subjects that are joined by a conjunction and that have the same verb. |

EXAMPLE The **time** and **place** for the prom will be announced tomorrow.

EXERCISE A In each of the following sentences, draw one line under the parts of the compound subject. Draw two lines under the conjunction or conjunctions joining those parts.

Example 1. Michael, Diane, and Martin will help make the prom decorations.

1. Some freshmen and a few sophomores will convert the gym into an ocean liner.

2. Either Ms. Lyle or another teacher will supervise the conversion.

3. Balloons, streamers, and other colorful decorations will adorn the gym.

4. Not only the walls but also the ceiling will sparkle with gold glitter.

5. The night before the prom, the gym floor and the bleachers will be waxed.

6. On prom night both students and chaperones will appreciate the prom committee's efforts.

7. Will Sheila, Eddie, or Douglas introduce the band at the prom?

8. Carlos and I do not want to be the first ones on the dance floor.

9. There are neither songs nor activities planned that aren't related to the ocean-liner theme.

10. The king and queen of the prom will be crowned by the principal.

EXERCISE B On the line provided, rewrite each pair of sentences as one sentence with a compound subject. You may need to change some verbs and pronouns to agree in number with the subject.

Example 1. Gunda is an excellent dancer. Alex is also an excellent dancer. _____

Both Gunda and Alex are excellent dancers.

11. "Do You Want to Dance?" is a favorite song of mine. "Respect" is also one of my favorites. ___

_____

12. The stroll is a dance that I like. The cha-cha is a dance that I like, too. _____

_____

13. Ms. Hall, a chaperone, danced at the prom. Mr. Contri, another chaperone, danced at the prom.

_____

14. Tanita may have won the door prize. Chauncey may have won it. Mavis may have won it. ___

_____

15. Denise played guitar in the band. Don played guitar in the band. _____

Compound Verbs

13g. A *compound verb* consists of two or more verbs that are joined by a conjunction and that have the same subject.

    EXAMPLE One helicopter **could fly, land,** or **navigate** on its own.

EXERCISE A In the following sentences, draw one line under the parts of the compound verbs. Draw two lines under the conjunctions that join the parts of the compound verbs.

Example 1. The International Aerial Robotics Competition <u>welcomes</u> <u><u>and</u></u> <u>supports</u> students.

1. Model helicopters and blimps must be built and operated by student inventors.

2. Each aircraft must depart from a small area, fly over a field, identify objects, and retrieve them.

3. Two Canadian students had consulted the Internet and found the IARC Web page.

4. They had not designed, engineered, or flown robotic aircraft before.

5. The boys talked about ideas, studied catalogs, and shopped for equipment.

6. Dave and Pawel received donations from some businesses but borrowed other equipment.

7. Could the boys or their computer fly and command the model helicopter?

8. At the competition the boys' helicopter flew well but could not retrieve the target objects.

9. A demonstration machine could fly rapidly, bank, hover, and land gracefully.

10. Many businesses would not only enjoy but also profit from advances in aerial robotic designs.

EXERCISE B Rewrite each of the following sets of sentences as one sentence with a compound verb. Use the conjunction or conjunctions given in parentheses to connect the parts of the compound verb.

Example 1. The judges will conduct the final tests. The judges will evaluate the results. *(and)* __

      The judges will conduct the final tests and evaluate the results.

11. That scientist works in a laboratory. That scientist also tutors students. *(not only . . . but also)* __

_____

12. Inventors may think of new ideas. They may use old ideas in new ways. *(either . . . or)* _____

_____

13. The two students entered the contest. They did not win. *(but)* _____

_____

14. Eugene and I designed this robot. Eugene and I programmed it, too. *(both . . . and)* _____

_____

15. Susan built a blimp. She refined its design. She entered the invention in the contest. *(and)* ____

_____

Compound Subjects and Verbs

13f. A *compound subject* consists of two or more subjects that are joined by a conjunction and that have the same verb.

13g. A *compound verb* consists of two or more verbs that are joined by a conjunction and that have the same subject.

COMPOUND SUBJECT   Both **Bianca** and **Kevin** want to become architects.
COMPOUND VERB   **Can** you **sing** or **play** a musical instrument?

A sentence may contain both a compound subject and a compound verb.

EXAMPLE   **Janetta** and **Ahmad** carefully **performed** the experiment and **recorded** the results.

EXERCISE A   In the following sentences, draw one line under each subject and two lines under each verb.

Example 1. Blue and white are our school colors.

1. That store not only sells but also repairs computer equipment.

2. Both the blue whale and the humpback are endangered species.

3. At the Freshmen Follies, Lucia and Ramon sang a duet.

4. Either *Androcles and the Lion* or *A Midsummer Night's Dream* will be our school's spring play.

5. Alex and Isaac left for summer camp this morning and will be there for two weeks.

EXERCISE B   On the line provided, rewrite each group of sentences as one sentence with a compound subject or a compound verb or both.

Example 1. At the state fair Dale rode in a hot-air balloon. I also rode in the hot-air balloon. ____

At the state fair Dale and I rode in a hot-air balloon.

6. The committee discussed the problem. The committee proposed no viable solution. _____

_____

7. The table on the patio is in need of repair. The chairs on the patio are in need of repair. _____

_____

8. I will talk to my guidance counselor. Then I will make my decision. _____

_____

9. Gnats were unusually troublesome last summer. Mosquitoes were unusually troublesome, too.

_____

10. Lin Sing saw the movie. Jalene saw it, too. They have been talking about it ever since. _____

_____

for **CHAPTER 13: THE PARTS OF A SENTENCE**   *pages 427–28*

Complements

13h.   A *complement* is a word or word group that completes the meaning of a verb.

A complement may be a noun, a pronoun, or an adjective, and may also be compound.

EXAMPLES   The first European to visit the Society Islands was **Samuel Wallis.** [noun]

I read **that** in the encyclopedia. [pronoun]

The article about the islands was **informative** and **thorough.** [adjectives]

EXERCISE   In each of the following sentences, write *S* above the *subject*, *V* above the *verb*, and *C* above the *complement*. Some sentences may have more than one complement.

Example 1. The Society Islands are part of French Polynesia.

1. Tahiti is one of the principal islands of the Society Islands.

2. The capital city is Papeete, on the island of Tahiti.

3. Papeete appears gracious and colorful.

4. Some aspects of Polynesian culture may seem unusual to tourists.

5. Polynesians settled the islands hundreds of years ago.

6. The islands must have seemed a paradise to those original settlers.

7. The island's exotic fruits may have tasted strange but delicious to them.

8. The French government claimed the fourteen islands.

9. Various writers and artists have illustrated the beauty of Tahiti.

10. Tahiti has spectacular waterfalls and streams.

11. Our first island adventure was a visit to a coral reef.

12. The island air smelled fresh and clean.

13. Islanders were selling fresh papayas.

14. During a hike in the mountains, I observed many kinds of wildlife.

15. The tropical vegetation was remarkable.

16. I saw bananas, coconuts, and papayas there.

17. Most of the islands' inhabitants are Polynesian.

18. Tahiti is certainly an extraordinary part of the world.

19. Our vacation in the Society Islands was too short.

20. This trip remains my all-time favorite vacation.

ELEMENTS OF LANGUAGE | Third Course

The Subject Complement: Predicate Nominatives

13i. A *subject complement* is a word or word group that is in the predicate and that describes or identifies the subject.

A *predicate nominative* is a word or word group that is in the predicate and that identifies the subject or refers to it.

EXAMPLES   Greta has been my **pen pal** for two years. [*Pen pal* identifies the subject *Greta*.]

The soccer team's co-captains are **Jamaal** and **he**. [*Jamaal* and *he* are a compound predicate nominative identifying the subject *co-captains*.]

EXERCISE   Underline the predicate nominatives in the following sentences.

Example 1. Is that your new bicycle?

1. Your lab partner will be either Michael or she.

2. Buenos Aires is the capital of Argentina.

3. The people who volunteered to help us were Moira and he.

4. Is Julie a sophomore or a junior?

5. Everyone in that ballet is an excellent dancer.

6. Two members of the wrestling team are Leslie and Jesse.

7. Beth is the tennis player whom I am coaching.

8. You have been a loyal friend to me!

9. Rodrigo, in my opinion, would be the best person to call for this job.

10. Barbara is the only soprano auditioning for the role.

11. Was she the one who called?

12. Is Leon your first name or your middle name?

13. The only applicants for the job were Josh, Enrique, and I.

14. Agoraphobia is the fear of being in large open places.

15. Is the current president of the United States a Democrat or a Republican?

16. Are you and Willis close friends?

17. We have always been avid fans of ice hockey.

18. Spanish is one of the Romance languages.

19. Is French a Romance language, too?

20. A fine mess this is!

The Subject Complement: Predicate Adjectives

13i. A *subject complement* is a word or word group that is in the predicate and that describes or identifies the subject.

A *predicate adjective* is an adjective that is in the predicate and that modifies the subject.

 EXAMPLES This loaf of bread smells **fresh** to me. [fresh loaf]

     Your essay is **clear** and **concise.** [clear and concise essay]

EXERCISE Underline the predicate adjectives in the following sentences.

 Example 1. Is that volcano <u>extinct</u>?

1. This song was popular during the summer of 1999.

2. In my opinion, your plan is more reasonable than any of the others.

3. All of the contestants appear calm and confident.

4. Does that salsa taste too spicy?

5. Are these horses free to roam the ranch?

6. The poetry of Shel Silverstein is delightful.

7. My stepsister is two years older than I am.

8. Why are you reluctant to express your opinion?

9. Usually, the children remain quiet and still during storytelling time.

10. Not all of the protagonist's actions, however, are heroic.

11. All summer the weather here has been hot and dry.

12. Why does the cellar always smell dank and musty?

13. Keep this information, for it may be helpful to you later.

14. The strawberries should be ripe in a few days.

15. Are any of these library books overdue?

16. This whole-grain cereal is not only delicious but also good for you.

17. The audience grew restless waiting for the concert to begin.

18. Both of the students seemed genuinely sorry for what they had said.

19. The actor portraying the dragon in the play did not feel comfortable in the elaborate costume.

20. Long, narrow, and winding was the unpaved road leading to the castle.

Predicate Nominatives and Predicate Adjectives

13i.   A *subject complement* is a word or word group that is in the predicate and that describes or identifies the subject.

> **EXAMPLES**   Lasagna is my favorite **food.** [predicate nominative identifying *Lasagna*]
> That sauce tastes **rich** and **tangy.** [compound predicate adjective describing *sauce*]
> How **delicious** this lasagna is! [predicate adjective describing *lasagna*]

EXERCISE A   Underline each subject complement in the following sentences. Then, above each write *PN* for *predicate nominative* or *PA* for *predicate adjective.*

                                       PN   *PN*

Example   1.   The best cooks are <u>she</u> and <u>Paulo</u>.

1.   This is a fine restaurant.

2.   The Marliave Ristorante has always been my favorite one.

3.   The prices at the Marliave seem reasonable and affordable.

4.   The chefs are Esther DeFalco and her brother.

5.   Their recipes are traditional.

6.   The ingredients smell and taste fresh.

7.   The pasta in their lasagna is homemade and light.

8.   "Be careful when rolling out the pasta dough," Esther says.

9.   "The lasagna pasta must be paper-thin," Vinicio points out.

10.   For the DeFalcos, the making of pasta remains an art.

EXERCISE B   On the lines provided, make the following word groups into complete sentences by adding the kinds of subject complements identified in parentheses.

Example   1.   *(predicate adjective)*   Sailing away from home to a strange land seems <u>*frightening*</u> .

11.   *(predicate adjective)*   For some immigrants, the voyage to the United States was _____.

12.   *(predicate nominative)*   Was the decision to immigrate _____?

13.   *(compound predicate adjective)*   The immigrants must have been _____.

14.   *(predicate nominative)*   The task of adapting to a new way of life is _____.

15.   *(compound predicate nominative)*   Two of the families who immigrated with the DeFalcos were

_____.

GRAMMAR

Direct Objects

13j. A *direct object* is a noun, pronoun, or word group that tells who or what receives the action of a verb or shows the result of the action.

A direct object answers the question "What?" or "Whom?" after a transitive verb.

EXAMPLES Did you attend the football **game**? [You did attend what? Game.]

Did you meet **Jason** and **Molly** there? [You did meet whom? Jason and Molly.]

EXERCISE Underline the direct objects in the following sentences.

Example 1. Many reporters interviewed the winning quarterback.

1. In 1967, Los Angeles hosted the first Super Bowl game.

2. More than sixty thousand fans attended the game at Memorial Coliseum.

3. Kansas City played Green Bay in the first Super Bowl game.

4. Green Bay defeated Kansas City by twenty-five points.

5. Before the Super Bowl became an annual event, the two best teams from the National Football League played a championship game.

6. In 1960, the American Football League formed and held its first annual championship.

7. Eventually, the AFL and NFL championship teams played each other at the end of the season.

8. A 1970 merger created the National Football Conference and the American Football Conference.

9. Has the NFC or the AFC won more Super Bowl titles?

10. Millions of fans watch it on television.

11. Many spectators find the halftime shows entertaining.

12. Do you know any amazing records set during Super Bowl games?

13. In 1994, Steve Christie kicked a 54-yard field goal.

14. How many records did Jerry Rice set?

15. In the early 1990s, the Buffalo Bills made appearances in four consecutive Super Bowls.

16. How many teams have won consecutive Super Bowl games?

17. Winners of more than one Super Bowl include San Francisco, Dallas, and Pittsburgh.

18. Which team won the Super Bowl last year?

19. Did you have tickets for the game?

20. What a terrific game those two teams played!

Indirect Objects

13k. An *indirect object* is a noun, pronoun, or word group that often appears in sentences containing direct objects. An indirect object tells *to whom* or *to what* (or *for whom* or *for what*) the action of a transitive verb is done.

EXAMPLE I showed **Mom** and **Dad** my report. [Showed to whom? Mom and Dad.]

EXERCISE A Underline the indirect objects in the following sentences.

Example 1. Mr. Greico gave us a quiz in math today.

1. I lent Yolanda my baseball glove.

2. Maxine baked us a vegetable pizza.

3. The Nineteenth Amendment gives women the right to vote.

4. Nathan bought his grandfather leather gloves for Christmas.

5. At the concession stand, Tim bought himself a bag of popcorn and a bottle of water.

6. The store manager offered each of the applicants a part-time job.

7. Every Monday morning, our parents hand us our allowances for the week.

8. Ms. Wong told the children the story about Damocles and the sword.

9. I am weaving my aunt and uncle a tapestry with pictures of hummingbirds and magnolias.

10. My neighbor pays me twenty-five dollars for mowing his lawn.

EXERCISE B Rewrite the following sentences, making each underlined phrase an indirect object.

Example 1. Please give this message to Terrence or Scott. *Please give Terrence or Scott this*
message.

11. Heather knitted a pair of socks for her baby brother. _____

_____

12. The camping trip provided plenty of exciting moments for the hikers. _____

_____

13. Did you send invitations to Rebecca and him? _____

_____

14. The judges awarded gold medals to both Kristi and Carl. _____

_____

15. Tomás showed his large collection of baseball cards to Armand and me. _____

_____

Direct and Indirect Objects

13j. A **direct object** is a noun, pronoun, or word group that tells who or what receives the action of a verb or shows the result of the action.

    EXAMPLE   Gayle visited an **island** in Florida. [Gayle visited what? Island.]

13k. An **indirect object** is a noun, pronoun, or word group that often appears in sentences containing direct objects. An indirect object tells *to whom* or *to what* (or *for whom* or *for what*) the action of a transitive verb is done.

    EXAMPLE   Give **Tish** and **me** your tickets. [Give to whom? Tish and me.]

EXERCISE A   Decide whether the underlined words in the following sentences are direct objects or indirect objects. Above each underlined word, write *DO* for *direct object* or *IO* for *indirect object.*

                                   IO   *IO*

Example **1.** Who gave the <u>teachers</u> and <u>students</u> the maps showing the farm's location?

1. The juniors planned a <u>trip</u> to Belle Grove, a nineteenth-century farm.

2. Farm children performed many <u>chores</u> before school each day.

3. They gave the <u>chickens</u> feed and milked the cows.

4. All family members had specific <u>duties</u> in the barn and fields.

5. Farmhands scattered <u>straw</u> over the barn floor.

6. A blacksmith pounded the <u>steel</u> with his hammer.

7. He told <u>us</u> his experiences as the village blacksmith.

8. The students asked <u>him</u> many questions.

9. Farm women made <u>lace</u> and embroidered during the winter.

10. One woman showed <u>me</u> her handmade shawl.

EXERCISE B   In the following sentences, underline direct objects once and indirect objects twice. Not all sentences contain both a direct object and an indirect object.

Example **1.** The librarian showed my <u><u>friend</u></u> and <u><u>me</u></u> the biography <u>section</u>.

11. The Pulitzer Prize Board awarded Alex Haley a special citation for *Roots* in 1977.

12. In *Roots,* Haley presents a heroic saga about African Americans.

13. The book provides Americans some insight into the horrors of slavery.

14. Haley's book inspired a popular television miniseries.

15. Various organizations gave the miniseries prestigious awards.

Parts of a Sentence

Every sentence contains a *subject* and a *verb*. Some sentences may also contain *complements*—direct objects, indirect objects, predicate nominatives, or predicate adjectives. Any of these sentence parts may be compound.

EXERCISE   In each of the following sentences, underline the sentence part or parts given in parentheses.

Example 1. *(direct object)*   Give your <u>tickets</u> to the person at that window.

1. *(direct object)*   Have you ever visited a county fair?

2. *(compound subject)*   Last year, my best friend and I attended a fair in our state capital.

3. *(predicate adjective)*   The playful antics of the rodeo clowns were quite entertaining.

4. *(verb)*   Then we wandered around the fairgrounds.

5. *(compound subject)*   Animal pens and displays of food and crafts filled the large exhibit halls.

6. *(verb)*   In one area sheep were lying about in small pens.

7. *(direct object)*   A ranchhand noticed our interest in the sheep and spoke to us.

8. *(predicate nominative)*   "These animals can be good pets," said the ranchhand.

9. *(compound direct object)*   Until then, I had considered only cats, dogs, or fish as pets.

10. *(indirect object)*   The friendly ranchhand brought the sheep some food.

11. *(predicate adjective)*   "By now these sheep are hungry."

12. *(indirect object)*   "Would you give them lunch?"

13. *(indirect object)*   The ranchhand gave each of us a handful of food pellets.

14. *(compound verb)*   The sheep, apparently ravenous, chewed the food quickly and looked for more.

15. *(direct object)*   The sheep gave me a brilliant idea.

16. *(compound predicate adjective)*   Yardwork certainly can become tiresome and dull.

17. *(direct object)*   Sheep, however, happily eat grass.

18. *(predicate nominative)*   In other words, a sheep is a natural lawn mower!

19. *(subject)*   There was only one problem with this idea.

20. *(direct object)*   The city has zoning laws against sheep ranching!

Classifying Sentences by Purpose

13l. A sentence may be classified, depending on its purpose, as *declarative, imperative, interrogative,* or *exclamatory.*

DECLARATIVE	Keiko is painting a watercolor in the style of the Japanese masters.
IMPERATIVE	Be sure to recycle those boxes.
INTERROGATIVE	At what time does the concert begin?
EXCLAMATORY	What a spectacular game that was!

EXERCISE   Classify each of the following sentences by purpose. On the line provided, write *DEC* if the sentence is *declarative, IMP* if it is *imperative, INT* if it is *interrogative,* or *EXC* if it is *exclamatory.*

Example *IMP* **1.** Please step onto the stage.

_____ **1.** Shana's dream has come true, for all summer long Shana will be the magician's assistant at Worlds of Entertainment.

_____ **2.** Imagine spending your summer being sawed in half and pulling rabbits out of a hat.

_____ **3.** What fun that would be!

_____ **4.** Have you heard the best part of all?

_____ **5.** At one point during the show, the magician makes Shana seem to float in the air.

_____ **6.** How does the magician make Shana float?

_____ **7.** Somehow, the curtain must cover the table on which Shana rests.

_____ **8.** What a fantastic trick that is!

_____ **9.** After the show, ask the magician and Shana for their autographs.

_____ **10.** Would you like to work with a magician?

_____ **11.** I am interested in the history of magic.

_____ **12.** Anthropologists think ancient civilizations believed in magic.

_____ **13.** Didn't the ancient Egyptians create amulets for magical purposes?

_____ **14.** Pass me that book about alchemists in the Middle Ages.

_____ **15.** In other times, thousands of people were accused of being witches and executed.

_____ **16.** What strange times those must have been!

_____ **17.** Have advances in science weakened belief in magic?

_____ **18.** Do superstitions indicate a belief in magic?

_____ **19.** Please tell me what you think.

_____ **20.** How puzzling some superstitions are!

Review A: Sentences and Sentence Fragments

EXERCISE Identify each of the following groups of words as a sentence or a sentence fragment. On the line provided, write *S* for *sentence* or *F* for *sentence fragment*.

Example ___*F*___ **1.** The city of Pamplona in the northern part of Spain.

_____ **1.** Pamplona, Spain, the site of Las Fiestas de San Fermín.

_____ **2.** This annual week-long celebration begins at noon on July 6.

_____ **3.** After a fireworks mortar has been fired.

_____ **4.** Perhaps the best-known part of the festival is the daily running of the bulls.

_____ **5.** The running of the bulls begins promptly at 8:00 A.M.

_____ **6.** City officials block off several streets.

_____ **7.** One of which is the *calle de la Estafeta*.

_____ **8.** The bulls run through streets leading to the *plaza de toros*.

_____ **9.** Traditionally, ahead of the bulls runs a crowd of young men.

_____ **10.** The daring runners wearing white shirts and pants and red bandannas and sashes.

_____ **11.** Obviously, this is very dangerous.

_____ **12.** Each day at noon, through the city's streets several people in elaborate costumes.

_____ **13.** The two people wearing tall costumes.

_____ **14.** One of the costumes is that of a king.

_____ **15.** The other costume that of a queen.

_____ **16.** Other costumes, which include enormous heads.

_____ **17.** Especially enjoying this part of the festivities are the children.

_____ **18.** Dancing, singing, and celebrating continue throughout the night.

_____ **19.** A traditional snack called *sopa de ajo*.

_____ **20.** A garlic soup that is served cold.

_____ **21.** *Sopa de ajo* is a mixture of mashed raw garlic, bread crumbs, water, salt, vinegar, and olive oil.

_____ **22.** For a week the participants in the festival spend very little time sleeping.

_____ **23.** In Ernest Hemingway's novel *Fiesta* is a description of the running of the bulls.

_____ **24.** Have you ever been to Spain?

_____ **25.** If you've ever heard of Las Fiestas de San Fermín.

Review B: **Subjects and Predicates**

EXERCISE A For each of the following sentences, underline the simple subject once and the verb twice. Before the numeral, write *(you)* if the subject is understood. Be sure to include all parts of any verb phrases and all parts of compound subjects or verbs.

Example 1. Neither my cousin nor I will ever forget my visit to his city last spring.

1. Last spring, I saw a fire.

2. My cousin, a nurse at a state hospital, had invited me down for the weekend.

3. Like him, I am studying for a career as a nurse.

4. He lives in a comfortable nurses' residence next to the hospital.

5. For our Saturday dinner, my cousin and I had bought fish fillets.

6. At six o'clock he put the fillets under the broiler.

7. Meanwhile, I was happily making a Waldorf salad.

8. Suddenly, his name was called over the public address system.

9. He groaned, rose to his feet, and gave me instructions.

10. "Just watch television in my room for a while."

EXERCISE B For each of the following sentences, underline the complete subject once and the complete predicate twice. Circle each simple subject and verb.

Example 1. I turned on one of my favorite programs.

11. I had already seen that episode of the television program.

12. I soon fell asleep on the sofa.

13. What woke me?

14. A loud wail of sirens came from the street below.

15. To my horror, the kitchen was full of black, acrid smoke.

16. Three figures in smoke masks charged past me.

17. They ran into the kitchen and opened the oven.

18. The firefighters extinguished the remains of the fish and cleared away the smoke.

19. The kitchen was a mess.

20. My cousin and I cleaned the kitchen.

ELEMENTS OF LANGUAGE | Third Course

Review C: Complements

EXERCISE A In each of the following sentences, decide what kind of complement the underlined word is. Above each underlined word, write *DO* for *direct object*, *IO* for *indirect object*, *PN* for *predicate nominative*, or *PA* for *predicate adjective*.

                                                 IO

Example 1. The Internet can provide <u>researchers</u> valuable information.

1. Computers are useful <u>machines</u> for problem solving and for information processing.

2. However, some people fear <u>computers</u>.

3. To these people, computers seem too <u>complicated</u>.

4. Generally speaking, people appreciate the <u>capabilities</u> of computers.

5. Computers can give <u>people</u> the ability to work more efficiently.

6. The Internet provided <u>me</u> much information for my report on archaeology.

7. Archaeologists uncover the <u>remains</u> of ancient civilizations.

8. Studying artifacts can give <u>archaeologists</u> information about past cultures.

9. This information is <u>useful</u> to historians and sociologists.

10. In fact, many people study these <u>data</u>.

EXERCISE B Each of the following sentences contains at least one complement. Underline each complement, and then identify it by writing above it *DO* for *direct object*, *IO* for *indirect object*, *PN* for *predicate nominative*, or *PA* for *predicate adjective*.

                                 IO   *DO*

Example 1. The reporter had asked <u>us</u> an interesting <u>question</u> about current fads.

11. Are most people conformists?

12. Many students merely follow the crowd.

13. Awareness of fads or fashions is important to most of us.

14. We follow school fads in dress, slang, and behavior.

15. Such fads are a normal part of teenage life.

16. Knowledge of current fads gives many people a sense of belonging.

17. What are some of the current fads?

18. Describe a current fad, Jesse.

19. Does popular slang still include such words as *cool*, *dude*, and *awesome*?

20. Fads of today may seem silly to us a few years from now.

Grammar, Usage, and Mechanics: Language Skills Practice **55**

Review D: **Sentence Fragments, Kinds of Sentences**

EXERCISE Decide whether each of the following groups of words is a sentence or a sentence fragment. On the line provided, write *S* for *sentence* or *F* for *fragment*. Then, identify each complete sentence by writing on the line provided one of these abbreviations:

DEC for *declarative sentence*   INT for *interrogative sentence*
EXC for *exclamatory sentence*   IMP for *imperative sentence*

Example _S, INT_ **1.** Have you read any of Barbara Kingsolver's works?

_____ **1.** Ms. Osaka is one of the art teachers at my school.

_____ **2.** Didn't you receive my e-mail message?

_____ **3.** How extraordinary your performance was tonight!

_____ **4.** Some of the mementos of our trip.

_____ **5.** Signal me when you are ready to begin singing.

_____ **6.** What a thoughtful person you are!

_____ **7.** Have you been practicing your saxophone lessons?

_____ **8.** How many languages can you speak?

_____ **9.** On our way home we stopped at the bakery to buy some bagels.

_____ **10.** The last short story that I read.

_____ **11.** Please show me how to program this VCR.

_____ **12.** What a clever trick that was!

_____ **13.** In major-league baseball, who holds the record for hitting the most home runs in a season?

_____ **14.** That restaurant serves Thai food.

_____ **15.** As soon as Anthony and I arrived.

_____ **16.** Call this number, and ask for Dr. Parker.

_____ **17.** If you can speak Spanish, you may find French easier to understand.

_____ **18.** Which freedoms does the First Amendment guarantee?

_____ **19.** Because all of the tickets for the concert had already been sold.

_____ **20.** Carmela, having decided that she would rather be a marine biologist than a chemical engineer.

for **CHAPTER 13: THE PARTS OF A SENTENCE**   pages 413–36

Literary Model: Dialogue

> Before the mirror, she let the wraps fall from her shoulders to see herself once again in all her glory. Suddenly she gave a cry. The necklace was gone.
>
> Her husband, already half undressed, said, "What's the trouble?"
>
> She turned toward him despairingly, "I . . . I . . . I don't have Mme. Forestier's necklace."
>
> "What! You can't mean it! It's impossible!"
>
> They hunted everywhere, through the folds of the dress, through the folds of the coat, in the pockets. They found nothing.
>
> He asked, "Are you sure you had it when leaving the dance?"
>
> "Yes, I felt it when I was in the hall of the Ministry."
>
> "But if you had lost it on the street, we'd have heard it drop. It must be in the cab."
>
> "Yes, quite likely. Did you get its number?"
>
> "No. Did you notice it, either?"
>
> "No."
>
> They looked at each other aghast. Finally Loisel got dressed again.
>
> "I'll retrace our steps on foot," he said, "to see if I can find it."
>
> —from "The Necklace" by Guy de Maupassant

Exercise A

1. What kinds of sentences (*declarative, imperative, interrogative,* or *exclamatory*) does Madame

Loisel (the second speaker) use in the passage? _____

_____

2. What kinds of sentences does her husband use? _____

_____

3. What kinds of sentences does the narrator use? _____

_____

4. What kind of sentence do neither the characters nor the narrator use? _____

Exercise B

1. Compare the kinds of sentences that Madame Loisel and her husband use. How do the

different kinds of sentences they use reflect their feelings? _____

_____

Literary Model (continued)

_____
_____
_____

2. Why do you think the kinds of sentences Mr. Loisel uses change in the second half of the passage? _____

_____
_____
_____

EXERCISE C   Write a short dialogue in which one character realizes that he or she has lost something and the other character tries to help him or her remember where the item was lost.

_____
_____
_____
_____
_____
_____
_____
_____
_____
_____
_____

EXERCISE D

1. What kinds of sentences did you use in your dialogue? _____
_____

2. In the dialogue, how did you use sentences of different purposes to show how the characters felt about losing the item and trying to find it? _____
_____
_____

Writing Application: Summary

We could probably communicate in English with a relatively small group of verbs—*be, do, go, eat, drink, sleep,* and a few others. Think, though, how boring communication would be!

    LESS INTERESTING   I went to the cafe on the corner and drank a lemonade.

    MORE INTERESTING   I hightailed it to the cafe on the corner and guzzled down a lemonade.

Fortunately, the English language contains thousands of verbs you can choose from to enliven your writing. Using well-chosen verbs, you, as a writer, can help your reader to visualize what you are describing.

WRITING ACTIVITY

Have you ever decided not to see a movie because you were afraid it would be as boring as the summary of it that you just read? A well-written summary often helps readers decide to view a movie. Think of a movie that impressed you and that you wanted to recommend to everyone you knew. Write a summary of the movie; to keep your writing interesting, be sure to include at least five well-chosen, precise, and lively verbs.

PREWRITING   Spend a few minutes remembering the plot and details of the movie and jotting down notes about what you remember. Pay extra attention to those aspects of the movie that first come to your mind, since they are probably what made the movie so memorable and what you will want to emphasize in your summary. Brainstorm for verbs that express the actions portrayed in the movie. In addition, consider the tone you will adopt. For instance, do you want to sound casual or formal?

WRITING   Decide how you will structure your summary. Will you arrange your ideas in some order other than chronological? If other ideas or details occur to you as you write, add them.

REVISING   Examine your draft to determine whether you can replace some of the verbs with others that are more precise or lively. A thesaurus can help you with this step, but double-check a dictionary to make sure that a word suggested by the thesaurus is appropriate for the sentence. Try out your draft on a friend to see whether your summary makes him or her want to see the movie.

PUBLISHING   Check your summary for errors in grammar, usage, punctuation, and spelling. Make sure you have followed capitalization and punctuation rules for movie titles. Consider submitting your summary for publication in your school newspaper or on a Web site concerned with movies. Find out submission dates and what the guidelines are for length.

EXTENDING YOUR WRITING

You may want to develop this writing activity further. You could write a review of the movie and include part or all of your summary in the review. Submit your piece to a newspaper, magazine, or Web site that publishes movie reviews.

for **CHAPTER 14: THE PHRASE** *pages 442–62*

Choices: Examining Phrases

The following activities challenge you to find a connection between phrases and the world around you. Do the activity below that suits your personality best, and then share your discoveries with your class.

MUSIC

Do Re Mi

Musicians use phrases. If you are a musician, tell the class what a musical phrase is. Be sure to play some examples. Then, create a chart that shows how grammatical phrases and musical phrases are used in similar ways. Use at least three examples to demonstrate the similarities.

HISTORICAL RESEARCH

Attila the Hun

Throughout history, there have been people who were known by their names and an appositive. Attila the Hun is one. Gather as many of these names as you can find. You should be able to find at least five, but try to come up with as many as ten. Then, using appositives, write a very short biography for each person. Be sure to point out which names use commas with their appositives and which do not.

CREATIVE WRITING

You, Wonderful You

If someone were writing about you twenty-five years from now, what appositives might be used? Be that someone. Write at least twenty sentences that use appositives (for the future you, of course). Include some short appositives and some quite long ones.

GAMES

Game Show Host

Divide the class into groups. Have each group brainstorm participles and some nouns that they commonly modify, such as *burnt toast, greased lightning,* and *roasted peanuts.* At the end of two minutes, collect each list. Then, write each participle and noun on the board, and answer any objections to the pairings. Eliminate any that are impossible or illogical. The team with the most participles modifying nouns wins!

WRITING

Mission Possible

If you've got a purpose and somebody asks you what it is, chances are you'll use an infinitive or two to answer the question. Working with your classmates, use infinitives to write five possible mission statements for the class. Then, with your teacher's permission, post your statements in your classroom.

RESEARCH

In the Pink

Phrases play a big role in idioms. Idioms like *in hot water, wearing your heart on your sleeve,* and *reading between the lines* can make people who aren't familiar with them frown and scratch their heads. However, they do make more sense if you know the story behind them. Start by brainstorming a list of at least ten idioms that are phrases or that contain phrases. Then, research the stories behind a few of these phrases. Report your findings to the class.

ART

Running Shoes

If you like a joke and you can draw, try this project. Illustrate at least five expressions that use participles and that conjure up humorous images, such as a *walking stick,* or *baked Alaska.* Then, display your images, but without the participial phrase. Let your classmates write their guesses at the bottom of each picture.

ORIGINAL PROJECTS

It's up to You

You have good ideas. Pick one, and create your own project. Use infinitives to write a list of your lifetime goals. Make a list of participles used in cooking. Compose a list of gerunds used in careers or sports. Whatever you decide to do, be sure to get your teacher's approval before you start.

Phrases

| **14a.** | A *phrase* is a group of related words that is used as a single part of speech and that does not contain both a verb and its subject. |

EXAMPLES   would have arrived [no subject]

in the deep blue sea [no subject or verb]

EXERCISE A   On the line provided, write *P* if the word group is a phrase or *NP* if it is not a phrase.

Example ___P___ **1.** throughout the seventeenth century

_____ **1.** in the government

_____ **2.** Rhode Island was a charter colony

_____ **3.** granting a charter

_____ **4.** without representation

_____ **5.** a charter was written

_____ **6.** the colonies united

_____ **7.** to leave early

_____ **8.** in Providence

_____ **9.** the revolution began

_____ **10.** in the public interest

_____ **11.** before the American Revolution

_____ **12.** along the Atlantic coast

_____ **13.** in Narragansett Bay

_____ **14.** it became a thriving center

_____ **15.** among the colonies

_____ **16.** to settle the colony

_____ **17.** in the dense forests

_____ **18.** the banishing of the colonists

_____ **19.** for religious freedom

_____ **20.** many years have passed

EXERCISE B   On the line provided, write *P* if the underlined word group is a phrase or *NP* if it is not a phrase.

Example ___P___ **1.** This engine converts heat energy <u>into mechanical energy</u>.

_____ **21.** In 1845, two Englishmen built an aircraft powered <u>by a lightweight steam engine</u>.

_____ **22.** The Englishmen used a steam engine, <u>the only type of engine available at that time</u>.

_____ **23.** <u>Working with an unsuitable engine</u>, the plane never got off the ground.

_____ **24.** <u>An engine is needed</u> to fly a long distance.

_____ **25.** Many inventors had been working <u>on the problem</u> of an airplane engine.

_____ **26.** <u>Lacking an engine</u>, a glider could stay afloat for only a short time.

_____ **27.** Over the next fifty years, <u>people tried to make steam-powered planes fly</u>.

_____ **28.** Do you know <u>what kind of engine was successful</u>?

_____ **29.** <u>Inventing compact gas engines</u> made airplane flight possible.

_____ **30.** It would take many years <u>before that invention occurred</u>.

Prepositional Phrases

14b. A *prepositional phrase* includes a preposition, the object of the preposition, and any modifiers of that object.

> **EXAMPLES** **at** the hobby shop
> **because of** them

14c. The noun or pronoun in a prepositional phrase is called the *object of the preposition.*

> **EXAMPLE** Is that a letter **from the Department of Education**? [The compound noun *Department of Education* is the object of the preposition *from.*]

EXERCISE A Underline the prepositional phrases in the following sentences. Then, circle the object of each preposition. Hint: Some sentences have more than one prepositional phrase.

Example 1. Stamp collecting involves citizens with their government.

1. What is the story behind a United States commemorative stamp?

2. A citizen submits to the Citizens' Stamp Advisory Committee an idea for a new stamp.

3. Members of this committee are artists, stamp collectors, and businesspersons.

4. First, the idea for the new design is approved by the committee.

5. Then, the idea is sent to the postmaster general.

6. Without the approval of these two parties, the stamp cannot be created.

7. The next step in the process is the selection of an artist.

8. The chosen artist gives the design to an artist from the Bureau of Engraving and Printing.

9. From this artwork, the bureau's artist completes the design of the stamp.

10. The new stamp will include the abbreviation for the United States of America, the price of the

stamp, and a title that tells about the stamp.

EXERCISE B On the line provided, add at least one prepositional phrase to each of the following sentences. Circle the object of the preposition in each phrase you write.

Example 1. _____At six o'clock in the morning_____ , we began our road trip to Atlanta.

11. We had been traveling _____ for hours.

12. We had finally reached the state line _____ .

13. _____ we were ready for lunch.

14. We stopped _____ to eat the sandwiches we had bought.

15. _____ we were quite comfortable.

The Adjective Phrase

14d.   A prepositional phrase that modifies a noun or pronoun is called an **adjective phrase.**

> **EXAMPLES**   The life cycle **of the piranha** is interesting. [The phrase *of the piranha* modifies *life cycle*.]
>
> Some **of the dangerous fish** are upstairs. [The phrase *of the dangerous fish* modifies *Some*.]
>
> Some frogs secrete poison from glands **in their skin.** [The phrase *in their skin* modifies *glands*, the object of the preposition *from*.]

EXERCISE   Underline the adjective phrases in the following sentences. Then, draw an arrow from each adjective phrase to the word it modifies. Hint: Some sentences have more than one adjective phrase.

Example 1. The variety of fish in the aquarium intrigues us.

1. My visit to the aquarium was fascinating.

2. There, I found information about creatures in the world's oceans.

3. There are fish with undeserved bad reputations.

4. Puffers in the ocean can look striking.

5. Puffers as a meal can be dangerous.

6. The tank near the center of the exhibit hall contains three small sharks.

7. Many species of sharks are perfectly harmless.

8. Only some of the world's sharks are dangerous.

9. The giant octopus from the waters off the Pacific Northwest coast appears dangerous.

10. The many suckers on the tentacles of the octopus look frightening.

11. Do the tentacles of a jellyfish resemble those of an octopus?

12. The suckers along the arms of the starfish help it move around.

13. Lobsters have two kinds of claws.

14. The manta is one of the more entertaining creatures in the ocean.

15. Another playful creature in the sea is the dolphin.

16. The aquarium also features a large exhibit of eels.

17. Some of the eels are six feet long.

18. Are fish from the depths of the ocean brightly colored?

19. Did you see every exhibit at the aquarium?

20. Here is a brochure with pictures of some of the exhibits.

The Adverb Phrase

14e. A prepositional phrase that modifies a verb, an adjective, or an adverb is called an *adverb phrase.*

An adverb phrase tells *how, when, where, why,* or *to what extent.*

EXAMPLES   **Through his poetry** Langston Hughes reveals something of the African American experience. [*Through his poetry* modifies the verb *reveals,* telling *how.*]

Hughes became well known **as Harlem's poet laureate.** [*As Harlem's poet laureate* modifies the adjective *known,* telling *how.*]

Later **in life** Hughes wrote several plays. [*In life* modifies the adverb *Later,* telling *when.*]

EXERCISE Underline the adverb phrases in the following sentences. Then, draw an arrow from each adverb phrase to the word or words it modifies.

Example 1. For many years Mark Twain has been famous for his adventure novels.

1. Mark Twain was born in Florida, Missouri.

2. When he was young, Twain lived in Hannibal, Missouri.

3. Hannibal is located on the Mississippi River.

4. Twain felt happy when he was on the Mississippi.

5. Early in his career Twain worked as a newspaper writer.

6. He traveled around the United States and in Europe.

7. In 1867, Twain traveled from New York to Europe and the Holy Land.

8. His travels resulted in a book, which he titled *The Innocents Abroad.*

9. The book was published after his return.

10. In a short time the book became popular.

11. Twain became famous early in his career.

12. He became well known as a humorist.

13. Look for Twain's name in this anthology.

14. In this book you can find Twain's best-known short story.

15. Many writers have been influenced by Twain's works.

16. If you are fond of humor, you will enjoy reading Twain's fiction.

17. *The Adventures of Tom Sawyer* and *The Adventures of Huckleberry Finn* are loved by many.

18. In how many novels do Tom Sawyer and Huck Finn appear?

19. Are the characters Tom Sawyer and Huck Finn based on real persons?

20. I could easily read Twain's fiction for hours.

for **CHAPTER 14: THE PHRASE** *pages 443–46*

Adjective and Adverb Phrases

14d. A prepositional phrase that modifies a noun or a pronoun is called an **adjective phrase.**

> **EXAMPLE** The woman **in the seat next to Mr. Holt** is our guest speaker. [*In the seat* modifies the noun *woman*, and *next to Mr. Holt* modifies the noun *seat*.]

14e. A prepositional phrase that modifies a verb, an adjective, or an adverb is called an **adverb phrase.**

> **EXAMPLE** **During spring break** we traveled **to Washington, D.C.** [Both prepositional phrases modify the verb *traveled*.]

EXERCISE A In the following sentences, draw an arrow from each underlined prepositional phrase to the word or words it modifies. Then, identify the phrase by writing above it *ADJ* for *adjective phrase* or *ADV* for *adverb phrase.*

Example 1. On Tuesday our science class took a field trip to the planetarium.

1. On the first night, the hikers camped near the Salinas River.

2. Most of this artwork was created by ninth-grade students.

3. Everyone I have met at my new school has been extremely kind to me.

4. Throughout the summer, I worked as a landscape gardener.

5. For dinner we will serve baked chicken with red beans and rice.

EXERCISE B Underline the two prepositional phrases in each of the following sentences. Draw an arrow from each phrase to the word or words it modifies. Then, identify each phrase by writing above it *ADJ* for *adjective phrase* or *ADV* for *adverb phrase.*

Example 1. Scott works at the pet shop in the mall.

6. Near the entrance to the cave, we discovered an old map.

7. The movie's ending took everyone in the theater by surprise.

8. What are some of the differences between the African elephant and the Asian elephant?

9. According to this recipe, the casserole should be baked for thirty minutes.

10. All of these lovely quilts were made by hand.

11. The development of the Internet has changed our lives in many ways.

12. Through the telescope we could see clearly the rings around Saturn.

13. In the living room, Sam chased the kitten around the couch.

14. After sunset is there still enough light for photography?

15. Austin, Texas, has been the capital both of a state and of a country.

GRAMMAR

The Participle

| **14f.** | A *participle* is a verb form that can be used as an adjective. |

(1) Present participles end in *–ing*.

EXAMPLE   The **screaming** fans spurred the team to victory. [*Screaming* modifies the noun *fans.*]

(2) Past participles usually end in *–d* or *–ed*. Other past participles are formed irregularly.

EXAMPLES   This restaurant's specialty is **grilled** salmon. [*Grilled* modifies the noun *salmon.*]
The lake appears **frozen.** [*Frozen* modifies the noun *lake.*]

EXERCISE   In each of the following sentences, underline the participle that is used as an adjective. Then, draw an arrow from the participle to the word it modifies.

Example 1. During the trial, the defendant recanted his signed confession.

1. The pacing lion made us nervous.

2. A part of the broken bat nearly hit the runner on third base.

3. Our football team had a winning season.

4. The hunted animal camouflaged itself.

5. All new employees must first complete a six-week training program.

6. The road sign read, "Watch for falling rocks!"

7. I had forgotten to add diced onions to the salad.

8. One movie critic called the movie disturbing.

9. Throughout the storm the little puppy remained under the bed, whimpering.

10. Would you please remove the whistling teakettle from the burner?

11. Typed hastily, the report contained several errors.

12. Harper Lee's only published novel is *To Kill a Mockingbird*.

13. Our cat's paw prints appear all over the freshly painted picnic table.

14. Startled, the young deer bounded across the creek.

15. Lying in the shade, the dog quickly fell asleep.

16. Lifting the piano, the worker pulled a muscle in his back.

17. When I proofread my report, I found two misspelled words.

18. On the windshield of every parked vehicle was an advertisement for the county fair.

19. The interviewer asked the celebrated author about her recent novel.

20. According to the legend, no one ever found the buried treasure.

The Participial Phrase

| **14g.** | A *participial phrase* is used as an adjective and consists of a participle and any complements or modifiers the participle has. |

EXAMPLES   We just saw Carlos **playing soccer in the park.** [The participial phrase, which consists of the present participle *playing*, the direct object *soccer*, and the prepositional phrase *in the park*, modifies the noun *Carlos*.]

The crew of the space shuttle **launched on Friday** will repair the satellite. [The participial phrase, which consists of the past participle *launched* and the prepositional phrase *on Friday*, modifies the noun *space shuttle*.]

EXERCISE   Underline the participial phrase in each of the following sentences. Then, draw an arrow to the word the phrase modifies.

Example 1. Climbing over the fence, the scout leader ripped his uniform.

1. On vacation we stayed at an inn built in the late eighteenth century.

2. Working for the florist, Langston learned about many varieties of plants.

3. The woman standing behind the podium is Ms. Kwan, our principal.

4. Is a baseball card autographed by Sammy Sosa very valuable?

5. The dog, searching for food, roamed the neighborhood.

6. Through my binoculars I spotted a hummingbird feeding on the nectar of a gladiolus.

7. The horse, walking slowly, approached the trainer.

8. We saw ahead of us a deer leaping across the highway.

9. The students, disturbed by the noise outside, could not concentrate on their class work.

10. Walking along the beach, we looked for colorful seashells.

11. Ontario, situated between Quebec and Manitoba, is Canada's most populous province.

12. Some literary critics consider that novel the best one ever written.

13. Walking through my new neighborhood, I met many friendly people.

14. Completed about 1506, *Mona Lisa,* Leonardo da Vinci's masterpiece, now hangs in the Louvre.

15. Glenn found on the Internet several good articles related to the topic of his science report.

16. Blowing her whistle, the lifeguard signaled the swimmers to get out of the pool.

17. Enchanted by the story, the children pleaded with Mr. Torres to tell another.

18. The student sitting at the first desk in the second row is an exchange student from Brazil.

19. Boarding *Air Force One,* the president smiled and waved at the enthusiastic crowd.

20. Training hard, the gymnasts practiced their floor exercises.

Participles and Participial Phrases

14f. A *participle* is a verb form that can be used as an adjective.

There are two kinds of participles: *present participles*, which end in *–ing,* and *past participles,* which end in *–d* or *–ed* or are irregularly formed.

14g. A *participial phrase* is used as an adjective and consists of a participle and any complements or modifiers the participle has.

> EXAMPLE **Disappointed with my performance,** I asked my opponent for a rematch. [The participial phrase, which consists of the past participle *Disappointed* and the prepositional phrase *with my performance,* modifies the pronoun *I.*]

EXERCISE A In each of the following sentences, underline the participle that is used as an adjective. Draw an arrow from the participle to the word it modifies.

Example 1. Soaring ticket sales made the team owners happy.

1. The participating players gathered on the field.

2. Cheering fans shouted the names of favorite players.

3. When Reginald came on the field, the delighted crowd roared.

4. Swaggering, he waved to the crowd.

5. Later, the winning team rushed off the field.

EXERCISE B Underline the participial phrases in the following sentences. Draw an arrow from each participial phrase to the word it modifies.

Example 1. Sifted at the site, the mounds of dirt yielded pieces of pottery and glass.

6. The archaeologist worked slowly, examining each particle of dirt carefully.

7. Artifacts buried in the site were valuable.

8. Serving as clues to early life, artifacts are like puzzle pieces.

9. The archaeologist, recording all efforts and observations, logged her progress.

10. A computer, given certain data, can help her date her findings.

11. We saw the archaeologist brushing dirt off an old statue.

12. Examining the statue, the archaeologist estimated its value.

13. Doesn't this artifact resemble one uncovered earlier?

14. Everyone working at the archaeological excavation was learning a great deal about the past.

15. An archaeological excavation would be an exciting experience for anyone interested in past cultures.

The Gerund

| **14h.** | A *gerund* is a verb form ending in *–ing* that is used as a noun. |

Like other nouns, gerunds are used as subjects, predicate nominatives, direct objects, indirect objects, and objects of prepositions.

EXAMPLES **Writing** requires patience. [subject]

My hobby is **writing.** [predicate nominative]

I enjoy **writing.** [direct object]

EXERCISE Underline the gerund in each of the following sentences. Then, identify the function of the gerund by writing above it one of these abbreviations: *S* for *subject*, *PN* for *predicate nominative*, *DO* for *direct object*, *IO* for *indirect object*, or *OP* for *object of a preposition*.

Example 1. Jogging is an excellent aerobic exercise.

1. My favorite pastime is stargazing.

2. After Dad and I grew tired of shopping, we went to a movie.

3. Do you enjoy fishing?

4. Teaching is a noble profession.

5. On my essay, my teacher wrote, "You should give careful proofreading more attention."

6. Either team has a good chance of winning.

7. Laughing easily helps to relieve stress.

8. I am not looking forward to moving.

9. The puppy's constant whimpering worried us.

10. The baby sitter talked to the children about the importance of sharing.

11. What does your mother do for a living?

12. A sizable part of the corporation's budget is spent on advertising.

13. My favorite pastime is definitely reading.

14. Helping others makes me feel good, too.

15. The sign read, "Loitering is not allowed."

16. The ceremony begins and ends with giving thanks.

17. Dancing is an important part of the ceremony.

18. You should give singing professionally very serious consideration.

19. Whistling always lifts my spirits.

20. The moral of the fable is "One should never stop dreaming."

The Gerund Phrase

14i. A *gerund phrase* consists of a gerund and any modifiers or complements the gerund has. The entire phrase is used as a noun.

Like other nouns, gerunds and gerund phrases are used as subjects, predicate nominatives, direct objects, indirect objects, or objects of prepositions.

EXAMPLES **Walking briskly** is good exercise. [subject]

How much did the mechanic charge for **repairing the car**? [object of the preposition]

EXERCISE   Underline the gerund phrase in each of the following sentences. Then, identify the function of the phrase by writing above it *S* for *subject*, *PN* for *predicate nominative*, *DO* for *direct object*, *IO* for *indirect object*, or *OP* for *object of a preposition*.

Example 1. He was four years old when he began playing golf. *[DO]*

1. Feeding the animals at the petting zoo was fun.

2. Meryl's hobby is raising tropical fish.

3. The Wildcats have a good chance of becoming state champions.

4. Every day, I get a good workout by walking through the park.

5. One of my weekly chores is cleaning the gerbil cage.

6. After talking to her guidance counselor, Katrina decided to take a course in auto mechanics.

7. Climbing to the summit of the mountain took the explorers nearly a week.

8. Finding a good part-time job has been difficult.

9. Your mistake was making a promise that you could not keep.

10. The artist James Whistler is best known for painting a portrait of his mother.

11. As soon as I came home, I started studying for the math test.

12. Would you be interested in trying out for the school's soccer team?

13. We especially enjoyed dining in the exotic atmosphere of the Rainforest Cafe.

14. We should give saving money for the trip our top priority.

15. Chris's responsibility is supervising the other workers.

16. Pablo and I are in charge of planning the family reunion.

17. At the age of six, Len began taking karate lessons.

18. Only one of my friends succeeded in tricking me on All Fools' Day.

19. The highlight of our visit to Washington, D.C., was touring the Smithsonian Institution.

20. Our class is looking forward to taking the field trip.

Gerunds and Gerund Phrases

14h.	A *gerund* is a verb form ending in *–ing* that is used as a noun.

14i.	A *gerund phrase* consists of a gerund and any modifiers or complements the gerund has. The entire phrase is used as a noun.

Like other nouns, gerunds or gerund phrases are used as subjects, predicate nominatives, direct objects, indirect objects, and objects of prepositions.

> **EXAMPLES**   Both of us enjoy **working.** [*Working* is the direct object of the verb *enjoy.*]
>
> **Working after school** has taught us the importance of **using our spare time wisely.**
> [*Working after school* is the subject of the verb *has taught. Using our spare time wisely* is the object of the preposition *of.*]

EXERCISE A   Underline the gerund in each of the following sentences. On the line provided, write *S* for *subject, PN* for *predicate nominative, OP* for *object of a preposition, DO* for *direct object,* or *IO* for *indirect object.*

Example _____DO_____ **1.** I learned <u>cooking</u> from my father.

_____ **1.** Moving is a big job and takes time.

_____ **2.** What is the point of hurrying?

_____ **3.** Singing is a tradition in our family.

_____ **4.** Was there a good reason for the scolding?

_____ **5.** His favorite outdoor chore is mowing.

_____ **6.** Ms. Santora enjoys teaching.

_____ **7.** We like bowling.

_____ **8.** The most popular sport around here is hiking.

_____ **9.** Rena and Opal both love ice skating.

_____ **10.** To earn extra money, we could give pet sitting a try.

EXERCISE B   Underline the gerund phrase in each of the following sentences. On the line provided, write *S* for *subject, PN* for *predicate nominative, DO* for *direct object,* or *OP* for *object of a preposition.*

Example _____S_____ **1.** <u>Our studying immigration</u> led to a discussion about Jane Addams.

_____ **11.** Founding Hull House was one of Jane Addams's greatest achievements.

_____ **12.** She began her work by obtaining a large, old house.

_____ **13.** Her work was encouraging people who lived in the slums to improve their lives.

_____ **14.** She also provided training in social work.

_____ **15.** Another of Addams's achievements was receiving the Nobel Peace Prize in 1931.

Participial and Gerund Phrases

14g. A *participial phrase* is used as an adjective and consists of a participle and any complements or modifiers the participle has.

EXAMPLE   **Restoring the historic home,** the new owners discovered some valuable artifacts.

14i. A *gerund phrase* consists of a gerund and any modifiers or complements the gerund has. The entire phrase is used as a noun.

EXAMPLE   **Restoring the historic home** will cost about fifty thousand dollars.

EXERCISE   In each of the following sentences, identify the underlined phrase by writing above it *PART* for *participial phrase* or *GER* for *gerund phrase*.

                                                   GER

Example 1. The dog would not stop barking at the snake.

1. The tour guide took snapshots of us standing in front of the Aztec pyramid.

2. Raising money for new uniforms proved more difficult than the band members had expected.

3. The scouts are looking forward to exploring the cavern.

4. Creating the family tree with his grandmother, Derek learned a great deal about his ancestors.

5. As treasurer, Jody is responsible for collecting the membership dues.

6. A cloud of black smoke rising above the treetops alarmed the campers.

7. In our spare time, Sarita and I enjoy making beaded moccasins.

8. Packing for my trip to the beach, I suddenly remembered that I hadn't bought any sunscreen.

9. Flying over the mountains in a helicopter was very exciting.

10. One of my duties as stage manager is giving the actors their cues.

11. Flying from Washington, D.C., to San Diego, California, we traveled through four time zones.

12. I wrote my pen pal a letter telling her about the fiesta.

13. Darcy is writing a poem about picking apples.

14. A snake slithering through the grass frightened the horse away.

15. With everyone offering me different advice, I became more confused than ever.

16. Planning activities for the school carnival was no easy task.

17. The name *Ohio* is an Iroquois word meaning "fine or great river."

18. When did you start taking tai chi lessons?

19. Winning the game would certainly boost our team's morale.

20. Everyone tried solving the riddle, but only Diego was successful.

The Infinitive

14j. An *infinitive* is a verb form that can be used as a noun, an adjective, or an adverb. Most infinitives begin with *to*.

NOUN	Would you like **to dance**? [*To dance* is the direct object of the verb *would like*.]
ADJECTIVE	This is a good place **to camp**. [*To camp* modifies the noun *place*.]
ADVERB	The performers were eager **to rehearse**. [*To rehearse* modifies the adjective *eager*.]

EXERCISE Underline the infinitive in each of the following sentences. Then, identify the use of the infinitive by writing above it *N* for *noun*, *ADJ* for *adjective*, or *ADV* for *adverb*.

N
Example 1. Where would you like to go?

1. John's refusal to participate surprised us.

2. Chen and I went to the library to study.

3. To travel in space is Sonia's ambition.

4. The Sorensons were the first guests to arrive.

5. My sister likes to swim.

6. Every one of my friends is willing to help.

7. A fascinating city to visit is San Antonio.

8. Dr. Simmons, our family's physician, has decided to retire.

9. At first, the witness appeared reluctant to testify.

10. In your opinion, what is the easiest word-processing program to use?

11. If you want to wait, Ms. Hobson will meet with you in a few minutes.

12. For any writing assignment, you should allow yourself time to proofread.

13. "Time is too valuable to waste," our teacher reminded us.

14. Is that the only way to solve the problem?

15. To celebrate, Coach Pierce and her team went to a restaurant after the game.

16. The explorers agreed that the journey would be too dangerous to undertake.

17. Which career do you intend to pursue?

18. According to my grandmother, sweet-potato pie is easy to prepare.

19. If you enjoy mysteries, Agatha Christie's *Witness for the Prosecution* is a good play to read.

20. Am I too late to volunteer?

The Infinitive Phrase

14k. An *infinitive phrase* consists of an infinitive and any modifiers or complements the infinitive has. The entire phrase can be used as a noun, an adjective, or an adverb.

NOUN	Lusita likes **to play chess with her grandmother.** [The phrase is the direct object of the verb *likes*.]
ADJECTIVE	Christopher's determination **to do the job well** impressed his boss. [The phrase modifies the noun *determination*.]
ADVERB	Chen has gone to the store **to buy paints.** [The phrase modifies the verb *has gone*.]

Sometimes the sign of the infinitive, *to*, is omitted in a sentence.

EXAMPLE	Jenna did not dare **go out without a raincoat.** [The infinitive phrase is the direct object of the verb *did dare*.]

EXERCISE A In each of the following sentences, identify the use of the underlined infinitive phrase by writing above it *N* for *noun*, *ADJ* for *adjective*, or *ADV* for *adverb*.

Example 1. Do you intend <u>to audition for the school play</u>? *(N)*

1. Trevor has the opportunity <u>to go to Japan next summer</u>.

2. <u>To become a journalist</u> is her ambition.

3. We worked late into the night <u>to finish the project</u>.

4. I need <u>to finish my homework</u> before I go to the game.

5. The band appeared eager <u>to perform an encore</u>.

EXERCISE B Underline the infinitive phrase in each of the following sentences. Then, identify the function of the phrase by writing above it *N* for *noun*, *ADJ* for *adjective*, or *ADV* for *adverb*.

Example 1. The comedian's attempts <u>to be funny</u> proved futile. *(ADJ)*

6. To earn our own spending money, my sister and I began a pet-care service.

7. The person to ask that question is Kathryn.

8. Do you like to play computer games?

9. The efforts to save the bald eagle from extinction have succeeded.

10. The manufacturer is planning to change the design of the car next year.

11. Carolyn's dream is to visit Spain.

12. The Riveras were the first ones to volunteer their services.

13. "I am very happy to be here with you this evening," the guest speaker said.

14. Are you sure this is the correct way to keep score?

15. Will Chris help us cook dinner tonight?

GRAMMAR

Infinitives and Infinitive Phrases

14j. An *infinitive* is a verb form that can be used as a noun, an adjective, or an adverb. Most infinitives begin with *to*.

14k. An *infinitive phrase* consists of an infinitive and any modifiers or complements the infinitive has. The entire phrase can be used as a noun, an adjective, or an adverb.

> **EXAMPLES** I cannot decide which puppy **to adopt.** [*To adopt* is an adjective modifying the noun *puppy.*]
>
> Is a beagle difficult **to train**? [*To train* is an adverb modifying the adjective *difficult.*]
>
> **To train any dog** requires patience. [*To train any dog* is the subject of the verb *requires.*]

EXERCISE A In each of the following sentences, identify the function of the underlined infinitive by writing *N* for *noun, ADJ* for *adjective,* or *ADV* for *adverb.*

Example _*ADV*_ **1.** The children were happy <u>to go</u>.

_____ **1.** Our cabin on the lake is the perfect place <u>to concentrate</u>.

_____ **2.** We were eager <u>to leave</u>.

_____ **3.** <u>To win</u> is Rodrigo's main goal.

_____ **4.** He absolutely loves <u>to compete</u>.

_____ **5.** It was a perfect book <u>to review</u>.

EXERCISE B Underline the infinitive phrase in each of the following sentences. Then, identify its function. On the line provided, write *N* for *noun, ADJ* for *adjective,* or *ADV* for *adverb.*

Example _*N*_ **1.** Monica's grandfather had not wanted <u>to leave his homeland</u>.

_____ **6.** Her grandfather, a lawyer, came to the United States in the 1950s to escape tyranny.

_____ **7.** To practice law in the United States was his dream.

_____ **8.** He worked hard to accomplish his goal.

_____ **9.** He struggled continually to learn the language.

_____ **10.** He faced the difficult task of finding a place to practice law.

_____ **11.** Still, he was grateful to be in a free country.

_____ **12.** One of his dreams is to visit his homeland.

_____ **13.** Monica is eager to write about her grandfather's life.

_____ **14.** Her grandfather will give her some details to include in the biography.

_____ **15.** Here are the best pictures to include in the report.

Verbal Phrases A

14g. A *participial phrase* is used as an adjective and consists of a participle and any complements or modifiers the participle has.

14i. A *gerund phrase* consists of a gerund and any modifiers or complements the gerund has. The entire phrase is used as a noun.

14k. An *infinitive phrase* consists of an infinitive and any modifiers or complements the infinitive has. The entire phrase can be used as a noun, an adjective, or an adverb.

EXERCISE A In each of the following sentences, identify the underlined verbal phrase by writing above it *PART* for *participial phrase, GER* for *gerund phrase,* or *INF* for *infinitive phrase.*

                                                                     GER

Example 1. The children soon grew tired of <u>playing the game</u>.

1. I look forward to <u>singing carols every Christmas</u>.

2. <u>To break the school record for the 50-meter dash</u> is one of Tyrone's goals.

3. One of my household chores is <u>taking out the trash</u>.

4. Dr. Bannerjee, <u>known for her skill at surgery</u>, performed the operation.

5. <u>Published in 1998</u>, the book remained on the bestseller list for nearly a year.

EXERCISE B Underline the verbal phrase in each of the following sentences. Then, identify the function of each phrase by writing above it *N* for *noun, ADJ* for *adjective,* or *ADV* for *adverb.*

                                               N

Example 1. Helen wants <u>to see the circus before it leaves town</u>.

6. A successful project requires researching the topic carefully.

7. Do you intend to plant a vegetable garden?

8. At the end of the summer, I will have saved enough money to buy a new stereo.

9. Riding along the bike trail, Matthew spotted a coyote on the ridge.

10. This young woman teaches water-skiing for beginners.

11. Someday Masud hopes to play the cello with a symphony orchestra.

12. From the kitchen window we saw an armadillo burrowing under the fence.

13. Interrupting others is rude.

14. The thought of speaking to the school assembly frightens me a little.

15. Hundreds of people were in line to buy tickets.

Verbal Phrases B

14g.	A *participial phrase* is used as an adjective and consists of a participle and any complements or modifiers the participle has.
14i.	A *gerund phrase* consists of a gerund and any modifiers or complements the gerund has. The entire phrase is used as a noun.
14k.	An *infinitive phrase* consists of an infinitive and any modifiers or complements the infinitive has. The entire phrase can be used as a noun, an adjective, or an adverb.

EXERCISE A   In each of the following sentences, identify the underlined verbal phrase by writing above it *PART* for *participial phrase,* *GER* for *gerund phrase,* or *INF* for *infinitive phrase.*

Example 1. A few months ago, I began <u>looking for a hobby</u>. *(GER)*

1. I needed a hobby <u>to fill my extra time</u>.

2. I made several attempts <u>to find a hobby that was right for me</u>.

3. <u>Finding an enjoyable hobby</u> was not easy.

4. <u>Impressed by my sister's enthusiasm for macramé</u>, I decided to take it up as a hobby.

5. However, <u>getting all knotted up</u> wasn't for me.

EXERCISE B   Underline the verbal phrase in each of the following sentences. Then, identify the function of each phrase by writing above it *N* for *noun,* *ADJ* for *adjective,* or *ADV* for *adverb.*

Example 1. <u>Washing the dishes</u> took only a few minutes. *(N)*

6. Maxine gets her exercise by dancing at least three hours a week.

7. To pass the time, Eddie makes model ships for his friends.

8. I watched the carpenter repairing our roof.

9. Yolanda went to get her book.

10. The man pushing that grocery cart is my karate instructor.

11. Winning the contest was a thrill for our cheerleaders.

12. We went to the theater to see a new play.

13. Richard's job is delivering groceries to the hospital.

14. Tired of the noise outside, we closed the windows.

15. Preparing for that test took several hours.

The Appositive

14l. An *appositive* is a noun or a pronoun placed beside another noun or pronoun to identify or describe it.

EXAMPLES   My best friend, **Toshiro,** is teaching me to play the ukulele. [*Toshiro* identifies the noun *friend*.]

The person in charge of the workshop is the librarian, **Ms. Epstein.** [*Ms. Epstein* identifies the noun *librarian*.]

EXERCISE   In each of the following sentences, draw one line under the appositive and two lines under the word or words it identifies or describes.

Example 1. My brother Richard attends Duke University.

1. The Mexican painter David Alfaro Siqueiros created large murals on public buildings.

2. Ramon, this is my cousin Lim Sing.

3. One of my favorite books, *The Yearling,* was made into a movie in 1946.

4. Terence won the spelling bee when he correctly spelled the word *aficionado.*

5. The artist Faith Ringgold rose to fame with her story quilts.

6. Our dance instructor told us about the first time she saw the dancer Maria Tallchief perform.

7. The Greek god Poseidon ruled the sea.

8. Have you read the Seneca myth "Sky Woman"?

9. Doesn't your uncle Jeremy play the accordion in a zydeco band?

10. August Wilson won a Pulitzer Prize for his play *The Piano Lesson.*

11. I am reading a book about the aviator Amelia Earhart.

12. Charles Lutwidge Dodgson is better known by his pen name, Lewis Carroll.

13. This magazine features some of the buildings designed by the architect I. M. Pei.

14. The name *Oklahoma* is from Choctaw words meaning "red people."

15. In social studies we have been studying the life of the Hindu leader Mohandas Gandhi.

16. How much larger than Earth is the planet Jupiter?

17. My English teacher, Mr. Olmos, also directs plays at the community theater.

18. Julia's essay, "The Job of a Border Patrol Officer," was expertly researched.

19. The first space shuttle, *Columbia,* was launched on April 12, 1981.

20. Where is the famous painting *The Last Supper* displayed?

The Appositive Phrase

14m. An *appositive phrase* consists of an appositive and any modifiers it has.

EXAMPLE Dad is making baklava, **our family's favorite dessert.** [*Dessert* is the appositive identifying *baklava*. *Our*, *family's*, and *favorite* modify the appositive.]

EXERCISE In each of the following sentences, draw one line under the appositive phrase and two lines under the word or words to which it refers.

Example 1. Don't they live in Oak Park, a suburb of Chicago?

1. Our trip included a visit to Stratford-upon-Avon, the birthplace of Shakespeare.

2. The baby's "blankie," a scrap of chewed flannel, must always be nearby.

3. Yellowstone National Park, the oldest national park in the United States, covers parts of Wyoming, Montana, and Idaho.

4. We held Amy's surprise party on December 10, the day before her birthday.

5. At the restaurant, I ordered sashimi, a traditional Japanese dish of raw fish and soy sauce.

6. Tashunca-uitco, a chief of the Lakotas, is perhaps better known as Chief Crazy Horse.

7. Mount Everest, the world's highest mountain peak, is part of the Himalayas.

8. Ms. Anaya, my next-door neighbor, volunteered to coach the softball team.

9. Jimmy Carter, a former U.S. president, devotes time each year to Habitat for Humanity.

10. In Greek mythology, the phoenix, a beautiful old bird in the Arabian Desert, set itself on fire and then rose from its ashes to live again.

11. Is Phoenix, the capital of Arizona, named for the bird in Greek mythology?

12. In 1999 Eileen Collins, a lieutenant colonel in the United States Air Force, became the first woman to command a space shuttle.

13. The Dragon, one of the roller coasters at the amusement park, is a thrilling ride!

14. Derrick Mitchell, our team's quarterback, is a freshman.

15. After the performance, there will be a reception, an informal party for close friends.

16. Michael Jordan, the legendary basketball player, also played professional baseball for a while.

17. Ms. Estevez won first prize, a trip to Hawaii.

18. Chau Yong, a new student from Vietnam, speaks fluent English.

19. Do you know Tom, the boy next door?

20. Sarah Langford, a police officer, will be tonight's guest speaker.

Appositives and Appositive Phrases

14l. An *appositive* is a noun or pronoun placed beside another noun or pronoun to identify or describe it.

14m. An *appositive phrase* consists of an appositive and any modifiers it has.

EXAMPLES   The Greek author **Homer** is best known for his epic poems.

I have read Homer's *Iliad*, **an epic poem about the Trojan War.**

EXERCISE A   Underline the appositive or appositive phrase in each of the following sentences.

Example 1. Helen, King Menelaus's wife, was kidnapped.

1. Paris, the son of the Trojan king, had kidnapped Helen.

2. Agamemnon, the brother of King Menelaus, led his warriors to Troy to rescue her.

3. The king of the gods, Zeus, tried to remain impartial.

4. How was the Greek goddess Athena involved in the Trojan War?

5. Thetis, Achilles' mother, tried to protect her son from death.

6. She dipped him into the Styx, a sacred river.

7. Achilles killed Hector, the Trojan king's son.

8. The king of Troy, Priam, saw this spectacle and wept.

9. Achilles mourned the death of his friend Patroclus.

10. Achilles, a brave Greek warrior, was killed by a poisoned arrow that pierced his heel.

EXERCISE B   Underline the appositive phrase in each of the following sentences.

Example 1. *Alaska* comes from *Alax̂sxax̂*, an Aleutian word meaning "mainland."

11. San Francisco, home of the famed cable cars, was named for St. Francis.

12. Pennsylvania is named for William Penn, one of its founders.

13. Quebec City, a Canadian city in the province of Quebec, is a seaport.

14. New York City, a mixture of many ethnic groups, is the largest city in the United States.

15. *Montreal*, the name of a city in Quebec Province, means "Mount Royal."

16. Lake Champlain, a lake in upstate New York, was named for Samuel de Champlain.

17. *San Jose,* the name of a city in California, is Spanish for "Saint Joseph."

18. The Spanish, early settlers of California, left their mark with these place names.

19. American Indian place names abound in Oklahoma, home of the Choctaw and other peoples.

20. Reflections of history, all these names provide clues about the past.

Review A: **Identifying Phrases**

EXERCISE A In each of the following sentences, underline the two prepositional phrases. Draw an arrow from each phrase to the word or words it modifies. Then, on the line provided, identify each phrase by writing *ADJ* for *adjective* or *ADV* for *adverb*.

Example _ADV, ADJ_ **1.** The report began with an allusion to a classical myth.

_____ **1.** At times we treat objects as if they were living creatures with human traits.

_____ **2.** In reports writers often give mythological names to heavenly bodies.

_____ **3.** Imagine how drab the reports of asteroids would be without mythical names.

_____ **4.** We might read in our daily newspapers, "Asteroid Approaches Surface of Sun."

_____ **5.** Instead, we can read livelier headlines like this one: "Icarus Flies Toward Sol."

EXERCISE B In each of the following sentences, identify the underlined verbal phrase by writing above it *PART* for *participial phrase*, *GER* for *gerund phrase*, or *INF* for *infinitive phrase*.

Example **1.** We certainly would not want to relive the experience!

6. As I found out last summer, living through a hurricane is a nerve-shattering experience!

7. The hurricane winds, reaching speeds of one hundred miles an hour, pounded our town.

8. After wading through ankle-deep water for a mile, we took refuge in a school building.

9. The school building, solidly constructed of brick and steel, sustained little damage.

10. We were happy to discover that everyone had survived!

EXERCISE C Most of the following sentences contain an appositive phrase. Draw one line under each appositive phrase and two lines under the word or words to which the phrase refers. If the sentence contains no appositive phrase, write *None* at the end of the sentence.

Example **1.** Henry W. Longfellow wrote "Paul Revere's Ride," a poem about the beginning of the American Revolution.

11. The Cullinan diamond, the largest rough diamond ever found, was cut into about a hundred smaller stones.

12. Have you ever read "Dreams," a short poem by Langston Hughes?

13. I read a moving speech by Chief Joseph, the famous leader of the Nez Perce.

14. The Museum of Science and Industry, located in Chicago's Hyde Park neighborhood, is near the University of Chicago.

15. The lady-slipper, a common American wildflower, is a species of orchid.

Review B: Identifying Phrases

EXERCISE A　In each of the following sentences, underline the two prepositional phrases. Draw an arrow from each phrase to the word or words it modifies. Then, on the line provided, identify each phrase by writing *ADJ* for *adjective* or *ADV* for *adverb*.

Example　*ADV, ADJ*　**1.** For the past year I have been keeping a journal of my ideas.

_____　**1.** I have developed some of those ideas into short stories.

_____　**2.** I wrote a story about an imaginary train ride across the country.

_____　**3.** The finest entry in my journal is an account of a young astronaut's moonwalk.

_____　**4.** Someday I might send a copy of the story to a magazine.

_____　**5.** At the present time I am the only reader of my journal.

EXERCISE B　In each of the following sentences, identify the underlined verbal phrase by writing above it *PART* for *participial phrase, GER* for *gerund phrase,* or *INF* for *infinitive phrase.*

Example　**1.**　Have you ever tried to plan a surprise birthday party? *INF*

6. Throwing a birthday party is no small feat.

7. Last June, I planned a grand bash to surprise my brother.

8. My first problem was gathering a list of his friends.

9. My brother was surprised by our shouting "Happy birthday!"

10. Stunned for a moment, he quickly recovered and began laughing wildly.

EXERCISE C　Most of the following sentences contain an appositive phrase. Draw one line under each appositive phrase and two lines under the word or words to which the phrase refers. If the sentence contains no appositive phrase, write *None* at the end of the sentence.

Example　**1.**　In a recent poll, Sally Ride, the first female American astronaut, was named a good

role model for girls.

11. My grandfather believes that turquoise, a blue-green mineral, should be classified as a

precious gem.

12. Famous baseball players are inducted annually into the Hall of Fame, located in Cooperstown,

New York.

13. The film is based on *Frankenstein,* a novel by Mary Shelley.

14. *I Wonder as I Wander,* the autobiography of Langston Hughes, is a fascinating book.

15. Jefferson City, the capital of Missouri, is on the banks of the Missouri River.

Review C: **Identifying Phrases**

EXERCISE A In each of the following sentences, underline the two prepositional phrases. Draw an arrow from each phrase to the word or words it modifies. Then, on the line provided, identify each phrase by writing *ADJ* for *adjective* or *ADV* for *adverb*.

Example *ADJ, ADV* **1.** Some of those CDs belong to Terry.

_____ **1.** I will call you after the game between the Bulldogs and the Wildcats.

_____ **2.** In October, the trees here burst with color.

_____ **3.** The meeting will be held at 3:30 P.M. in the school library.

_____ **4.** Ms. Leguizamo has been the principal of the school for fifteen years.

_____ **5.** We are planning a trip to Mammoth Cave National Park in Kentucky.

EXERCISE B Underline the verbal phrase in each of the following sentences. Then, identify the phrase by writing above it *PART* for *participial phrase,* *GER* for *gerund phrase,* or *INF* for *infinitive phrase.*

Example 1. Each year, many African Americans celebrate the holiday called Kwanzaa.

6. African Americans began observing Kwanzaa in 1966.

7. The celebration, lasting from December 26 to January 1, is a special time for African Americans.

8. Many take time to reflect upon their African heritage.

9. Seven candles, representing the seven principles of Kwanzaa, are placed in a *kinara,* a candleholder.

10. Lighting one of the candles is a daily ritual.

EXERCISE C Most of the following sentences contain an appositive phrase. Draw one line under the appositive phrase and two lines under the word or words to which the phrase refers. If the sentence contains no appositive phrase, write *None* at the end of the sentence.

Example 1. Ottawa, the capital of Canada, is situated in Ontario Province.

11. Mount Rushmore, part of the Black Hills of South Dakota, is a popular tourist attraction.

12. Featured on the one-dollar coin is the image of Sacagawea, the Shoshone guide for the Lewis and Clark expedition.

13. For dinner we are preparing kimchi, a tasty Korean dish.

14. The winners of the writing contest were Justin and Leah.

15. An early twentieth-century American artist, Grant Wood is best known for painting *American Gothic.*

Literary Model: Description

> In a forest of mixed growth somewhere on the eastern spurs of the Carpathians, a man stood one winter night watching and listening, as though he waited for some beast of the woods to come within the range of his vision and, later, of his rifle. But the game for whose presence he kept so keen an outlook was none that figured in the sportsman's calendar as lawful and proper for the chase; Ulrich von Gradwitz patrolled the dark forest in quest of a human enemy.
>
> —from "The Interlopers" by Saki

EXERCISE A   In the above paragraph, identify each underlined prepositional phrase as an *adverb* phrase or an *adjective* phrase and give the word that each phrase modifies. The first prepositional phrase has been identified for you as an example.

1. *In forest—adverb—stood*
2. _____
3. _____
4. _____
5. _____
6. _____
7. _____
8. _____
9. _____
10. _____
11. _____

EXERCISE B

1. Rewrite the last three lines of the text without any of the prepositional phrases.

   _____

   _____

   _____

   _____

2. Is the paragraph easier or more difficult to understand without the phrases? What kind of information is missing without them?

   _____

   _____

   _____

   _____

for **CHAPTER 14: THE PHRASE** | pages 442–62

Literary Model (continued)

EXERCISE C Rewrite the paragraph, replacing each of the prepositional phrases you identified in Exercise A with a prepositional phrase of your own invention. Your phrases may modify different words but should function in the same way as the originals (as either adjective or adverb phrases). Feel free to change any other words so that your new phrases make sense.

_____

_____

_____

_____

_____

_____

_____

_____

_____

_____

_____

EXERCISE D

1. Did your phrases change the setting and tone of the original passage? If so, how? If not, could the setting and tone have been changed if you had used other phrases?

_____

_____

_____

_____

2. Consider what adverb phrases tell about the words they modify. Why did changing the adverb phrases affect the setting of the original passage?

_____

_____

_____

_____

GRAMMAR | Language in Context: Writing Application

Writing Application: Speech

A subject and predicate that agree and express a complete thought make up the bare bones of a sentence. To add details, writers often use prepositional phrases.

LESS SPECIFIC   People have not always known about dinosaurs.

MORE SPECIFIC   Before the 1822 discovery of a giant fossilized tooth by Mary Ann Mantell in England, people did not know about dinosaurs. The giant reptiles were not given the name of "terrible lizard" by Richard Owen until 1841.

Eight prepositional phrases in the second and third sentences tell how, when, and where people first became aware of the dinosaur fossil record.

WRITING ACTIVITY

You have volunteered to accompany a class of fourth-graders on their field trip to your city's museum of natural history. For fourth-graders, the highlight of the field trip will be visiting the fossil exhibit. Prepare a five-minute speech to tell the children about fossils. Use prepositional phrases to add details to your speech.

PREWRITING   Consult print reference sources, the Internet, or both to learn about the discovery of the fossil record. (Two facts to get you started appear in the example above.) Take notes on what you find, picking out the facts that are most basic to the children's understanding and that fourth-graders will find most interesting. Think of times when you have enjoyed listening to speakers. How did they keep your attention?

WRITING   Write your presentation, organizing the information so it is easy to follow. Remember, because you are speaking to fourth-graders, you will have to choose words that they will understand.

REVISING   Read your presentation aloud slowly and clearly to several people, and ask them to take brief notes. Then, look at their notes—did they list all of your main points? If not, you may need to emphasize those points more in your presentation.

PUBLISHING   Even though your audience will not see your written product, check it for spelling and punctuation errors that may trip you up while reading it aloud. Read your presentation to your class, using the classroom as an imaginary museum.

EXTENDING YOUR WRITING

You may wish to develop this writing exercise further. Schools and museums welcome volunteer efforts. You could expand your research and presentation into a script for museum guides, or you could add illustrations and create a booklet for a museum to give to students on field trips to the museum.

Choices: Exploring Clauses

The following activities challenge you to find a connection between clauses and the world around you. Do the activity below that suits your personality best, and then share your discoveries with your class.

MUSIC

If I Had the Wings of an Angel

Subordinating conjunctions begin many popular songs. Compile a list of opening lines that begin with a subordinating conjunction, and post the list in the classroom. Be sure to underline each subordinate clause and highlight each subordinating conjunction.

REPRESENTING

Around and Around We Go

Show your classmates how adverb clauses can often be moved from the end of a sentence to the beginning or vice versa. Write a sentence that includes two parts: an independent clause and an adverb clause. Using all lowercase letters and no punctuation, write or print out several copies of each clause. Cut out each clause so it is on its own strip of paper. Then, tape the strips together, alternating your two clauses. Ta-da! You have an endless statement that makes sense, no matter which clause comes first. Give two copies of each clause to your classmates, and ask them to capitalize and punctuate both possible versions of the sentence.

DRAMA

He Said, She Said

Write a dialogue between two people who are deciding where to go on Saturday night. One speaks only in independent clauses; the other speaks only in subordinate clauses. Videotape your dialogue, or perform it for the class.

MATHEMATICS

One Times One Plus One

Forge a connection between mathematical clauses and grammatical clauses. Plan and conduct a short seminar in mathematical clauses. Begin with an independent clause—a simple equation. Then, add parenthetical expressions that make the equation more complex.

PERFORMANCE

Start a Chain Reaction

Try this project if you like surprises! First, make sure everyone in the class has a list of subordinate conjunctions and relative pronouns. Then, you start the ball rolling by giving one classmate an independent clause. He or she adds on a subordinate clause and passes on the sentence to the next person. When the last person adds a clause, you'll have an incredibly long sentence that will probably be a very strange and funny story. You can do this project aloud or by passing around a sheet of paper. If you do the project on paper, be sure to read the story to the class.

REPRESENTING

Decisions, Decisions

Make a flowchart showing the process of deciding whether a word group is a phrase or an independent or a subordinate clause. Naturally, you'll have steps for finding the subject and the verb. You'll want a step for determining whether the word group is a complete thought, too. Neatly transfer your flowchart to poster board. Feel free to jazz up your chart with colors and designs.

ORIGINAL PROJECTS

Have It Your Way

Create a project of your own. Write and teach a marching song about clauses to the class. Write a monologue composed only of subordinate clauses, such as *If only I had. . . .* Look up the etymology and definitions of the word *clause*, and report what you learn. Find out what the legal term *clause* means. Color-code the adverb and adjective clauses in a page of writing. Cut up some complex sentences into clauses, and ask your classmates to put them back together. Be sure to get your teacher's approval before starting your project.

Clauses

15a. A *clause* is a word group that contains a verb and its subject and that is used as a sentence or as part of a sentence.

Although every clause contains a subject and a verb, not every clause expresses a complete thought. Clauses that do are called *independent clauses*. Clauses that do not are called *subordinate clauses*.

EXAMPLES   many people will attend the banquet [independent clause]

because many people will attend the banquet [subordinate clause]

Do not mistake a phrase for a clause. A phrase does not contain both a verb and a subject.

PHRASE   before the banquet [no verb]

CLAUSE   before the banquet began [subject—*banquet;* verb—*began*]

PHRASE   to decorate the banquet hall today [no subject]

CLAUSE   we need to decorate the banquet hall today [subject—*we;* verb—*need*]

EXERCISE   Decide whether each of the following word groups is or is not a clause. On the line provided, identify the word group by writing *I* for *independent clause, S* for *subordinate clause,* or *N* for *not a clause.*

Example ___*S*___ **1.** where the banquet would be held

_____ **1.** until the school year is over

_____ **2.** until the end of the school year

_____ **3.** the school year is over

_____ **4.** the arrival of spring

_____ **5.** when spring comes

_____ **6.** because I prefer warm weather

_____ **7.** I prefer warm weather

_____ **8.** my preference for warm weather

_____ **9.** to win the game this Friday

_____ **10.** if we win the game this Friday

_____ **11.** whom I have never met

_____ **12.** after meeting them

_____ **13.** to be a mechanical engineer someday

_____ **14.** she wants to be an engineer

_____ **15.** what she wants to be

_____ **16.** pleased with their performance

_____ **17.** with their performance

_____ **18.** was he pleased with their performance

_____ **19.** at the end of the race

_____ **20.** before the race ended

_____ **21.** the hiding cat

_____ **22.** the cat is hiding

_____ **23.** when we were happy

_____ **24.** happy about the celebration

_____ **25.** we were happier then

Independent Clauses

15b. An *independent* (or *main*) *clause* expresses a complete thought and can stand by itself as a sentence.

EXAMPLES **Harambee is an annual holiday.**

Harambee is an annual holiday that many African Americans celebrate.

My cousin Leon, an aspiring artist, enjoys this holiday, for **on display at a Harambee party are works of art** that other African Americans have created.

EXERCISE A   For each of the following sentences, decide whether or not the clauses, labeled A and B, are independent clauses. Circle the letter of each independent clause. Hint: One sentence contains more than one independent clause.

Example 1. (A) *Harambee* is a Swahili word **(B)** that means "unity."

1. **(A)** Harambee is celebrated on October 31, **(B)** which is the same date as Halloween.

2. **(A)** As you know, **(B)** on Halloween many people, especially children, dress in costumes and go from door to door requesting treats.

3. **(A)** Although Halloween is a popular tradition, **(B)** many African Americans celebrate Harambee instead.

4. **(A)** The originators of this holiday were some African Americans **(B)** who lived in Dallas, Texas.

5. **(A)** At a Harambee party, families and friends gather to celebrate their culture; **(B)** they play music, sing, dance, and discuss the exhibits of artwork.

EXERCISE B   Underline each independent clause in the following sentences.

Example 1. <u>Many athletes remember Alice Coachman</u> because she helped break down barriers for both women and African Americans.

6. When she was a child, Alice Coachman sneaked away from her chores to play basketball.

7. While she was at Tuskegee Institute High School in the 1940s, Coachman captured national track-and-field championships in four events.

8. As World War II ended, Coachman looked forward to entering international competitions.

9. The 1948 Olympics were held in London, England, and Alice Coachman was there.

10. Winning first place in the high jump was a feat that won her recognition as the first African American woman to win an Olympic gold medal.

Subordinate Clauses

| **15c.** | A *subordinate* (or *dependent*) *clause* does not express a complete thought and cannot stand by itself as a sentence. |

Although every clause contains a subject and a verb, not every clause expresses a complete thought. Generally, clauses that begin with *when, whom, because, which, that, if,* or *until* do not express complete thoughts.

SUBORDINATE CLAUSE   what we need to repair first

SENTENCE   **What we need to repair first** is the roof.

EXERCISE   Underline the subordinate clause in each of the following sentences.

Example   1. "Be careful about <u>what you wish for</u>," warned my aunt Lucy.

1. After we ate lunch at the Japanese tearoom, we browsed the gift shop for souvenirs.

2. A monument has been erected at the site where the battle occurred.

3. Although Beethoven lost his hearing, he continued to compose music.

4. My friend Malcolm, whose opinion I value highly, recommended this book.

5. Because I have not seen the movie, please do not tell me about the ending.

6. Ava gave me a jar of her homemade salsa, which won a blue ribbon at the state fair.

7. What our guest speaker said sparked a lively discussion.

8. According to Benjamin Franklin, "Three may keep a secret if two of them are dead."

9. The wide receiver was tackled as soon as he caught the pass.

10. Remind me to take a camera along when we go camping again.

11. Whether the school can provide new computers depends largely upon the fund-raisers.

12. The beach was closed to the public because a shark had been sighted.

13. Soledad attends Stanford University, where she is studying to become a civil engineer.

14. We searched the Internet for a Web site that would give us information about jogging.

15. You can invite whomever you want to the Cinco de Mayo party.

16. If that painting is still for sale, I will buy it.

17. My cousin Eduardo, whom you will meet at the party, wants to audition for our band.

18. Today I left soccer practice early so that I would not be late for my dentist appointment.

19. A technician at the electronics shop told me that my CD player was beyond repair.

20. Before we left for the airport, we called the airline to confirm the departure time of our flight.

Independent and Subordinate Clauses

| **15b.** | An *independent* (or *main*) *clause* expresses a complete thought and can stand by itself as a sentence. |

| **15c.** | A *subordinate* (or *dependent*) *clause* does not express a complete thought and cannot stand by itself as a sentence. |

SUBORDINATE CLAUSE   when the explorers returned to their campsite
INDEPENDENT CLAUSE   they discovered some unusually large footprints

EXERCISE In each of the following sentences, identify the underlined clause by writing on the line provided *I* for *independent clause* or *S* for *subordinate clause.*

Example ____*S*____ **1.** Chess, <u>which requires skill and concentration</u>, is a challenging game.

_____ **1.** Anyone <u>who wants salad</u> should order it separately.

_____ **2.** Bonus points will be awarded to <u>whoever turns in the assignment early</u>.

_____ **3.** <u>The puppy</u> that is sitting in the corner <u>seems very shy</u>.

_____ **4.** <u>What Dr. Chan said</u> has started to worry me.

_____ **5.** Because there are many kinds of burritos, <u>we enjoy having them for dinner once a week</u>.

_____ **6.** The tennis player Bjorn Borg, who was a calm player, <u>was called "The Iceman."</u>

_____ **7.** Judy Garland first appeared onstage <u>when she was only five years old</u>.

_____ **8.** Do you know <u>whether the media center has any CD-ROMs about volcanoes</u>?

_____ **9.** Unless the weather improves, <u>the trail ride will be canceled</u>.

_____ **10.** Tomorrow <u>Tamala will give her presentation</u>, which is about opera.

_____ **11.** Commercial art is <u>what Russell will study in college</u>.

_____ **12.** <u>John Field is the composer</u> whose works Cheryl enjoys performing.

_____ **13.** Of course, the award should go to <u>whoever is the most deserving</u>.

_____ **14.** <u>Since the prime minister of Canada is giving a speech at the convention center</u>, there will probably be a parking problem downtown.

_____ **15.** After our class, Pedro, Kevin, and I decided <u>that we would go fishing</u>.

_____ **16.** As the French army withdrew from Russia in 1813, <u>Napoleon lost 500,000 soldiers</u>.

_____ **17.** The mayor refunded the Garzas <u>the money</u> that they had spent to beautify the park.

_____ **18.** If you want to <u>pursue a career in music</u>, you should practice more often than you do.

_____ **19.** Please give whoever calls <u>this message</u>.

_____ **20.** Someone told me <u>that you intend to run for class president</u>.

GRAMMAR

Adjective Clauses A

15d.   An *adjective clause* is a subordinate clause that modifies a noun or a pronoun.

An adjective clause usually follows the word or words it modifies and tells *what kind* or *which one.*

> **EXAMPLES**   White-water rafting is a sport **that you might enjoy.** [The adjective clause modifies the noun *sport,* telling *what kind.*]
>
> White-water rafting is a sport **you might enjoy.** [The relative pronoun *that* is omitted.]
>
> This is the site **where we will begin our rafting trip.** [The adjective clause modifies *site,* telling *which one.*]

EXERCISE A   In each of the following sentences, draw an arrow from the underlined adjective clause to the word it modifies.

Example 1. Uncle Theo, who is an experienced rafter, introduced me to the sport.

1. The head of the river, which lies north of here, contains relatively calm water.

2. Our guide, whom we know well, showed us photographs of her last rafting trip.

3. Our guide then showed us a chart of the course we would follow.

4. The part of the river where we rafted was not too dangerous.

5. We rode on a raft that my uncle Theo had built.

EXERCISE B   Underline the adjective clause in each of the following sentences. Then, draw an arrow from the clause to the word it modifies.

Example 1. A guide who has been carefully trained takes new rafters out.

6. Areas of the river that can be hazardous are marked on a chart.

7. You must learn techniques that minimize danger.

8. Guides who are especially skilled reassure inexperienced people.

9. Some beginners have spectators take snapshots, which they can enjoy later.

10. Would you like to see photos of the first time I went rafting?

11. Some rafters spend hours writing reports that friends will read.

12. One report, which I particularly enjoyed, described an unexpected onrush of white water.

13. Everyone who loves a challenge in the outdoors should consider rafting.

14. Several people whom I respect have recommended the sport to me.

15. It is a sport that you should try in the company of an experienced guide.

for **CHAPTER 15: THE CLAUSE**   *pages 473–74*

Adjective Clauses B

15d. An *adjective clause* is a subordinate clause that modifies a noun or a pronoun.

An adjective clause usually follows the word or words it modifies and tells *what kind* or *which one.*

    EXAMPLES   Is this the medication **that you take for your allergies**? [The adjective clause modifies the noun *medication,* telling *which one.*]

                  That was the year **when they buried the time capsule.** [The adjective clause modifies *year,* telling *which one.*]

EXERCISE A   In each of the following sentences, draw an arrow from the underlined adjective clause to the word it modifies.

Example 1. The chief products <u>that Costa Rica exports</u> are coffee, bananas, and sugar.

1. I have a friend <u>whose mother is an archaeologist</u>.

2. James Thurber wrote several amusing stories in a style <u>that resembles that of Aesop's fables</u>.

3. Everyone <u>who attended the Fourth of July celebration</u> dressed in red, white, and blue.

4. The Surgeon General described the health problems <u>that smoking can cause</u>.

5. The only e-mail message <u>you have</u> is from Mr. Salinger.

EXERCISE B   Underline the adjective clause in each of the following sentences. Then, draw an arrow from the clause to the word the clause modifies.

Example 1. Where is the user's guide <u>that came with the VCR</u>?

6. Komodo dragons, which are indigenous to the jungles of Southeast Asia, are the world's largest living lizards.

7. Today, Uncle Regis, who loves card tricks, taught me a few of them.

8. The name *Chicago* is an Algonquian word that means "place of the onion."

9. Josh drew this family tree, which shows the history of seven generations of his family.

10. Carol, who is the new president of the Wilderness Club, has already organized a camping trip.

11. Who will be responsible for raising the flag on days when you are absent from school?

12. The Kentucky Derby, which is held on the first Saturday in May, is considered the first jewel in the Triple Crown of horse racing.

13. Can you tell me the year the first space shuttle was launched?

14. Is it a stalactite that extends from the roof of a cave?

15. Wheat, corn, and sugar beets are among the crops that farmers in Chile grow.

Relative Pronouns

15d. An *adjective clause* is a subordinate clause that modifies a noun or a pronoun.

An adjective clause is often introduced by a *relative pronoun,* which relates the clause to the word or words the clause modifies.

> **EXAMPLES** Aunt Salma, **who has worked hard all her life,** is someone **for whom I have great respect.** [*Who* relates to *Aunt Salma* and functions as the subject of the verb *has worked. Whom* relates to *someone* and functions as the object of the preposition *for.*]
>
> Uncle Diego, **whose recipes should be published,** makes the best paella **that I have ever eaten.** [*Whose* relates to *Uncle Diego* and functions as a possessive pronoun. *That* relates to *paella* and functions as a direct object of the verb *have eaten.*]

EXERCISE A Underline the adjective clause in each of the following sentences. Then, draw an arrow from the relative pronoun to the word to which the pronoun relates.

Example 1. One desert animal that is poisonous is the Gila monster.

1. Those who want to participate in the readathon should sign up in the library.

2. Did the oak saplings that you planted last spring survive the summer drought?

3. The pharmacist for whom Allison worked encouraged her to pursue a career in medicine.

4. Do you know the artist who painted these watercolors?

5. My grandfather is one person to whom I always go for advice.

6. The movie is quite different from the book on which it is based.

7. Is basketball the only sport that you like to play?

8. General Colin Powell is the person whom I have selected as the subject of my essay.

9. The president of our Ecology Club wrote the song that we sang at the Earth Day celebration.

10. Do the jobs for which you have applied pay more than minimum wage?

EXERCISE B For each of the following sentences, identify the function of the relative pronoun within the underlined adjective clause. Above the relative pronoun, write *S* for *subject, DO* for *direct object, OP* for *object of a preposition,* or *PP* for *possessive pronoun.*

Example 1. Laura is the candidate *OP* for whom I will vote.

11. The chapter that the class is reading now discusses American life during the Great Depression.

12. He was the only celebrity whose autograph I could get.

13. The two deer, which had ambled down to the river, suddenly retreated into the woods.

14. The troubled queen to whom the poet is referring is Mary, Queen of Scots.

15. An arachnophobe is someone who has an abnormal fear of spiders.

Adverb Clauses A

15e.   An **adverb clause** is a subordinate clause that modifies a verb, an adjective, or an adverb.

An adverb clause generally tells *how, when, where, why, how much, to what extent,* or *under what condition* the action of a verb takes place.

EXAMPLE   **If the rain stops soon,** we will continue the game. [The adverb clause modifies the verb *will continue,* telling *under what condition* we will continue the game.]

Adverb clauses are introduced by *subordinating conjunctions*—words that show the relationship between an adverb clause and the word or words the clause modifies. Common subordinating conjunctions include *after, although, as, as if, as long as, as soon as, because, if, since, so that, than, unless, until, when, whenever, where, wherever, whether,* and *while.*

EXERCISE A   Underline the adverb clause in each of the following sentences. Then, circle the subordinating conjunction.

Example 1. Dad and I hid the gift (so that) we could surprise my sister.

1. After the owners of the store reduced prices, more people shopped there.

2. Call me if you need any help organizing the recycling campaign.

3. Carole performed a more difficult dive than any of her challengers did.

4. I made several errors on the test because I had misread the instructions.

5. Although televised newscasts are informative, I prefer reading the newspaper.

6. Jorge carries his laptop computer wherever he goes.

7. Cathy plays tennis better than I do.

8. You may go whenever you finish your homework.

9. As we drove up the mountain, the fog grew heavier.

10. A few of the guests at the party acted as if they were bored.

EXERCISE B   Complete each of the following sentences by writing in the blank provided a subordinating conjunction that shows a logical relationship between the ideas in the sentence.

Example 1. Tranh called about the part-time job ____as soon as____ I told him about it.

11. Jill will be moving to Miami _____ she graduates from high school.

12. Armand and Tony set up the tent _____ Travis and I gathered firewood.

13. May I use your computer _____ I can type my essay?

14. _____ you show your student identification at the ticket booth, you will receive a

   discount.

15. Robert could not play in the game _____ he had injured his wrist.

Grammar, Usage, and Mechanics: Language Skills Practice

Adverb Clauses B

15e. An *adverb clause* is a subordinate clause that modifies a verb, an adjective, or an adverb.

An adverb clause generally tells *how, when, where, why, how much, to what extent,* or *under what condition* the action of a verb takes place.

> **EXAMPLE** **Since the weather is so pleasant,** we should have a picnic by the lake. [The adverb clause modifies the verb *should have,* telling *why* we should have a picnic.]

Adverb clauses are introduced by *subordinating conjunctions*—words that show the relationship between an adverb clause and the word or words the clause modifies. Common subordinating conjunctions include *after, although, as, as if, as long as, as soon as, because, if, since, so that, than, unless, until, when, whenever, where, wherever, whether,* and *while.*

EXERCISE A Underline the adverb clause in each of the following sentences. Then, circle the subordinating conjunction.

Example 1. (As) the *Titanic* was sinking, the musicians continued to play.

1. Our nervousness subsided after the first round of the contest ended.

2. If you want to try out for the golf team, contact Coach Atkins by Friday.

3. A solar eclipse occurs when the moon comes between the sun and the earth.

4. Although he was seasick at times, Jules enjoyed most of the cruise.

5. Rosalie has been playing chess since she was four years old.

6. I need to stay after school today so that I can finish my science project.

7. The food drive may not be successful unless more people volunteer to help.

8. Annie had shown little interest in an acting career until she attended college.

9. In the gentle breeze the scarecrow looked as if it were dancing.

10. Put the vegetables wherever you can find room in the refrigerator.

EXERCISE B Complete each of the following sentences by writing in the blank provided a subordinating conjunction that shows a logical relationship between the ideas in the sentence.

Example 1. Why are you acting _____*as if*_____ you don't trust me?

11. Mr. Yan cannot be at school today _____ he has been called for jury duty.

12. _____ she returns, I will give her your message.

13. The audience applauded and cheered _____ the director joined the cast onstage.

14. Our two dogs raced alongside us _____ we ran to catch the school bus.

15. _____ we do not work tomorrow, we may not finish the project on time.

Subordinating Conjunctions

Adverb clauses are introduced by *subordinating conjunctions*—words that show the relationship between an adverb clause and the word or words the clause modifies.

Do not mistake a prepositional phrase for an adverb clause. Some words can be used as a preposition or a subordinating conjunction.

PREPOSITION	Where did you go **after** the movie?
SUBORDINATING CONJUNCTION	Where did you go **after** you watched the movie?

EXERCISE A Identify each of the following word groups by writing on the line provided either *PREP* for *prepositional phrase* or *ADV* for *adverb clause*.

Examples *PREP* **1.** before the ceremony

  ADV **2.** before the ceremony began

_____ **1.** after the boat capsized

_____ **2.** after the boating accident

_____ **3.** since the sixteenth century

_____ **4.** as if we needed any help

_____ **5.** unless the library closes early

_____ **6.** since it was already dark

_____ **7.** as the team's quarterback

_____ **8.** until we meet again

_____ **9.** until our next meeting

_____ **10.** although we were late

EXERCISE B Underline the adverb clause in each of the following sentences. Then, circle the subordinating conjunction.

Example 1. (When) they visit a museum, some people become confused.

11. They should study the museum guide before they begin looking at the exhibits.

12. Most visitors stop where the skeletons of prehistoric animals stand.

13. If you are curious about dinosaurs, you can learn much about them.

14. One day, as we approached the exhibit on prehistoric birds, another visitor told us about the discovery of the remains of a dinosaur in South America in the late 1990s.

15. This friendly visitor certainly knew more about prehistoric birds than we did.

16. Because some of the features of the dinosaur resemble those of a bird, the researchers called the creature *Unenlagia*, meaning "half bird."

17. The creature probably did not fly, though its forelimbs are similar to a bird's wings.

18. Scientists are still unsure whether Unenlagia had feathers.

19. Because dinosaurs can be difficult to imagine, museum models help museum visitors.

20. You will probably want to read more about dinosaurs after you visit the museum.

GRAMMAR

Adjective and Adverb Clauses

15d.   An *adjective clause* is a subordinate clause that modifies a noun or a pronoun.

> **EXAMPLE**   John R. Erickson has written several novels **in which the principal character is named Hank the Cowdog.** [The adjective clause modifies the noun *novels*.]

15e.   An *adverb clause* is a subordinate clause that modifies a verb, an adjective, or an adverb.

> **EXAMPLE**   **Although the novels are considered children's literature,** adults enjoy reading them as well. [The adverb clause modifies the verb *enjoy*.]

EXERCISE A   Identify the underlined clause in each of the following sentences by writing above it *ADJ* for *adjective clause* or *ADV* for *adverb clause*.

Example 1.   A bibliophile is someone who enjoys collecting books. *[ADJ]*

1. When the optometrist examined my eyes, she found no signs of astigmatism.

2. In Greek mythology, Thetis immersed her son, Achilles, in the river Styx so that he would be invulnerable to injury.

3. Everyone who volunteered to decorate for Pumpkinfest should report to the gym after school.

4. Years later, she returned to the African village where she had been a Peace Corps volunteer.

5. The scientists cannot solve the problem until they have identified the cause of it.

EXERCISE B   Underline each subordinate clause in the following sentences. Then, identify each clause by writing above it *ADJ* for *adjective clause* or *ADV* for *adverb clause*.

Example 1.   Childe Hassam was an impressionist, an artist who strives to show the changing *[ADJ]* effects of light on a subject.

6. Before Hassam became a painter, he worked as an engraver and later as an illustrator for a magazine.

7. When he moved into a studio in Paris, Hassam found some paintings that the previous occupant, another artist, had left behind.

8. The artist who had created the paintings was Pierre Auguste Renoir, the great French impressionist.

9. Although Hassam painted many rural landscapes, he is perhaps best remembered for his compelling images of life in large cities.

10. In each painting, Hassam strove to make known the emotion that the subject of the painting evoked in him.

Noun Clauses A

15f. A *noun clause* is a subordinate clause that is used as a noun.

A noun clause may be used as a subject, a predicate nominative, a direct object, an indirect object, or an object of a preposition.

EXAMPLES **That Marie Curie changed modern science** is well known. [subject]
We sent **whomever we contacted** a letter of appreciation. [indirect object]

Sometimes, the introductory word in a noun clause is omitted but understood.

EXAMPLE I said **I had already heard the news.** [*That* is understood.]

EXERCISE A Underline the noun clause in each of the following sentences.

Example 1. According to my teacher, I can write my report about <u>whomever I want</u>.

1. I have decided that I will write about the life of George Washington Carver.

2. What Carver wanted to become was an artist.

3. He showed that he had talent for painting.

4. Where he could go to college depended on the restrictive laws of his time.

5. Horticulture was what he studied in college.

6. That he was intelligent, talented, and hardworking is obvious.

7. Carver was whom Booker T. Washington at Tuskegee Institute chose as the first director of its agriculture department.

8. Did you know that Carver developed hundreds of uses for peanuts, potatoes, and soybeans?

9. From Carver's "school on wheels," many farmers learned how they could improve their soil.

10. In 1923, the National Association for the Advancement of Colored People (NAACP) awarded Carver its Spingarn Medal for what he had achieved.

EXERCISE B Underline the noun clause in each of the following sentences. Then, on the line provided, identify the function of the clause by writing *S* for *subject*, *PN* for *predicate nominative*, *DO* for *direct object*, *IO* for *indirect object*, or *OP* for *object of a preposition*.

Example _*DO*_ **1.** Will you show me <u>how you solved the last problem</u>?

_____ **11.** The researchers remained puzzled by what they had discovered.

_____ **12.** A physical therapist is what Tina has always wanted to be.

_____ **13.** Do you know who wrote the national anthem of the United States?

_____ **14.** Alex will give whoever finds his class ring a cash reward.

_____ **15.** That you have not missed one day of school in ten years is remarkable.

Noun Clauses B

15f. A *noun clause* is a subordinate clause that is used as a noun.

EXAMPLES **That the band had to cancel its concert** disappointed many fans. [subject]

Ed's duties at the shop are not **what he had expected.** [predicate nominative]

I believe **that their new address is 6541 Spring Street.** [direct object]

The teacher gave **whoever solved the riddle** five extra points. [indirect object]

I am sorry for **what I said to you earlier.** [object of a preposition]

Sometimes, the introductory word in a noun clause is omitted but understood.

EXAMPLE I believe **their new address is 6541 Spring Street.** [*That* is understood.]

EXERCISE A Underline the noun clause in each of the following sentences.

Example 1. Can you tell me <u>when the compact disc was invented</u>?

1. We fans could not understand why the referee had called a technical foul on the coach.

2. The director gave whichever actors were present first choice of rehearsal times.

3. The nutritionist explained which vegetables are richest in vitamin C.

4. Guess what my grandparents gave me for my birthday.

5. The winner will be whichever team finds the most items.

6. What became of the English colony on Roanoke Island in 1587 remains a mystery.

7. Many people are interested in whom the presidential candidate will select as a running mate.

8. That Ms. Arquette had decided to withdraw from the mayoral race surprised even her campaign manager.

9. My mother offered a special surprise to whoever finished cleaning first.

10. The teacher showed me how I could better organize the ideas of my research paper.

EXERCISE B Underline the noun clause or clauses in each of the following sentences. Then, on the line provided, indicate how each noun clause is used. Write *S* for *subject,* *PN* for *predicate nominative, DO* for *direct object, IO* for *indirect object,* or *OP* for *object of a preposition.*

Example __*DO*__ **1.** Do you know <u>who is responsible for starting the rumors</u>?

_____**11.** Whether the class goes on the field trip depends on the weather conditions.

_____**12.** I did not know that the brown pelican is an endangered species.

_____**13.** The principal was pleased with what the student council had achieved.

_____**14.** The restaurant manager will pay whoever works this weekend a bonus of fifty dollars.

_____**15.** What the players want to know is who their new coach will be.

Kinds of Subordinate Clauses

15d.	An **adjective clause** is a subordinate clause that modifies a noun or a pronoun.
15e.	An **adverb clause** is a subordinate clause that modifies a verb, an adjective, or an adverb.
15f.	A **noun clause** is a subordinate clause that is used as a noun.

ADJECTIVE CLAUSE	Sherman Alexie, **who is an award-winning novelist,** is one of my favorite authors.
ADVERB CLAUSE	I waited **until the sun set.**
NOUN CLAUSE	Is this **what you need**?

EXERCISE Underline the subordinate clause in each of the following sentences. Then, above each clause, classify it by writing *ADJ* for *adjective clause*, *ADV* for *adverb clause*, or *N* for *noun clause.*

                                    ADV

Example 1. After he saw a program about Easter Island, Uncle Jim visited the island.

1. At first Uncle Jim did not know what would be required, so he did some research.

2. After he had read several books about the island, he discussed the idea with my family.

3. Where he would stay there was my mother's main concern.

4. He remembered that my aunt Victoria has camped all over the world, so he called her.

5. Aunt Victoria is happy to help anyone who shows an interest in traveling and camping.

6. She helped Uncle Jim choose the tent and equipment that he would use on the island.

7. He made a supply list so that he would remember to get everything at the camping store.

8. He decided to buy a small camp stove that could burn several types of fuel.

9. He packed his equipment and double-checked his packing list before he left.

10. After he flew to Chile from Florida, he waited several hours before flying to Easter Island.

11. Did you know that Easter Island is over two thousand miles west of Chile?

12. As soon as he arrived, he went to look at some *moai,* the famous stone heads of Easter Island.

13. Many of the *moai* stand on *ahu,* which are long stone platforms.

14. Because he was curious about the statues, Uncle Jim took many pictures of them.

15. The statues were carved out of the rock at Rano Raraku, which is an extinct volcano.

16. Where he set up his tent was a campground at the foot of the volcano.

17. He spent a week at Rano Raraku and lived in the tent while he studied the statues.

18. When the sun came up each morning, Uncle Jim photographed the giant stone heads.

19. He was pleased about how well his trip to Easter Island went.

20. Uncle Jim is happy to show his Easter Island photographs to whoever wants to see them.

GRAMMAR

Simple Sentences and Compound Sentences

15g(1). A *simple sentence* contains one independent clause and no subordinate clauses. It may have a compound subject, a compound verb, and any number of phrases.

> **EXAMPLE** Songkran, the Water Festival of Thailand, lasts for four days.

15g(2). A *compound sentence* contains two or more independent clauses and no subordinate clauses.

> **EXAMPLE** During the festival, colorfully decorated cars carry large statues of Buddha from temple to temple, and the people along the streets sprinkle water on the statues. [two independent clauses joined by a comma and the coordinating conjunction *and*]

EXERCISE A On the line provided, write the number of independent clauses (*1, 2,* or *3*) in each of the following sentences.

Example ___2___ **1.** My cousin Carlotta was born in Los Angeles, California, but for most of her life, she has lived in Guadalajara, Mexico.

_____ **1.** Last March, I had the opportunity to travel to Guadalajara and visit Carlotta.

_____ **2.** Each year, Carlotta can hardly wait until November, for the Día de los Muertos occurs during that month.

_____ **3.** In November, Carlotta prepares an altar in honor of deceased relatives, for the Día de Los Muertos is the "day of the dead."

_____ **4.** During this Mexican festival, families decorate an altar with photographs and candy skulls, prepare special foods, and light candles.

_____ **5.** During the festival, shops sell special items, performers dance, and children play.

EXERCISE B On the line provided, classify each of the following sentences by writing *S* for *simple sentence* or *CD* for *compound sentence.*

Example ___S___ **1.** The Industrial Revolution began in England in the eighteenth century.

_____ **6.** With the start of the Industrial Revolution came a heightened need for child labor laws.

_____ **7.** Many children worked for long hours in factories and mines, and most of them received extremely low wages.

_____ **8.** In addition, the children often suffered dangerous working conditions.

_____ **9.** Charles Dickens, a popular author at the time, saw the problem in England, and like many others, he sought to abolish the abuses.

_____ **10.** The efforts of Dickens and other citizens eventually resulted in more effective labor laws.

Complex Sentences and Compound-Complex Sentences

15g(3). A *complex sentence* contains one independent clause and at least one subordinate clause.

> **EXAMPLE** In India, Holi is a day of frivolity [independent clause] that is celebrated every year in late February or early March [subordinate clause].

15g(4). A *compound-complex sentence* contains two or more independent clauses and at least one subordinate clause.

> **EXAMPLE** During Holi, both young and old sing and dance [independent clause]; they also sprinkle each other's clothes with colored water [independent clause] until their attire becomes a hodgepodge of brilliant dyes [subordinate clause].

EXERCISE A In each of the following sentences, draw one line under each independent clause and two lines under each subordinate clause.

Example 1. John Zweifel is a miniaturist, an artist who creates very small works of art.

1. When Zweifel created a replica of the White House, he got help from his family and friends.

2. This model, which measures sixty feet by twenty feet, contains reproductions of all the White House furnishings, from rugs and furniture to oil paintings and crystal goblets.

3. Zweifel added 1,589 feet of wiring so that the 548 tiny light bulbs and 6 televisions would work.

4. Although the replica is complete, it remains a work in progress, for whenever there is a change in the actual White House, Zweifel duplicates the change in the replica.

5. Perhaps you have seen this famous replica, which many consider a masterpiece of miniature art; it has toured not only the United States but also Europe and Japan.

EXERCISE B Classify each of the following sentences by writing above it *CX* for *complex sentence* or *CD-CX* for *compound-complex sentence.*

Example 1. *CD-CX* Dr. Turner is an anthropologist, and last year he traveled to Canada, where he lived with a Cree family for several months.

6. While he lived with the family, Dr. Turner learned much about Cree history and culture.

7. Although most Cree live in Canada, about two thousand live on a reservation in Montana.

8. The woodlands of eastern and northern Canada were once home to all of the Cree; then in the mid-1700s some Cree bands moved west, where they became hunters.

9. Today, many Cree work on reservations, while others live in cities in Canada.

10. As Dr. Turner discovered, some Cree are employees of the Canadian government; they generally serve as teachers, clerks, or health-care workers.

Review A: Independent and Subordinate Clauses

EXERCISE A Underline the subordinate clause in each of the following sentences. Then, identify that clause by writing above it *ADJ* for *adjective clause*, *ADV* for *adverb clause*, or *N* for *noun clause*.

                         ADV
Example 1. As soon as we saw the cat, we wanted to adopt him.

1. My family and I adopted a Siamese cat, whom we named Chang.

2. That we have pampered Chang is an understatement.

3. Chang certainly senses that he is an important member of our family.

4. At times, in fact, he treats us as if we were his pets.

5. When we sit down to eat, Chang leaps promptly to the top of a nearby table.

6. Sitting there quietly, he purrs his contentment with the food that we give him.

7. Chang usually will eat what we like to eat.

8. Although he prefers tuna, he also enjoys other kinds of food.

9. Chang does not leave his table until we have cleared away the dishes from our meal.

10. After eating, Chang lies down in his basket, where he sleeps until snack time.

EXERCISE B Identify the underlined clause in each of the following sentences by writing above it *I* for *independent clause*, *ADJ* for *adjective clause*, *ADV* for *adverb clause*, or *N* for *noun clause*.

                                               N
Example 1. Chang never doubts for a moment that he is entitled to go with us on trips.

11. Aunt Jo has a fox terrier that becomes a nervous wreck on seeing Jo packing for a vacation.

12. Chang does not quiver a whisker, though, for he believes that cats always go on vacations.

13. When our car is packed and ready, he hops in cheerfully.

14. He avoids the driver's seat, willingly leaving the driving to whoever wants to drive.

15. Sleeping is what Chang likes best about a car trip.

16. He slips under the front seat to take the long midday nap that every other sensible cat takes.

17. He curls up politely and gives whoever is sitting in the front seat plenty of legroom.

18. That the rest of us remain awake probably baffles him.

19. In his view, the smartest traveler is one who arrives at his or her destination with the least worry and trouble.

20. Chang always seems content when we arrive at our destination.

Review B: **Clauses and Their Functions**

EXERCISE A Underline the subordinate clause in each of the following sentences. Then, identify that clause by writing above it *ADJ* for *adjective clause,* *ADV* for *adverb clause,* or *N* for *noun clause.*

Example 1. I went to a dance <u>that was sponsored by the American Field Service Club.</u> *(ADJ)*

1. At the dance I met Michelle, a student whose hometown is Paris.

2. When Michelle first arrived, her English was somewhat stilted.

3. Since we met, her speech has improved.

4. Michelle understands that it is important to practice English.

5. Sometimes, though, what she says surprises me.

6. Because she is athletic, Michelle loves sports jargon.

7. She readily learns the new terms that we teach her.

8. Baseball, which is my favorite game, confuses her.

9. However, she "talks" soccer as if she were a professional player.

10. What Michelle wants to become is a sports announcer.

EXERCISE B Identify the underlined clause in each of the following sentences by writing above it *I* for *independent clause,* *ADJ* for *adjective clause,* *ADV* for *adverb clause,* or *N* for *noun clause.* For each adjective or adverb clause, circle the word or words that the clause modifies. For each noun clause, indicate how the clause is used by writing above it *S* for *subject,* *DO* for *direct object,* *IO* for *indirect object,* *PN* for *predicate nominative,* or *OP* for *object of a preposition.*

Examples 1. What has a long, silky coat, a plumed tail, and flared (ears) <u>that resemble butterflies?</u> *(ADJ)*

2. Did you know <u>that a papillon is not just a butterfly?</u> *(N—DO)*

11. I laughed <u>when my father brought home a papillon.</u>

12. Don't you think <u>that a cat or a dog would make a better pet?</u>

13. That is <u>what I asked upon hearing of his strange purchase.</u>

14. <u>Imagine my surprise at the time</u> when I learned the truth.

15. Papillon, <u>which is French for "butterfly,"</u> is also the name of a breed of dog.

16. <u>What distinguishes the papillon from other toy spaniels</u> is its unusual, butterflylike ears.

17. A breed <u>that is becoming popular in the United States,</u> the papillon is an intelligent dog.

18. <u>If one can judge from our Papou,</u> the breed is also very friendly.

19. Our Papou, for example, readily responds to <u>whoever takes note of him.</u>

20. More than a show dog, he gives <u>whoever loves him</u> plenty of affection in return.

Grammar, Usage, and Mechanics: Language Skills Practice

Review C: **Sentence Structure**

EXERCISE Classify each of the following sentences by writing on the line provided *S* for *simple sentence,* *CD* for *compound sentence,* *CX* for *complex sentence,* or *CD-CX* for *compound-complex sentence.*

Example _____*S*_____ **1.** I use the *Dictionary of American Biography* to research famous Americans.

_____ **1.** If you like to read about contemporary people, you might enjoy *Current Biography.*

_____ **2.** Actually, *The Guinness Book of World Records* is my favorite source of biographical trivia.

_____ **3.** Because Philo T. Farnsworth helped invent television, his name is in encyclopedias.

_____ **4.** A statue of Buddha in Tokyo, Japan, is the world's tallest statue.

_____ **5.** In 1946, Estée Lauder founded a cosmetics firm and marketed beauty care products.

_____ **6.** In 1871, the entertainer P. T. Barnum opened a circus, which he later called "The Greatest Show on Earth"; he was later elected mayor of Bridgeport, Connecticut.

_____ **7.** In 1955, the cartoonist Charles Schulz won the Reuben Award from the National Cartoonists Society; he won the award again in 1964.

_____ **8.** The baseball player Sadaharu Oh, who has hit more than eight hundred home runs in his career, has been called the "Babe Ruth of Japan."

_____ **9.** I know that in 1998 Mark McGwire set a record for hitting the most home runs in a season, but I am not sure whether he still holds that record.

_____ **10.** *The Guinness Book of World Records* includes many other interesting facts and figures.

_____ **11.** With twenty-two letters, *superextraordinarisimo* is the longest word in Spanish.

_____ **12.** I learned that every known language includes the sound "ah," as in the word *father.*

_____ **13.** *Chi-n-chi-ku-ri-n,* which means "a very short person," is the longest word in Japanese.

_____ **14.** The English language includes approximately 1,016,500 words; that any English speaker uses more than 60,000 of these words is highly unlikely.

_____ **15.** William Shakespeare, a playwright and poet, had a vocabulary of about 33,000 words.

_____ **16.** Are you interested in geographical trivia?

_____ **17.** Hilo, Hawaii, is the southernmost city in the U.S., and Barrow, Alaska, is the northernmost.

_____ **18.** Covering about forty-five acres, the Quetzalcóatl Pyramid near Mexico City is not only the world's largest pyramid but also the largest monument ever built.

_____ **19.** The Gateway to the West arch is the world's tallest monument; it rises 630 feet.

_____ **20.** I like trivia games that are challenging; so does Irene.

Review D: **Clauses and Sentence Structure**

EXERCISE A Underline the subordinate clause in each of the following sentences. On the line provided, identify the clause by writing *ADJ* for *adjective clause*, *ADV* for *adverb clause*, or *N* for *noun clause*.

Example __*ADV*__ **1.** While we were shopping, we lost one of our packages.

_____ **1.** The forest fire started because someone had not smothered a campfire.

_____ **2.** The family that bought the house next door is from Seattle.

_____ **3.** Did you know that Joel is the new team captain?

_____ **4.** Mr. O'Brien will buy the store if the bank will lend him the money.

_____ **5.** The girl who won the golf match has practiced diligently.

EXERCISE B For each of the following sentences, underline each independent clause once and each subordinate clause twice. Then, identify each sentence according to structure. On the line provided, write *S* for *simple sentence*, *CD* for *compound sentence*, *CX* for *complex sentence*, or *CD-CX* for *compound-complex sentence*.

Example __*CX*__ **1.** I've enjoyed this class since we've been studying Yellowstone National Park.

_____ **6.** Did you know that Yellowstone National Park is the oldest of our national parks?

_____ **7.** I don't know if you have ever visited Yellowstone, but you should plan to see it soon.

_____ **8.** The first recorded trip to the Yellowstone geysers was made in 1807 by John Colter.

_____ **9.** Colter's reports of rainbow-colored pools, spouting geysers, and boiling mudholes were dismissed as hallucinations.

_____ **10.** After 1810, a number of trappers and scouts visited the region, but few people believed the stories that these explorers brought back.

_____ **11.** In 1870, an expedition that was headed by Henry D. Washburn and Nathaniel P. Langford finally discovered the truth behind the stories.

_____ **12.** The next year, Dr. Ferdinand Hayden, head of the U.S. Geological Survey, led a scientific expedition to Yellowstone; he brought with him an artist and a photographer.

_____ **13.** Their reports captured the interest of the nation, and Congress quickly acted to preserve the region as a national park.

_____ **14.** In 1988, much of Yellowstone's forest and meadowland was consumed by fire, which was allowed to burn unchecked.

_____ **15.** In the event of fire, park policy is to let nature take its course.

Literary Model: Poetry

GRAMMAR | Language in Context: Literary Model

When I heard the learn'd astronomer,
When the proofs, the figures, were ranged in columns before me,
When I was shown the charts and diagrams, to add, divide, and measure them,
When I sitting heard the astronomer where he lectured with much applause in
     the lecture room,
How soon unaccountable I became tired and sick,
Till rising and gliding out I wandered off by myself,
In the mystical moist night air, and from time to time,
Looked up in perfect silence at the stars.

—"When I Heard the Learn'd Astronomer" by Walt Whitman

Exercise A

1. On the lines below, write the subject and verb of each clause in the poem. Next to the subject and verb, write *S* if the clause is subordinate or *I* if the clause is independent. One clause from the last four lines has been indentified for you.

    I wandered, looked—S

_____

_____

_____

_____

2. It may surprise you to realize that the poem is one long sentence. Based on the clauses you identified in Item 1, what kind of sentence is it: simple, compound, complex, or compound-complex?

_____

Exercise B   As you can see, the poem begins with a series of increasingly longer clauses. How might the length and number of these clauses indicate how the speaker feels about the astronomer's lecture?

_____

_____

_____

_____

ELEMENTS OF LANGUAGE | Third Course

Literary Model (continued)

EXERCISE C   Write a short poem describing a lecture or a speech you once heard and how you felt about it. Make your poem one long sentence as Whitman did.

_____

_____

_____

_____

_____

_____

_____

_____

_____

EXERCISE D

1. On the lines below, write the subject and verb of each clause you used in your poem. Next to the subject and verb, write *S* if the clause is subordinate or *I* if the clause is independent.

_____

_____

_____

_____

_____

2. What kind of sentence is your poem: simple, compound, complex, or compound-complex?

_____

3. Explain how your use of clauses helps describe the lecture or speech. For instance, did you use subordinate clauses for less important ideas and independent clauses for more important ones? Did you use long or short clauses to help express your meaning? Explain your answers.

_____

_____

_____

_____

Writing Application: Instructions

Characteristics such as age and level of experience influence a person's ability to understand a set of instructions. For example, a teenager who has been cooking and creating recipes since the age of seven will probably find it easier to understand instructions for how to make lasagna than another teenager whose cooking experience consists of heating a frozen dinner in a microwave oven. The writing used in the instructions given to the beginner should contain more simple sentences and fewer compound, complex, and compound-complex sentences.

SIMPLE	Let eggs reach room temperature. Beat four eggs for one minute. Add them to the batter.
COMPOUND-COMPLEX	Beat for one minute four eggs that have reached room temperature; then, add them to the batter.

In any kind of writing—but especially in informative pieces of writing—consider your audience when you choose sentence structures.

WRITING ACTIVITY

Think of something that you know how to do or make that would be appropriate for both children and adults. Write two sets of instructions for your activity: one that a group of second-grade students can follow without any difficulty, and the other that a group of adults can successfully follow. Be sure to tailor your choice of sentence structures according to the audience.

PREWRITING　Use a flowchart or some other type of diagram to list all the steps and materials that need to be included in your instructions. Then, while visualizing yourself actually performing the task, check that you have included every step and material in the diagram.

WRITING　Use what you have written in your diagram to guide you as you write a draft of each set of instructions. Remember to choose sentence structures according to whether the instructions are intended for the second-grade students or the adults. You should use mostly simple sentences in your instructions for the children.

REVISING　Read your two drafts to two classmates to see whether they can tell which set of instructions is intended for which audience. If it is not completely obvious, then you need to revise sentence structures. You will also need to make sure your vocabulary is appropriate for each audience. If your classmates are not familiar with your topic, ask them whether they think the instructions are clear enough.

PUBLISHING　Put your two sets of instructions aside for a while, then proofread them slowly later. Check that all your sentences are complete sentences and that you have correctly used punctuation in your compound, complex, and compound-complex sentences. Proofread for other errors in grammar, usage, spelling, and punctuation. Then, use one set of instructions to demonstrate the steps of your activity to the class.

EXTENDING YOUR WRITING

Along with one or two of your classmates, turn your instructions into a handy guidebook. First, your group needs to determine the audience of your guidebook: adults, children, or a combination of the two. Write a brief but helpful introduction that explains the content of your guide. Decide which instructions to include, come up with the best way to bind them together, and illustrate the pages and cover of your book.

for **CHAPTER 16: AGREEMENT** | *pages 490–512*

Choices: Exploring Agreement

The following activities challenge you to find a connection between subject-verb agreement and pronoun-antecedent agreement and the world around you. Do the activity below that suits your personality best, and then share your discoveries with your class.

BUILDING BACKGROUND KNOWLEDGE

Rock-and-Roll

There are quite a number of pairs of nouns that go together. They actually name only one thing. These pairs are called *binomials*. Get together with a friend and brainstorm a list of binomials. You could start with *macaroni and cheese* or *horse and carriage*. When you're done, pass out copies of your list for your classmates to insert in their English notebooks.

GRAPHICS

Neither Fish nor Fowl

Some indefinite pronouns really are indefinite; they can be singular or plural. You know the ones—*all, any, more, most, none,* and *some.* Design a poster to show your classmates. Choose five indefinite pronouns that can be singular or plural. For each pronoun, write two sentences: one for each context.

FOREIGN LANGUAGES

¿Habla Español?

Interview a few people who speak or are learning a foreign language. Find out if other languages require subjects and verbs to agree. Make a handout of examples for your classmates, and report back to the class.

CONTEST

STOP!

Prepare a dialogue or monologue on audio- or videotape. Sprinkle subject-verb errors and pronoun-antecedent agreement errors throughout the tape. Then, divide the class into two teams. Play your tape. When someone hears an error, he or she yells "STOP!" Stop the tape and ask the person to correct the error. Proper corrections earn a point. Incorrect stops lose a point. The team with the most points wins.

MATHEMATICS

The Latest Statistics

Some people say that we live in the age of statistics. Studies, statistical analyses, and polls on every possible subject are being made daily. Pick one recent statistical analysis. (They're in newspapers all the time.) Study it and write out some of the facts that the study found. Be sure to use percentages and fractions as subjects and antecedents. Then, report on the topic, and give your classmates a chance to hear how percentages and fractions sound when they agree with verbs and antecedents.

DRAMA

Collective Decisions

Sometimes deciding whether collective nouns are singular or plural is easy, and sometimes it's not. Make it easy for your classmates. In a group, act out a few situations. First, write a half-dozen sentences, each of which is a scenario that your group acts out. Write three in which the group acts as a unit and three in which the group members act individually. Make sure you write the sentence that you are acting out on the board.

ORIGINAL PROJECTS

Blaze Your Own Trail

There are plenty of lists you could compile for this chapter—lists of plural nouns that actually are singular, plural nouns *(pants)* that name only one thing, titles that are plural *(Wuthering Heights),* and many more. Compile one of these lists or come up with your own activity. Go on a scavenger hunt for agreement errors in magazines and newspapers. Write a riddle or a limerick. Design a brochure. Perform a comedy routine. If you want to do something new, do it! Just make sure your activity relates to agreement.

Number

USAGE

16a.	A word that refers to one person, place, thing, or idea is *singular* in number. A word that refers to more than one is *plural* in number.

SINGULAR	building	he	woman	knife	country
PLURAL	buildings	they	women	knives	countries

EXERCISE A   On the line, write *S* for each singular word and *P* for each plural word.

Example ___P___ **1.** several

_____ **1.** vegetables
_____ **2.** valley
_____ **3.** it
_____ **4.** mice
_____ **5.** we
_____ **6.** wrenches
_____ **7.** chicken
_____ **8.** honesty
_____ **9.** children
_____ **10.** ourselves

_____ **11.** contest
_____ **12.** strawberries
_____ **13.** dandelion
_____ **14.** monkey
_____ **15.** office
_____ **16.** men
_____ **17.** wolves
_____ **18.** them
_____ **19.** peach
_____ **20.** loss

_____ **21.** somebody
_____ **22.** pennies
_____ **23.** her
_____ **24.** catalogue
_____ **25.** wharves
_____ **26.** anything
_____ **27.** truth
_____ **28.** few
_____ **29.** piano
_____ **30.** oats

EXERCISE B   On each line, complete each word group with a correct singular or plural word. Write *S* after a singular word and *P* after a plural word.

Example 1. those breathtaking ___photographs P___

31. twelve strange _____
32. an excellent _____
33. several satisfied _____
34. neither of the _____
35. these interesting _____
36. many talented _____
37. another large _____
38. thirty-five _____
39. some mysterious _____
40. a pair of _____

41. a delicious _____
42. a few more _____
43. a thousand _____
44. every _____
45. a herd of _____
46. numerous _____
47. that small _____
48. each of the _____
49. many important _____
50. not even a single _____

Agreement of Subject and Verb A

16b. A verb should agree in number with its subject.

(1) Singular subjects take singular verbs.
(2) Plural subjects take plural verbs.

SINGULAR	**He takes** music lessons.	**She has been sleeping.**
PLURAL	**They take** music lessons.	**They have been sleeping.**

16c. The number of the subject usually is not determined by a word in a phrase or clause following the subject.

EXAMPLES   That **dog** with big teeth **scares** me.

           Earl, as well as his older sister, **is** a fantastic athlete.

USAGE

EXERCISE A In each of the following sentences, two verbs appear in parentheses. Underline the verb that agrees with its subject.

Example 1. Some members of the Spanish club (*has, have*) been studying Mexico.

1. The capital of Mexico (*is, are*) Mexico City.

2. The plaza at the center of the city (*covers, cover*) the site of an ancient Aztec temple.

3. Today, people (*calls, call*) the plaza the Zócalo.

4. Many buildings of historical and architectural interest (*surrounds, surround*) the Zócalo.

5. The City Hall, as well as the National Palace, (*is, are*) on the Zócalo.

6. The offices of the government (*is, are*) in the National Palace.

7. The National Palace (*was, were*) built over three hundred years ago.

8. Inside the Palace (*is, are*) several murals by Diego Rivera.

9. One of them, titled *El Mundo Azteca*, (*depicts, depict*) people from the ancient culture.

10. The citizens, together with tourists, (*enjoy, enjoys*) visiting the National Palace.

EXERCISE B Each of the sentences in the following paragraph contains an error in subject-verb agreement. Cross out each incorrect verb and write the correct verb above it.

Example [1] The arts of illusion ~~is~~ *are* essential in the world of moviemaking.

[11] Few viewers of the film *Superman: The Movie* knows how Christopher Reeve soars through the air. **[12]** Credit for the flying scenes go to special-effects crews. **[13]** These masters of illusion creates the tricks to make the impossible appear to happen. **[14]** Superman, together with Lois Lane, were suspended on wires from huge cranes. **[15]** The actors in the scene were moving only their heads and arms while films of rushing scenery was projected onto large screens behind them.

Grammar, Usage, and Mechanics: Language Skills Practice

Agreement of Subject and Verb B

16b. A verb should agree in number with its subject.

(1) Singular subjects take singular verbs.
(2) Plural subjects take plural verbs.

SINGULAR **He sings** in the choir. **She has been drawing.**
PLURAL **They sing** in the choir. **They have been drawing.**

16c. The number of the subject usually is not determined by a word in a phrase or clause following the subject.

EXAMPLE The **documentary** on runners in Kenya **was** fascinating.

EXERCISE In each sentence below, underline the verb that agrees with its subject.

Example 1. The name of the student with the highest grades (*has, have*) been announced.

1. The vase of flowers (*is, are*) on the table.

2. The photographs on the table (*reminds, remind*) me of our recent trip.

3. The pole vault, as well as the high jump, (*is, are*) Abdul's specialty.

4. Bears (*lives, live*) in those mountains.

5. Rome, together with Venice, (*has, have*) many interesting sights.

6. Lemon (*enhances, enhance*) the flavor in fish.

7. The tigers at our hometown zoo (*roams, roam*) freely on an island.

8. Spinach, in addition to squash, (*is, are*) very nourishing.

9. The highest mountains in the world (*rises, rise*) in the Himalayas.

10. The plays we read in speech class (*is, are*) based on historical events.

11. The grass on the lawns (*gets, get*) parched when we have a hot, dry summer.

12. Anaba, along with her brothers, (*wants, want*) to learn some traditional songs.

13. That pair of scissors with the orange handles (*is, are*) missing.

14. My aunt from the Netherlands (*loves, love*) to travel.

15. Three students in my math class (*is, are*) going to the state finals.

16. Coyotes, rattlesnakes, and lizards (*thrives, thrive*) in the Mexican desert.

17. Many beautiful fish near the reef in Cozumel (*swims, swim*) lazily below us.

18. The grandparents of my best friend (*has, have*) always lived in Guadalajara.

19. Dust mites in the air (*is, are*) a problem for people with allergies.

20. The top of those bushes (*reaches, reach*) almost to the second story.

Agreement of Subject and Verb C

16d. The following indefinite pronouns are singular: *anybody, anyone, anything, each, either, everybody, everyone, everything, neither, nobody, no one, nothing, one, somebody, someone,* and *something.*

> **EXAMPLE** **Everyone** in the cast **is** at rehearsal today.

16e. The following indefinite pronouns are plural: *both, few, many,* and *several.*

> **EXAMPLE** **Several** of the athletes **were** at the banquet.

16f. The indefinite pronouns *all, any, more, most, none,* and *some* may be singular or plural, depending on their meaning in a sentence.

> **EXAMPLES** **Most** of our vacation **is** over. [*Most* refers to the singular noun *vacation*.]
>
> **Most** of the days **have passed.** [*Most* refers to the plural noun *days*.]

EXERCISE A Each of these sentences has an indefinite pronoun as a subject. Write *S* above the pronoun if it is singular and *P* if it is plural. Then, underline the correct form of the verb in parentheses.

                P
Example 1. Some of my neighbors *(has, have)* installed extra lights.

1. Neither of the contestants *(knows, know)* the answer to the question.

2. *(Has, Have)* all of the ice melted?

3. Everybody in the theater *(is, are)* standing and cheering.

4. Many of the tickets to the play *(has, have)* been sold.

5. Both of the candidates for the job *(seems, seem)* capable.

6. No one at the party *(recognizes, recognize)* Stefan.

7. Each of the Maramoto brothers *(has, have)* applied for a scholarship.

8. Most of the musicians *(respects, respect)* the conductor.

9. Some of the story *(was, were)* difficult to understand.

10. *(Is, Are)* either of the doctors available for an appointment tomorrow?

EXERCISE B In each of the following sentences, two verbs appear in parentheses. Underline the correct verb form. Then, circle the subject of the sentence.

Example 1. (All) of Suzi's kittens *(was, were)* adopted.

11. Everything about the concert *(was, were)* thrilling.

12. *(Is, Are)* any of the peaches ripe yet?

13. Few of the boys *(responds, respond)* well to criticism.

14. None of the dessert baked by my sisters *(is, are)* left.

15. Several of the new students *(speak, speaks)* Spanish.

USAGE

Agreement of Subject and Verb D

16d. The following indefinite pronouns are singular: *anybody, anyone, anything, each, either, everybody, everyone, everything, neither, nobody, no one, nothing, one, somebody, someone,* and *something.*

EXAMPLE **Neither** of the girls **is** here now.

16e. The following indefinite pronouns are plural: *both, few, many,* and *several.*

EXAMPLE **Both** of us **were** excited to attend the concert.

16f. The indefinite pronouns *all, any, more, most, none,* and *some* may be singular or plural, depending on their meaning in a sentence.

EXAMPLES **All** of the salad **has been eaten.** [*All* refers to the singular noun *salad.*]

All of the oranges **are** gone. [*All* refers to the plural noun *oranges.*]

EXERCISE A If the verb in a sentence does not agree with its subject, cross out the incorrect verb and write the correct verb above it. If a sentence is already correct, write *C* above it.

Example 1. Many of the drivers in the race ~~was~~ *were* European.

1. Most of the children does their homework in study hall.

2. Some of the television program were interesting.

3. Neither of the team captains have told us what to do.

4. Does both of the writers want to attend the workshop?

5. Everyone who likes to sing usually joins in on the choruses.

6. Nothing in these books contradict your theory.

7. Everybody already know how to solve the problem.

8. Several of the band members is planning to audition for the orchestra.

9. None of us wants to go there in the winter.

10. Each of the girls swim every day during the summer.

EXERCISE B In each of the following sentences, two verbs appear in parentheses. Underline the correct verb form. Then, circle the subject of the sentence.

Example 1. *(Is, Are)* any of the boys playing soccer this afternoon?

11. Some of the guests *(was, were)* friends of his brother.

12. Everything in your notebooks *(is, are)* graded weekly.

13. *(Does, Do)* all of the tires on the car need air?

14. Neither of the girls *(is, are)* planning to stay late.

15. *(Is, Are)* both of them studying right now?

USAGE

Agreement of Subject and Verb E

USAGE

16g. Subjects joined by *and* generally take a plural verb.

  EXAMPLE   **Justin Leonard** and **Annika Sörenstam are** famous professional golfers.

Compound subjects that name only one person, place, thing, or idea take a singular verb.

16h. Singular subjects joined by *or* or *nor* take a singular verb. Plural subjects joined by *or* or *nor* take a plural verb.

  EXAMPLE   Either a **doctor** or a **nurse checks** on the hospital patients each morning.

16i. When a singular subject and a plural subject are joined by *or* or *nor*, the verb agrees with the subject nearer the verb.

  EXAMPLES   Neither the band members nor the **singer feels** ready for the performance.
  Neither the singer nor the band **members feel** ready for the performance.

EXERCISE A   Underline the verb that agrees with the compound subject of the sentence.

Example 1. Macaroni and cheese (*is, are*) on the menu for lunch today.

1. Three women and a man (*makes, make*) up the conference committee.

2. The leading actor and dancer (*is, are*) Gregory Hines.

3. Neither her play nor her novels (*is, are*) widely read.

4. Maya Angelou and Joan Didion (*writes, write*) about personal experiences.

5. Neither the actors nor their director (*has, have*) staged a play by Wilson before.

6. Neither the pitcher nor the outfielders (*is, are*) playing well today.

7. Recycling and paper drives (*is, are*) helpful for the environment.

8. The conductor and the musicians of the symphony (*is, are*) very talented.

9. Either the eggs or the milk (*seems, seem*) spoiled.

10. Neither the trees nor the flowers (*fares, fare*) well in this heat.

EXERCISE B   Circle the subject and underline the verb that agrees with the subject.

Example 1. The (producer) and (director) of the film (*is, are*) Steven Spielberg.

11. Neither the managers nor the workers (*agrees, agree*) with the negotiator.

12. Jason Granholm and Ty Nguyen (*is, are*) the winners of the poetry contest.

13. Either the puppies or their mother (*has, have*) torn a hole in that chair.

14. Neither Beatriz nor her sisters (*attends, attend*) Southdale High School.

15. Those plants and the ones next to the window (*blooms, bloom*) each spring.

Agreement of Subject and Verb F

16g.	Subjects joined by *and* generally take a plural verb.

Compound subjects that name only one person, place, thing, or idea take a singular verb.

EXAMPLE   My **mother** and **father cook** excellent meals.

16h.	Singular subjects joined by *or* or *nor* take a singular verb. Plural subjects joined by *or* or *nor* take a plural verb.

EXAMPLE   Neither the **guests** nor the **hosts are dancing.**

16i.	When a singular subject and a plural subject are joined by *or* or *nor*, the verb agrees with the subject nearer the verb.

EXAMPLES   Neither the players nor the **coach is** happy with the game.
Neither the coach nor the **players are** happy with the game.

EXERCISE A   Circle the subject and underline the verb that agrees with the subject.

Example 1. Either (Tom) or (Susan) *(live, lives)* on the next street.

1. The singer and songwriter of the CD *(is, are)* a talented artist.

2. Neither Beth nor her parents *(is, are)* able to come to the concert.

3. Cynthia or Tania *(want, wants)* to go hiking this weekend.

4. Either the club members or the president *(has, have)* the right to make the decision.

5. Beverly and Rafael *(agrees, agree)* that the house needs to be painted.

EXERCISE B   If a verb does not agree with its subject, cross out the incorrect verb and write the correct verb above it. If a verb is already correct, write *C* above it.

Example 1. Neither my mother nor my aunts ~~has~~ *have* perfect vision.

6. Both Cocheta and Amalia buys their clothes with money from their jobs.

7. Either Will Rogers or James Thurber are the author of that quotation.

8. Neither the residents nor the governor want the bridge to be built.

9. Does the Arnolds or the MacLeods always bring the salsa?

10. Neither my sister nor my mom are willing to go with me.

11. Neither Delores nor any of the other girls wants to go surfing with me.

12. Neither the ghosts nor the pirates in the haunted house scares me.

13. Either the mail carrier or the meter readers have been leaving my gate open.

14. The hamster and the mouse seems healthier since we got the new feeders.

15. The room and board at the dormitory seem reasonable.

Agreement of Subject and Verb G

16j. The contractions *don't* and *doesn't* should agree with their subjects.

The word *don't* is the contraction of *do not*. Use *don't* with all plural subjects and with the pronouns *I* and *you*.

EXAMPLES **I don't** speak French well. **Doesn't she** like spinach?

USAGE

EXERCISE In each of these sentences, the contractions *don't* and *doesn't* appear in parentheses. Underline the contraction that agrees in number with its subject.

Example 1. She *(don't, doesn't)* ski very often.

1. A desert *(don't, doesn't)* get much rain.

2. *(Don't, Doesn't)* these kinds of fruit contain a lot of vitamin C?

3. Some of the spectators watching the magician *(don't, doesn't)* realize he is creating illusions.

4. The dancer performing the slow moves *(don't, doesn't)* impress me as much as the other one.

5. Macaroni and cheese *(don't, doesn't)* taste bad at all.

6. *(Don't, Doesn't)* he know that I want a new bicycle for my birthday?

7. Many of the players *(don't, doesn't)* mind practicing more often.

8. *(Don't, Doesn't)* the time go by fast when you're having fun?

9. If Juan Pablo and his brother *(don't, doesn't)* get here on time, we're leaving.

10. It really *(don't, doesn't)* matter to me whether we leave now or in fifteen minutes.

11. That CD player you bought yesterday *(don't, doesn't)* sound too good.

12. The leaves on the pecan tree typically *(don't, doesn't)* start falling off until mid-October.

13. *(Don't, Doesn't)* one of you belong to that national organization?

14. The jazz band at María's school *(don't, doesn't)* perform every month.

15. My friend, who is from the Philippines, *(don't, doesn't)* mind eating my mother's Southern cooking.

16. One of the girls *(don't, doesn't)* intend to go to the football game.

17. You and she *(don't, doesn't)* have to coordinate your plans.

18. *(Don't, Doesn't)* every person in the group have to participate to the fullest extent?

19. Those *(don't, doesn't)* offer the same benefits.

20. The last song on that set of CDs *(don't, doesn't)* sound like the rest.

Agreement of Subject and Verb H

16k. A collective noun may be either singular or plural, depending on its meaning in a sentence.

> **EXAMPLES**   The **committee is meeting** today. [*Committee* is thought of as a unit.]
>
> The **committee are discussing** several issues. [*Committee* is thought of as individuals.]

EXERCISE A   For each of the following sentences, choose the correct form of the verb in parentheses.

Example 1. The audience (*express, expresses*) its enthusiasm by applauding loudly.

1. Each Christmas, Marco's family (*exchange, exchanges*) gifts with one another.

2. The committee in charge of the project (*make, makes*) its decision at 3:00 P.M. tomorrow.

3. Graziella's class (*has, have*) chosen its theme for the annual dance.

4. Far off the shore, a fleet of ships (*move, moves*) away from the island one by one.

5. The team (*is, are*) happy because each member has been given a victory award.

EXERCISE B   Select five collective nouns, and write five pairs of sentences that show clearly how the nouns you chose may be singular or plural. Select from the following: *army, audience, class, club, committee, fleet, flock, group, public,* and *team.*

Examples 1. *The herd of cattle cautiously moves away from the barn.*

     2. *Hearing the loud noise, the herd of cattle quickly move in separate directions.*

6. _____

_____

7. _____

_____

8. _____

_____

9. _____

_____

10. _____

_____

for **CHAPTER 16: AGREEMENT**   pages 502–503

Agreement of Subject and Verb I

| **16l.** | A verb agrees with its subject, but not necessarily with a predicate nominative. |

EXAMPLES My favorite **vegetable is** peas.   **Peas are** my favorite vegetable.

| **16m.** | When the subject follows the verb, find the subject and make sure that the verb agrees with it. |

EXAMPLES   Where **is** your **plate?**   Here **are** some **sandwiches** for you.
                      Where **are** your **friends?**   Where**'s** your **friend?**

USAGE

EXERCISE For each of the following sentences, underline the correct form of the verb in parentheses. Then, underline the subject of the sentence twice.

Example 1. The <u>order</u> we made <u>(was, were)</u> three pizzas.

1. Where (is, are) the line to purchase tickets for the movie?

2. The team's mission (is, are) victories.

3. When (was, were) the new CD releases announced?

4. There (is, are) the list of items you wanted.

5. The items (was, were) a list of ingredients for cooking paella.

6. Achievements (is, are) the main objective of that company.

7. Here (is, are) the samples you requested.

8. The New Orleans jazz bands performing at the festival (was, were) a popular appeal.

9. There (is, are) never enough time to do all that you want to do.

10. Why (is, are) the squirrels in our backyard so friendly?

11. The main attraction at the circus (is, are) usually the acrobats.

12. Where (is, are) the soccer team traveling for the next game?

13. A popular food in south Louisiana (is, are) red beans and rice.

14. There (was, were) more visitors expected at the exhibit this year.

15. In biology, why (is, are) those birds a distinct category?

16. For my mother, peas and carrots (is, are) traditional side dishes.

17. A collection of old stamps (was, were) an interest of many visitors at the exhibit.

18. There (is, are) the list of topics for the project.

19. Here (is, are) the roster of names of those who plan to attend the ceremony.

20. That group of insects (is, are) a special class.

Agreement of Subject and Verb J

USAGE

16n. An expression of an amount (a measurement, a percentage, or a fraction, for example) may be singular or plural, depending on how it is used.

EXAMPLES **Six weeks is** a long vacation. [Amount is thought of as a unit.]
Six dollars were lying on the street. [Amount is thought of as individual pieces.]
Eighty-five percent of the seniors **are going** on the class trip. [Percentage is plural because it refers to the plural word *seniors*.]
One quarter of the term **is** over. [Fraction is singular because it refers to the singular word *term*.]

EXERCISE For each of the following sentences, choose the correct form of the verb in parentheses.

Example 1. Three fourths of my classmates (*is, are*) studying Spanish.

1. Three months (*is, are*) the training period for Susan's new job.

2. Half of the men (*was, were*) barefoot.

3. Two eighths (*is, are*) the same as one fourth.

4. The teacher said that 50 percent of the grade (*is, are*) this essay.

5. Half of an orange (*was, were*) enough for me.

6. Aren't you surprised that almost 100 percent of the children (*know, knows*) the answer?

7. Two thirds of a cup of flour (*was, were*) more than enough to thicken the sauce.

8. Nine cents (*was, were*) found under the couch cushion.

9. Only 10 percent of the members (*wants, want*) to spend money on that project.

10. Only thirty weeks (*remain, remains*) until summer vacation.

11. Half of the apples (*was, were*) rotten.

12. Five dollars an hour (*is, are*) not even minimum wage.

13. Of the tomatoes, two thirds (*has, have*) already been eaten.

14. Ten days (*is, are*) the limit for returning the merchandise after purchase.

15. I think 60 percent of the paper (*has, have*) been written.

16. One third of the employees (*plans, plan*) to attend the training session.

17. Seventy dollars (*is, are*) a lot to pay for a shirt.

18. The director said that about one fifth of the time (*was, were*) spent scouting for locations.

19. One tenth of the compound (*consist, consists*) of hydrogen.

20. Fifty percent of the scientist's time (*is, are*) spent doing research.

Agreement of Subject and Verb K

| **16o.** | Some nouns that are plural in form take singular verbs. |

EXAMPLES   The **news is** on at six o'clock.

The **scissors were left** on the counter.

| **16p.** | Even when plural in form, the title of a creative work (such as a book, song, film, or painting), the name of an organization, or the name of a country or city generally takes a singular verb. |

EXAMPLE   ***The Grapes of Wrath* is** a novel by John Steinbeck.

EXERCISE   For each of the following sentences, choose the correct form of the verb in parentheses.

Example   1. The news about the earthquake (*was*, *were*) a shock to everyone.

1. The coach explained that gymnastics (*is*, *are*) a good sport for improving flexibility.

2. Linguistics, the study of language, (*include*, *includes*) social and nonsocial aspects of language.

3. How much (*do*, *does*) those binoculars cost?

4. My new pajamas (*fits*, *fit*) me very loosely.

5. "Night and Day" (*is*, *are*) a song by one of the great American songwriters, Cole Porter.

6. Checkers (*is*, *are*) my cousin Ignacio's favorite game.

7. The scissors in the top drawer (*has*, *have*) to be repaired.

8. The blues, thought to have been developed after the Civil War, (*is*, *are*) traditionally an African American form of music.

9. Statistics, a branch of mathematics, (*is*, *are*) used to organize and interpret numerical data.

10. The acoustics in the auditorium (*was*, *were*) excellent; we had no trouble hearing the choir.

11. Ernest Hemingway's *The Torrents of Spring* (*was*, *were*) published in 1926.

12. My braces (*has*, *have*) to be adjusted by the dentist in four weeks.

13. The shears in the garage (*is*, *are*) rusting because of the damp weather we have been having.

14. Dominoes (*is*, *are*) my grandfather's favorite pastime during the hot summer.

15. Ethics (*use*, *uses*) reason to address questions of what is right and what is wrong.

16. Jane says that economics (*is*, *are*) what her son has decided to study.

17. Politics, the science of government, (*is*, *are*) Rafael's primary interest.

18. *The Outsiders* (*is*, *are*) my brother Tom's favorite movie.

19. The shorts I wore yesterday (*was*, *were*) inexpensive.

20. Girls' athletics (*has*, *have*) become popular at my high school.

Agreement of Subject and Verb L

16q. Subjects preceded by *every* or *many a* take singular verbs.

> **EXAMPLE** **Many a** concert **was performed** at that arena.

16r. When the relative pronoun *that, which,* or *who* is the subject of an adjective clause, the verb in the adjective clause agrees with the word to which the relative pronoun refers.

> **EXAMPLES** The home **that is** on the tour is next door. [*That* refers to the singular noun *home.*]
> The homes **that are** on the tour are in my neighborhood. [*That* refers to the plural noun *homes.*]

EXERCISE A For each of the following sentences, choose the correct form of the verb in parentheses.

Example 1. Every teacher and student (*is, are*) invited to the auditorium for the concert.

1. Many a family (*has, have*) either a dog or cat as a pet.

2. Every girl and boy in the class (*receive, receives*) merit points for good conduct.

3. Many a play (*is, are*) produced at the Little Theater in my hometown.

4. Every film at the festival (*was, were*) reviewed by a dozen critics.

5. Many a farmer (*grow, grows*) corn or soybeans in this part of the country.

EXERCISE B For each of the following sentences, underline the correct form of the verb in parentheses. Then, underline twice the word or word group with which the verb agrees.

Example 1. Here is the picture that (*show, shows*) all my friends at my birthday party.

6. The stadium that (*is, are*) located downtown seats up to forty thousand spectators.

7. Everyone who (*visits, visit*) that monument is amazed by its grandeur.

8. Improvisation, which (*is, are*) the ability to create spontaneous music, is characteristic of jazz.

9. Mark, who (*know, knows*) he has a lot to do, has decided to prioritize.

10. That is the building that (*house, houses*) all the offices of the computer company.

Agreement of Pronoun and Antecedent A

16s. A pronoun should agree in number and gender with its antecedent.

EXAMPLES **Gloria Estefan** records **her** songs in Spanish and in English. [*Her* is a singular, feminine pronoun referring to the antecedent *Gloria Estefan*.]

My **cousins** brought **their** backgammon game. [*Their* is a plural pronoun referring to the antecedent *cousins*.]

EXERCISE Complete each of the following sentences by inserting at least one pronoun that agrees with its antecedent. Then, underline the antecedent.

Example 1. Each girl waited for _____ *her* _____ mother outside the building after school.

1. The boy in the blue sweater just dropped _____ notebook and calculator.

2. Resting on the branch of the tree, the robin fluttered _____ wings.

3. I try to wash _____ car every weekend when the weather is pleasant.

4. The women entered _____ offices at about the same time.

5. Neither man was wearing _____ name tag at the meeting.

6. The treasurer needs to keep good records so that _____ knows how much money has been spent.

7. Did the forwards on the girls' soccer team do _____ best?

8. We never ride _____ bicycles on the main road.

9. Mr. Robinson gave _____ dog a treat for being so obedient.

10. Daniel and Roseanne said _____ would be late.

11. Sophia said that *To Kill a Mockingbird* is _____ favorite novel.

12. Ryan said _____ would report on the films of the director Billy Wilder.

13. My aunt Catherine's cat always licks _____ paws after eating.

14. The students said that _____ were happy with the results of the vote.

15. Each member presented _____ position on the issue in an unbiased fashion.

16. María walks _____ dog every morning and every evening.

17. How many friends is Claire going to invite to _____ party?

18. Eric's car had _____ back window broken during the hail storm.

19. We would like to add _____ names to the petition.

20. Three of the girls will take _____ college entrance exam tomorrow.

Agreement of Pronoun and Antecedent B

16t. Some indefinite pronouns are singular, and some are plural. Other indefinite pronouns can be either singular or plural, depending on their meaning in a sentence.

> **SINGULAR** **Each** of the girls thinks **she** can help.
> **Someone** forgot **his or her** jacket.
> **PLURAL** **Both** of my brothers left on **their** bikes.
> **Few** of the class said **they** had finished.

EXERCISE Complete each of the following sentences by inserting at least one pronoun that agrees with its antecedent.

Example 1. Several of the boys were awarded medals for _____*their*_____ charity work.

1. One of the lizards on the patio had a twig in _____ mouth.

2. Did all of the people invited to the party bring _____ CDs?

3. Someone will have to give up _____ seat.

4. Both of the trained gymnasts moved _____ bodies with ease and grace.

5. Everyone in my family puts lots of syrup on _____ pancakes.

6. Most of the houses appear to have icicles on _____ eaves.

7. None of the cereal is left because _____ has all been eaten.

8. Only one of the women has finished packing _____ suitcase for the trip.

9. Many live _____ lives without ever taking serious risks.

10. Someone has left _____ car headlights on.

11. In spite of the bad weather, neither of the girls altered _____ plans.

12. Each of the boys was happy with _____ grades.

13. All of the water in the pond is gone; _____ evaporated in the heat.

14. Would one of the sopranos like to perform _____ favorite song?

15. Rosa just bought a new tennis racket, and _____ intends to use it in the next game.

16. One of the fish in the tank swims around _____ food before eating it.

17. Several of the writers were praised for _____ eloquence and style.

18. Neither of the girls blamed _____ for the accident.

19. No one forgot to bring _____ pencil to the exam.

20. We really enjoyed those pears and mangos; _____ were perfectly ripe.

Agreement of Pronoun and Antecedent C

16u. Use a singular pronoun to refer to two or more singular antecedents joined by *or* or *nor*.

    EXAMPLE **Max or Kai** will bring **his** hibachi for the cookout.

16v. Use a plural pronoun to refer to two or more antecedents joined by *and*.

    EXAMPLE **Marlys and Simone** are practicing **their** duet because **they** perform tonight.

USAGE

EXERCISE A For each of the following sentences, underline the pronoun in parentheses that agrees with its antecedent.

Example 1. Mary and Pam will have the opportunity to prove *(herself, themselves)* at the concert.

1. Neither Marco nor Juan agreed to give *(his, their)* opinion on the subject.

2. Sandra or Lucia will have to meet Jim at the station so that *(she, they)* can drive him home.

3. The waiters and the manager at the restaurant will do *(his, their)* best to assist you.

4. The singer and the orchestra performed *(its, their)* selection of songs with great care.

5. Paul or Dennis arranged to have *(his, their)* car repaired by the mechanic.

6. The coach and the goalie wanted to have *(its, their)* picture taken.

7. Neither Mr. Lund nor Mr. Hebert believed that *(his, their)* job was at stake.

8. Neither Scott nor his brother would have blamed *(themselves, himself)* for the mistake.

9. My sister and her husband arrived late because *(their, his and her)* train was delayed.

10. Eduardo or William will lend me one of *(his, their)* jackets if the weather turns cool.

EXERCISE B The following sentences contain blanks where pronouns should be. Complete the sentences by inserting pronouns that agree with their antecedents.

Example 1. Either Patrick or Ted will bring _____ *his* _____ CD player to the party.

11. Neither my aunt Barbara nor my aunt Margaret liked _____ new haircut.

12. Where will Sam and Nicholas take _____ parents tonight?

13. Jessica or Sarah will deliver the food to the homeless shelter; then _____ will

    return to the school.

14. Katie and Claire pride _____ on _____ knowledge of history.

15. Charlie and Albert said that _____ thought _____ game strategy

    was best.

Agreement of Pronoun and Antecedent D

USAGE

16w. The number of a relative pronoun (such as *who, which,* or *that*) is determined by its antecedent.

EXAMPLES Aluhani is a **girl who** is loyal to **her** friends. [*Who* refers to the singular noun *girl.* Therefore, the singular form *her* is used to agree with *who.*]

The **students who** finished **their** projects early were allowed to go to the library. [*Who* refers to the plural noun *students.* Therefore, the plural form *their* is used to agree with *who.*]

EXERCISE A For each of the following sentences, underline the pronoun in parentheses that agrees with its antecedent.

Example 1. The bees that were in *(its, their)* hive came out and stung Fernando.

1. My uncle Joe is a person who treats *(their, his)* friends with the utmost kindness.

2. Those who achieve recognition in *(his, their)* field typically have to work hard.

3. Dogs that obey *(its, their)* owners are often given tasty treats.

4. My neighbor who has *(their, her)* own unicycle rides it around the park every day.

5. Theresa, who decorates *(their, her)* house every Fourth of July, enjoys the holidays a lot.

EXERCISE B Complete each of the following sentences by inserting a pronoun that agrees with its antecedent. Then, circle the word to which the relative pronoun *who* refers.

Example 1. The (students) who received _____*their*_____ diplomas this year entered college in the fall.

6. Cameron is a boy who always promises to do _____ best.

7. People who use _____ time wisely usually find that they have more free time.

8. Anyone who would like to turn in _____ report early is encouraged to do so.

9. Many who offered _____ assistance after the hurricane were given awards.

10. The girl who forgot _____ notebook has not returned yet.

Agreement of Pronoun and Antecedent E

16x. A collective noun is singular when it refers to the group as a unit and plural when it refers to the individual members of the group.

EXAMPLES The **flock** of birds wended **its** way south. [*Flock* is thought of as a unit.]

The **flock** of birds were grooming **themselves.** [*Flock* is thought of as individuals.]

16y. An expression of an amount (a measurement, a percentage, or a fraction, for example) may be singular or plural, depending on how it is used.

EXAMPLES **Two minutes** is a long time; **it** seems long when you're on hold. [The amount is thought of as a unit.]

Two of the ten minutes were already used up; we had spent **them** reading the agenda. [The amount is thought of as individual pieces or parts.]

16z. Singular pronouns are used to refer to some nouns that are plural in form.

EXAMPLES We like books about **politics** and **its** effects on communities.

These **pants** fit; **they** fit better than the ones you tried on yesterday. [Plural pronouns are used to refer to some nouns that end in *s* but refer to a single item.]

EXERCISE For each of the following sentences, underline the pronoun that agrees with its antecedent.

Example 1. I am very interested in civics. I have been studying *(it, them)* for several years.

1. The pride of lions take turns resting in the sun after *(their, its)* successful hunt.

2. One half of the employees decided *(it, they)* needed to speak to the boss about the situation.

3. The scissors are in the top drawer. But watch out! *(It, They)* may be sharp!

4. About one fourth of the squirrels in the park grabbed the peanuts I offered *(it, them)*.

5. *Guys and Dolls* opened on Broadway in 1950. *(They, It)* proved to be a big success.

6. The soccer team at our high school won seventeen of *(their, its)* games last season.

7. The soccer team proved *(their, its)* remarkable abilities when each member scored a point.

8. Listening to the news on the radio, we found *(them, it)* very troubling.

9. One third of the committee members left the room. *(It, They)* returned two minutes later.

10. My aunt and uncle live in Arlington Heights; they find *(it, them)* to be very pleasant.

Grammar, Usage, and Mechanics: Language Skills Practice

129

Review A: Subject-Verb Agreement

USAGE

EXERCISE A Change the following sentences according to the directions given in parentheses. If necessary, change the forms of verbs, pronouns, or other words in the sentences. Cross out words you are changing, and write the new words above the old words.

only one enjoys

Example 1. Of all the students in my class, ~~perhaps one or two enjoy~~ being the star of the class play. *(Change perhaps one or two to only one.)*

1. Most of the students in the class want to work on the play, however. *(Change Most of the students to Almost every student.)*

2. There is at least one major speaking role in this year's play. *(Change at least one major speaking role to several major speaking roles.)*

3. The hero and the heroine, naturally, have more lines than the supporting members of the cast. *(Change The hero and the heroine to The hero or the heroine.)*

4. Two of my friends were thrilled that they were assigned to the stage crew. *(Change Two to One.)*

5. At every performance of our play, two of my three lines earn laughs from the audience. *(Change two to one.)*

EXERCISE B In most of the following sentences, a verb does not agree with its subject. Strike through each wrong verb. Then, write the correct form above it. If a verb form is already correct, write C above it.

have

Example 1. Nancy and her sister ~~has~~ tickets to the play.

6. My aunt and I like to play tennis, although neither of us are really very good at it.

7. Everybody likes to spend some free time relaxing.

8. Some of the prize-winning costumes was very original.

9. Mathematics are an easy subject for some students, but to most students either history or English seems easier.

10. Everybody in the movie theater were laughing hysterically.

11. The chef and his assistant cooks excellent dishes.

12. Neither the waiters nor the cook expect customers to return food.

13. Paul's closest friend doesn't find him to be ill-tempered.

14. My family agrees that our last two trips was a big success.

15. Here's the pictures we took at the beach.

Review B: **Pronoun-Antecedent Agreement**

USAGE

EXERCISE Complete each sentence by underlining the pronoun that agrees with its antecedent. Then, underline the antecedent twice. If the antecedent is a relative pronoun, circle the word to which the relative pronoun refers.

Example 1. How many (people) who have *(his or her, their)* driver's licenses live in a big city?

1. I like studying economics. I find *(them, it)* very interesting.

2. Each of my three stepsisters will update *(their, her)* diary tonight.

3. Neither Jane nor Clarissa will say what *(their, her)* middle name is.

4. The jazz musicians won great praise for *(its, their)* remarkable performance.

5. Startled by the thunder, the flock of sheep huddled against each other and made *(its, their)* way to shelter.

6. Sarah Vaughan, a popular jazz singer, was known for *(her, their)* rich voice and inventive ability to improvise.

7. One half of the musicians arrived late. I think *(they, it)* must have gotten caught in the traffic.

8. One of my brothers said that *(they, he)* just had a haircut.

9. Lola or Carmen will bring salad to the potluck dinner on Friday night. *(She, They)* will also pick up Rafael on the way.

10. Alex is a man who treats all of *(their, his)* friends with a great deal of respect.

11. The flock of sea gulls descended one by one to *(their, its)* nests on the cliff.

12. Our teacher said that physics will fascinate us. *(They, It)* is a very important area of study.

13. Nearly one fifth of the players received *(its, their)* awards for outstanding performance.

14. Most of this shoreline and *(their, its)* natural beauty is under threat.

15. Li-yun and Chao, two Taiwanese friends of mine, invited us to dinner at *(her, their)* grand-parents' home.

16. The car that had *(its, her)* headlights on would no longer start.

17. Few of the boys had time to eat *(his, their)* lunch before the bell rang.

18. Many consider "St. Louis Blues" a classic song. I believe *(it, they)* must be admired by many.

19. My grandfather said that fifteen dollars was a lot of money to pay for a CD. He would never pay *(it, them)*.

20. The class gathered all *(its, their)* backpacks and headed toward the auditorium for the assembly.

for **CHAPTER 16: AGREEMENT**   *pages 491–512*

Review C: **Subject-Verb and Pronoun-Antecedent**

EXERCISE For each of the following sentences, underline the correct form of the verb or pronoun in parentheses.

Example 1. Two thirds of our assignment *(has, have)* been completed.

1. Almost every game we play in gym *(is, are)* strenuous.

2. The jury believes that *(it, they)* may have reached a decision.

3. Few people claim that iguanas or lizards *(is, are)* among their favorite pets.

4. In this band everyone can play *(their, his or her)* favorite instrument.

5. In this novel, there *(is, are)* at least one main theme.

6. If I get home before 3:00 P.M., my sister or my brother *(don't, doesn't)* have to walk the dog.

7. Visitors who eat in *(its, their)* hotel rooms will miss a great deal of sightseeing.

8. Neither Jim nor Matt knew that *(his, their)* wallet had been lost.

9. Based on his first trip to the United States, Dickens' *American Notes (is, are)* widely read.

10. The researcher announced that genetics *(is, are)* going to be the topic of the next seminar.

11. Despite many hours of grueling practice, neither of the teams *(is, are)* ready for the playoffs.

12. All of the birds who visited our birdbath chirped happily while *(it, they)* bathed.

13. Don't you think that 70 percent of the votes *(is, are)* going to be in our favor?

14. Either Lucia or Susan will need to call *(their, her)* parents for a ride.

15. *(Has, Have)* Tanya and Jeffrey been told about the change in plans?

16. Many a neighbor *(decorate, decorates)* his or her yard for the holiday.

17. Most of the money *(are, is)* in the bank account.

18. Both of the books were recommended by the librarian. I had already read *(it, them)* last year.

19. Very few of the boys played as well as *(he, they)* could.

20. Lists of terms relating to economics *(appears, appear)* in that book of technical jargon.

Proofreading Application: Report

Good writers are generally good proofreaders. Readers tend to admire and trust writing that is error-free. Make sure that you correct all errors in grammar, usage, spelling, and punctuation in your writing. Your readers will have more confidence in your words if you have done your best to proofread carefully.

Journalists aren't the only people who write reports. Many jobs require daily reports as well as monthly and quarterly reports. Very likely, you will write reports when you enter the work-force as an adult.

When you write reports, make sure that you proofread carefully for agreement. Your subjects and verbs or pronouns and antecedents must agree. Otherwise, you will not be able to convey accurate information. For instance, if you use a singular subject with a plural verb, your readers will think that something has been left out. Consequently, they will question the accuracy of your facts.

PROOFREADING ACTIVITY

In the following report, find and correct the agreement errors. Use proofreading symbols such as those on page 901 of *Elements of Language* to make your corrections.

Example   Since September, the goal of the school beautification committee

          has
          ~~have~~ been to create a garden.
          ∧

That garden, thanks to the help of many people, are almost

completed. Many businesses in our town is to be thanked for their

contribution to this project. For example, Garden Furnishings promise

to deliver a beautiful concrete bench this week.

    Amber O'Hara and Franklin Gibson worked hard on her and his

spectacular design for the garden. Everybody on the committee has given

their free time to create fifty custom stepping stones for a walkway.

The mosaics of broken tile that decorate each stone is especially appre-

ciated because the design incorporates our school mascot.

    Three myrtle trees or a young maple are still needed to shade the

area. Trees Galore have agreed to donate whatever we need for our

project. Don't anyone know where we can get the free truckload of gravel

that we still need? The grand opening of the ninth grade's contribution

to the school grounds are scheduled for March 17.

USAGE | Language in Context: Literary Model

Literary Model: Poetry

Because I could not stop for Death
By Emily Dickinson

Because I could not stop for Death—
He kindly stopped for me—
The Carriage held but just Ourselves—
And Immortality.

We slowly drove—He knew no haste
And I had put away
My labor and my leisure too,
For His Civility—

We passed the School, where Children strove
At Recess—in the Ring—
We passed the Fields of Gazing Grain—
We passed the Setting Sun—

Or rather—He passed Us—
The Dews drew quivering and chill—
For only Gossamer, my Gown—
My Tippet—only Tulle—

We paused before a House that seemed
A Swelling of the Ground—
The Roof was scarcely visible—
The Cornice—in the Ground—

Since then—'tis Centuries—and yet
Feels shorter than the Day
I first surmised the Horses Heads
Were toward Eternity—

EXERCISE A   Name the two pronouns that refer exclusively to Death in the above poem.

_____

_____

EXERCISE B

1. When an antecedent is an abstract noun, generally the neuter third-person singular pronouns *it* and *its* are used to refer to it. Why do you think Emily Dickinson chose to use pronouns that indicate masculine gender to refer to Death?

_____

_____

2. If Dickinson had indicated, through the use of pronouns, that Death had a feminine persona, how might the poem have been different?

_____

_____

_____

Literary Model (continued)

EXERCISE C The subject of Dickinson's poem is the abstract quality or idea of Death. Think of a different quality or idea—for example, beauty, truth, strength, or goodness—and write a poem that has this idea as the poem's subject. Determine whether the persona of the quality or idea you have chosen is masculine or feminine, and use the appropriate pronouns when referring to it.

_____

_____

_____

_____

_____

_____

_____

_____

_____

_____

_____

_____

_____

_____

_____

_____

_____

_____

_____

_____

_____

_____

_____

_____

EXERCISE D Analyze your choice of gender for the persona of the quality or idea that is the subject of your poem.

_____

_____

_____

Grammar, Usage, and Mechanics: Language Skills Practice

Writing Application: Report

Language is never static. Although changes in a language happen slowly, they do occur. For instance, nowadays in informal conversation you'll often hear plural personal pronouns being used to refer to singular antecedents that can be either masculine or feminine. That is, it's not uncommon to hear "Everyone at that table is wearing *their* letter jacket." This usage might have been totally unacceptable to a nineteenth-century English grammarian. Yet such usage is gradually becoming more common in writing, and someday it may become acceptable as standard written English. For the present, though, you should avoid this and all other instances of nonstandard usage in formal writing and speaking, including those instances related to subject-verb agreement.

NONSTANDARD	Neither of us like big trucks.
STANDARD	Neither of us likes big trucks.

WRITING ACTIVITY

How much does a person's favorite type of vehicle reveal about his or her personality? It might reveal nothing at all—but it can be a fun topic to explore. Poll several friends or classmates about their favorite vehicles, and write a paragraph describing the results and your interpretation of the survey.

PREWRITING   Ask four to six friends or classmates which three adjectives best describe their personalities and what their favorite types of vehicles are. Record this information on a chart that you have prepared prior to beginning your survey. Classifying responses by means of the chart will help you write your paragraph logically. After completing the survey, think about the tone you want your writing to have.

WRITING   Using the information in your chart, write your draft freely, yet at the same time try to express your ideas clearly. Analyze your survey results to determine the topic sentence for your paragraph.

REVISING   Read your paragraph several times, first concentrating on content, then on organization, and finally on style. Make sure that your topic sentence is adequately supported by details. Ask yourself if the writing will hold the attention of your reader.

PUBLISHING   Identify the subject(s) and verb(s) in each sentence, and check for any errors in subject-verb agreement. Also, check for other errors in usage and mechanics. Be sure you have capitalized all proper nouns. Create a chart as a visual aid to accompany your report. Publish your report and chart and, with your teacher's permission, post it on the board or on your class Web site.

EXTENDING YOUR WRITING

You may wish to conduct a more extensive survey and then develop this writing exercise into a longer essay. Do an Internet search for online publications of student writing, and submit your essay.

Choices: Investigating Verbs

The following activities challenge you to find a connection between sentences and the world around you. Do the activity below that suits your personality best, and then share your discoveries with your class.

LINGUISTICS

Strike Out!

Some verbs have more than one past or past participle form, although the forms are not always interchangeable. The past participle of *strike*, for example, may be *struck* or *stricken*. Get together with several friends and research a list of other verbs that have alternative past or past participle forms. Then, prepare a handout for your classmates that includes the verbs, the alternative forms, and example sentences using the alternatives if they have different meanings.

DISCUSSION

Yo!

The way people talk with their friends on a relaxed Sunday afternoon is often quite different from the way they talk at the office or in school bright and early Monday morning. Why does this difference exist? What purpose does it serve? How might a listener react to informal speech in a formal situation? How might a listener react to formal speech in an informal situation? Lead a discussion of these and related questions.

VIDEO

Three of a Kind

Be a movie star! Working with two friends, write and videotape a dialogue among three people. One person speaks only in the present tense, one speaks only in the past tense, and the other speaks only in the future tense. Before you begin writing, talk about the kind of outlook on life that each of these three characters might have. Ask yourself how they might come into conflict. Then, videotape your dialogue. When you've finished taping, show your video to the class. Then, sit back and bask in the applause!

ART

A Work in Progress

Illustrate several different stages of an event to help you and your classmates understand how the tenses are used. If you have access to a computer, you could use a paint program. Under each picture, write a sentence describing the action, underline the verb, and label its tense.

STUDY AIDS

Fuel Injection

Some people remember the different tenses easily, but others may need a way to speed up the process. Write a poem or rap, or devise some other kind of study aid to help your classmates master these tenses. Begin by writing down and studying the rules for each tense. When you've got your study aid ready, share it with your class.

ART

The Setting Sun

Create small posters illustrating the proper use of the troublesome verbs *lie/lay, sit/set,* and *rise/raise.* For instance, you could find or draw pictures of the sun setting and rising. If you want to go hog-wild, you could design a deck of playing cards, with each card illustrating a situation in which one of these verbs is used correctly. Naturally, you will need to include a sentence that each picture illustrates.

ORIGINAL PROJECT

Made to Order

Create your own project. Speak using archaic or obsolete verbs for a day, and dress the part. Better yet, put on a play in which modern English speakers go through a time warp and meet English speakers from earlier times and hear the way they *spake,* not *spoke.* Poll English teachers for their opinions on the most misused verbs and brainstorm ways to improve usage. What will you do? Whatever you decide, be sure to get your teacher's approval first.

Grammar, Usage, and Mechanics: Language Skills Practice

The Principal Parts of Verbs

17a. The four *principal parts* of a verb are the *base form,* the *present participle,* the *past,* and the *past participle.*

BASE FORM	PRESENT PARTICIPLE	PAST	PAST PARTICIPLE
hope	[is] hoping	hoped	[have] hoped
walk	[is] walking	walked	[have] walked
sing	[is] singing	sang	[have] sung

EXERCISE A In each of the following sentences, identify the principal part of the underlined verb by writing above it *BF* for base form, *Pres P* for present participle, *P* for past, or *Past P* for past participle.

                                Past P

Example 1. I have just heard about an exciting exhibit.

1. The Smithsonian Institution has sponsored a traveling exhibition titled "We Shall Overcome."

2. The exhibition is going to many cities in the United States.

3. The display will present seventy-five photographs.

4. The Smithsonian organized these photographs of events and people of the Civil Rights era.

5. The Smithsonian placed the words of Dr. Martin Luther King, Jr., Fannie Lou Hamer, Julian

Bond, Medgar Evers, and James Baldwin beside the photographs.

6. The staff has compiled a diverse group of photographs.

7. The Civil Rights era extended from 1954 through 1968.

8. Is the exhibit showing literacy training, marches, and voter registration?

9. The Smithsonian has certainly created an exhibit that challenges us to think about that time.

10. The exhibit is traveling around the United States for quite a while.

EXERCISE B In each of the following sentences, identify the principal part of the underlined verb by writing above it *BF* for base form, *Pres P* for present participle, *P* for past, or *Past P* for past participle.

                                Past P

Example 1. The Smithsonian is headquartered in Washington, D.C.

11. The Smithsonian is mounting traveling exhibitions to share its enormous collections.

12. The Smithsonian Institution has become the largest museum complex in the world.

13. Have you gone to see the Smithsonian's permanent collections?

14. The Smithsonian has published a special guide for exploring African American heritage

through its vast collections.

15. The Smithsonian's Center for African American History and Culture merged with the

Anacostia Museum in 1995.

Regular Verbs

17b. A *regular verb* forms its past and past participle by adding *–d* or *–ed* to the base form.

> **EXAMPLES** Leo **wanted** to see a movie on his birthday.
> The horse **trotted** to the gate.

USAGE

EXERCISE In each of the following sentences, write the correct past or past participle form of the verb in parentheses above the verb.

worked
Example 1. Have Yoshi and Sam *(work)* at the kennel with you a long time?

1. Takara *(want)* to know which languages are spoken in Ecuador.

2. We have *(roll)* all the napkins we will need for the banquet.

3. The Supreme Court has finally *(hand)* down its verdict in that case.

4. Darlene *(travel)* to Australia last year as a member of the soccer team.

5. Have I *(answer)* your question about what to use to remove grass stains?

6. Mu Lan had already *(apply)* for a passport before she won the trip.

7. As the flag passed by, we *(place)* our right hands over our hearts.

8. We *(bake)* sweet potatoes last night.

9. Have you *(wonder)* why I had to miss school yesterday?

10. Have you ever *(fish)* for your supper?

11. Do you think he has already *(try)* this strategy?

12. The burro *(kick)* wildly whenever anyone came near.

13. I'm sure he has been *(employ)* for at least six months.

14. The canary *(escape)* while Jane was cleaning the cage.

15. Those children *(play)* in the backyard for hours.

16. Many explorers have *(risk)* their lives for adventure.

17. He *(search)* for hours, but he could not find his wallet.

18. When the little girl blew out the candles, she *(wish)* for a new kitten.

19. My aunt and my cousins *(drop)* by to visit on Saturday.

20. What time did you say they *(arrive)*?

USAGE

Irregular Verbs A

17c. An *irregular verb* forms its past and past participle in some other way than by adding −*d* or −*ed*.

An irregular verb forms its past and past participle in one of these ways: changing consonants, changing vowels, changing vowels *and* consonants, or making no change at all.

EXAMPLES   The bird **built** its nest high in the tree.   I had **thought** so.

Robbie **swam** across the lake.   The bubble had **burst.**

EXERCISE   In each of the following sentences, underline the correct form of the verb in parentheses.

Example 1. Have you (*eated, eaten*) all your vegetables?

1. We (*seen, saw*) porpoises following the ferryboat to the island.

2. Pearl Bailey (*sang, sung*) in clubs, in Broadway shows, and in films.

3. Health officials have (*taked, taken*) precautions against an outbreak of the flu.

4. Only one boat (*sank, sinked*) in the storm.

5. The ambassador had (*gave, given*) an eloquent speech.

6. Luisa (*brought, brang*) me a gift from Puerto Rico.

7. Many northern birds have (*flied, flown*) to Mexico for the winter.

8. The members of the basketball team (*chose, choosed*) Abdul as their captain.

9. How much has the creek cleanup (*cost, costed*)?

10. The mayor (*rang, ringed*) the bell to begin the Independence Day festivities.

11. David (*become, became*) the first member of our family to finish college.

12. Sean, Hasan, Mina, and I have (*written, wrote*) the parts for our scene in the skit.

13. Today, Justin and Eileen (*begun, began*) their report on the Trail of Tears.

14. We (*drank, drunk*) ice-cold lemonade.

15. Ms. Hatcher (*teached, taught*) us some sign language.

16. For the last two years, I have (*growed, grown*) tomatoes, squash, beans, and onions.

17. As a result of her research, Jasmine (*telled, told*) us how to find the secret room.

18. Look what Nabil has (*finded, found*) among the bits of broken pottery!

19. Felicia (*did, done*) the whole report on her own.

20. As we watched, Sammy (*swum, swam*) all the way back to the dock.

Irregular Verbs B

USAGE

| **17c.** | An *irregular verb* forms its past and past participle in some other way than by adding –d or –ed. |

An irregular verb forms its past and past participle in one of these ways: changing consonants, changing vowels, changing vowels *and* consonants, or making no change at all.

EXAMPLES   They **sent** flowers.   The sun had **gone** down.

             I **knew** the song.   Where has he **put** the pliers?

EXERCISE A   On the line provided, change the verb forms given below. If the base form is given, change it to the past form. If the past form is given, change it to the past participle. Use *have* before the past participle form.

Example   _____*have begun*_____   **1.** began

_____   **1.** became   _____   **6.** draw

_____   **2.** feel   _____   **7.** ate

_____   **3.** teach   _____   **8.** grow

_____   **4.** win   _____   **9.** wrote

_____   **5.** rang   _____ **10.** had

EXERCISE B   In each of the following sentences, underline the correct form of the verb in parentheses.

Example **1.** Has the counselor *(spoke, spoken)* to you yet about your schedule?

11. The committee *(held, holded)* a meeting to nominate candidates for president.

12. Nina *(keeped, kept)* a log as we worked out each stage of our group's project.

13. Which clothes have you *(wore, worn)* on previous camping trips?

14. Although we stacked the firewood carefully, some of it *(fell, fallen)* out of the pickup.

15. The afternoon has *(gone, went)* by too quickly!

16. Has the president ever *(flew, flown)* on a Concorde jet?

17. Since lunch hour is over, please be sure you have *(throwed, thrown)* away your trash.

18. The Senate committee *(struck, striked)* a bargain with the lobbyists.

19. The wool sweater has *(shrank, shrunk)* too much after being washed.

20. My aunt has *(gave, given)* me a Christmas ornament every year since I was born.

Irregular Verbs C

17c. An *irregular verb* forms its past and past participle in some other way than by adding *–d* or *–ed*.

An irregular verb forms its past and past participle in one of these ways: changing consonants, changing vowels, changing vowels *and* consonants, or making no change at all.

EXAMPLES The sapling **bent** in the wind.   Jo has **caught** the flu.

They **sang** loudly.   Have they **set** a record?

EXERCISE A Choose the correct form of the verb in parentheses in each of the following sentences.

Example 1. Rafiq's uncle (*teached, taught*) several of my friends how to play the guitar.

1. After Jeremy stretched, he (*went, gone*) outside to jog around the neighborhood.

2. My friend (*rang, rung*) the doorbell and left a birthday gift on the steps.

3. Have you ever been (*stinged, stung*) by a bee?

4. My younger brother had (*written, wrote*) ten short stories by the time he was nine years old.

5. Last night, I heard a loud clap of thunder a few seconds before the lightning (*striked, struck*).

6. Did you know that the artist (*drawed, drew*) twenty different versions of that landscape?

7. Melissa and her cousin have never (*flown, flew*) on an airplane.

8. Someone has (*stealed, stolen*) the key to the secret passage.

9. In our lifeguard training session today, we (*swam, swum*) laps while holding a ten-pound brick.

10. The baby hugs his favorite teddy bear so often that the bear's ears have (*worn, wore*) thin.

EXERCISE B In the following paragraph, write the correct verb form over each underlined base form.

Examples Our need for a first-aid kit **[1]** become [*became*] evident several years ago after my brother

Jeremy had **[2]** fall [*fallen*] and sprained his ankle.

Because we did not know whether Jeremy had **[11]** break his ankle, we **[12]** make splints and bandages from anything we **[13]** have handy. After that, Mom **[14]** feel we should have a first-aid kit. A medical supply company we ordered from **[15]** send us tongue depressors to use as finger splints and other, longer wood splints. One salesclerk **[16]** tell us where to get triangular bandages. Every time we went to the grocery store, we **[17]** keep our eyes open for baking soda, salt, antiseptic soap, paper cups, and adhesive bandages. Mom **[18]** find sheets and towels on sale. By the time we completed our first-aid kit, we had **[19]** buy adhesive tape, bandages, aspirin, and an eyedropper. As his contribution, Dad had **[20]** bring home scissors, tweezers, and needle-nose pliers from the hardware store.

Irregular Verbs D

USAGE

17c. An *irregular verb* forms its past and past participle in some other way than by adding *–d* or *–ed*.

An irregular verb forms its past and past participle in one of these ways: changing consonants, changing vowels, changing vowels *and* consonants, or making no change at all.

> **EXAMPLES** We **made** fried rice.   I had **torn** my jeans.
> The dog **ran** home.   Larry has **hit** a home run.

EXERCISE On the line provided, write the correct past or past participle form of the italicized verb given before each sentence.

Example 1. *run*   Had she ever _____*run*_____ for office before that election?

1. *fly*   How many miles has that pilot _____ this month?

2. *win*   Our business plan _____ first place on Career Day.

3. *choose* Eddie _____ a two-week trip to Alaska as his graduation gift.

4. *wear*   Sixteen people have _____ this service badge in our department's history.

5. *freeze* Arleta has _____ several trays of ice cubes for the party.

6. *throw* The pitcher _____ a no-hitter again last night.

7. *come*   Many of you have _____ here to visit with our older adults.

8. *break* Ramai was so nervous that she had already dropped and _____ two dishes.

9. *light* Caroline _____ the candles as Nathan set the plates on the table.

10. *ride*   Only Tamika and Benjamin have _____ through white-water rapids before.

11. *fight* How many women _____ in the French Resistance?

12. *draw* Henry _____ the sketch that will be the basis for our mural.

13. *sing* What was the name of the song they _____ after the pep rally?

14. *lead* Terry and Lance _____ the cyclists into the last lap.

15. *shake* Mom _____ her head in amazement at the low cost for the repairs.

16. *tear* As soon as it had arrived, the girls had quickly _____ open the unusual box.

17. *swim* During our warm-ups, Keeshia _____ two more laps than Liona did.

18. *eat*   Once Granddad had _____ lunch, he took a short walk.

19. *write* Last year their pen pals from Portugal _____ to them twice a month.

20. *see*   When we opened the door, we _____ the package on the steps.

Irregular Verbs E

| **17c.** | An *irregular verb* forms its past and past participle in some other way than by adding –*d* or –*ed*. |

An irregular verb forms its past and past participle in one of these ways: changing consonants, changing vowels, changing vowels *and* consonants, or making no change at all.

EXAMPLES   Matt had **lent** me his book.   Antonio **left** for Argentina.

Sandra **bought** the mangos.   They had **spread** the news.

EXERCISE   In each of the following sentences, underline the verb. Be sure to include any helping verbs. If a verb form is incorrect, write the correct form above the main verb. If a verb form is already correct, write *C* above the main verb.

                                                      become
Example 1. Gardening has became more and more popular since the 1940s.

1. Kara knew the answer to the question.

2. Have they already maked the salad for the party?

3. We have rode our bikes on this street many times.

4. You must have heared that noise last night.

5. Someone left the tools out in the rain.

6. He had ringed the doorbell twice.

7. Sam has already swum fifty laps this week.

8. Had he wrote that note on the chalkboard?

9. Sarita had putted the milk in the refrigerator.

10. The children slided all the way to the bottom of the hill.

11. Have you saw my shoes?

12. Jarrell sung a solo in last night's concert.

13. Those girls had ate all the popcorn.

14. The trees shaked during the storm.

15. Has a yellow jacket ever stinged anyone in your family?

16. Lightning striked the tall pine tree on the ridge of the hill.

17. Some students have drawed illustrations for their reports.

18. My uncle taked me to the movies last weekend.

19. I have weared my favorite jacket to school every day this month.

20. Mr. Williams teached geography last year.

USAGE

Tense

| **17d.** | The *tense* of a verb indicates the time of the action or of the state of being expressed by the verb. |

| **17e.** | Each of the six tenses has its own special uses. |

PRESENT I speak	**PRESENT PERFECT** I have spoken
PAST I spoke	**PAST PERFECT** I had spoken
FUTURE I will (shall) speak	**FUTURE PERFECT** I will (shall) have spoken

The *progressive form* of each tense expresses continuing action. It consists of a form of the verb *be* plus the present participle of a verb.

EXERCISE Change the tense of the verb in each of the following sentences to the tense indicated in parentheses. Cross out the verb in the sentence, and write the new verb form above the original one.

Example 1. She ~~sits~~. (*present perfect progressive*)   has been sitting

1. I need a hat. (*past*)

2. They buy a car. (*present perfect*)

3. She gives a speech. (*future*)

4. You go home. (*past perfect progressive*)

5. We eat lunch. (*past progressive*)

6. He studies for three hours. (*future perfect progressive*)

7. They sing in the choir. (*future progressive*)

8. I walk to the store. (*present progressive*)

9. You hand me the book. (*past perfect*)

10. We will vote by tomorrow. (*future perfect*)

11. You do your homework. (*present perfect progressive*)

12. She brings the groceries in. (*future*)

13. He leaves it here. (*past progressive*)

14. I rake the yard. (*past perfect*)

15. We write letters. (*future progressive*)

16. She does the dishes. (*future perfect*)

17. The alarm rings early. (*past*)

18. She tells the story. (*past perfect progressive*)

19. The clock strikes one. (*present perfect*)

20. I throw the ball. (*present perfect progressive*)

Consistency of Tense A

17f. Do not change needlessly from one tense to another.

When describing events that occur at the same time, use verbs in the same tense. When describing events that occur at different times, use different tenses to show clearly the order of events.

EXAMPLES   He **turned** around and **spoke** to me. [*Turned* and *spoke* are both in the past tense.]

She **thought** she **had locked** the door that morning. [Because the action of locking the door was completed before the action of thinking, *had locked* is in the past perfect tense, and *thought* is in the past tense.]

EXERCISE   In each item below, one of the verbs should be changed to make the tenses consistent. Draw a line through the verb you are changing, and write above it a verb that makes sense.

Example   1. I was in my seat before the bell ~~rings~~. *rang*

1. She had ridden a bicycle for ten years before she starts to ride a unicycle.

2. Carlos scored the winning point and the fans had cheered with excitement.

3. Jared rushed into the room and stops to catch his breath.

4. Why didn't he shut the window before he leaves the house?

5. The cat twitched its tail once, curled into a ball, and quickly falls asleep.

6. Karinna has already finished her research and wrote most of her report.

7. My mother came in, takes one look at the mess in the kitchen, and sat down in a chair.

8. We will need to return this book to the library after we had finished it.

9. The sailboat sank because its hull breaks.

10. After we drank the milk, we will eat all the apples.

11. Every day, he takes out the trash, sweeps the floor, and wiped off the counter.

12. I will sing the alto part if Wynne will have sung the soprano part.

13. Cassie has dropped the glass of water when the door slammed behind her.

14. The sun broke through the clouds shortly after the rain stops.

15. On Saturdays, we usually visit our grandparents and ate lunch at a restaurant.

16. If you will bring the shirt to my house, I will have sewed on the button.

17. He had been knocking on the door for ten minutes before they open it.

18. I sought a safe shelter whenever I see lightning in the sky.

19. You either left your shoes on the front porch or had thrown them under the bed.

20. The child laughed, covered her eyes, and has begun counting to a hundred.

Consistency of Tense B

17f. Do not change needlessly from one tense to another.

When describing events that occur at the same time, use verbs in the same tense.

> **EXAMPLE** The dog **yawned** and **settled** down to sleep in the shade. [*Yawned* and *settled* are both in the past tense.]

When describing events that occur at different times, use different tenses to show clearly the order of events.

> **EXAMPLE** By the time my friends **arrived,** I **had** already **cleaned** the living room. [Because the action of cleaning was completed before the action of arriving, *had cleaned* is in the past perfect tense, and *arrived* is in the past tense.]

EXERCISE In the following paragraph, write the correct form of the verb in parentheses above the verb. Be sure the tenses are consistent throughout the paragraph and that they make sense. Look at the other verbs in the paragraph for clues about the order of events. Be sure to include helping verbs whenever necessary.

Example As soon as the electricity came back on, I **[1]** *(call)* my friend Jakob.
called

I can't wait to tell you about my exciting weekend! My family **[1]** *(plan)* a quiet weekend. We had only a few errands to run, and we **[2]** *(think)* a picnic would be fun. We **[3]** *(take)* out the map and chose a park not far from here. Then we **[4]** *(fill)* our cooler with food and drinks, **[5]** *(load)* everything into the car, and started off. Well, we **[6]** *(get)* about ten miles when we realized that dark clouds **[7]** *(begin)* to gather overhead. We turned the car around and **[8]** *(head)* back home. After we **[9]** *(eat)* our lunch, we **[10]** *(look)* at the movie schedules. Everyone **[11]** *(get)* back in the car, and off we **[12]** *(drive)* again. When we arrived at the theater, however, we **[13]** *(realize)* that the movie already **[14]** *(start)*. My brother **[15]** *(look)* at an old newspaper and the schedule had changed! By the time we **[16]** *(reach)* the house again, the storm **[17]** *(be)* really raging. The lights were out because the storm **[18]** *(knock)* down some power lines earlier. We **[19]** *(spend)* the rest of the afternoon and night sitting in the dark, listening to the wind and the rain, and telling stories. We will probably never forget the weekend when absolutely nothing **[20]** *(go)* according to plan!

Active and Passive Voice

17g. A verb in the *active voice* expresses an action done by its subject. A verb in the *passive voice* expresses an action done to its subject.

> **ACTIVE VOICE** Dorothy Parker **wrote** many humorous poems. [The subject, *Dorothy Parker*, performs the action.]
>
> **PASSIVE VOICE** Many humorous poems **were written** by Dorothy Parker. [The subject, *poems*, receives the action.]

EXERCISE On the line provided, write *AV* if the sentence is in the active voice. Write *PV* if it is in the passive voice.

Example _*PV*_ **1.** The lawn was mowed today by Alyssa.

_____ **1.** The new bill was presented to Congress by Senator Thompson.

_____ **2.** Montreal was defeated by Pittsburgh, eight to two.

_____ **3.** Low-flying airplanes impaired our television reception.

_____ **4.** The delicate glass was dropped accidentally by Maria.

_____ **5.** The novel *Ethan Frome* was written by Edith Wharton.

_____ **6.** Excessive heat and a lack of rain ruined the crops last summer.

_____ **7.** The pitcher is throwing fast curve balls.

_____ **8.** The play *Romeo and Juliet* was performed by the drama class last week.

_____ **9.** The best-actor award had been won by a newcomer to the screen.

_____ **10.** Carlo Rinelli was elected president of the Student Council by the student body.

_____ **11.** Both of the boys finished the homework in an hour.

_____ **12.** What kind of cake has he baked for the party?

_____ **13.** Hooray! We have been given another week for this assignment.

_____ **14.** The deer trotted warily to the side of the highway.

_____ **15.** Most of us have learned a little French.

_____ **16.** Most of these stories were written in the 1920s.

_____ **17.** Did you take an earlier bus?

_____ **18.** Announcements are read daily at three o'clock.

_____ **19.** My grandparents were raised on a cattle ranch.

_____ **20.** Please take that wet dog out of the house!

USAGE

Using the Passive Voice

In general, avoid using the passive voice—it is less direct, less forceful, and less concise than the active voice.

PASSIVE VOICE   A motorcycle **was ridden** everywhere by Jake.

ACTIVE VOICE   Jake **rode** a motorcycle everywhere.

The passive voice is useful when you do not know the performer of the action, do not want to reveal the performer of the action, or want to emphasize the receiver of the action.

EXAMPLE   Mabel **was chosen** May queen. [to emphasize receiver of action]

EXERCISE A   The following sentences are in the passive voice. Above each sentence, rewrite it in the active voice.

Mel brought the food into the room.

Example   1. The food was brought into the room by Mel.

1. All of us were given a tour of the ranch by my grandfather.

2. The pictures had been developed by the new technician.

3. These buildings were designed by a well-known architect.

4. The words were looked up in a dictionary by the students.

5. We were driven to the movies by Jeff's parents.

EXERCISE B   The following sentences are all in the passive voice. For each sentence, determine whether the sentence would be better (more direct, forceful, or concise) in the active voice. If so, rewrite it in the space above the sentence. If you think the sentence should stay in the passive voice, write *PV* on the line provided.

Annie and James brought the old clothes.

Example _____ **1.** The old clothes were brought by Annie and James.

_____ **6.** The letter was sent anonymously.

_____ **7.** Our team was awarded the trophy.

_____ **8.** A grasshopper was caught by the bird.

_____ **9.** The performance was appreciated by many in the audience.

_____ **10.** Corinne was elected president by an overwhelming majority.

_____ **11.** A few drops of the chemical were added to the solution.

_____ **12.** All the streets were swept today in preparation for the parade.

_____ **13.** Multiplication problems were answered by the students.

_____ **14.** Wasn't the garbage picked up this morning?

_____ **15.** The festive lanterns were hung by my brother and Anthony.

Lie and *Lay*

USAGE

17h. The verb *lie* means "to rest," "to recline," or "to remain in a lying position." *Lie* does not take an object. The verb *lay* means "to put" or "to place (something somewhere)." *Lay* generally takes an object.

> **EXAMPLES** The dog **lay** sleeping on the rug. [past tense of *lie*]
> The builders quickly **lay** the bricks. [present tense of *lay*]

EXERCISE On the line provided, write the correct form of *lie* or *lay*.

Example 1. Have you ___*laid*___ the pencils on the counter?

1. The contractor had _____ the house plans on the table.

2. Whose homework paper is _____ on top of the stack?

3. After the storm, a large branch _____ across the driveway.

4. Next, _____ a tile over the glue and press down firmly.

5. Last night, Fran _____ a bag of sand and an ice scraper beside the front door.

6. The paintbrushes have _____ in the cleaner long enough.

7. Has Mom been _____ these magazines over here?

8. We should have _____ down our menus sooner.

9. _____ here and rest until your headache has gone away.

10. The wreckage of the freighter now _____ under twenty feet of water and mud.

11. I have no idea how long I had _____ there in a daze.

12. How long have those shoes been _____ there?

13. The raccoon _____ the apple down and scurried into the woods.

14. My mother told my sister to go upstairs and _____ down.

15. The lioness _____ in the shade and watched her cubs.

16. Tomorrow, my uncles will be _____ a brick foundation for the new house.

17. She was sure that she had _____ the book on the car seat.

18. By this time tomorrow afternoon, we will be _____ on the beach.

19. _____ that stack of papers on the shelf, please.

20. The old map _____ undisturbed for decades.

USAGE

Sit and Set

17i. The verb *sit* means "to rest in an upright, seated position." *Sit* seldom takes an object. The verb *set* means "to put" or "to place (something somewhere)." *Set* generally takes an object.

EXAMPLES **Sit** down and enjoy your dinner. [present tense of *sit*]

Set the napkins next to the plates. [present tense of *set*]

EXERCISE On the line provided, write the correct form of *sit* or *set*.

Example 1. Have you ____*set*____ the stones along the sides of the path?

1. In five minutes we will have _____ the table for you.

2. Jake _____ his books on the couch and then sat down there himself.

3. _____ the roses on the counter and the ivy on the floor, please.

4. Which athlete is _____ new track records this season?

5. DeVon was stiff because she had been _____ too long in the same position.

6. At the end of shop class, Roger _____ the sander under the workbench.

7. For most printing jobs, we no longer _____ type in a tray letter by letter.

8. The clown had _____ on the low end of the seesaw.

9. _____ with us and admire the colors of this sunset.

10. How long have you _____ there waiting for us?

11. The hikers reached the mountaintop just as the sun was _____.

12. The old man came in, _____ down, and began to tell an amazing story.

13. Before she went to bed, she _____ the alarm clock.

14. The passengers had been _____ patiently for an hour before the train left the station.

15. Had Tamara _____ in that row before?

16. The owl _____ on the branch for a few minutes and then flew away.

17. He adjusted the oven temperature, _____ the timer, and left the kitchen.

18. I wish we could go outside and _____ under those trees.

19. What is the name of the man who is _____ behind your father?

20. Before you _____ the table, please wash your hands.

Rise and *Raise*

USAGE

| **17j.** | The verb *rise* means "to go in an upward direction." *Rise* does not take an object. The verb *raise* means "to move (something) in an upward direction." *Raise* generally takes an object. |

EXAMPLES   The audience **rose** in praise of the performance. [past tense of *rise*]

Our group **raised** enough money for the trip. [past tense of *raise*]

EXERCISE   On the line provided, write the correct form of *rise* or *raise*.

Example 1. The sun appeared quite red as it _____*rose*_____ this morning.

1. _____ the curtain so the actors can take their bows.

2. The temperatures had _____, not fallen, throughout the day.

3. Do you think we should _____ the voting age?

4. Antonio had _____ from his chair to answer Mr. MacIntyre's question.

5. Our parents are _____ us to be polite and well-mannered.

6. The bread dough in that recipe will _____ more slowly in a cool room.

7. Steam quickly _____ and built up pressure in the radiator.

8. At the sound of crackling leaves, the mysterious woman _____ her head.

9. _____ and be recognized to testify before us in this session.

10. The pole vaulter had _____ the bar by two notches for his practice.

11. Emil has been _____ an hour earlier than usual each morning.

12. Jeanine's family had _____ wheat for generations.

13. When the full moon _____, the whole forest was illuminated.

14. Daniel was _____ his hand to answer the question.

15. The council member has _____ an important issue.

16. Prices may be _____ faster than wages.

17. The sailors _____ the sails and headed across the bay.

18. He _____ from the couch, crossed the room, and shut the window.

19. She was up and dressed an hour before the sun had _____.

20. Have they ever _____ sheep or goats on their ranch?

USAGE

Six Troublesome Verbs

17h. The verb *lie* means "to rest," "to recline," or "to remain in a lying position." *Lie* does not take an object. The verb *lay* means "to put" or "to place (something somewhere)." *Lay* generally takes an object.

17i. The verb *sit* means "to rest in an upright, seated position." *Sit* seldom takes an object. The verb *set* means "to put" or "to place (something somewhere)." *Set* generally takes an object.

17j. The verb *rise* means "to go in an upward direction." *Rise* does not take an object. The verb *raise* means "to move (something) in an upward direction." *Raise* generally takes an object.

EXERCISE A   In each of the sentences below, two pairs of verbs appear in parentheses. Underline the verb that completes each sentence correctly.

Example 1. Aurelio (*rose, raised*) and then (*set, sat*) down again when his aunt entered the room.

1. Franco was (*lying, laying*) on the sofa, and Tim was (*sitting, setting*) nearby.

2. Bette (*raised, rose*) from her chair as Carmen (*raised, rose*) the flag.

3. Please (*sit, set*) the plates on the table and (*lay, lie*) napkins next to them.

4. As I (*set, sat*) down, he (*laid, lay*) down on the couch across the room.

5. Gloria had (*raised, risen*) early, but her brother had (*laid, lain*) in bed until noon.

EXERCISE B   The following paragraph contains five errors in the use of the six troublesome verbs. Draw a line through each error, and write the correct verb above it.

Example   Rather than ~~lay~~ *lie* around and watch TV, we went to see a play.

We set in the balcony for the performance of *Les Misérables*. Before the curtain raised, the

orchestra began to play. The play raises many issues about right and wrong. A man has laid in jail

for many years for stealing a loaf of bread. Now out of jail, he cannot find work. Tired, hungry,

and desperate, he steals, among other things, two candlesticks that are laying in a cupboard at a

church. Although the man spends his life doing kind deeds for others, a police officer trails him

endlessly, trying to lie the old case to rest.

USAGE

Mood

17k.   *Mood* is the form a verb takes to indicate the attitude of the person using the verb.

(1) The *indicative mood* is used to express a fact, an opinion, or a question.

EXAMPLE   Deborah **is** an excellent swimmer.

(2) The *imperative mood* is used to express a direct command or request.

EXAMPLE   **Go** to the store and **buy** some more flour, please.

(3) The *subjunctive mood* is used to express a suggestion, a necessity, a condition contrary to fact, or a wish.

EXAMPLE   Our choir director insisted that we **be** on time for the concert.

EXERCISE A   On the line before each sentence, identify the mood of the underlined verb by writing *IND* for indicative, *IMP* for imperative, or *SUBJ* for subjunctive.

Example   _SUBJ_   **1.** If I <u>were</u> you, I would buy tickets as soon as possible.

_____   **1.** <u>Do</u> not <u>miss</u> this show by the José Greco II Flamenco Dance Company.

_____   **2.** The company <u>is</u> famous for its strength and artistry.

_____   **3.** <u>Tell</u> me whether you like the show.

_____   **4.** José Greco II, also called "Pepe," <u>wants</u> to strengthen flamenco tradition.

_____   **5.** If he <u>were</u> to define his work, he might say "trying for better and more."

_____   **6.** It is essential that flamenco dances <u>include</u> intense footwork.

_____   **7.** <u>Notice</u> the influence of his training with the National Ballet of Spain.

_____   **8.** He wishes to leave his own mark on this dance form, as his father <u>did</u>.

_____   **9.** <u>Can</u> you <u>tell</u> me how long his company has been on tour?

_____   **10.** He may wish he <u>were</u> able to be at home more than one month a year.

EXERCISE B   On the line provided, write the correct form of the italicized verb given before each sentence.

Example   1. *know*   I wish I ___*knew*___ how to prepare as many dishes as Malcolm does.

11. *go*   Yesterday, Malcolm and I _____ into the kitchen to make a tossed salad.

12. *wash*   "First," said Malcolm, "_____ the raw vegetables very well."

13. *put*   He continued, "Now, _____ all the vegetables in the bowl."

14. *be*   He said, "I only wish Jane _____ here to enjoy this delicious salad with us."

15. *Pass*   "I know. Oh, well," I said. "_____ me the dressing and the tongs so I can start tossing!"

Review A: **Verb Forms**

EXERCISE A   Each of the items below is a set of expressions that contain verbs. Underline the expression that contains an incorrect verb form. Write the correct form of the verb above the incorrect form.

sold

Example 1. we have raised, I selled, they have risked, they'd be gone

1. we swam, they have took, the lake was frozen, it was stolen

2. I had drunk, the box bursts, has it began, she has never ridden

3. the pen is lying there, you have lain in the sun, they laid the books here, the dog laid down

4. they have went, he raised his price, we sat down, raise it

5. set it there, it was setting on the step, they have chosen me, she has gone

6. we have swam there, the box had sat there, would have set it, she has thrown

7. the wreck occurred, had instruct the jury, the fog lay low, we had struck

8. both ran well, it has shrank, she sat down, we have sought

9. we seen him, they had awakened, we drove, which were blown down

10. the plane rose, they have worn, she came in, we had throwed them out

EXERCISE B   On the line provided, write the correct form (past or past participle) of the verb given in italics.

Example 1. *fly*   Have you ever ____*flown*____ in a small plane?

11. *ask*   Last summer, while we were visiting in New Jersey, Aunt Maura _____ if I would like to go for a plane ride.

12. *speak*   She had already _____ to my parents about it.

13. *choose* She _____ the hottest day of the year for the plane ride.

14. *begin*   I had just _____ thinking of ways to keep cool, such as going to the beach or to a movie.

15. *give*   I _____ up my other plans immediately.

16. *eat*   As soon as we had _____ lunch, we set out for the airport.

17. *lie*   The airport _____ on the edge of town.

18. *rise*   Heat waves _____ from the hot asphalt of the streets.

19. *come*   The wind that _____ in through the open windows of the car was like a furnace blast.

20. *ride*   We _____ in the small plane for two glorious hours.

USAGE

Review B: Consistency of Tense; Voice

USAGE

EXERCISE A   Read the following passage. Decide whether it should be written in the present or the past tense. Above the underlined verb, write the correct form of any verb that needs to be changed. Write *C* above the underlined verb if it is already in the correct tense.

Example   An embarrassing thing **[1]** <u>happens</u> on the trip I took to Wisconsin.
happened (above happens)

Last summer, I **[1]** <u>was invited</u> to spend a week with my cousins at their summer cottage in Wisconsin. My sister drove me to Chicago and **[2]** <u>puts</u> me on the train for Milwaukee. Just as the train was about to pull out, my sister **[3]** <u>gave</u> me my ticket. She **[4]** <u>reminds</u> me to take good care of it, but I told her that I **[5]** <u>am</u> not a baby and that I **[6]** <u>didn't need</u> advice about what to do with a train ticket. After a few moments the train **[7]** <u>started</u>, and soon the conductor came down the aisle with his ticket punch. Looking in my wallet, I **[8]** <u>realized</u> with horror that my ticket was not there. The conductor, with a puzzled look on his face, **[9]** <u>watches</u> me searching frantically through my pockets. Finally he **[10]** <u>says</u>, "If you're looking for your ticket, it's lying on the seat beside you. May I have it, please?"

EXERCISE B   On the line provided, write *PV* if the sentence is in the passive voice or *AV* if it is in the active voice. Above each sentence in the passive voice, rewrite the sentence in the active voice.

Example   __*PV*__ **1.** The beds were made by Clarita.
Clarita made the beds. (above sentence)

_____ **11.** The bell was rung by Ramash.

_____ **12.** Clarence is pouring the milk.

_____ **13.** The mail was brought by our new carrier.

_____ **14.** The curtains were ironed by Darob.

_____ **15.** The security guard has sounded the alarm.

_____ **16.** Nina was chosen as class representative by the principal.

_____ **17.** The cat curled up by the fireplace.

_____ **18.** We will have finished this project by 2:30.

_____ **19.** That fire was put out by volunteer firefighters.

_____ **20.** A mess was made by my brother's friends.

Review C: Verb Forms

EXERCISE A Each of the items below is a set of expressions that contain verbs. Underline the expression that contains an incorrect verb form. Write the correct form of the verb above the incorrect form.

> *sunk*
Example 1. we gave, it had <u>sank</u>, they'd supposed, I'm going

1. you have swam, I threw it, the water froze, the pipes burst

2. I have done it, you drove, she has known, I seen it

3. he has took, they were broken, it was known, they wrote

4. you had throwed it out, they have taken, he has worn, she has sung

5. I have flown, he has went, they rose at dawn, the flag is raised

6. I ate, the horns blew, she has spoke, they drank

7. she is lying, they have seen, it has burst, it begun

8. the book is lying here, it has laid under the desk, they laid the trap, I was laying it down

9. set the alarm, you have been chosen, I have sat it down, it has gone

10. the cloth has wore out, you have run, the bell rang, she has fallen

EXERCISE B On the line provided in each of the following sentences, write the correct form (past or past participle) of the verb given in italics.

Example 1. *go*   Have you ever ___*gone*___ to the circus?

11. *become*   I _____ interested in being a dancer after seeing a performance by the Alvin Ailey American Dance Theater.

12. *lie*   Grassy plains once _____ at the edge of that forest.

13. *know*   That stranger looks like someone I have _____ for many years.

14. *ride*   I have never _____ in a hot-air balloon.

15. *rise*   The fog _____ from the lake and drifted toward the house.

16. *catch*   Nikhil _____ a very bad cold this winter.

17. *freeze*   As I looked up at the trees, I noticed that the water had _____ on the branches.

18. *speak*   The person chosen to address the audience had _____ to us three weeks earlier.

19. *begin*   By the time we finished unpacking, it had _____ to rain.

20. *bring*   She had _____ far more books than we could read in a week's time.

Review D: **Consistency of Tense; Voice**

USAGE

EXERCISE A   Read the following passage. Decide whether it should be written in the present or the past tense. Underline any verbs that are not in the correct tense, and write the correct tense above the verb.

Example   **[1]** When my mother was a teenager, she is pretty impulsive.
(was written above "is")

[1] Once she amazes her family and friends by flying to Los Angeles to see the 1984 Olympics.

[2] Her decision to go comes as a shock, since she had never flown before. **[3]** Her sister teased her

about changing her mind until the moment the family leaves her in the airport waiting room.

[4] To Mother's relief, the flight is uneventful. **[5]** The Olympics are not. **[6]** Los Angeles was so

packed that she has problems finding a hotel room. **[7]** Fortunately, she had cousins there who

invite her to stay with them. **[8]** From the start, she hopes to see Carl Lewis run, so she was

thrilled to learn that her cousins had an extra ticket to the 100-meter dash. **[9]** For ten long seconds

Mom sat on the edge of her seat, keeps her fingers crossed, and cheered loudly. **[10]** It is thrilling

for her to see Lewis win one of his four gold medals.

EXERCISE B   On the line provided, write *PV* if the sentence is in the passive voice or *AV* if it is in the active voice. Above each sentence in the passive voice, rewrite the sentence in the active voice.

Example   _PV_   **1.** The whole garden was hoed by me and my sister.
(My sister and I hoed the whole garden. written above)

_____ **11.** The doctor was applauded by the students.

_____ **12.** Rocky has taken the picture.

_____ **13.** The juice was poured by the nurse.

_____ **14.** The play was seen by hundreds of people.

_____ **15.** An important lesson was learned by all the students.

_____ **16.** The racing yacht was sailed by an experienced crew.

_____ **17.** I get home from school around 4:00 P.M.

_____ **18.** Anna put the book by the door.

_____ **19.** The marks on the floor were made by dirty shoes.

_____ **20.** Have you found that book?

for **CHAPTER 17: USING VERBS CORRECTLY** pages 516–47

Proofreading Application: Letter

Good writers generally are good proofreaders. Learn to become a careful proofreader so that you can correct errors in grammar, usage, spelling, and punctuation. Readers will have more trust in what you're communicating if you do your best to make sure that your writing is error-free.

Many times in your life, you will want or need to write about past events. For instance, you might write a letter to a friend and tell about the things that have happened. You may write about your work experiences for an application. Or you may need to write a report at work when you are older.

Whenever you write about past events, be particularly careful about using correct verb forms and tenses. Correct verb forms allow readers to focus on the meaning of your writing. Was the first event over before the second one began? Is the first event still going on? What is happening now? Don't leave these questions in your readers' minds. Proofread your verbs carefully.

PROOFREADING ACTIVITY

In the following excerpt from a letter of application, correct the errors in verb form and tense. Use proofreading symbols such as those on page 901 of *Elements of Language* to make your corrections.

Example My skills and interest in engineering ^*make* ~~makes~~ me an ideal candidate for your summer program in engineering.

I wanted to be an engineer before I had known what engineers are. When I had been only five years old, I builded a system of roads and waterways in my backyard. The system included waterwheels and, later, a lock for the canal to the "lake" that I created. My mother has took pictures of many of my projects, and I am enclosing copies of these photographs. As I had grown, I moved on to metal and plastic models, and those with moving parts always were my favorites. Eventually, I begun to design my own animated models. I have maked cranes, conveyor belts, pistons, merry-go-rounds, and many other structures. My father has teached me basic computer programming, which I had used to direct several robots.

I always show up on time, worked hard, and set my standards high. Please consider me for your upcoming summer session.

Literary Model: Narration

> On December the third, the wind changed overnight, and it was winter. Until then the autumn had been mellow, soft. The leaves had lingered on the trees, golden-red, and the hedgerows were still green. The earth was rich where the plow had turned it.
>
> Nat Hocken, because of a wartime disability, had a pension and did not work full time at the farm. He worked three days a week, and they gave him the lighter jobs: hedging, thatching, repairs to the farm buildings.
>
> —from "The Birds" by Daphne du Maurier

EXERCISE A Underline the verbs in the passage above.

EXERCISE B

1. In the list below, circle each verb tense that is used in the passage.

present tense   past tense   future tense

present perfect tense   past perfect tense   future perfect tense

2. Why does the author need to use more than one verb tense in the passage?

_____

_____

_____

_____

_____

_____

_____

_____

_____

3. In the first paragraph, what two words signal that the verb tense is about to change?

_____

for **CHAPTER 17: USING VERBS CORRECTLY**   *pages 528–29*

Literary Model (continued)

EXERCISE C Have you ever suddenly realized that what is happening to you at the present moment had been foreshadowed by events in the past? Perhaps a roomful of people have just shouted "Surprise!" at you, and you realize that last week when you thought your best friend was avoiding you, she actually had been planning your surprise party. Using an experience like this one or an event that you make up, write a passage in which you use at least two verb tenses to narrate an event.

_____

_____

_____

_____

_____

_____

_____

_____

_____

_____

_____

_____

EXERCISE D

1. Which verb tenses did you use in your passage?

_____

_____

2. Did you use words or phrases to signal that the tense was about to change? If so, what are they? If not, what are some words or phrases you could have used?

_____

_____

3. Why is it sometimes more effective to use a change in verb tense, such as in a flashback, than it is to tell a story or event in strict chronological order?

_____

_____

_____

_____

Grammar, Usage, and Mechanics: Language Skills Practice

Writing Application: Personal Essay

Events in personal essays, just as in real life, can happen in the past, present, or future. In English the tense of the verb indicates the time of the action or of the state of being that the verb is expressing. You, as a writer, can help your reader understand when the events in a personal essay take place by using verb tense correctly. Sometimes you will need to use different tenses in a paragraph or even in the same sentence.

> **EXAMPLE**   The house had not been wired to code, and the inevitable result was that it caught on fire and was completely destroyed. Whatever will become of the unfortunate family who lived next door?

You can also help your reader understand the timing of events in your personal essay by not changing needlessly from one tense to another.

INCONSISTENT TENSE   The house catches on fire. The firefighters quickly arrived.

CONSISTENT TENSE   The house **caught** on fire. The firefighters quickly **arrived.**

WRITING ACTIVITY

What is a hobby, sport, or other activity that you presently enjoy doing and have enjoyed doing for several years? Think back to when you first started doing this activity. Then, consider why you have continued to do it over a period of time. Write a personal essay in which you describe what your initial experience with the activity was like; whether your appreciation of the activity has grown and, if so, how; and what you expect your relationship to the activity to be like as you grow older. Use at least four different verb tenses in your essay.

PREWRITING   Use a clustering or webbing technique to break your topic down into smaller parts. Consider having the following radiate from the central topic circle: one cluster of ideas that deals with your initial experience with the activity, another cluster dealing with your present relationship to it, and a third cluster that deals with your future relationship to it. Before you begin writing your draft, determine who your audience will be.

WRITING   Using the information in the cluster diagram, write your draft freely, without concentrating too much on errors in grammar, usage, spelling, and punctuation. Ask yourself whether chronological order is the best way to arrange your ideas.

REVISING   Have a classmate read your draft. Ask him or her to tell you its strengths and weaknesses, as well as a few suggestions for improving it. In an effort to make your writing as focused as possible, make sure your draft is not repetitive or wordy.

PUBLISHING   Check that you have used at least four verb tenses, that they are all used correctly, and that you have not used tenses inconsistently. Use a dictionary or your textbook to verify the spelling of irregular verb forms. Then, share your essay with someone else who leads or participates in this activity.

EXTENDING YOUR WRITING

Are there any newsletters or magazines that publish articles on the kind of hobby, sport, or other activity that you wrote about? Revise your essay to appeal to that publication's audience, and submit your essay for publication.

Choices: Investigating Pronouns

The following activities challenge you to find a connection between pronoun usage and the world around you. Do the activity below that suits your personality best, and then share your discoveries with your class.

HISTORY

Junkyard or Antique Shop?

Whatever happened to those old-fashioned *thee*'s and *thou*'s? They wound up in the junkyard of English. There can be a lot of good stuff at a junkyard, though. Writers can make poetry out of such out-of-date words. Make a poster titled "Language Junkyard" or "Antique Shop of English." On it, write words and expressions that are no longer used or that are no longer considered standard. Don't limit yourself to pronouns. Anything goes. With your teacher's permission, hang your poster in the hall.

SURVEY

The Hit Parade

With permission, tape-record conversations. Then, count the number of personal pronouns used. Which personal pronoun is used the most often in your experiment? Which ones are most often used incorrectly? Which ones are most often used correctly? Present the class with an ordered listing of your results. Present, too, your opinions about the results you obtained.

FOREIGN LANGUAGES

Él y Ella

How do other languages handle pronouns? Do other languages have nominative, objective, and possessive cases? What about second- and third-person singular and plural? How are these handled in, say, Spanish? Find out, and share your finding with your classmates.

BUILDING BACKGROUND KNOWLEDGE

Close Relatives

Look up the word *nominative*. What is its root word? Then, brainstorm as many words as you can that share this same root word. Use each of these words in a sentence. Next, create a poster. Write the root word in the center, and create a chart showing how each word relates to the root word.

RESEARCH

Street Lingo

Standard English does not have a special pronoun for second-person plural. However, nonstandard varieties of English do. In fact, there are several. List some expressions that include these special pronouns. In what geographical region or regions are they used? Let your classmates know the answers to these questions.

CONVERSATION

Dialogue

What would conversations sound like if people used *whom* as often as standard usage requires? Write a ten-line dialogue that involves one person who always uses *who* and another person who always uses *whom*. As you alternate from one speaker to the other, make sure to use *who* or *whom* correctly at least once in each line of conversation.

WRITING

Travel Article

Just how important are pronouns, anyway? Find out by trying to write a few paragraphs without using any pronouns. Pretend you are a travel writer whose assignment is to describe a trip you have taken with your friends or family. Give detailed descriptions of the scenery, activities, and people you encountered. Don't hold back, but remember—absolutely no pronouns allowed!

ART

In Black and White

Elliptical clauses can be tricky. Take, for instance, *He liked the movie more than her.* Does this sentence mean that she didn't like the movie as much as he did or that he liked the movie more than he liked her? Find or create a few of these confusing sentences. Then, draw cartoons illustrating the situations that the sentences describe. Don't forget to include the unintended results!

Grammar, Usage, and Mechanics: Language Skills Practice

Case

18a.   *Case* is the form that a noun or pronoun takes to show its relationship to other words in a sentence.

NOMINATIVE	**He** and his **mother** will be bringing the salads.
OBJECTIVE	Marilyn brought my **dog** back to **me.**
POSSESSIVE	**Heather's** horse hurt **its** leg.

EXERCISE   Above each underlined noun or pronoun, identify its case by writing *NOM* for *nominative case,* *OBJ* for *objective case,* or *POS* for *possessive case.*

Example   1.   Will the <u>class's</u> new teacher be <u>she</u>?
                    POS   *NOM*

1. <u>They</u> don't know whether the <u>team's</u> uniforms have arrived.

2. The <u>mechanic</u> promised to deliver <u>our</u> car by noon.

3. Today, Adele put the <u>books</u> on the shelves for <u>me</u>.

4. We gave Allen and <u>her</u> our tape, which <u>they</u> will preview tonight.

5. The <u>trees</u> are shedding <u>their</u> leaves.

6. The <u>coach's</u> speech gave <u>them</u> all something to consider.

7. The newly elected class <u>president</u> is <u>she</u>.

8. Darryl volunteered to help <u>us</u> at the senior citizens' <u>center</u>.

9. How may <u>I</u> order the <u>plans</u> for your water conservation system?

10. Please inform <u>your</u> parents of the <u>principal's</u> new rules about homework.

11. The <u>president</u> of the chess club is offering <u>lessons</u>.

12. <u>Their</u> <u>uniforms</u> are different this year.

13. Please write <u>your</u> <u>opinions</u> about the book.

14. The newest member of <u>my</u> team is <u>Alicia</u>.

15. <u>They</u> help homeless <u>veterans</u> find work.

16. Next year, Carla and <u>she</u> will be on the <u>school's</u> soccer team.

17. A <u>cheetah</u> can run fast enough to catch <u>its</u> prey.

18. Our <u>city's</u> animal rescue group helps <u>people</u> find new pets.

19. <u>She</u> studied hard and learned the new <u>material</u>.

20. <u>Their</u> history <u>book</u> contains many useful maps.

USAGE

The Case Forms of Personal Pronouns

18a. *Case* is the form that a noun or pronoun takes to show its relationship to other words in a sentence.

In English there are three cases: *nominative*, *objective*, and *possessive*.

Personal Pronouns

NOMINATIVE CASE	I, you, she, he, it, we, you, they
OBJECTIVE CASE	me, you, her, him, it, us, you, them
POSSESSIVE CASE	my, mine, your, yours, her, hers, his, its, our, ours, their, theirs

EXERCISE A All the pronouns in each of the following groups have the same case form. Identify the form of each group by writing on the line provided *NOM* for *nominative case*, *OBJ* for *objective case*, or *POS* for *possessive case*.

Example _POS_ **1.** hers, its, their

_____ **1.** me, you, them

_____ **2.** I, she, they

_____ **3.** mine, your, its

_____ **4.** he, you, we

_____ **5.** her, him, us

EXERCISE B Identify the case of the underlined pronouns in each of the following sentences by writing above the pronoun *NOM* for *nominative case*, *OBJ* for *objective case*, or *POS* for *possessive case*.

Example 1. Yesterday, my grandparents bought their tickets for the playoff games.

6. The waiter brought him and me a pitcher of water.

7. I was curious about the neatly wrapped packages, so I opened one of them.

8. She owns over one thousand videotapes; I have never seen so many of them in one room!

9. After the meal, our table contained many more dishes than theirs did.

10. After lunch, we completed the worksheets our teacher had given us.

11. Terry and she gave their old newspapers to the neighbors.

12. Before we reached the stable, the horse had bruised its leg.

13. This paper is mine; that one is yours.

14. His parents and they visited our house last week.

15. Did you tell them about the garage sale?

The Nominative Case A

18b. The subject of a verb should be in the nominative case.

    EXAMPLES   **They** thought that **we** would be afraid to go into the cave.
                    Have **Alia** and **she** finished their homework?

18c. A predicate nominative should be in the nominative case.

    EXAMPLE   Could the famous detectives be **Mary** and **she**?

EXERCISE A   In the following sentences, underline the correct one of the two pronouns in parentheses.

Example 1. Among the volunteers are Karla and (*I, me*).

1. Bruce and (*me, I*) often study together after school.

2. Did you say that Jeff Draper and (*her, she*) live down the street?

3. Neither (*him, he*) nor Ben knew the telephone number.

4. The girl in the red and white kimono was (*I, me*).

5. That must be (*he, him*) at the door now.

6. It was (*he, him*) who decided to have a picnic.

7. Doug and (*them, they*) went to buy some CD's.

8. Either Stuart or (*her, she*) will be class president.

9. Could the culprits be (*them, they*)?

10. By the time Gary and (*her, she*) returned from the store, the movie had ended.

EXERCISE B   Revise each of the following sentences by replacing the underlined word or words with a pronoun. Cross out the underlined word or words, and write the pronoun above them.

Example 1. ~~Maisie and I~~ *We* searched for our map.

11. My mother and my uncle took the ferry to Lantua.

12. The only one who brought a camera was my uncle.

13. My uncle and I hiked down the long hill.

14. Is that Mother in the restaurant?

15. Next time, my mother and I want to try fishing.

The Nominative Case B

18b. The *subject of a verb* should be in the nominative case.

> **EXAMPLES**   **We** were proud when **she** qualified for the state science fair.
> Are **he** and **I** supposed to use these suitcases?

18c. A *predicate nominative* should be in the nominative case.

> **EXAMPLE**   Will the club's officers be **Gabrielle** and **he**?

EXERCISE   On the line before each of the following sentences, write the nominative case pronoun that will correctly replace the underlined word or words.

Example ___*she*___ **1.** My roommates will be Elena and Andrea.

_____ **1.** Are you and Timothy leaving early?

_____ **2.** The mysterious caller was Cathy.

_____ **3.** Antonio and I will join the team.

_____ **4.** Was that Karen who called?

_____ **5.** It must have been Kevin who left the message.

_____ **6.** Jaime and I are learning to paint with watercolors.

_____ **7.** The biologist who wrote this article was Susan.

_____ **8.** The dancers who won the contest were Tsiyoshi and Mitsi.

_____ **9.** Tomorrow morning, Connie and Janice will come over.

_____ **10.** Could the gymnast on the balance beam be Rachel?

_____ **11.** Ricky and Debbie are in the band.

_____ **12.** The new mascot will be Maurice.

_____ **13.** Lisa and Franco and I attended the track meet.

_____ **14.** Is it Rosa that won first prize?

_____ **15.** I was happy when Susan returned from Europe.

_____ **16.** Because Lee had left the the door open, the hornets were able to fly into the house.

_____ **17.** It might have been Tamika who wrote the mysterious note.

_____ **18.** Jeff and Katy are going to Japan this summer.

_____ **19.** The students who went to the library are Gail and Michael.

_____ **20.** Could the Count of Monte Cristo be Edmond Dantès?

USAGE

The Objective Case A

18d. A *direct object* should be in the objective case.

EXAMPLE   Luis visited **her** and **me** in Chicago last week.

18e. An *indirect object* should be in the objective case.

EXAMPLE   The manager handed **him** and **me** applications.

18f. An *object of a preposition* should be in the objective case.

EXAMPLE   Donna offered some grapes to **us** and **them**.

EXERCISE A   In the following sentences, identify each underlined pronoun by writing above it *DO* for direct object, *IO* for indirect object, or *OP* for object of a preposition.

Example 1. The landscape designer showed us three shrubs for our garden.

1. People gave him the nickname Satchmo.

2. I saw Charles and him at the meeting.

3. A messenger in a blue uniform handed a sealed package to her.

4. Most of us liked the new biology book.

5. Aunt Flo sent Howard and me a magazine subscription.

EXERCISE B   In the following sentences, underline the correct pronoun in parentheses.

Example 1. Terrell asked *(they, them)* about the class officer elections.

6. Dad scolded *(we, us)* for being late to dinner.

7. After the second interview, Mr. Seiko offered *(he, him)* the job.

8. At the door, the students handed him and *(me, I)* the completed ballots.

9. Except for Anoki and *(I, me)*, the room was empty.

10. His companion dog climbs on the bus ahead of *(he, him)*.

11. She gladly gave *(they, them)* the book.

12. Dolores and her sister entered *(us, we)* in the contest.

13. They gave *(he, him)* a new watch.

14. Mrs. Peters told my brother and *(I, me)* a funny story.

15. Deanna gave *(her, she)* guitar lessons for free.

USAGE

The Objective Case B

18d.   A *direct object* should be in the objective case.

     EXAMPLE   The ski instructor will take **them** and **me** to the easiest slope first.

18e.   An *indirect object* should be in the objective case.

     EXAMPLE   Did the band leader give **them** and **him** praise for a job well done?

18f.   An *object of a preposition* should be in the objective case.

     EXAMPLE   Louisa's friends cooked a wonderful birthday dinner for **her.**

EXERCISE Replace the underlined word or words in the following sentences with the appropriate objective case pronoun. Cross out the underlined words, and write the correct pronouns above them. Avoid using *you* or *it*.

Example 1. Are you going to take ~~your pets~~ *them* with you on the trip?

1. At the end of the controversial experiment, the studious assistant described the long-awaited results for the professor.

2. Didn't you invite Darla, Francine, and Kenny?

3. Kevin, have you shown your grandparents the math project you put together for next week's school fair?

4. Mr. Friedman gave the class a helpful lesson in the differences between business letters and personal letters.

5. Instead of asking Tamisha again, why not ask Barry to be on the cleanup committee?

6. Asked about a career in medicine, the counselor advised Justin to take as many high school science courses as possible.

7. Tomorrow, would you take Sally and me with you to see the historical exhibits on the Seminole and Cherokee?

8. Joe showed Marty and Hal his magazine and newspaper clippings about the eclipse.

9. Among my family and friends, the seven days of Kwanzaa are celebrated with gift-giving and storytelling.

10. For extra credit, did Mrs. Jamison say that she wants you and me to read "Misspelling" by Charles Kuralt?

Grammar, Usage, and Mechanics: Language Skills Practice

for **CHAPTER 18: USING PRONOUNS CORRECTLY**   *pages 550–55*

Nominative and Objective Case Pronouns

USAGE

18b.	The *subject of a verb* should be in the nominative case.
18c.	A *predicate nominative* should be in the nominative case.
18d.	A *direct object* should be in the objective case.
18e.	An *indirect object* should be in the objective case.
18f.	An *object of a preposition* should be in the objective case.

EXERCISE For each of the following sentences, underline the correct pronoun in parentheses.

Example 1. Do Mark and *(he, him)* read books to children at the library?

1. Kiyo and *(she, her)* have been friends since third grade.

2. On stage, a magician mysteriously sawed *(she, her)* in half.

3. Studying the martial arts taught Sara and *(me, I)* valuable skills.

4. The one with the most baseball cards is *(he, him)*.

5. There is an empty lot between the river and *(we, us)*.

6. Ahmed and *(he, him)* sliced the cantaloupe.

7. The conductor showed *(we, us)* how to use a baton.

8. There are some differences of opinion between Bill and *(I, me)*.

9. The yoga instructor taught *(we, us)* new stretches.

10. Will the next volunteer be *(she, her)*?

11. Siamack and *(he, him)* speak Farsi.

12. The Clarks gave the puppy to Sandra and *(she, her)*.

13. The customers who ordered juice were Becky and *(she, her)*.

14. It was *(I, me)* who wanted to speak to you.

15. The captain of the football team is *(he, him)*.

16. May Mark and *(I, me)* borrow your paintbrushes?

17. I lent *(he, him)* my favorite jacket.

18. Did you see *(she, her)* before she left?

19. Were *(they, them)* your grandparents?

20. Jason and Susan helped Sarah and *(he, him)* with their homework.

ELEMENTS OF LANGUAGE | Third Course

The Possessive Case

18g(1). The possessive pronouns *mine, yours, his, hers, its, ours,* and *theirs* are used as parts of a sentence in the same ways in which the pronouns in the nominative and the objective cases are used.

> EXAMPLES **Mine** is the one with the broken clasp. [subject]
>
> That small yellow lunch box is **his.** [predicate nominative]
>
> Harold and Mark brought **theirs** with them. [direct object]
>
> Mother gave **ours** a quick proofreading last night. [indirect object]
>
> I think my jacket is underneath **hers.** [object of preposition]

18g(2). The possessive pronouns *my, your, his, her, its, our,* and *their* are used as adjectives before nouns.

> EXAMPLES Was that **their** dog that was howling all night?
>
> **His** going outside gave me the opportunity to prepare the surprise.

USAGE

EXERCISE A Complete the following sentences by writing an appropriate possessive pronoun on each of the lines provided. Use a variety of possessive pronouns.

Example 1. We didn't know how long ____*their*____ vacation would last.

1. Who can tell me the name of _____ state capital?

2. Look how bright the comet is and how long _____ tail is!

3. Sandra, please be sure that book is _____ before you write your name in it.

4. Some trees do not lose _____ leaves in the fall and winter.

5. After comparing the maps, we decided _____ would help us the most.

6. What convinced Marie Curie to continue _____ search for radium?

7. A skunk shows _____ annoyance by releasing a strong-smelling spray.

8. _____ speech teacher lived in Virginia Beach, Virginia, at one time.

9. Of all the answers that we received for this question, _____ is the best.

10. The recipe that uses rice noodles, tofu, and vegetables is _____.

EXERCISE B Complete the following sentences by writing an appropriate possessive pronoun on each of the lines provided. Use a variety of pronouns.

Example 1. ____*His*____ winning the race impressed us all.

11. Is that his hamster, or is it _____?

12. The shoes in the corner are _____; I took them off a few minutes ago.

13. We felt that our approach would work better than _____.

14. _____ piano sounds bad; we should have it tuned.

15. _____ falling asleep so quickly surprised his mother.

Grammar, Usage, and Mechanics: Language Skills Practice

171

Case Forms A

18a. *Case* is the form that a noun or pronoun takes to show its relationship to other words in a sentence.

> **EXAMPLE** **He** told **me** that **his** sister was in town. [*He* is in the nominative case; *me* is in the objective case; *his* is in the possessive case.]

EXERCISE A In the following sentences, underline the correct pronoun in parentheses. Identify the case of the correct pronoun by writing above it *NOM* for *nominative, OBJ* for *objective,* or *POS* for *possessive.*

Example 1. Is my lab partner Kelly or (*him,* <u>*he*</u>)? *[NOM]*

1. Mr. Matthews called Melanie and (*she, her*) up to the stage at the awards ceremony.

2. Karl announced that (*they, their*) tour guide would be Sandy.

3. We sold Tom and (*they, them*) the late-edition newspapers.

4. Does (*he, him*) know the shortcut to the sports auditorium?

5. Your new student council president is (*she, her*).

6. Three reviewers praised Kate's and (*my, mine*) performances in the new play.

7. Could my uncle James have served with (*they, them*) in the navy?

8. With one minute left, Juanita interrupted the debate between (*we, us*) and them.

9. After sundown, Peter and (*him, he*) set up the telescope.

10. The judges announced that first prize in the canned goods category was (*her, hers*).

EXERCISE B In each of the following sentences, identify the case of the underlined pronoun. Write *NOM* for *nominative, OBJ* for *objective,* or *POS* for *possessive* above the underlined word.

Example 1. Was it <u>she</u> who was asking for me? *[NOM]*

11. Marcus wrote a script for <u>us</u> this year.

12. The play is dedicated to <u>our</u> energetic and devoted teacher.

13. The president of the drama club is <u>she</u>.

14. The leading male in this spring's production will be <u>he</u>.

15. <u>His</u> stage voice is powerful and confident.

16. Do you think <u>their</u> new play was as appealing as the last one?

17. Could it have been <u>she</u> who directed the last play?

18. We watched <u>him</u> set up the stage.

19. Did each actress remember <u>her</u> long, difficult lines?

20. Are <u>they</u> the main characters in the play?

USAGE

Case Forms B

18a. *Case* is the form that a noun or pronoun takes to show its relationship to other words in a sentence.

NOMINATIVE	**I, you, he, she, it, we, they**
OBJECTIVE	**me, you, him, her, it, us, them**
POSSESSIVE	**my, mine, your, yours, his, her, hers, its, our, ours, their, theirs**

EXERCISE Using the clues in the passage, insert correct pronouns on the lines provided.

Example **[1]** The grandparents love to have their grandchildren visit _____*them*_____.

[1] Mr. and Mrs. Thibodaux built _____ new house near the Atchafalaya Basin.

[2] _____ like living near the water. **[3]** Mr. Thibodaux brings _____ canoe to the swamp.

[4] Sometimes his grandchildren accompany _____. **[5]** Mr. Thibodaux takes _____ bass

fishing. **[6]** One time _____ saw an alligator nearby. **[7]** The children were afraid, but

_____ remained calm. **[8]** The alligator wasn't trying to harm _____. **[9]** Soon, the alligator

retreated and Mr. Thibodaux laughed with _____ grandchildren.

[10] Mrs. Thibodaux plays accordion with _____ friends. **[11]** _____ music has a happy

sound and a fast beat. **[12]** When her grandchildren visit, _____ join in and play. **[13]** Mrs.

Thibodaux teaches _____ new tunes on an accordion. **[14]** One of her grandsons always

brings _____ fiddle. **[15]** He wrote a new song for his grandmother and played it for

_____. **[16]** He appreciates his grandmother, for it was _____ who taught him to play the

fiddle. **[17]** He still asks for _____ advice when he plays.

[18] The grandchildren visit _____ grandparents as often as possible. **[19]** The grandchildren

bring _____ photographs and gifts. **[20]** For Mr. and Mrs. Thibodaux, spending time with

_____ family is of great importance.

Who and *Whom*

| **18h.** | The use of *who* or *whom* in a subordinate clause depends on how the pronoun functions in the clause. |

EXAMPLES   Who was that girl **whom** you were speaking to yesterday? [*Whom* is the object of the preposition *to* and is in the objective case.]

The snacks will go to **whoever** gets here first. [*Whoever* is the subject of *gets* and is in the nominative case.]

EXERCISE   Underline the correct pronoun in parentheses in the following sentences.

Example 1. Do you know (*who*, *whom*) she's going to be for Halloween?

1. Carol wondered (*who*, *whom*) she should ask for directions.

2. The artist (*who*, *whom*) painted that mural was Diego Rivera.

3. I don't even know (*who*, *whom*) she is.

4. Lily had to figure out (*who*, *whom*) sent her the surprise package.

5. Jesse didn't know (*who*, *whom*) we were talking about at first.

6. You may invite (*whoever*, *whomever*) you wish.

7. Mr. Chow, to (*who*, *whom*) I made the phone call, is a real-estate broker.

8. (*Whoever*, *Whomever*) solves the mystery gets a free copy of the book.

9. Do you know (*who*, *whom*) your new neighbors are?

10. That woman to (*who*, *whom*) you gave the packages looks ill.

11. Did you see Judd Hirsch, (*who*, *whom*) we met on the tour, autograph his picture?

12. Ask (*whoever*, *whomever*) scores the winning goal for an interview.

13. How does the conductor know from (*who*, *whom*) he must collect tickets?

14. Mrs. Park, (*who*, *whom*) I know well, gave me a ride home.

15. Except for Anoki and me, (*who*, *whom*) did you expect to meet here today?

16. Is this the lady (*who*, *whom*) made an appointment?

17. We will go fishing with (*whoever*, *whomever*) wants to join us.

18. The man (*who*, *whom*) you were talking to is my uncle.

19. For (*who*, *whom*) was the song written?

20. Bill will give the book to (*whoever*, *whomever*) he chooses.

Appositives

18i. A pronoun used as an appositive is in the same case as the word to which it refers.

EXAMPLES The troop leaders, **he** and **I,** stayed late. [The pronouns are in the nominative case because they are used as appositives of the subject, *leaders*.]

Ms. Barrientos gave the troop leaders, **him** and **me,** the papers for the meeting. [The pronouns are in the objective case because they are used as appositives of the indirect object, *leaders*.]

We students will play against the faculty. [*We* is the subject of the sentence and is in the nominative case. The appositive *students* identifies the pronoun *We* but does not affect its case.]

EXERCISE A Underline the correct pronoun in parentheses in the following sentences.

Example 1. She chose her teammates, Sarah and (I, <u>me</u>).

1. The best friends, Robert and *(he, him)*, left together.

2. She looked for the brothers, Todd and *(he, him)*.

3. The new club members, Pearl and *(I, me)*, were introduced to the group.

4. They gave prizes to the winners, Minnie and *(I, me)*.

5. She forgot to give the students, Patricia and *(she, her)*, their books.

6. The nurses, Mrs. Reynolds and *(she, her)*, arrived early.

7. They offered the boy scouts, Mike and *(he, him)*, new caps.

8. The passengers, Charles and *(I, me)*, left at noon.

9. Will the journalists, Henry and *(he, him)*, be here?

10. The teacher gave *(we, us)* students an extra day to complete the project.

EXERCISE B For each of the following, write a sentence that correctly uses the words in parentheses as an appositive.

Example 1. *(he and Jane)* *Two students, he and Jane, entered a project in the statewide science fair.*

11. *(she and Tom)* _____

12. *(him and me)* _____

13. *(he and Carl)* _____

14. *(Megan and them)* _____

15. *(my cousin and I)* _____

USAGE

Pronouns in Incomplete Constructions

18j. After *than* and *as* introducing an incomplete construction, use the form of the pronoun that would be correct if the construction were completed.

EXAMPLES   We thanked him more than **she** [did].

We thanked him more than [we thanked] **her.**

USAGE

EXERCISE A   Underline the correct pronoun in parentheses in the following sentences.

Example 1. She runs faster than *(he, him)*.

1. We appreciate the other players as much as *(they, them)*.

2. Shelly and Paul practice more often than *(we, us)*.

3. After the race, I was as tired as *(she, her)*.

4. The nurse told us that she works more hours than *(he, him)*.

5. Mike can whistle more loudly than *(she, her)*.

6. She paid more attention to me than *(they, them)*.

7. Are we as prepared as *(they, them)*?

8. I wrote more letters than *(she, her)*.

9. The older students didn't prepare as many lunches for the field trip as *(they, them)*.

10. Will the mayor speak to the city council for as long as *(he, him)*?

EXERCISE B   Underline the correct pronoun in parentheses in the following sentences. Then, on the line provided, write the sentence's understood clause.

Example 1. Frank plays chess better than *(I, me)*. *than I play chess* _____

11. Jill has visited me more often than *(him, he)*. _____

12. Is Samantha as diligent as *(they, them)*? _____

13. Sarah is taller than *(him, he)*. _____

14. Are you as confident as *(them, they)*? _____

15. He collected as many canned goods as *(she, her)*. _____

for **CHAPTER 18: USING PRONOUNS CORRECTLY**   pages 559–64

Special Pronoun Problems

18h. The use of *who* or *whom* in a subordinate clause depends on how the pronoun functions in the clause.

     OBJECTIVE   Is that the boy **whom** you saw? [*Whom* is the direct object of *saw.*]

     NOMINATIVE   **Whoever** comes in first will win a prize. [*Whoever* is the subject of *comes.*]

18i. A pronoun used as an **appositive** is in the same case as the word to which it refers.

     OBJECTIVE   Haley gave her best friends, Alyx and **me,** her word. [*Me* is an appositive identifying *friends,* the indirect object of *gave.*]

     NOMINATIVE   Her best friends, Alyx and **I,** planned Haley's party. [*I* is an appositive identifying *friends,* the subject of *planned.*]

18j. After *than* and *as* introducing an incomplete construction, use the form of the pronoun that would be correct if the construction were completed.

     OBJECTIVE   I like crossword puzzles more than [I like] **him.**

     NOMINATIVE   I like crossword puzzles more than **he** [does].

EXERCISE   Underline the correct pronoun in parentheses in the following sentences.

Example 1. She is the professor (*who*, *whom*) teaches biology and botany.

1. Camila told her best friends, Tina and (*I, me*), the secret.

2. Is she the doctor (*who, whom*) you recommended?

3. The new volunteers had many more questions than Martina and (*I, me*).

4. He can teach golf to (*whoever, whomever*) wants to learn.

5. The defending lawyers, Robert and (*she, her*), worked hard on the case.

6. (*Whoever, Whomever*) wrote this letter didn't sign it.

7. Did you know that the new cashiers are even younger than Rob and (*she, her*)?

8. You may work with (*whoever, whomever*) you prefer.

9. Mrs. Greenwood made breakfast for her new neighbors, who are as friendly as Kelly and (*he, him*).

10. Please ask (*whoever, whomever*) wants to join us to arrive early.

USAGE

Clear Pronoun Reference A

18k(1–2). A pronoun should refer clearly to its antecedent. Avoid using ambiguous or general references.

AMBIGUOUS	Ms. Dean asked Sheree to photocopy the report after she had read it.
CLEAR	After Ms. Dean had read the report, she asked Sheree to photocopy it.
GENERAL	I washed the dishes and dusted, and that made me feel better.
CLEAR	I washed the dishes and dusted, and doing those chores made me feel better.

EXERCISE Revise each of the following sentences, correcting each inexact pronoun reference. Write your revisions on the lines provided.

Example 1. We brought gifts and a cake, and this completely surprised Mom.

That we brought gifts and a cake completely surprised Mom.

1. Whenever our pet gander is near our old truck, it runs around honking.

_____

2. My aunt called my sister to discuss the theme for her party.

_____

3. Carla needs to read an entire novel this weekend, but she says that it will be no problem.

_____

4. Lucy didn't want to tell Amanda that she had brought the wrong basket to the picnic.

_____

5. Katherine told Mary that she needed to change the oil in her car.

_____

6. Bill met with James at his house.

_____

7. She has many ambitions, and it helps her remain motivated.

_____

8. The city council are divided about the sales tax rate, which is upsetting to many citizens.

_____

9. Has Mona asked Teri if she could sell twenty tickets for our fund-raiser?

_____

10. It rained the day of the party, and that upset the children.

_____

USAGE

Clear Pronoun Reference B

18k(3–4). A pronoun should refer clearly to its antecedent. Avoid using indefinite or weak pronoun references.

USAGE

WEAK	Jill is good at programming computers; she wants this to be her career.
CLEAR	Jill is good at programming computers; she wants computer programming to be her career.
INDEFINITE	In the instructions they included a sketch of all the parts for the model.
CLEAR	The instructions included a sketch of all the parts for the model.

EXERCISE Revise each of the following sentences, correcting each inexact pronoun reference. Write your revisions on the lines provided.

Example 1. I'm afraid of flying, but I'm trying to get over it.

   I'm afraid of flying, but I'm trying to get over my fear.

1. She is superstitious; one of them is about walking under ladders.

_____

2. Every time Tyrone saw an ice-skating event, he wanted to be one.

_____

3. Gilda loves traveling in the United States and can never decide which one to visit next.

_____

4. In our straw vote, it showed that most students favor wearing uniforms.

_____

5. I hope my reading books during story hour helps them want to read more.

_____

6. Last night on the weather forecast, they predicted a record number of hurricanes this season.

_____

7. We began watching the meteor shower at sundown but didn't see any until after midnight.

_____

8. She loves the theater but hasn't seen any lately.

_____

9. In the article, they described a blue moon as the second full moon in a calendar month.

_____

10. They had run so long it had winded them.

_____

Clear Pronoun Reference C

18k(1–4). A pronoun should refer clearly to its antecedent. Avoid using ambiguous, general, indefinite, and weak pronoun references.

USAGE

EXERCISE   On the lines after each of the following sentences, rewrite the entire sentence to clarify the pronoun reference.

Example 1. Carla was angry, and it made it difficult for her to concentrate.

Carla's anger made it difficult for her to concentrate. _____

1. Martha called Mrs. Kent when she arrived. _____

_____

2. Cassandra went to the computer store but didn't buy one. _____

_____

3. Martin got the new job for which Paul had also applied, and it was more interesting than his

old one. _____

_____

4. William wrote to Marcos when he arrived in Boston. _____

_____

5. Luc is loyal, and this makes him a good friend. _____

_____

6. Celeste loves art, so she bought one for her apartment. _____

_____

7. In the interview, they asked the judge about her decision. _____

_____

8. Berta gave Sarah a rose before she left. _____

_____

9. Frank learned how to ski, and that was helpful during his vacation. _____

_____

10. I bought new software, but they don't say how to install it. _____

_____

Review A: **Case Problems**

EXERCISE A Each of the following sentences contains two pronouns in parentheses. Underline the correct pronoun. Then, tell how the pronoun is used in the sentence by writing above it *S* for *subject, PN* for *predicate nominative, DO* for *direct object, IO* for *indirect object,* or *OP* for *object of the preposition.*

Example 1. Do you write as well as (*he*, *him*)?

1. Ahulani and *(me, I)* like to play chess.

2. Both of *(we, us)* play it rather well.

3. My grandparents gave *(we, us)* a beautiful new chessboard.

4. As for my parents, we can play much better than *(they, them)*.

5. "This is a good game for *(they, them)*," my father said," since they have plenty of time."

6. My mother and *(him, he)* taught me how to play the game.

7. It is *(he, him)* and Ahulani who hate most to lose.

8. "Play *(she, her)* again," my mother says after I defeat him.

9. It is *(she, her)* whom I most enjoy defeating because her game is always carefully played.

10. My father doesn't play Ahulani and *(I, me)* often.

EXERCISE B On the line provided, write *who* or *whom* to complete each of the following sentences correctly.

Example 1. _____*Whom*_____ are you going to the dance with Friday night?

11. _____ was the first American grandmaster?

12. Neither Liseli nor I know _____ it was.

13. To _____ would you go to learn this fact?

14. Our school librarian, _____ knows where to look, told us.

15. I admire Bobby Fischer, _____ I've never met.

16. _____ do you suppose I'll defeat this week?

17. Fischer, _____ became World Champion in 1972, played aggressively.

18. Unlike some chess players, I like everybody _____ challenges me.

19. Some chess players dislike any opponent _____ they play.

20. I only momentarily dislike anyone _____ defeats me.

Review B: **Clear Reference**

EXERCISE Rewrite each sentence to clarify the inexact pronoun reference.

Example 1. Frank showed Tom a sketch of the moon after he finished dinner.

After Frank had finished dinner, he showed Tom a sketch of the moon.

1. Throughout the movie it shows phases of the moon. _____

_____

2. Dani enjoyed my drawings of the moon; she thinks I should take it as an elective. _____

_____

3. I confuse the hay moon of July with the grain moon of August, and that frustrates me. _____

_____

4. On the CD-ROM they use high-speed photography to show the phases of the moon. _____

_____

5. Did you read my poem about the moon? Do you think I should consider that as a career? ____

_____

6. My uncle told my father a joke about the strawberry moon of June when he walked in the door.

_____

7. Amateur astronomers may have trouble on rainy nights, but they shouldn't let that bother

them. _____

_____

8. My sister and mother decided to plant seeds on the first day she observed a new moon. _____

_____

9. February has fewer days than the moon's cycle of 29.2 or 29.9 days; this occasionally causes a

February without a full moon. _____

_____

10. An understanding of both mathematics and physics as well as a passion for the night sky are

important; these make a strong, competent astronomer. _____

_____

USAGE

Review C: **Using Pronouns Correctly**

EXERCISE A Some of the following sentences contain errors in pronoun usage. If a sentence is correct, write *C* on the line provided. If a sentence is incorrect, underline the pronoun error. Then, write the correct pronoun on the line provided.

Example ___*I*___ **1.** By the time she and <u>me</u> finished our argument, we were best friends.

_____ **1.** Was it my sister or me who first played chess well?

_____ **2.** My father and us beginners soon were playing well.

_____ **3.** It was he who first realized how complex a game it is.

_____ **4.** Between my sister and me, there arose a bitter rivalry.

_____ **5.** Before long, my father and her were also bitter rivals.

_____ **6.** The person whom enjoyed the rivalry least was my mother.

_____ **7.** Everyone except she agreed that rivalry is good for anyone who plays.

_____ **8.** "You must remember that there are many people who don't enjoy bickering the way you do," she said.

_____ **9.** My mother is a person who you can't argue with for long.

_____ **10.** Father and her seldom argue because she dislikes arguments.

EXERCISE B Each of the following sentences contains two pronouns in parentheses. Underline the correct pronoun. Then, determine the case of the pronoun (nominative, objective, or possessive). Above the word, write *NOM* for *nominative, OBJ* for *objective,* or *POS* for *possessive.*

Example 1. The principal presented the medals to the two winners, Franklin and *(she,* <u>her</u>). *(OBJ)*

11. Carlos and *(her, she)* like to discuss their future careers.

12. To *(who, whom)* did the clerk give the package?

13. It is *(he, him)* who enjoys hair-raising carnival rides.

14. Do you know *(who, whom)* left this book on the table?

15. Samantha admires marine biologists and wants to learn more about *(they, their)* work.

16. Seeing videotapes of astronauts has given Shelly and *(him, he)* inspiration.

17. Danny, *(whom, who)* I met yesterday, is an interesting person.

18. Carol has convinced my sister and *(I, me)* that traveling to Spain would be exciting.

19. Carla hopes that someday *(she, her)* and Carlos and I will travel to Mars together.

20. She sends toys to her nephews *(who, whom)* aren't old enough to read.

Review D: **Using Pronouns Correctly**

EXERCISE A Some of the following sentences contain errors in pronoun usage. If a sentence is correct, write *C* on the line provided. If a sentence is incorrect, underline the pronoun error. Then, write the correct pronoun on the line provided.

Example ___*I*___ **1.** In the morning, my brother Kele is usually more alert than me.

_____ **1.** Kele and me run to catch the school bus each morning.

_____ **2.** It is he who makes sure that I am on time.

_____ **3.** Together, he and I have managed to be punctual every day.

_____ **4.** Anyone whom misses the bus has to walk.

_____ **5.** Sally is one student whom will be late.

_____ **6.** Nobody except Hononi and she misses the bus more than once a week.

_____ **7.** I think that Kele and me should help them.

_____ **8.** Us two can sprint to the bus stop when we're late.

_____ **9.** However, there aren't many people who can run as fast as we can.

_____ **10.** Perhaps we could call Hononi and she early every morning.

EXERCISE B On the line below each sentence, rewrite the entire sentence to clarify the pronoun reference.

Example 1. Miko lost her keys, and it upset her.

Losing her keys upset Miko.

11. In the article, they asked Maya Angelou many questions.

_____

12. Paolo loves cooking and wonders if he should become one.

_____

13. Sergei bought a new car, and it made his life easier.

_____

14. Alejandro asked Jacob if he should rent a car.

_____

15. Rebecca is an honest person, and this makes her easy to trust.

_____

Proofreading Application: Speech

Good writers are generally good proofreaders. Readers tend to admire and trust writing that is error-free. Make sure that you correct all errors in grammar, usage, spelling, and punctuation in your writing. Your readers will have more confidence in your words if you have done your best to proofread carefully.

Throughout your school and work careers, you will make speeches. Pronoun errors in speeches are particularly troublesome because listeners cannot go back and listen to the speech again. Whether your speech is short or long, take special care to proofread for correct pronoun case and references. Correct pronoun usage ensures that your ideas will get the hearing they deserve.

PROOFREADING ACTIVITY

In the following speech, find any errors in pronoun use and correct them. Use proofreading symbols such as those on page 901 of *Elements of Language* to make your corrections. You may need to rewrite some of the sentences.

Example   Is Mr. Valdez the teacher ~~whom~~ *who* is retiring?

As most of you know, Mr. Valdez is retiring this year. When Mrs. Adams asked me if I would give a speech about he and his work, I was honored. I have heard nothing but kindhearted comments about Mr. Valdez, no matter who I have asked. He has given mine fellow students and I more than respect; he has given us hope for the future. In our school yearbooks over the past twenty years, they show dozens of pictures of Mr. Valdez surrounded by a crowd of admiring students.

The photographs reminded me, as they would remind any of we students, of many lively scenes from Mr. Valdez's class. I will never forget the day Principal Huffman came to Mr. Valdez's classroom to announce that he'd won the district's Educator of the Year award. Those of you whom are seniors can remember the countless hours that Mr. Valdez has spent listening to problems and helping we to understand mathematics. Because we had the chance to experience the humor and inspiration of Mr. Valdez, you and me are extremely lucky. Thank you, Mr. Valdez.

Literary Model: Poetry

The Secret
by Denise Levertov

Two girls discover
the secret of life
in a sudden line of
poetry.

5 I who don't know the
secret write
the line. They
told me

(through a third person)
10 they had found it
but not what it was
not even

what line it was. No doubt
by now, more than a week

15 later, they have forgotten
the secret,
the line, the name of
the poem. I love them for
finding what
20 I can't find,
and for loving me
for the line I wrote,
and for forgetting it
so that
25 a thousand times, till death
finds them, they may
discover it again, in other
lines

in other
30 happenings. And for
wanting to know it,
for
assuming there is
such a secret, yes,
35 for that
most of all.

EXERCISE A

1. To whom do the pronouns *I* and *me* refer in the poem?

   _____

2. What is the antecedent of the pronouns *they* and *them*?

   _____

3. To what antecedents does the pronoun *it* refer at different points in the poem?

   _____

   _____

   _____

   _____

   _____

   _____

EXERCISE B

1. What is the effect of using *it* throughout the poem to refer to different antecedents at different times?

   _____

   _____

   _____

   _____

2. How might the ambiguity over what *it* refers to relate to the theme and title of the poem?

   _____

   _____

   _____

   _____

   _____

   _____

Literary Model (continued)

EXERCISE C Write a short poem about a secret or a mystery. Experiment with using ambiguous pronoun references to heighten the sense of not knowing what the secret or mystery is.

_____

_____

_____

_____

_____

_____

_____

_____

_____

_____

EXERCISE D

1. What kinds of unclear pronoun references did you use, and why are they unclear?

_____

_____

_____

_____

2. How did your use of ambiguous pronoun references contribute to the theme of your poem?

_____

_____

_____

3. How would your poem be different if you revised it to avoid the ambiguous pronouns?

_____

_____

_____

_____

for **CHAPTER 18: USING PRONOUNS CORRECTLY**   pages 549–65

Writing Application: Biographical Sketch

What would we do without pronouns? For one thing, we would be making statements like this: *Marsha prefers to stay in Marsha's room, but Marsha's mom wants Marsha and Marsha's sister Samantha to spend more time with the family.* Since pronouns take the place of nouns, they can eliminate instances of repetition. However, when you use pronouns in your writing, you should help out your readers by not using too many of them and by making sure that each one you use refers clearly to its antecedent.

CONFUSING   Marsha brought Samantha some flowers. As she walked through the kitchen, she smelled and admired them. They were very pretty.

CLEAR   Marsha brought Samantha some flowers. As Marsha walked through the kitchen, she smelled and admired the bouquet. The daffodils in particular were very pretty.

WRITING ACTIVITY

Which historical figure do you most admire? The person who first comes to your mind must have done so for some good reasons—considering how many historical figures you've learned about over the years. Write a biographical sketch or short essay about this person. Use a variety of pronouns (at least eight of them) as subjects, predicate nominatives, direct and indirect objects, and objects of prepositions.

PREWRITING   Consider using a time line to organize information chronologically. Since you are writing a biographical sketch or short essay, you will need to focus on a limited number of events in the person's life—preferably those that have the most significance for you. Then, increase your readers' interest level in your writing by including many attention-holding details about each event. Consult print and online encyclopedias and other reference materials to discover additional information about the person.

WRITING   After you have written an introductory paragraph, use each event as the topic sentence of a paragraph. Support the topic sentence with the details you already knew and those you learned in reference materials. Make sure that your admiration for the person is evident in your writing.

REVISING   After you have finished your draft, leave it alone for a while; then, read it aloud to yourself. Reading aloud may help you notice rough spots that could be improved. Replace any weak words with more precise ones.

PUBLISHING   Check that at least eight pronouns appear in your sketch or essay and that they are used in different positions. Be sure that each one is in the correct case and refers clearly to its antecedent. Also, check your essay for errors in spelling and punctuation. With your teacher's permission, post your essay in the classroom.

EXTENDING YOUR WRITING

You might develop this writing exercise into a longer biographical essay. Then you could collect your classmates' essays and, adding your own, create an anthology. The anthology could be presented to a middle school or elementary school library.

Choices: Exploring Modifiers

The following activities challenge you to find a connection between modifiers and the world around you. Do the activity below that suits your personality best, and then share your discoveries with your class.

VISUAL

Go with the Flow

Sometimes a picture makes everything clear. If identifying adverbs and adjectives is easy for you, consider this project. Make a flow chart detailing the steps in identifying a modifier as an adjective or an adverb. With your teacher's permission, hang your chart in the classroom.

BUILDING BACKGROUND KNOWLEDGE

There's Always an Exception

Some adverbs do not end in *–ly*. For instance, we don't say, "He ran fastly." Can you think of other adverbs that don't end in *–ly*? Brainstorm a list of these adverbs, use each one correctly in a sentence, and give everybody in the class a handout for their notebooks.

CONTEST

Just for Laughs

Misplaced modifiers are often funny, even though the writer may not have intended readers to laugh. Hold a contest to see who can write (and correct) the most hilarious misplaced modifier. You'll need a panel of judges. Make sure the winner's entry receives an award.

GROUP DEMONSTRATION

Human Flashcards

Don't worry, shy people, these are nonspeaking parts. Take one or two sentences containing one-word modifiers such as *only, just,* and *even* and prepare large flashcards for each word in the sentences. Make a special card for the one-word modifiers, perhaps using a red, not black, marker. One person holds each card, and everyone stands in sentence order in front of the class. Then, the spotlight falls on the person with the one-word modifier card. He or she gets to move around, creating different meanings and some rather strange errors.

WORD ASSOCIATION

The Best of the Best

Everybody has an opinion. Find out what your classmates' thoughts are on these topics: movies, books, fictional characters, and places to visit. Create a list of superlatives such as *funniest, coldest, happiest, most impressive,* or *most memorable.* Get into groups of four or fewer, and have each group member share his or her own idea of the most memorable place to visit, funniest movie, and so on.

WRITING

"I Before E . . ."

Do you remember that old rhyme, "*I* before *e* except after *c* . . ." It was and is a big help in spelling. Write a similar rhyme for comparisons, one that will help your classmates remember when to use the comparative form and when to use the superlative form.

ART

The Man with the Dog in the Gray Flannel Suit

Draw a cartoon illustrating your favorite misplaced modifier and, with your teacher's permission, post it in the hall where everybody can appreciate it.

GAME

Concentration

Do you remember those memory games—the ones with the cards turned face down? Here's a new twist on that old game. Write appropriate words on four groups of cards: nouns, adjectives, verbs, and adverbs. Then, lay all the cards out face down. Each player turns over two cards. If one card cannot sensibly modify the other, turn the cards back over. The player with the most matches wins.

Grammar, Usage, and Mechanics: Language Skills Practice

Modifiers

A *modifier* is a word or word group that makes the meaning of another word or word group more specific. A modifier may consist of one word, a phrase, or a clause. The two kinds of modifiers are *adjectives* and *adverbs*.

19a. An adjective makes the meaning of a noun or pronoun more specific.

19b. An adverb makes the meaning of a verb, an adjective, or another adverb more specific.

ADJECTIVES   **Waking early,** he put on **clean** clothes **that were hanging in his closet.** [The participial phrase *Waking early* modifies the pronoun *he;* the adjective *clean* modifies the noun *clothes;* the adjective clause *that were hanging in his closet* modifies the noun *clothes.*]

ADVERBS   **Before he left,** he checked his homework **very carefully.** [The adverb clause *Before he left* modifies the verb *checked;* the adverb *very* modifies the adverb *carefully;* the adverb *carefully* modifies the verb *checked.*]

EXERCISE A   Identify each underlined word or word group below by writing *ADJ* for *adjective* or *ADV* for *adverb* on the line provided.

Example   *ADV*   **1.** At the circus <u>yesterday</u> the trapeze artist walked timidly.

_____ **1.** We enjoyed the <u>silent</u> night at the cabin.

_____ **2.** The winner of the first-place trophy is smiling <u>broadly</u>.

_____ **3.** <u>Because the power went out last night</u>, my alarm clock did not wake me.

_____ **4.** That tiny frog can jump farther <u>than I would have guessed</u>.

_____ **5.** The candle <u>on the nightstand</u> has a beautiful blue design.

EXERCISE B   Identify the underlined modifiers in the paragraph below by writing above each one *ADJ* for *adjective* or *ADV* for *adverb.*

Example   Augustin Jean Fresnel is remembered **[1]** <u>for his experiments</u> **[2]** <u>that increased the</u>
                                                      ADV   ADJ

     <u>amount of light provided by lighthouses.</u>

The **[1]** <u>glass</u> parts **[2]** <u>of Fresnel lenses</u> produced a brighter light than that provided **[3]** <u>by oil</u> <u>lamps with simple reflectors.</u> **[4]** <u>As the glass parts captured lamplight</u>, they directed that light **[5]** <u>onto the "bull's-eyes"</u> at the centers of the beehive-shaped lenses. Sailors **[6]** <u>who were as far</u> <u>away as twenty miles out to sea</u> were warned quite easily **[7]** <u>about the coastline</u> that they were approaching. **[8]** <u>Before long</u>, the Fresnel lenses were made in seven sizes. The **[9]** <u>three</u> largest lens types were primarily for use in lighthouses along the seacoast. **[10]** <u>For harbor or bay areas</u>, the smaller lens sizes were more suitable.

One-Word Modifiers

19a. An adjective makes the meaning of a noun or pronoun more specific.

EXAMPLES **Only** you have seen **those rare** birds here. [The adjective *Only* makes the meaning of the pronoun *you* more specific, and the adjectives *those* and *rare* make the meaning of the noun *birds* more specific.]

19b. An adverb makes the meaning of a verb, an adjective, or another adverb more specific.

EXAMPLES Did**n't** the birds work **diligently** to build a nest that was large? [The adverb *not* (*–n't*) makes the meaning of the verb *Did work* more specific; the adverb *diligently* makes the meaning of the verb *Did work* more specific.]

EXERCISE A Identify each underlined word below by writing *ADJ* for *adjective* or *ADV* for *adverb* on the line provided.

Example __*ADJ*__ **1.** noisy toy

_____ **1.** brave woman

_____ **2.** joyously cheered

_____ **3.** gave generously

_____ **4.** proud parent

_____ **5.** most brilliant color

EXERCISE B In the sentences below, underline each adjective once and each adverb twice. Do not include the articles *a, an,* and *the.*

Example 1. Didn't you ever find your numbered, signed copy of that unusual book?

1. *The Diary of a Sparrow* reminds us to recognize the most ordinary people.

2. Enji, a grandfather of Kazuko Watanabe, kept a diary for nearly seventy years.

3. In this outstanding book, Watanabe excerpts eight compelling events about Enji.

4. How did Enji first react to the surprising voices and music on the "sound-making" box?

5. He must surely have felt amazed when he saw the first Japanese airplane fly in 1911!

6. Enji clearly depicts the unprecedented development and prosperity of the early 1900s.

7. Many readers could readily understand the terrible pain of losing a son in World War II.

8. Ms. Watanabe has skillfully provided the English translation of the Japanese text in the diary.

9. Appropriately, abstract illustrations by Watanabe accompany the hand-printed stories.

10. Read the book in the traditional manner or, optionally, view it as three-dimensional art.

Adjective or Adverb?

While many adverbs end in –*ly*, others do not. Furthermore, not all words with the –*ly* ending are adverbs. Some adjectives also end in –*ly*. To decide whether a word is an adjective or an adverb, determine how the word is used.

| ADJECTIVES | I may be **late**. | This is a **fast** train. |
| ADVERBS | I may arrive **late**. | This train goes **fast**. |

19c. If a word in the predicate modifies the subject of the verb, use the adjective form. If it modifies the verb, use the adverb form.

| ADJECTIVES | Teresa was **angry**. | The children seemed **happy**. |
| ADVERBS | Teresa shouted **angrily**. | The children played **happily**. |

EXERCISE A   In the following sentences, determine whether the adjective or adverb form should be used. Then, underline the correct form of the word in parentheses.

Example 1. During the children's birthday party, the clown danced (*happy*, *happily*).

1. One of the children asked (*loud*, *loudly*) if the clown was going to sing.

2. The children laughed when the clown pretended to be (*angry*, *angrily*).

3. The awkward clown had just tripped (*clumsy*, *clumsily*) over a teddy bear.

4. It was very (*humorous*, *humorously*) when he blamed the teddy bear.

5. The children giggled (*excited*, *excitedly*) when the clown made his dramatic exit.

EXERCISE B   In the following sentences, underline all adjectives once and adverbs twice. Then, draw an arrow from each adjective or adverb to the word or words that it modifies. Do not include the articles *a*, *an*, and *the*.

Example 1. Today, Chen could hardly wait to describe the new job assignment.

6. Tomorrow, Chen begins a different part-time job at the skating rink.

7. He will work nightly during the week and on some weekends.

8. Initially, Chen will skate behind the ice-resurfacing machine to check for problem areas.

9. Various repairs will again smooth the chipped, pockmarked surface of the skating rink.

10. If Chen does this tedious job well, he will eventually earn greater responsibilities.

11. He may even be allowed to operate the huge resurfacing machine.

12. Under a large cover, a blade precisely scrapes a thin layer of ice up onto spinning conveyors.

13. Meanwhile, water jets flush dirt and other debris toward a vacuum hose.

14. The dirty water will be filtered to be reused on the skating-rink surface.

15. Other jets send out hot water that is spread over the icy surface by a large towel.

Phrases Used as Modifiers

Like one-word modifiers, phrases can also be used as adjectives and adverbs.

ADJECTIVES   **Filmed overseas,** the movie **about the Civil War** was the one **to watch.** [The participial phrase *Filmed overseas* and the prepositional phrase *about the Civil War* both modify the noun *movie*. The infinitive *to watch* modifies the pronoun *one*.]

ADVERBS   **During the last month,** Helen has taken her little sister **to see three movies.** [The prepositional phrase *During the last month* and the infinitive phrase *to see three movies* both modify the verb *has taken*.]

EXERCISE A   In the following sentences, underline each adjective phrase and adverb phrase. Then, draw an arrow to the word or word group that each adjective phrase or adverb phrase modifies.

Example 1. My friend Callie rents old movies to watch over and over.

1. She knows by heart all the lyrics from songs in *Showboat.*

2. Do you enjoy old movies in black and white?

3. The ones to see for humorous antics are the films with Charlie Chaplin.

4. Because of special effects, movies can include almost any setting or character.

5. See how the director used color highlights to emphasize the black-and-white setting.

6. The setting looks artistic enough to be a painting.

7. A number of films use clouds or fog to set the stage for a person's dream.

8. Behind the actors, the scaled-down model of a town created a mood.

9. Computer graphics have added flexibility to the range of special effects.

10. For some roles, actors might require several hours to put on their costumes and makeup.

EXERCISE B   On the lines provided, write an adjective phrase or an adverb phrase to complete each of the following sentences.

Example 1. Actors rehearse many hours *to make the scenes believable* .

11. Isabel watched that film again _____.

12. The plot was very difficult _____.

13. Some writers are good _____.

14. _____, writers may have to rewrite the script many times.

15. What is your favorite movie _____?

Clauses Used as Modifiers

Like words and phrases, clauses can also be used as adjectives and adverbs.

ADJECTIVE   A factory **that was built in the state of Sonora in Mexico** resulted in better jobs for the Choctaws of Mississippi. [The adjective clause *that was built in the state of Sonora in Mexico* modifies the noun *factory*.]

ADVERB   **Since he became chief executive of tribal business,** Chief Philip Martin has brought jobs to the reservation and encouraged development more successfully **than anyone had before.** [The adverb clause *Since he became chief executive of tribal business* modifies the verb *has brought*. The adverb clause *than anyone had before* modifies the adverb *successfully*.]

EXERCISE A   Underline the adjective or adverb clause in each of the following sentences. Then, identify the clause by writing above it *ADJ* for *adjective* or *ADV* for *adverb*.

Example 1. The crew reviewed the weather conditions ADV before they left for the launch pad.

1. Ruby memorized the poem, which was forty lines long.

2. As soon as we can after the banquet, Al and I will fold up the chairs and tables.

3. Mr. Kendall described the chemical mixture that had caused the rotten-egg smell.

4. We'll have room to grow pumpkins if we add two more loads of dirt to the garden.

5. Of the chores that were on Mom's list, Tara has finished all except one.

6. She stayed at the library until she grew tired.

7. Because the directions were unclear, we couldn't follow them.

8. The vegetarian dishes cooked more quickly than the meat dishes did.

9. After he finished his five-mile run, Jacob took a long nap.

10. When we arrived at the park, all of the picnic areas had been claimed.

EXERCISE B   Identify each underlined clause in the sentences below as an adjective clause or an adverb clause. In the blank before each sentence, write *ADJ* for *adjective clause* or *ADV* for *adverb clause*.

Example _ADJ_ **1.** She sang a beautiful song that brought tears to our eyes.

_____ **11.** Anyone who has a paintbrush may begin working.

_____ **12.** Because she entered so silently, no one noticed her.

_____ **13.** The older cat purred more loudly than the kitten did.

_____ **14.** The magazine that you lent me is quite interesting.

_____ **15.** Numerous musicians who play the violin attended the show.

Phrases and Clauses Used as Modifiers

Like one-word modifiers, both phrases and clauses may be used as adjectives and adverbs.

ADJECTIVE **Working by himself,** Jake set the timer **on the sprinkler system we had installed.**
[The participial phrase *Working by himself* modifies the noun *Jake.* The prepositional phrase *on the sprinkler system we had installed* modifies the noun *timer.* The
clause *we had installed* modifies the noun *system.*]

ADVERB **After Virginia won the race,** she stood **in the shade** and rested **to catch her breath.**
[The clause *After Virginia won the race* modifies the verbs *stood* and *rested.* The
prepositional phrase *in the shade* modifies the verb *stood.* The infinitive phrase *to
catch her breath* modifies the verbs *stood* and *rested.*]

EXERCISE In the sentences below, identify each underlined phrase or clause by writing above it *ADJ
phrase, ADJ clause, ADV phrase,* or *ADV clause.*

Example 1. Ships following the east-west shipping lanes use the Panama Canal <u>to shorten their</u>
                                                                                 ADV phrase

trips.

1. The Panama Canal is an essential structure because the canal is necessary <u>to allow ships easy

passage between oceans.</u>

2. <u>Depending on traffic patterns</u>, varying amounts of time are needed to travel through the canal.

3. Opened in 1914, the canal takes ships through a series <u>of locks.</u>

4. The entire lock system, <u>which joins Colón and Panama City</u>, includes two lakes.

5. Each lake, Gatun and Miraflores, has the same name as the lock <u>next to it</u> does.

6. Almost at the midpoint <u>of the 50-mile-long canal</u> is the Galliard Cut.

7. Any ship <u>that is larger than 106 feet wide and 965 feet long</u> cannot navigate the canal.

8. <u>When the canal was run as a nonprofit utility</u>, it was successful.

9. Operation of the canal is complicated enough <u>to allow for numerous employment

opportunities.</u>

10. The canal is expensive to maintain, so profits from tariffs are essential <u>to keep the canal in

good condition.</u>

USAGE

Bad and Badly, Good and Well

Bad is an adjective. In most uses, *badly* is an adverb. *Good* is an adjective and should not be used to modify a verb. *Well* may be used either as an adjective or as an adverb. As an adjective, *well* has two meanings: "in good health" and "satisfactory." As an adverb, *well* means "capably."

EXAMPLES   The test results were **bad.**   Honi slept **badly** last night.

That was a **good** effort.   Is the poem **good**?

Carrie did **well** on her test.   Isn't Zina feeling **well** this morning?

EXERCISE   Underline the form of the modifier in parentheses that is correct according to the rules of standard, formal English.

Example 1. We had set out for the campsite before the weather looked (<u>bad</u>, *badly*).

1. My aunt and uncle had prepared (*good, well*) for the hike through the hills.

2. They didn't want anyone coming back (*bad, badly*) sunburned.

3. Whether I could set up camp (*good, well*) or not, hiking in the fresh air was relaxing.

4. "How (*bad, badly*) do we want to hike in this breeze?" I asked.

5. My uncle said that it feels (*good, well*) to hike when there's a breeze.

6. Aunt Lucy said, "With weather this gorgeous, no one's mood could be (*bad, badly*)."

7. I had brought old boots, but they didn't feel too (*bad, badly*) on my feet.

8. Actually, the boots helped me hike (*good, well*) on rocky parts of the trail.

9. My uncle had a map of the area that was drawn (*bad, badly*).

10. Fortunately, he knew the hills quite (*good, well*).

11. There were numerous trails, some of which were marked (*good, well*).

12. It was a (*good, well*) thing that I was learning about camping.

13. I felt that I was not doing too (*bad, badly*) at putting up the tent.

14. Because we shared the chores, we had time to rest (*good, well*) before cooking supper.

15. We couldn't see (*good, well*) enough by the firelight to notice the change in the clouds.

16. No one knew how (*bad, badly*) I wanted to tell my favorite ghost story.

17. A (*good, well*) blast of cool air and a few drops of rain sent us rushing into our tents.

18. Outside, the thunder and rain made the storm seem (*bad, badly*).

19. Because of the sound of the rain, I didn't sleep very (*good, well*).

20. Even so, I felt (*good, well*) when I woke up and saw the sunshine.

USAGE

Slow and Slowly, Real and Really

Slow is used as both an adjective and an adverb. *Slowly* is an adverb. In most adverb uses, it is better to use *slowly* than to use *slow*.

EXAMPLES   A **slow** wave rolled onto the beach.   The log drifted **slowly** in the sea.

Real is an adjective meaning "actual" or "genuine." *Really* is an adverb meaning "actually" or "truly."

EXAMPLES   Are you a **real** professional athlete?   She dribbled the ball **really** fast.

EXERCISE   Some of the sentences below have a form of modifier that is incorrect according to the rules of formal, standard English. If the form of a modifier is incorrect, cross it out and write the correct form above it. If a sentence has no errors, write *C* to the left of the numeral.

Example 1. How ~~slow~~ *slowly* do you scroll the images on your computer screen?

1. As we launched the sailboat, the wind blew really hard.

2. Devon won a slow game of chess against me.

3. The marathon runner crossed the finish line real quickly.

4. Did you notice how slow the water was flowing from that pipe?

5. Is it real difficult to locate a gardening expert?

6. That is a real good remedy for someone who is airsick.

7. During the movie, Derek got up slowly and left.

8. I had no idea that the traffic on this route to work was going to move this slow.

9. You need to know that this job requires real attention to detail.

10. Would you please drive slow as we pass the front of that shop?

11. Bess noticed that the birds flew real high above the canyon.

12. Fran painted the office while business was moving slow at the hardware store.

13. For the real answer to your question, we will need to check an encyclopedia.

14. Gerald always completes his assignments slow but thoroughly.

15. The posse slow moved through the blustery storm.

16. Her tennis skills were really improving.

17. Because of the holidays, this package will be delivered more slow than usual.

18. The diamond sparkled real nicely in the sunlight.

19. Eric sauntered slow into the dark room.

20. Does this train seem slow to you?

Eight Troublesome Modifiers

A word that modifies a noun or pronoun should be in *adjective* form. A word that modifies a verb, an adjective, or another adverb should be in *adverb* form.

ADJECTIVES	ADVERBS
Our trip got off to a **bad** start.	Our trip began **badly.**
The **good** doctor said I was **well.**	I should do **well** on that test today.
We played the video in **slow** motion.	Look first; then, back up **slowly.**
The **real** picture seems clearer.	Do we expect to hike **really** far?

EXERCISE Some of the sentences below have a form of modifier that is incorrect according to the rules of formal, standard English. If the form of a modifier is incorrect, cross it out and write the correct form above it. If a sentence has no errors, write *C* at the beginning of the sentence.

Example 1. Did her tears in the play seem ~~real~~ *really* convincing to you?

1. Theo threw the ball bad, but it still went into the hoop.

2. Our car came to a slow stop after the engine quit running.

3. Before adding the liquid ingredients, mix these together good.

4. How good did Arlo sing during the choir tryouts?

5. The computerized image of the lion looked real frightening.

6. Please explain why the milk tasted badly if it looked just fine.

7. Rain fell quite slow, soaking everything thoroughly.

8. Look for real juice when buying snacks for the children.

9. Watching cartoons interfered very bad with my homework.

10. Justine was surprised that her batting average was so good.

11. Moving at a slow pace, the snail eventually reached its destination.

12. Harry thought Denise's suggestion was real excellent.

13. What a good route this will be once the bridge is finished!

14. Marta put a picture of a real mouse beside her computer mouse.

15. Does that pace seem too slowly for this kind of relay?

16. The story she told was a good one.

17. Did I speak slow enough?

18. They did reasonably good on the exam.

19. Is the movie good enough to recommend?

20. I ate too much bread, and my stomach felt badly for a few minutes.

Regular Comparison

19d. Modifiers change form to show comparison.

POSITIVE	COMPARATIVE	SUPERLATIVE
quickly	more quickly	most quickly

USAGE

EXERCISE Complete the following chart by filling in the two missing forms for each given modifier. (Do not include decreasing comparisons.)

Example	Positive	Comparative	Superlative
1.	fast	faster	fastest

	Positive	Comparative	Superlative
1.	_____	_____	largest
2.	early	_____	_____
3.	_____	more popular	_____
4.	_____	fewer	_____
5.	_____	_____	most famous
6.	numerous	_____	_____
7.	_____	_____	clearest
8.	_____	_____	most mountainous
9.	_____	warmer	_____
10.	frequently	_____	_____
11.	pretty	_____	_____
12.	_____	more intense	_____
13.	beautiful	_____	_____
14.	_____	_____	most intelligent
15.	_____	more patient	_____
16.	_____	_____	most expensive
17.	cheap	_____	_____
18.	_____	_____	most talented
19.	_____	_____	funniest
20.	_____	more magnificent	_____

USAGE

Irregular Comparison

The comparative and superlative degrees of some modifiers are irregular in form.

POSITIVE	COMPARATIVE	SUPERLATIVE
bad	worse	worst
good	better	best
well	better	best
many	more	most
much	more	most
far	farther/further	farthest/furthest
little	less	least

EXERCISE Underline the correct form of the modifier in parentheses.

Example 1. Eric took (*littler, less*) time to give his report than I did.

1. Justin's tree has the (*most, mostest*) peaches.

2. The results were (*more bad, worse*) than we had expected.

3. Cara was obviously the (*most good, best*) runner on the team.

4. You bought (*more, manier*) clothes today than I bought all year!

5. Who has (*less, more little*) homework, you or Tim?

6. Of the three carpet samples, I liked the soft one the (*most good, best*).

7. Sara is feeling (*weller, better*) than she has in some time.

8. That color looks even (*worse, badder*) in daylight!

9. I was willing to carry the argument (*more far, further*) than he was.

10. We raised far (*more, mucher*) money this year than last.

11. What is the (*most little, least*) amount you could expect to pay?

12. Sami ran the (*most far, farthest*) of all of us.

13. After I took the medicine, I felt (*more bad, worse*) than I had before.

14. I think the blue corn chips are (*better, gooder*) than the yellow.

15. I have seen (*gooder, better*) illustrations in other books.

16. She drove (*farther, more far*) than the rest of us.

17. Does the squash dish taste (*better, more good*) than the spinach?

18. Which of the two clarinets is the (*most little, least*) expensive?

19. She understood the play (*better, more well*) than I did.

20. Boris played his (*baddest, worst*) game ever last week.

USAGE

Regular and Irregular Comparison A

19d. Modifiers change form to show comparison.

POSITIVE	COMPARATIVE	SUPERLATIVE
calm	calmer	calmest
quiet	quieter	quietest
decidedly	more decidedly	most decidedly
bad	worse	worst
far	further/farther	furthest/farthest
good/well	better	best
little	less	least

EXERCISE A In each sentence below, a modifier is underlined. Above the modifier, write *P* if it is the *positive* form, *C* if it is *comparative*, or *S* if it is *superlative*.

_C_
Example 1. Please put the <u>older</u> books on the shelf.

1. That plant has the <u>greenest</u> leaves of all the plants in the garden.

2. Walt arrived at the drama club meeting <u>early</u>, as he had planned.

3. The <u>sooner</u> you can get here, the more we will be able to get finished.

4. Give the name <u>most commonly</u> used to refer to this orange and black butterfly.

5. Bermuda grass is a tougher and <u>better</u> grass for the lawns in our climate.

EXERCISE B In each sentence below, a modifier is underlined. If the form of the modifier is incorrect, write the correct form above it. If it is already correct, write *C* above it.

worse
Example 1. When he got up, Benjamin felt <u>badder</u> than when he had gone to bed.

6. Yoshi shined the <u>brightest</u> of the spotlights on the actors at center stage.

7. This bicycle helmet offers <u>more good</u> protection than the old model did.

8. What was the <u>most bad</u> grade you have ever gotten on an essay?

9. Of all my friends, Phil and Ann stayed the <u>latest</u> to clean up after the party.

10. Modern science fiction movies have <u>gooder</u> special effects than early movies did.

11. Yesterday's tornado was the <u>baddest</u> of any we have seen this season.

12. We must be <u>quieter</u> so the groups around us can finish their work.

13. Lori is the <u>most good</u> three-point shooter on the basketball team.

14. Stephen felt much <u>more well</u> after he had a nap.

15. The only thing <u>worser</u> for a picnic than rain is an invasion of ants.

Regular and Irregular Comparison B

19d. Modifiers change form to show comparison.

POSITIVE	COMPARATIVE	SUPERLATIVE
short	shorter	shortest
sudden	more sudden	most sudden
excitable	less excitable	least excitable
bad	worse	worst
many/much	more	least
little	less	least

EXERCISE A Identify the form of each underlined modifier in the sentences below by writing above it *P* for *positive,* *C* for *comparative,* or *S* for *superlative.*

Example 1. She was known for being the $\overset{S}{\underline{quietest}}$ student in class.

1. Please cross out the <u>worst</u> example on the list.

2. Of the two answers, which one seems <u>worse</u>?

3. The new sewing machine is <u>quieter</u> than the old one.

4. She wondered if the speaker were the <u>least knowledgeable</u> person in the room.

5. If he does <u>well</u> on the exam, he won't have to retake it.

EXERCISE B On the lines provided, write the correct form of the word shown to the left of each sentence.

Example 1. comparative of *friendly*   This clerk is _____*friendlier*_____ than that one.

6. superlative of *generous*   Of the three, Suki was the _____.

7. comparative of *heavy*   These sacks are _____ than they were Friday.

8. superlative of *unusual*   Sam's tale was the _____ I've ever heard.

9. superlative of *long*   The reticulated python is the _____ of all snakes.

10. superlative of *good*   Of all the fruits, the melons look _____.

11. comparative of *favorable*   Tuesday's results were _____ than last week's.

12. superlative of *tall*   Alex is the _____ of my three brothers.

13. comparative of *well*   Aaron danced _____ than the others.

14. comparative of *slowly*   The tortoise moved _____ than the hare.

15. superlative of *bad*   That was the _____ movie I have ever seen.

USAGE

Using Comparative and Superlative Forms A

19e. Use the comparative degree when comparing two things. Use the superlative degree when comparing more than two.

    COMPARATIVE   Artist Henry Ossawa Tanner is **more famous** now than he was a decade ago.

    SUPERLATIVE   One of Tanner's **most famous** works shows a banjo lesson.

19f. Include the word *other* or *else* when comparing one member of a group with the rest of the group.

    EXAMPLE   My cousin Jack is taller than anyone **else** in the family.

EXERCISE Rewrite the following sentences to correct errors in the use of modifiers.

Example 1. The silk dress in the corner is softer than any dress in the store. *The silk dress in the corner is softer than any other dress in the store.*

1. I finished with a higher grade than any student in our class. _____

_____

2. Of the two pairs of sneakers, the red ones are best. _____

_____

3. In ancient Rome, a mile was shortest than it is today. _____

_____

4. The day I broke my arm has to be the worse day of my life. _____

_____

5. The moon is closer to earth than any object in our solar system. _____

_____

6. That actor sounded more convincing than anyone on the stage. _____

_____

7. Of all the stories in the collection, I find this one more interesting. _____

_____

8. Which one of the pair is largest? _____

_____

9. Of the two, Milo writes letters most frequently. _____

_____

10. Of the four colors, this one is better. _____

_____

Using Comparative and Superlative Forms B

19g. Avoid using double comparisons.

> **NONSTANDARD** This is the most deepest cave in the area.
> **STANDARD** This is the **deepest** cave in the area.

19h. Be sure your comparisons are clear.

> **UNCLEAR** Leon's bike is newer than Monty.
> **CLEAR** Leon's bike is newer than **Monty's** [bike].

EXERCISE Rewrite the following sentences to correct errors in the use of modifiers.

Example 1. Doug's joke was sillier than Helena. *Doug's joke was sillier than Helena's.*

_____

1. The mushroom is more smaller than the leaves around it. _____

_____

2. We saw pictures of the most hugest type of frog, called the Goliath frog. _____

_____

3. My mother's soup tastes better than the restaurant. _____

_____

4. I think the flag of South Korea has one of the most prettiest designs of any flag. _____

_____

5. Thai food is spicier than Germany. _____

_____

6. The most longest mountain chain in the world is the Andes. _____

_____

7. My neighbor's yard is better maintained than David. _____

_____

8. An Alaskan summer night is longer than Florida. _____

_____

9. Venus looks more brighter than any other planet. _____

_____

10. My grandmother's paintings are more abstract than my aunt. _____

_____

Using Comparative and Superlative Forms C

19e. Use the comparative degree when comparing two things. Use the superlative degree when comparing more than two.

19f. Include the word *other* or *else* when comparing one member of a group with the rest of the group.

19g. Avoid using double comparisons.

19h. Be sure your comparisons are clear.

USAGE

EXERCISE Rewrite each of the following sentences to correct any errors in comparison.

Example 1. The Italian temple was built before French.   *The Italian temple was built before the*
French temple.

1. She likes spinach more than her sister. _____

_____

2. Janice's skates are more expensive than Andrea. _____

_____

3. This clock is the most loudest in the house. _____

_____

4. Is Dr. Kean more knowledgeable than any doctor? _____

_____

5. Of Maria and her sister, Maria has always been the fastest runner. _____

_____

6. My aunt writes me more than my cousin. _____

_____

7. The temperature is more warmer than it was yesterday. _____

_____

8. The table is sturdier than any table in the room. _____

_____

9. Franco is taller than any boy on his team. _____

_____

10. Bootsie was the most smallest kitten in the litter. _____

_____

Grammar, Usage, and Mechanics: Language Skills Practice

Correcting Dangling Modifiers

19i. Avoid using dangling modifiers.

A modifying word, phrase, or clause that does not clearly and sensibly modify a word or a word group in a sentence is a *dangling modifier*.

DANGLING   To prevent fires, these rules are important. [Rules cannot prevent fires.]

CORRECT   To prevent fires, follow these important rules. [The understood subject, you, can prevent fires.]

EXERCISE   Most of the sentences below have dangling modifiers. If a sentence has a dangling modifier, rewrite the sentence to correct it. If a sentence is already correct, write *C* on the line provided.

Example 1. Approaching the house, the smell of fresh-baked bread is inviting. *Approaching the house, we found the smell of fresh-baked bread inviting.*

1. Looking up, the large umbrella blocked the sun. _____

_____

2. Researching the rain forest, the huge variety of trees and animals becomes apparent. _____

_____

3. Unexplored for years, the scientists are now making discoveries. _____

_____

4. Finding many trees in one area, an important discovery was made. _____

_____

5. Using cranes and climbing ropes, scientists study the tops of the trees. _____

_____

6. Full of insects, the researchers study many life forms. _____

_____

7. Buzzing and humming, we learned how the nests are made. _____

_____

8. Sinking its roots into a branch, a mistletoe plant grows high above the ground. _____

_____

9. Understanding just part of the rain forest, something becomes clear. _____

_____

10. To avoid destroying this sea of life, the rain forest must be protected. _____

_____

USAGE

Correcting Misplaced Modifiers

| **19j.** | Avoid using misplaced modifiers. |

A word, phrase, or clause that seems to modify the wrong word or word group in a sentence is a *misplaced modifier.*

MISPLACED   Lying in the middle of the road, I saw a large snake.

CORRECT   I saw a large snake lying in the middle of the road.

MISPLACED   The report is lying on my kitchen table that was due today.

CORRECT   The report that was due today is lying on my kitchen table.

EXERCISE Most of the sentences below contain misplaced modifiers. If a sentence has a misplaced modifier, revise the sentence to correct it. Circle each word group you are moving, and insert a caret (∧) to show where the word group belongs. If a sentence is already correct, write *C* at the end of the sentence.

Example 1. (Landing in a field,) I saw a huge hawk ∧ near the school.

1. We looked for the map in the back of the car that we needed.

2. An elm fell across the house that had been uprooted in the storm.

3. We saw a raccoon coming home from the movies.

4. The sapling in front of the window was growing rapidly.

5. We saw the Taj Mahal looking down from an airplane.

6. I bought a book at that store that describes the history of the Alamo.

7. While riding on the train, Christina did her homework.

8. The keys that she found belonged to her brother under the hedge.

9. My briefcase, which is full of books, is standing by the door.

10. My aunt served fish to Melvin and me broiled over hot coals.

11. To avoid driving through heavy traffic, the subway can help you.

12. The azalea belongs to my neighbor, which blooms early in the spring.

13. The deer looked at me with white spots.

14. Yolanda bought the shoes with the high heels.

15. Alice picked up the puppy with a grin.

16. The socks were knitted by my grandmother in the crib.

17. On the windowsill, I watched my cat sleep.

18. The mother went to pick up her son wearing her nurse's uniform.

19. While walking along the beach, I spotted a beautiful seashell.

20. The cat nibbled on the plant with long whiskers.

USAGE

Correcting Dangling and Misplaced Modifiers A

19i. Avoid using dangling modifiers.

DANGLING	The rainbow vanished, driving into the sunset. [Was the rainbow driving?]
CORRECT	The rainbow vanished **as we drove into the sunset.**

19j. Avoid using misplaced modifiers.

MISPLACED	Trees shaded the stroller that had long branches. [Did the stroller have long branches?]
CORRECT	Trees **that had long branches** shaded the stroller.

EXERCISE Rewrite each sentence below to correct the dangling or misplaced modifier.

Example 1. Even in first grade, ballet fascinated her. *Even when she was in first grade, ballet fascinated her.*

1. Removing the wrapping paper, the gift proved delightful. _____

_____

2. Hidden in the drawer, Hans found the notebook. _____

_____

3. Nancy washed and polished the car along with her sister. _____

_____

4. Alone, the lightning frightened him. _____

_____

5. Color-coded, Mark studied the map of the island. _____

_____

6. While preparing for a test, reading and reviewing notes will help. _____

_____

7. Bees are attracted to certain flowers that make honey. _____

_____

8. As a young boy, botany was interesting. _____

_____

9. To have a suggestion accepted, thorough understanding of a situation is essential. _____

_____

10. Gina searched the shelf for a magazine that was cluttered. _____

_____

ELEMENTS OF LANGUAGE | Third Course

Correcting Dangling and Misplaced Modifiers B

19i. Avoid using dangling modifiers.

> **DANGLING** Driving toward our house, our dog got excited. [Was the dog driving?]
> **CORRECT** Our dog got excited **while we were driving toward our house.**

19j. Avoid using misplaced modifiers.

> **MISPLACED** She poured the stew into a bowl that was tasty. [Was the bowl tasty?]
> **CORRECT** She poured the stew **that was tasty into a bowl.**

EXERCISE Rewrite each of the following sentences to correct the dangling or misplaced modifier.

Example 1. The horse was chosen by the photographer with the silvery mane and white tail.

The horse with the silvery mane and white tail was chosen by the photographer.

1. The village had become a favorite spot for tourists surrounded by mountains. _____

_____

2. Hiking in the woods, the squirrel scurried up a tree. _____

_____

3. Having mostly melted, we walked through the snow. _____

_____

4. Hopping about excitedly, I videotaped the kangaroos. _____

_____

5. The silver cups were a gift from my nephew in the cabinet. _____

_____

6. Without a care in the world, the tree was climbed. _____

_____

7. Blouses should be taken to the dry cleaner made of silk. _____

_____

8. Frightened, the door opened slowly. _____

_____

9. The art teacher painted the kitten who teaches senior art classes. _____

_____

10. Having finished supper, the dishes were washed. _____

_____

Review A: **Comparative and Superlative Forms**

USAGE

EXERCISE A   On the lines provided, write the comparative and superlative forms of each of the following modifiers. Do not include forms showing decreasing comparisons.

Example 1. bad   *worse, worst* _____

1. good   _____

2. closely   _____

3. rich   _____

4. useful   _____

5. many   _____

6. disgusted   _____

7. little   _____

8. systematic   _____

9. tightly   _____

10. strong   _____

EXERCISE B   For each of the following sentences, identify the form of the underlined modifier by writing above it *P* for *positive, C* for *comparative,* or *S* for *superlative.*

Example 1. He is as s̲m̲a̲r̲t̲ as his brother.

11. Some people thought the photograph of the dancer was m̲o̲r̲e̲ ̲b̲e̲a̲u̲t̲i̲f̲u̲l̲ than the painting of the landscape.

12. Our new mayor works h̲a̲r̲d̲, doesn't he?

13. It rains in Hawaii m̲o̲r̲e̲ ̲o̲f̲t̲e̲n̲ than anywhere else in the country.

14. Connie can still run f̲a̲s̲t̲e̲r̲ than Stephan.

15. That was the l̲o̲v̲e̲l̲i̲e̲s̲t̲ music I had ever heard.

16. These were the h̲i̲g̲h̲e̲s̲t̲ grades she made all year.

17. She was the s̲t̲r̲o̲n̲g̲e̲s̲t̲ rower on the team.

18. The dress is d̲a̲r̲k̲e̲r̲ than I had expected.

19. The violinist was t̲a̲l̲e̲n̲t̲e̲d̲, according to her colleagues.

20. Are these curtains p̲r̲e̲t̲t̲i̲e̲r̲ than the old ones?

Review B: Correcting Errors in Comparison

USAGE

EXERCISE Each of the sentences below contains an incorrect modifier. Cross out each incorrect modifier, and write the correct modifier above it. Hint: If the only correction needed is adding a missing word, place a caret (∧) where the word belongs, and then write the missing word above the caret.

                larger   *other*

Example 1. Is Texas ~~more larger~~ than any ∧ state in the Union?

1. Who is tallest, you or Arlon?

2. Our city park is much more cleaner than most of the parks in neighboring towns.

3. Which of the two high schools in your town is the largest?

4. My sister Marita is taller than anybody in my family.

5. I think I did worser on the first half of the test than on the second half.

6. Alaska is bigger than any U.S. state.

7. Which do you like best, a warm climate or a cold climate?

8. My hometown is prettier than any town its size in the entire state.

9. Which is the highest waterfall, Niagara or Yosemite?

10. The Grand Canyon is larger than any gorge in the United States.

11. To make our trip more easier, we got suitcases with wheels on them.

12. Her dog was much more calmer than mine.

13. Ana loves movies more than Marco.

14. The ice dancer was almost a foot taller than anyone in the show.

15. Of the two colleges, I will choose the most reputable.

16. My brother offered me more advice than Frank.

17. Some people thought that the princess was oldest than the prince.

18. Which of the twins is the most talented in dramatic arts?

19. The soprano's solo was more beautiful than all the solos presented.

20. Paula likes the dog more than her brother.

21. He tells me stories more often than Todd.

22. The people of this town are more friendlier than I had expected.

23. Who is the taller of all the boys on the team?

24. The village is the most smallest in the vicinity.

25. Katya sends me gifts more frequently than Marta.

for **CHAPTER 19: USING MODIFIERS CORRECTLY**   *pages 585–89*

Review C: **Correcting Dangling and Misplaced Modifiers**

USAGE

EXERCISE   Rewrite each of the following sentences to correct a misplaced or dangling modifier.

Example 1. At the age of six, my father decided that I was ready for my first camping trip.

When I was six, my father decided that I was ready for my first camping trip.

1. The campers watched the sunrise peacefully eating their breakfast. _____

_____

2. Seated in armchairs in front of their television sets, the problems of world leaders may look

simple to some people. _____

_____

3. A gift basket was carried into the living room that was filled to the top with fancy cheeses and

crackers. _____

_____

4. Sewing a hem in the dress, the needle broke. _____

_____

5. The police chief issued a warning to homeowners who carelessly leave their doors unlocked

about burglars. _____

_____

6. After climbing the mountain, a shooting star streaked across the sky. _____

_____

7. Circling the field, the women in the control tower watched the plane. _____

_____

8. Always check your work after you have finished for accuracy. _____

_____

9. Skating gracefully over the ice, the camera zoomed in. _____

_____

10. Some books in the school library seem surprisingly up-to-date that were written many years

ago. _____

_____

Review D: **Modifiers**

EXERCISE A Rewrite the following sentences to correct problems in the use of modifiers.

Example 1. Having fallen asleep, the television remained on. *Having fallen asleep, he was unaware that the television remained on.*

1. At the awards ceremony, the coach congratulated the soccer team for playing a real good season. _____

2. Franklin hoped the weather would not get more worse. _____

3. My mother assigned me more chores than my father. _____

4. Emily had read more books than anyone in her class. _____

5. Bandit seemed to be the faster of the three dogs. _____

EXERCISE B Rewrite each of the following sentences to correct the misplaced or dangling modifier.

6. The helicopter was used in the emergency rescue of three injured people that Georgina's uncle owned. _____

7. Roaming around the department store, a vase fell off a high shelf. _____

8. Noted for its plumage, the bird-watcher identified a rare species. _____

9. Tied securely to the boat, she handed him the anchor. _____

10. A lecturer described the development of written language to a fascinated audience in the ancient Near East. _____

Grammar, Usage, and Mechanics: Language Skills Practice

213

for **CHAPTER 19: USING MODIFIERS CORRECTLY** pages 572–89

Proofreading Application: Evaluation

Good writers are generally good proofreaders. Readers tend to admire writing that is error-free. Make sure that you correct all errors in grammar, usage, spelling, and punctuation in your writing. Your readers will have more confidence in your words if you have done your best to proofread carefully.

Whenever you make evaluations and comparisons, you use modifiers—adjectives and adverbs. If you don't use modifiers correctly, your readers may have trouble figuring out what they modify. Proofreading your modifiers will help you to communicate more effectively.

You can help your peers improve their writing by evaluating the content, organization, and usage in their writing. Make sure your evaluation uses modifiers correctly.

PROOFREADING ACTIVITY

In the following peer evaluation, find the errors in the use of modifiers and correct them. Use proofreading symbols such as those on page 901 of *Elements of Language* to make your corrections. If an item is already correct, write *C* above the item number.

Example **[1]** The writer's punctuation needs improvement ∧ bad.
                                                                              badly

[1] Overall, this opinion paper makes its point well. [2] Writing clearly and concisely, the thesis statement expresses the paper's content. [3] Another strong point is the description of works that were painted by Picasso in the opening paragraph. [4] The body of the paper is arranged logically, though a chronological order may have been more better. [5] Unfortunately, the emotional appeal in the conclusion was not as effective as in the introduction.

[6] Thinking back over the paper, the thing that impressed me most was my classmate's vocabulary. [7] This author seems to have a larger vocabulary than anyone in the class. [8] However, I had to read slow whenever I came across an unfamiliar word. [9] Some of the technical terms would have been least confusing if they had been defined.

[10] Nevertheless, in only five pages, the author does give an effective answer to the question, "Which twentieth-century artist expresses life in the twentieth century better?"

Literary Model: Poetry

Sylvan historian, who canst thus express
A flowery tale <u>more sweetly</u> than our rhyme:
> —from "Ode on a Grecian Urn"
> by John Keats

Heard melodies are <u>sweet</u>, but those unheard
Are <u>sweeter</u>; therefore, ye soft pipes play on;
> —from "Ode on a Grecian Urn"
> by John Keats

With <u>blackest</u> moss the flower-pots
Were <u>thickly</u> crusted, one and all;
> —from "Mariana"
> by Alfred, Lord Tennyson

Three years she grew in sun and shower,
Then Nature said, "A <u>lovelier</u> flower
On earth was never sown;
> —from "Three years she grew"
> by William Wordsworth

> Through what power,
Even for the least division of an hour,
Have I been so beguiled as to be blind
To my <u>most grievous</u> loss!—That thought's
  return
Was the <u>worst</u> pang that sorrow ever bore,
Save one, one only, when I stood forlorn,
Knowing my heart's <u>best</u> treasure was no
  more;
> —from "Surprised by Joy"
> by William Wordsworth

EXERCISE A Write each underlined modifier. Beside it, label it *positive*, *comparative*, or *superlative*.

_____

_____

_____

_____

_____

_____

_____

_____

_____

_____

EXERCISE B Write each underlined modifier. Beside it, write the word it modifies.

_____

_____

_____

_____

_____

_____

_____

_____

_____

_____

_____

_____

_____

_____

_____

for **CHAPTER 19: USING MODIFIERS CORRECTLY**   *pages 572–89*

Literary Model (continued)

EXERCISE C   Think about a memorable day of your life—a day that included good moments and not-so-good moments. Then, write a poem describing the day you have chosen. In your poem, be sure to use at least three comparative modifiers. (Try to use an interesting combination of positive, comparative, and superlative forms.) When you are finished, underline your modifiers that show comparison.

_____

_____

_____

_____

_____

_____

_____

_____

_____

_____

_____

_____

_____

_____

_____

_____

_____

_____

_____

_____

_____

EXERCISE D   Explain why it is sometimes more effective to use the comparative or superlative form of a modifier instead of the positive form (such as using *funniest* instead of *funny*).

_____

_____

_____

_____

_____

_____

_____

_____

Writing Application: Letter

You probably make at least one comparison a day—to say that basketball is a *more interesting* sport than soccer, to wonder why science seems so much *harder* than math, to announce that your favorite song is the *best* one on the air. Since comparing things seems to be an inherent part of human nature, you will naturally include comparisons when you write. Using comparisons that are clear and correctly formed will make any composition more polished.

UNCLEAR	Tamika wrote her aunt more often than her cousin Tara.
CLEAR	Tamika wrote her aunt more often **than she wrote her cousin Tara.**
CLEAR	Tamika wrote her aunt more often **than her cousin Tara did.**
NONSTANDARD	Arturo jumps higher than anyone on his team.
STANDARD	Arturo jumps higher than anyone **else** on his team.
NONSTANDARD	Your poem is more better than mine.
STANDARD	Your poem is **better** than mine.

WRITING ACTIVITY

Your best friend in fourth grade moved away at the end of that school year. The two of you have kept up a correspondence since then. The letter you received yesterday contained the announcement that your friend's family is moving back to your city. Your friend's parents know how much your city has grown and changed since they moved away, so they want feedback from you about which part of the city they should live in. In a personal letter to your friend, describe various parts of the real or imagined city you live in, using at least five comparative and five superlative forms of modifiers.

PREWRITING   Arrange your ideas before you begin writing. You might create a big sketch of your city and jot down notes about the positive and negative aspects of living in each area. If you want to categorize information in a chart, you can use the names of the areas as column heads and use topics such as "Transportation," "Access to Stores," and "Noise Level."

WRITING   As you write your draft, use the sketch or chart to help you make comparisons of the various parts of the city. Carefully choose comparative and superlative forms of modifiers so that each comparison will be clear to your friend.

REVISING   Have a classmate play the role of your best friend and read the draft of your letter. Ask him or her to make sure all your comparisons are clear. Revise any comparisons that are confusing.

PUBLISHING   Read your letter for errors in grammar, usage, spelling, and punctuation. Pay special attention to the spelling of comparative and superlative forms made by adding –er and –est. If you have included any of the eight troublesome modifiers discussed on pages 575–76 of your textbook, check that you have used them correctly. Then, neatly copy or print out your letter and add it to your portfolio.

EXTENDING YOUR WRITING

After completing your letter, work with a partner to create a brochure for an imaginary city. Your new city should have a combination of the best qualities that you and your partner described in your individual letters. Choose four or five of these qualities, then use text and illustrations to develop them.

Choices: Exploring Real-world Usage

The following activities challenge you to find a connection between usage and the world around you. Do the activity below that suits your personality best, and then share your discoveries with your class.

ART

Road Signs

Create road signs cautioning against errors in usage. Begin by sketching road signs you see every day. You can find examples of many of these in a state-issued driver's manual or in a driver's education textbook. You may be surprised to learn that the shape of a road sign has a meaning. Incorporate these meanings into your designs. When the signs are completed, ask for permission to hang them around your school.

ANTHROPOLOGY

Other Voices

Language is closely bound to a person's cultural identity. Put yourself in an entirely new cultural situation; perhaps visit a new neighborhood, a business office, or a community center. Listen to how people talk in this setting. What do you hear that is unfamiliar to you? What aspects of the language are familiar? Share your findings with the class.

WRITING

Easy to Remember

Help your friends (or yourself) remember the solution to one or two troublesome usage problems. Write a rap, a riddle, or some other rhythmic lines that highlight the correct use of at least two of the items listed in this chapter. Then, teach your memory aid to the class.

WRITING

Get It Down

Every type of speech, even slang, has rules. You probably know more than a little slang. Write a glossary of ten current slang expressions. Define each word or expression, and include an example sentence for each one. Check with your teacher to be sure the items you have chosen are appropriate in the classroom. Then, share your glossary with the class.

GEOGRAPHY

Map It!

Many regions of the English-speaking world have their own special ways of talking. Dictionaries usually label these special usages *dialect* or *regionalism*. Most of these usages are informal, not incorrect. Research some regional and dialectal usages (*reckon, a-going, fixing to, y'uns, y'all*). Pay particular attention to expressions from your own region. Then, write each word or expression on a small piece of paper and pin it to a United States or world map, in the region where it is used. Post your map in the classroom.

MUSIC

"Froggie Went A-Courtin'"

Traditional songs like "Froggie Went A-Courtin'" contain examples of informal and non-standard usage. In fact, nonstandard forms such as the prefix *a–* before a verbal can be quite useful to a songwriter because they add an extra beat. Write a humorous song in the traditional style. Include four or five informal or nonstandard items from the glossary chapter to help you maintain the rhythm or rhyme of your song. Then, play your song for the class. See if your classmates can identify the usage errors.

CREATIVE WRITING

Inside Out

You could say that English is really two languages—one for reading and writing and one for speaking. How well have you mastered both kinds of English? Find out. First, write a letter inviting friends to a casual dinner party. Use informal English in this letter. Next, use formal English to write a letter inviting friends and relatives to a very formal dinner party. Read both versions to the class.

Glossary of Usage A

Review pages 596–97 of the Glossary of Usage for information on the correct use of the following words or word groups:

a, an	*ain't*	*anyways, anywheres, everywheres,*
accept, except	*all the farther, all the faster*	*nowheres, somewheres*
affect, effect	*a lot*	*at*
	and etc.	*beside, besides*

USAGE

EXERCISE A In each sentence below, underline the word or expression in parentheses that makes the sentence correct according to the rules of formal, standard English.

Example 1. Do you know where my book bag (<u>is</u>, is at)?

1. This new medicine does have one side (affect, *effect*).

2. Call for a vote to determine how many members (beside, *besides*) us are for the change.

3. (A, *An*) heated debate occurred today in the Senate.

4. How long has it been since we have gone (anywheres, *anywhere*) interesting?

5. Andrea told me that two teaspoons of salt was (alot, *a lot*) for this recipe.

6. I found a tire pump in the garage, but it (ain't, *isn't*) mine.

7. I saved a seat for Carl right (besides, *beside*) mine.

8. Doesn't that change machine return anything (accept, *except*) dimes and nickels?

9. For the barbecue we will have chicken, potato salad, coleslaw, (and etc., *etc.*)

10. I'm afraid this is (all the farther, *as far as*) I can walk.

EXERCISE B In each of the sentences in the following paragraph, cross out each nonstandard expression. Above it write the word or word group that is correct according to the rules of formal, standard English.

Example [1] Olga follows her brother ~~everywheres~~. *everywhere*

[11] Olga has a older brother named Dietrich. [12] The two of them play sports, such as basketball, soccer, baseball, and etc. [13] Olga thinks that she ain't as good as Dietrich at most sports. [14] She says that sometimes when she wants to practice more, he's nowheres to be found. [15] Beside sports, Olga is interested in music and art. [16] However, her favorite place to be is right besides her older brother playing a tough game of soccer or basketball. [17] Olga knows that just watching sports won't effect her performance. [18] She certainly won't be able to run all the faster he can unless she works hard. [19] Therefore, Olga trains with her brother alot. [20] Dietrich has always had a good affect on her training habits and sense of sportsmanship.

Glossary of Usage B

Review pages 597–600 of the Glossary of Usage for information on the correct use of the following words:

between, among	*bust, busted*	*discover, invent*
borrow, lend, loan	*can, may*	*don't, doesn't*
bring, take	*could of*	*fewer, less*

EXERCISE A   In each sentence below, underline the word or expression in parentheses that makes the sentence correct according to the rules of formal, standard English.

Example 1. Do you know the difference *(between, among)* a tiger, a panther, and a cougar?

1. Was it you who *(discovered, invented)* the crystal cave on the ranch?

2. Our run was quite pleasant because there was *(fewer, less)* traffic early in the morning.

3. The police announced that they had *(busted, arrested)* the leader of the burglary ring.

4. He *(don't, doesn't)* know yet whether or not he wants to go with us.

5. Denisha, you *(can, may)* work on your Web site after you complete this practice exercise.

6. Hailey *(must have, must of)* guessed who had bought her that sweater.

7. *(Bring, Take)* these permission forms back to me tomorrow after your parents sign them.

8. Can you *(borrow, lend)* me two dollars until tomorrow?

9. The council debated *(among, between)* themselves in closed session.

10. Sean knew that Alexander Graham Bell *(discovered, invented)* the telephone.

EXERCISE B   In each of the sentences in the following paragraph, cross out each nonstandard expression. Above it write the word or word group that is correct according to the rules of formal, standard English.

Example [1] That bowler ~~don't~~ *doesn't* know how to keep score.

[11] Janet and Craig were trying to find out who discovered the game of bowling. [12] Last week, the librarian borrowed them a book about the rules of bowling. [13] Among the two of them, they read quite a bit about the sport. [14] Janet ought to of bought her own bowling ball. [15] Fortunately, Craig told her that she can use his whenever she wants. [16] Janet asked Craig to take the library book with him when he came to the bowling alley. [17] Craig and Janet could of scored higher if they had practiced more. [18] They knocked down less pins than they thought they would. [19] Among them they had a score of only eighty-five. [20] Craig joked that the police might bust them for bowling so poorly.

Glossary of Usage C

Review pages 600–604 of the Glossary of Usage for information on the correct use of the following words or word groups:

good, well	*kind, sort, type*	*leave, let*
had ought, hadn't ought	*kind of, sort of*	*like, as*
he, she, they	*learn, teach*	*like, as if, as though*
hisself, theirself, theirselves		

EXERCISE A In each sentence below, underline the word or word group in parentheses that makes the sentence correct according to the rules of formal, standard English.

Example 1. Our *(teacher he, teacher)* took us on a field trip last week.

1. You should never believe *(these kind, these kinds)* of stories.

2. After three days of the flu, finally on Friday I felt *(well, good)* enough to get out of bed.

3. *(Learn, Teach)* us how to trim bonsai plants, please, Mr. Takahashi.

4. The coach acted *(as though, like)* he had not heard Fran's question.

5. *(Leave, Let)* me choose the day, and you may choose the time.

6. *(Mom, Mom she)* took us ice-skating over the holidays.

7. You must be *(kind of, rather)* careful when you back out of the driveway.

8. Residents of the boarding house feel free to come and go *(like, as)* they please.

9. Our neighbors have just bought *(theirselves, themselves)* a new car.

10. Leonard *(hadn't ought, ought not)* to give up playing the clarinet when he is doing so well.

EXERCISE B In each of the sentences in the following paragraph, cross out each nonstandard expression. Above it write the word or word group that is correct according to the rules of formal, standard English.

           somewhat
Example **[1]** The students were ~~kind of~~ nervous about the exam.

    [11] Sergio said that he and his friends should do like their teacher suggested. **[12]** She learned them how to study for all sorts of tests. **[13]** Sergio said they simply needed to discipline theirself. **[14]** He said they had ought to study at least an hour each day. **[15]** These kind of studying allows students to learn the information in smaller blocks. **[16]** Sometimes Sergio asked his classmates to leave him study alone. **[17]** At such times, he needed to memorize facts, and doing so alone worked good for him. **[18]** At other times, however, studying in small groups was sort of more beneficial. **[19]** One student would act like he or she were the teacher and ask the others difficult questions. **[20]** Using these methods, Sergio and his friends taught theirselves better study habits.

USAGE

Glossary of Usage D

Review pages 604–606 of the Glossary of Usage for information on the correct use of the following words or word groups:

of	*supposed to, suppose to*	*this here, that there*
reason . . . because	*than, then*	*try and, try to*
some, somewhat	*them*	

EXERCISE A In each sentence below, underline the word or expression in parentheses that makes the sentence correct according to the rules of formal, standard English.

Example 1. Where did you find *(that there, that)* vintage coat?

1. When we finished shingling, I needed help getting *(off, off of)* the roof.

2. I think we should *(try and, try to)* study together for the big test.

3. *(This, This here)* package has been on the hall table since yesterday.

4. Is Albany farther from New York City *(than, then)* Buffalo is?

5. Aren't you *(suppose, supposed)* to finish your homework before you go out?

6. The reason we are honoring Chi is *(because, that)* she earned the top grades this year.

7. During this term, Andy has improved his understanding of chemistry *(some, somewhat)*.

8. *(Inside, Inside of)* the computer you will see a memory chip on the main circuit board.

9. When will the store let us know how much *(them, those)* tennis shoes cost?

10. Rashid will *(try and, try to)* read everything he can about creating Web sites.

EXERCISE B In each of the sentences in the following paragraph, cross out each nonstandard expression. Above it write the word or word group that is correct according to the rules of formal, standard English.

Example **[1]** The reason they played that game at the party is ~~because~~ *that* Susie requested it.

[11] The children at the party enjoyed themselves some watching cartoons, but soon they felt restless. **[12]** One of the children knew more games then the others. **[13]** She suggested they play this here word game. **[14]** Another child suggested that they try and think of a game that everyone could play together. **[15]** Unfortunately, all of them board games were for two to four players. **[16]** What were the children suppose to do? **[17]** They really didn't want to stay inside of the house. **[18]** Quickly, they decided to play outdoors rather then stay inside. **[19]** After tossing around that there soccer ball, they decided to play kickball. **[20]** The reason they chose that game was because everyone could participate.

Glossary of Usage E

Review pages 606–607 of the Glossary of Usage for information on the correct use of the following words or word groups:

used to, use to	*when, where*	*without, unless*
way, ways	*where*	*your, you're*
what	*which, that, who*	

EXERCISE A In each sentence below, underline the word or expression in parentheses that makes the sentence correct according to the rules of formal, standard English.

Example 1. Paula has a brother (*who, which*) is in the class play.

1. My cousin (*use to, used to*) say I had better luck than anyone else in our family.

2. Cara won't go to the party (*without, unless*) her friend Benita can go, too.

3. Franz had a long (*way, ways*) to go before he reached his grandparents' house.

4. She is the girl (*which, who*) plays first clarinet in the concert band.

5. I heard (*where, that*) Congress Avenue is going to be under construction for three years.

6. The story (*that, what*) I heard was different from the one you heard.

7. Isn't sunstroke (*when, a condition in which*) too much sun causes a form of heatstroke?

8. Is it true that (*your, you're*) going to be an uncle?

9. A fugue is (*where someone has, a state of*) psychological amnesia.

10. Our school has one bus (*who, that*) is never completely full.

EXERCISE B In each of the sentences in the following paragraph, cross out each nonstandard expression. Above it write the word or word group that is correct according to the rules of formal, standard English.

Example [1] The women went to the store ~~what~~ *that* had the best bargains.

[11] Ann and Marge use to go shopping at Carr's Department Store every month. [12] One day Ann said, "Your not going to believe it, but I've found a better place to shop!" [13] The two friends decided to try the new store on their next shopping trip without another store was having a sale that day. [14] Both women were pleased that the new store was not a long ways away from their neighborhood. [15] Marge was looking for a lamp who would fit on a small end table. [16] Quickly, they found a salesclerk which knew where the lamps were. [17] The salesclerk showed them a lamp what was just the right size. [18] "Your going to love the price, too!" the clerk said. [19] Ann had heard where the store was going to have a big sale the next weekend. [20] "We'll certainly be in you're store again soon," she told the clerk.

Double Negatives

In a *double negative,* two or more negative words are used when one is sufficient. Do not use double negatives in formal writing and speaking.

DOUBLE NEGATIVE	I don't have no idea.
STANDARD	I **have no** idea. [or I **don't have any** idea.]

EXERCISE A Read each sentence below, and decide whether it contains a double negative. On the line provided, write either *DN* for *double negative* or *S* for *standard*.

Example _*DN*_ **1.** The tour guide can't do nothing about our lost luggage.

_____ **1.** The shoe department don't have nothing left in your size.

_____ **2.** I haven't never seen this movie before.

_____ **3.** After this week, I have no more rehearsals!

_____ **4.** There weren't hardly any people standing in line for the late show.

_____ **5.** Our school hasn't had no cases of flu this year.

_____ **6.** Because of the noise of the engines, we couldn't scarcely hear each other talk.

_____ **7.** Although the library has many magazines, it had none on stamp collecting.

_____ **8.** Denise doesn't have no homework today.

_____ **9.** The box office doesn't have any more tickets for Saturday's concert.

_____ **10.** My dog won't do nothing but wag his tail.

EXERCISE B Revise each sentence below to correct the double negative.

Example 1. Henry could hardly do ~~nothing~~ *anything* because he was laughing so hard.

11. We don't have no milk in the house for breakfast.

12. Danny had hardly no time between classes today.

13. I won't hear nothing from Shani until next week.

14. Betty looked outside, but she didn't see nobody there.

15. The hikers hadn't scarcely any water left.

16. Don't you never dance?

17. In the afternoon, there aren't hardly any birds at the feeder.

18. Because he is shy, Ray doesn't never volunteer to read aloud.

19. This type of cactus doesn't have no spines.

20. Our Labrador retriever can't barely fit in that carrier.

Nonsexist Language

Nonsexist language applies to people in general, both male and female. Using nonsexist language will help you communicate effectively.

GENDER-SPECIFIC	fireman	housewife	man-made
NONSEXIST	firefighter	homemaker	synthetic

If the antecedent of a pronoun may be either masculine or feminine, use both masculine and feminine pronouns to refer to it. If the *his or her* construction is awkward, either substitute an article for the construction or use plural forms for both the pronoun and its antecedent.

> **EXAMPLES**   **Each** of the contestants will read **his or her** story aloud during today's assembly.
>
> **Each** of the contestants will read **a** story aloud during today's assembly.
>
> **All** of the contestants will read **their** stories aloud during today's assembly.

EXERCISE A In the following pairs, underline the nonsexist word or expression.

Example 1. postman   <u>mail carrier</u>

1. spokesperson   spokesman

2. stewardess   flight attendant

3. foreman   supervisor

4. server   waitress

5. chairman   chairperson

EXERCISE B Revise the sentences below to eliminate any sexist language. Cross out each sexist word, and write the nonsexist word above it.

Example 1. That ~~salesman~~ *salesclerk* can help you select a good pair of skis.

6. Keri was voted chairman of this year's book drive.

7. Is the job of a housewife difficult and demanding?

8. Mr. Stanley asked everyone to bring his costume to play rehearsal.

9. This man-made fabric can be washed like cotton but needs no ironing.

10. May the best man win in our school debate!

11. Several students in our class are considering becoming policemen.

12. Will there be any watchmen at the concert tonight?

13. I'm looking for a seamstress to alter this jacket.

14. The program teaches clients to become better businessmen.

15. Anyone can learn to play golf better if she practices.

Review A: **A Glossary of Usage**

USAGE

EXERCISE Revise each of the following sentences to reflect the rules of formal, standard English or to eliminate any sexist language. Cross out each nonstandard or sexist word, and write the standard or nonsexist word above it.

Besides
Example 1. ~~Beside~~ two courses in Spanish, Helen is taking a course in South American history.

1. For some reason, we have less track meets than most other high schools in the state do.

2. The bus stop is nowheres near my aunt's farm.

3. Our science teacher he took us on a field trip to the wildlife sanctuary.

4. The treasure hunters couldn't hardly believe their eyes when they saw the glittering coins.

5. There wasn't no one in the building except the guard.

6. We could hardly of solved the problem without some help from the teacher.

7. I can't go to the movies without I finish my homework first.

8. The captain insisted that the reward be distributed equally between all the crew members.

9. There wasn't no food left over from the picnic.

10. You should never believe these kind of stories.

11. Teresa ain't happy about the new chores.

12. Losing three games in a row had a bad affect on the team's morale.

13. There are others besides me who had ought to spend less time daydreaming.

14. Mr. Wilson is going to learn us how to grow plants in a greenhouse.

15. Jenny acted like she did not recognize you.

16. This here coat has been lying on the chair all day.

17. The coach won't leave you play in tonight's game if your ankle still hurts.

18. Leonard has been playing the piano much longer then we have.

19. Her home is a long ways from New York City.

20. The microphone was so bad that we couldn't scarcely hear the speaker.

21. What qualifications does a person need to become a policeman?

22. I didn't except the stranger's offer of a ride.

23. Was that a African elephant that we saw?

24. The company is looking for additional salesmen for the tri-state area.

25. My sister borrowed me her skates for the entire summer.

Review B: **A Glossary of Usage**

EXERCISE Revise each of the following sentences to reflect the rules of formal, standard English usage or to eliminate any sexist language. Cross out each nonstandard or sexist word, and write the standard or nonsexist word above it.

Besides
Example 1. ~~Beside~~ the bread, please pick up a quart of milk when you go to the store.

1. Without I finish my homework, I won't be able to go to the game tonight.

2. I hope he will except this gift that I bought him.

3. I don't want no help in completing this assignment.

4. Aren't none of you ready for the big game tomorrow?

5. I wish you would learn me how to type as fast as you do.

6. He couldn't scarcely see the difference between the two model cars.

7. Since she wasn't feeling well, Nancy asked her little brother to leave her rest.

8. You hadn't ought to cut things out of the newspaper before everyone has read it.

9. I have a long ways to go before reaching the park's border.

10. The polite guest acted like she didn't notice the messy room.

11. Did less people visit the Grand Canyon this year than last year?

12. My dog is much furrier then yours is.

13. That there library book is overdue.

14. What affect might a new governor have on the state?

15. The museum curator had an interest in these type of coins.

16. Mike couldn't hardly believe his ears when he heard that he had won the essay contest.

17. Between all of us, we ought to have enough money to pay for lunch.

18. My mother she asked me to be sure to invite you to the party tonight.

19. Yoko ought to of remembered to hand in her report today.

20. I bicycle everywheres in the neighborhood.

Review C: A Glossary of Usage

EXERCISE Each of the following sentences contains nonstandard usage or sexist language. Correct each sentence by crossing out nonstandard or sexist language and writing revisions above the original sentence. You may add words by inserting a caret (∧) and writing the added words above the caret.

Example 1. If a student studies hard, he ∧will do better on the exam.
or she

1. She will travel anywheres her sister recommends.

2. A officer reprimanded the enlisted men for not having shined their boots.

3. The reason she left early is because she had an appointment.

4. She doesn't want to drive to the coast without her friends go with her.

5. Bowling is a sport where players use a ball to knock down pins.

6. Kristen drove a long ways before finding her friend's house.

7. A doctor can't help me unless he's familiar with my condition.

8. That there lake contains plenty of fish.

9. Are you're friends coming with us?

10. The new bridge won't effect my travel time.

11. The teacher arrived earlier then we had expected.

12. Nobody accept Berta showed up for the rehearsal.

13. They hadn't ought to be late for the play.

14. She was sort of reluctant to ask the teacher a question.

15. Alot of tourists visit the local mall.

16. I know my keys are somewheres around here.

17. How many men will we need for the job?

18. When was the Mississippi River invented?

19. He hurt hisself while climbing the tree.

20. We were suppose to be here earlier.

Proofreading Application: Public Flyer

Good writers generally are good proofreaders. Readers tend to admire and trust writing that is error-free. Make sure that you correct all errors in grammar, usage, spelling, and punctuation in your writing. Readers will have more confidence in your words if you have done your best to proofread carefully.

Chances are that sooner or later you'll need to write a classified ad or a poster for your club or some other announcement. Your public statement is important to you. Proofread this type of document carefully so that usage errors do not threaten your success.

PROOFREADING ACTIVITY

Find and correct the errors in usage in the following flyer. Use proofreading symbols such as those on page 901 of *Elements of Language* to make your corrections.

Example Happyville schools need ⌃you're help!
                                    your

ATTENTION, Residents of Happyville!

Many schools in this district have no computers. The reason is because they are so expensive. Our classrooms were all suppose to have new computer systems by December of last year, but the money was spent on heating and cooling systems instead.

Students for Tomorrow, a group committed to our schools, must of already raised almost two thousand dollars. We've got a ways to go to reach our goal. We cannot succeed without you help us. Come to the

GIANT GARAGE SALE
on November 9 in the Happyville Middle School parking lot at 710 Oak Avenue.

Help Happyville students help theirselves. We need alot of donations! Give us that old toaster. Hand over them old tennis rackets. We need your white elephants. We won't turn down nothing. Your old televisions and radios are valuable to us; in fact, their our ticket to the technology of the future.

Drop off donations at Happyville Middle School, or call us at 555-6382! We pick up!

USAGE | Language in Context: Literary Model

Literary Model: Description

> They didn't know what to do. But like Cathy say, folks can't stand Granddaddy tall and silent and like a king. They can't neither. The smile the men smilin is pullin the mouth back and showin the teeth. Lookin like the wolf man, both of them. Then Granddaddy holds his hand out—this huge hand I used to sit in when I was a baby and he'd carry me through the house to my mother like I was a gift on a tray. Like he used to on the trains. They called the other men just waiters. But they spoke of Granddaddy separate and said, The Waiter. And said he had engines in his feet and motors in his hands and couldn't no train throw him off and couldn't nobody turn him around. They were big enough for motors, his hands were. He held that one hand out all still and it gettin to be not at all a hand but a person in itself.
>
> —from "Blues Ain't No Mockin Bird" by Toni Cade Bambara

The following exercises will help you both to identify several common usage errors used in the preceding passage and to understand why the author chose to use them.

EXERCISE A

1. Identify the three double negatives in the passage, and write them on the line below.

_____

2. Identify one use of *like* for which formal, standard usage would require *as*. Identify another use of *like* for which formal, standard usage would require *as if* or *as though*.

_____

EXERCISE B

1. You may notice that not every negative expression in the passage is a double negative. Why do you think the narrator uses double negatives in the three places where they are used?

_____

_____

_____

2. How would the tone of the passage be different if the narrator had consistently followed formal, standard usage rules regarding *like* and *as*?

_____

_____

Literary Model (continued)

EXERCISE C   Write a paragraph in which a narrator describes someone he or she admires. In your description, try using informal or nonstandard expressions in a few places to help give the narrator a special voice and the paragraph a distinct tone and style.

_____

_____

_____

_____

_____

_____

_____

_____

_____

_____

_____

_____

EXERCISE D

1. What informal or nonstandard expressions did you use in your paragraph?

_____

_____

_____

2. How did these informal or nonstandard expressions contribute to the voice of the narrator and affect the tone and style of the paragraph?

_____

_____

_____

3. How did using informal or nonstandard expressions allow you to say things differently than if you had avoided using them?

_____

_____

_____

for **CHAPTER 20: A GLOSSARY OF USAGE**   *pages 595–611*

Writing Application: Speech

When talking to friends, do you pay attention to whether you are using nonstandard or informal expressions? Of course, you don't. If you were talking to a potential employer during an interview, however, you would probably try to avoid all nonstandard and informal expressions in an effort to create a good impression.

INFORMAL/NONSTANDARD	Didja make it to the concert last night? I would of, but I had to stay home with my sister. I heard it was totally cool.
FORMAL/STANDARD	I would have preferred to work last summer as well, but I felt that it was more important to take the summer course work that will allow me to graduate a year in advance.

WRITING ACTIVITY

As student council representative for your class, you have been asked to present a four-minute speech to the school board on a topic of concern to students. In your speech, include at least five correct expressions covered in the standard usage guidelines in this chapter.

PREWRITING Determine the topic of your speech. Then, decide on a few questions you will ask your classmates about the topic. You will need to incorporate their opinions into your speech. Interview your classmates, and then categorize their responses in a chart. Then, create a rough outline using these responses, your own opinion, and other information needed to support the position you are expressing in the speech.

WRITING Use the outline to write a draft of your speech. Spend enough time on the introduction to make it grab your listeners' attention as you present your statement of opinion. Then, discuss each supporting point. Maintain your listeners' attention by making your speech focused and avoiding redundancy. Conclude your speech by restating your main point.

REVISING Ask a classmate to listen to your speech and to time it. Add or delete words to make the speech approximately four minutes long. Ask your classmate whether your position is clear, whether the speech is persuasive, and whether it contains any nonstandard or informal expressions that should be revised.

PUBLISHING Since this is a formal speech, check once more that it is free of usage problems and that you have used only formal, standard English. Use the glossary entries in this chapter to correct any common usage errors. With your teacher's permission, present your speech in front of the class.

EXTENDING YOUR WRITING

You could develop this writing exercise into a letter to the editor for your school, community, or school district newspaper.

Choices: Exploring Capitalization

The following activities challenge you to find a connection between capitalization and the world around you. Do the activity below that suits your personality best, and then share your discoveries with your class.

COMPUTER

Umbra BT

Computers have made wonderful and fantastic fonts, or alphabets, available to just about everyone who has access to a computer. If you have access, you probably have dozens of fonts. You can also find some very creative fonts in books of fonts. Pick out a few of the coolest ones, print them out, and label them. Not all fonts use lowercase letters. Which ones don't? Print them out, too. Then, post your printouts where everyone can see them.

VISUAL

Illuminated Manuscript

Go to the library, and find a copy of a page or two from the famous *Book of Kells*. Show the class how this beautiful manuscript uses capital letters. Point out differences between the way capital letters were used then and the way they are used now.

FOREIGN LANGUAGES

When in Rome

Research this question: Do all languages have capital letters? Which ones do not? Find an alphabet that does not use capital letters. Make a copy of the alphabet, and present your findings to the class.

RESEARCH

What's an Aitch, Anyway?

Answer this question. Then, explore the history of a capital letter, any letter. You'll be amazed! We owe the history of our letters to many cultures and peoples. Use a map as the basis of a poster illustrating the origins and development of just one capital letter.

REAL LIFE

Your Hometown

For each rule in this chapter, find a real-life example from your city or town. Then, write each rule, along with your hometown examples. Spice them up with some illustrations. Give your classmates copies for their notebooks.

DISCUSSION

Truth and Beauty

In the nineteenth century, English-language writers commonly capitalized a great many nouns. As time went on, this practice became more and more frowned upon. Generally, now only proper nouns are capitalized. However, nouns that refer to certain absolutes, such as Truth or Beauty, are still sometimes capitalized. Why do you suppose this change came about? To what political or cultural conditions would you attribute the change? Think about these questions. Then, lead your class in an exploration of these issues, using your opinions as a springboard for debate.

BUILDING BACKGROUND KNOWLEDGE

Under a Cabbage Leaf?

Research the words *uppercase* and *lowercase*. Where did these words originate? Prepare a report for the class about this interesting bit of historical background. Include illustrations, if possible.

REAL LIFE

In the Diplomatic Corps

Get a good secretarial dictionary, and check out the types of titles that people have in different parts of the world. How are these titles capitalized? Make a list of them, paying particular attention to interesting ones, as well as ones that you might actually have the need or opportunity to use in your life. Pass out copies of the list to your classmates for their notebooks.

Capitalizing First Words, *I*, and *O*

21a.	Capitalize the first word in every sentence.
21b.	Traditionally, the first word of a line of poetry is capitalized.
21c.	Capitalize the first word of a directly quoted sentence.
21d.	Capitalize the first word in both the salutation and the closing of a letter.
21e.	Capitalize the pronoun *I* and the interjection *O*.

EXERCISE A   In each of the following sentences, cross out any word that is incorrectly lowercased and correctly write the word above it.

              Oh   *I*
Example 1. ~~oh~~, Carmen and ~~i~~ visited the art museum yesterday.

1. last night after I got home, i read about civilization in the Indus Valley.

2. mom was oh so surprised that i had finally found a subject I liked.

3. she asked me, "where and when did this civilization exist?"

4. the Indus Valley civilization is rather old; it existed 4,500 years ago.

5. an old map showed that its region covered much of Pakistan and the western region of India.

6. skills that the people developed during that time were what i especially noticed.

7. scientists have uncovered remains that show that the people built brick buildings.

8. looking at pictures of a temple, I can almost hear a prayer, "We ask thee, o Great One. . . ."

9. these people built not only drainage systems, but, oh, heated bathing pools also.

10. oh, maybe someday I can visit the area and see this for myself.

EXERCISE B   In the following letter, cross out any word that has an error in capitalization and correctly write the word above it.

            She
Example [1] ~~she~~ received a letter from her younger sister.

[11] dear Kate,

    [12] thank you for the nice note you sent. **[13]** Bobby says, "have a very happy Valentine's

Day." **[14]** He even wrote this poem for you: "It can't be too late / to send love to Kate!"

                                      [15] sincerely,

                                        Debbie

MECHANICS

Proper Nouns and Proper Adjectives A

21f. Capitalize proper nouns and proper adjectives.

(1) Capitalize the names of persons and animals.

For names having more than one part, capitalization may vary. Always check the spelling of such a name with the person who has that name, or look in a reference source.

EXAMPLES **N**el **V**oorberg **L**assie **M**aria **de** la **V**ega **R**obert **O'C**onnor

(2) Capitalize initials in names and abbreviations that come before or after names.

EXAMPLES **M**s. Guerrera Albert **D. B.** Walker, **Jr.** LaKeeshia Smith, **D.D.S.**

EXERCISE For each of the following items, cross out any word that has an error in capitalization and correctly write that word above it. If the name is already correct, write *C*.

> *Red Deer*
Examples 1. Chief ~~red deer~~

> **2.** Ms. Aurora *C*

1. a short story by alice munro

2. fr. antoine lanager

3. wilhelm k. roentgen

4. samuel f. b. morse

5. a poem by Gwendolyn brooks

6. jeanne woodward, r. n.

7. mrs. o'leary

8. barry matthews, l.l.d.

9. st. francis of Assisi

10. augusta ada byron king

11. dr. martin luther king, jr.

12. elton john's piano

13. Prof. Stanley Fish

14. mr. baxter

15. j.r.r. tolkien

16. lawrence of Arabia

17. a horse named pinta

18. p. d. james

19. ms. Hartnett

20. scott of the Antarctic

21. my pet hamster, bernard

22. Doug hall, ph.d.

23. dr. mark chavana

24. c. s. lewis

25. franklin johnson, sr.

MECHANICS

Capitalizing Geographical Names

21f(3). Capitalize geographical names.

EXAMPLES   the **G**rand **C**anyon   **S**anta **C**ruz de la **S**ierra, **B**olivia
             Collin **C**ounty   **P**ainted **D**esert
             Sioux **F**alls, **S**outh **D**akota   the **N**orthwest
             444 **E**ast **T**hirty-third **S**t.   **G**ulf of **M**exico
             Yosemite **N**ational **P**ark   **M**ount **H**ood
             Europe   **I**sle of **W**ight

EXERCISE For each of the following items, cross out any word that has an error in capitalization and correctly write the word above it. If the word group is already correct, write *C*.

Examples **1.** ~~los~~ Alamos, ~~new~~ Mexico   *(Los, New written above)*

          2. the state of Idaho *C*

1. 1202 Elm ave.

2. a nation in Africa

3. Mount whitney

4. the midwest

5. niagara falls

6. a north carolina city

7. Great bear lake

8. Cape of good Hope

9. Everglades national park

10. Strait of Gibraltar

11. Sonoran desert

12. Blue hill, Maine

13. appalachian trail

14. Leeward islands

15. Republic of the Philippines

16. south Korea

17. Cross Island expressway

18. borough of Queens

19. Sri lanka

20. the Cascade range

21. Toledo bend reservoir

22. 12 west Forty-First street

23. gulf of Aden

24. bay of Bengal

25. a village in Vietnam

MECHANICS

Proper Nouns and Proper Adjectives B

21f(4). Capitalize the names of organizations, teams, government bodies, and institutions.

> **EXAMPLES**   **M**useum of **F**ine **A**rts, **B**oston   **N**ational **A**rbor **D**ay **F**oundation
> the **U.S. D**epartment of **A**griculture   the **D**etroit **T**igers
> **D**emocratic **P**arty (*or* **p**arty)   **YWCA** (**Y**oung **W**omen's **C**hristian **A**ssociation)

EXERCISE A For each of the following items, cross out any word that has an error in capitalization and correctly write the word above it. If the word or word group is already correct, write C.

                 Giants
Example 1. The New York ~~giants~~

1. National bureau of engraving

2. the Washington mystics

3. supreme Court

4. HuD

5. Los Angeles children's museum

6. United States naval observatory

7. Church of England

8. Department of justice

9. Smith college

10. U.S. senate

11. FBI

12. World bank

13. Audubon society

14. San Diego city council

15. Nelson high school

16. Library of congress

17. Cincinnati reds

18. Nba

19. university of Iowa

20. department of the Interior

EXERCISE B For each sentence in the following paragraph, cross out any word that has an error in capitalization and correctly write the word above it.

                          Louisiana State
Example [1] My father studied at ~~louisiana state~~ University.

[21] My father is a fan of the L.S.U. tigers. [22] My oldest brother is planning to study at L.S.U. and then work for the U.s. department of agriculture. [23] I'm hoping to study biology at L.S.U. and later work for the Museum of natural science. [24] My sister, however, wants to study at tulane university and work for the cia. [25] The only thing my family members have in common is that all of us are on the swim team at the ymca.

Proper Nouns and Proper Adjectives C

21f(5). Capitalize the names of historical events and periods, special events, holidays, and other calendar items.

The names of seasons are not capitalized unless they are personified or part of proper nouns.

EXAMPLES   the **A**merican **C**ivil **W**ar   the **F**ourth of **J**uly
                Annual **S**pring **F**ling   the **M**iddle **A**ges
                Walk **A**cross **A**merica   **S**aturday
                Valentine's **D**ay   a **w**inter evening

EXERCISE   For each of the following items, cross out any word that has an error in capitalization and correctly write the word above it. If the word or word group is already correct, write *C*.

Example 1. ~~presidents' day~~   *Presidents' Day*

1. New year's eve

2. Independence day

3. thanksgiving

4. a benefit for the Special olympics

5. founders' day

6. battle of waterloo

7. Yalta Conference

8. wednesday

9. grandparents' day

10. the roaring twenties

11. Rose of tralee festival

12. Industrial revolution

13. Pan-american day

14. the first day of Autumn

15. tournament of roses parade

16. Hollister county Spelling bee

17. the second week of october

18. February

19. veterans day

20. Hundred Years' war

21. New York World's Fair

22. Davis cup

23. Victory of General Zaragosa day

24. a summer day

25. Mardi Gras

Proper Nouns and Proper Adjectives D

21f(6). Capitalize the names of nationalities, races, and peoples.

EXAMPLES **A**ustralian   **L**akota   **Y**oruba   **Y**oruban   **N**ew **Y**orkers

21f(7). Capitalize the names of religions and their followers, holy days and celebrations, sacred writings, and specific deities.

The words *god* and *goddess* are not capitalized when they refer to the deities of ancient mythology, but the names of specific gods and goddesses are capitalized.

EXAMPLES **H**induism   **R**oman **C**atholic   **G**ood **F**riday

Feast of **R**amadan   **Y**om **K**ippur   the **B**hagavad-**G**ita

Koran   **B**uddha   the **g**oddess **H**era

EXERCISE For each of the following items, cross out any word that has an error in capitalization and correctly write the word above it. If the word or word group is already correct, write *C*.

Example 1. the ~~torah~~ *Torah*

1. a chicano artist

2. the teachings of Confucius

3. an italian opera

4. the russian language

5. north carolinians

6. a greek temple

7. the Roman goddess Demeter

8. taoism

9. the feast of epiphany

10. the zuni people

11. the book of genesis

12. a palestinian leader

13. the prophet Mohammed

14. written in the veda

15. a portuguese newspaper

16. the swiss

17. a canadian hockey team

18. Kwanzaa

19. the south american coast

20. a jewish holiday

21. a methodist church

22. a book of the new testament

23. an indian movie

24. the german language

25. praying to allah

Grammar, Usage, and Mechanics: Language Skills Practice

Proper Nouns and Proper Adjectives E

21f(8). Capitalize the names of businesses and the brand names of business products.

Do not capitalize a common noun that follows a brand name.

   EXAMPLES   **S**ears, **R**oebuck and **C**o.   a **S**ears lawn mower

21f(9). Capitalize the names of planets, stars, constellations, and other heavenly bodies.

The word *earth* is not capitalized unless it is used along with the names of other heavenly bodies that are capitalized. The words *sun* and *moon* generally are not capitalized.

   EXAMPLES   **M**ercury   the **P**leiades   **U**rsa **M**ajor   the **e**arth and the **m**oon

21f(10). Capitalize the names of ships, trains, aircraft, and spacecraft.

Proper names of boats or cars are generally capitalized.

   EXAMPLES   the **O**rient *Express*   **D**odge **C**aravan   the shuttle *Discovery*   **SS** *Iowa*

EXERCISE For each of the following items, cross out any word that has an error in capitalization and correctly write the word above it. If a word or word group is already correct, write *C.*

Examples 1. *Jupiter Earth* ~~jupiter, earth,~~ and *Mars* ~~mars~~

     2. where on *earth* ~~Earth~~

1. Chase bank

2. Bounty paper towels

3. whirlpool refrigerator

4. SS *united states*

5. a Fender Electric Guitar

6. *voyager 2*

7. Metro Plumbing Services

8. total eclipse of the Sun

9. *milwaukee arrow* (a train)

10. the constellation orion

11. lysol spray disinfectant

12. horseshoe nebula

13. *viking 1*

14. quaker oatmeal

15. the perseids

16. amtrak express metroliner

17. the shuttle *columbia*

18. *Skylab*

19. arm & hammer baking soda

20. the evening star venus

21. toyota camry

22. jupiter and saturn

23. a texaco station

24. capitol auto

25. the star polaris

MECHANICS

Proper Nouns and Proper Adjectives F

21f(11).   Capitalize the names of awards, memorials, and monuments.

EXAMPLES **N**obel **P**eace **P**rize	**C**ongressional **M**edal of **H**onor
Washington **M**onument	**H**eisman **M**emorial **T**rophy

21f(12).   Capitalize the names of particular buildings and other structures.

Generally, do not capitalize words like *hotel, theater, college, high school, post office,* and *courthouse* unless they are part of a proper name.

EXAMPLES **B**uckingham **P**alace	**B**rooklyn **B**ridge	**R**eed **H**igh **S**chool
a **p**alace	that new **b**ridge	a **h**igh **s**chool student

MECHANICS

EXERCISE   For each of the following items, cross out any word that has an error in capitalization and correctly write the word above it. If the word or word group is already correct, write *C*.

Example 1. Jefferson ~~memorial~~ *Memorial*

1. purple heart

2. Hancock tower

3. Ryman auditorium

4. golden globe award

5. the Empire State building

6. Newbery medal

7. Chamizal national memorial

8. a Bridge in Italy

9. Honolulu tower

10. Arlington national cemetery

11. the Globe Theatre

12. Vietnam veterans memorial

13. Pulitzer prize

14. the Courthouse in Falls City

15. the Ritz Hotel

16. national baseball Hall of Fame

17. Distinguished flying cross

18. Washington monument

19. Oakland Bay bridge

20. Hoover dam

21. taj mahal

22. the lincoln memorial

23. mount rushmore national memorial

24. the golden gate bridge

25. the space needle in Seattle

Names of School Subjects

21g. Do not capitalize the names of school subjects, except the names of language classes or course names that contain a number.

Do not capitalize the class names *freshman, sophomore, junior,* or *senior* unless they are part of a proper noun.

EXAMPLES   This year I take **S**panish, **g**eology, **A**rt 101, **b**iology, and **W**orld **H**istory II.

Many **f**reshman athletes serve on the **F**reshman Citizen Board.

EXERCISE   For each of the following sentences, cross out any word that has an error in capitalization and correctly write the word above it.

Example 1. Next year I will take ~~fine arts~~ II, ~~american~~ history, and ~~Advanced Algebra~~.
                     Fine Arts   *American*   *advanced algebra*

1. Most Sophomores are taking chemistry and algebra I.

2. Foreign language courses at our school include french, spanish, and japanese.

3. The teacher of our russian course spoke to the students in art history 104.

4. As a junior, Jacqui was the chairperson of the junior Prom Committee.

5. All seniors taking world literature I will read *Don Quixote*.

6. When Julio was a sophomore, he took both Creative Writing and poetry.

7. Because she was good at math, she took geometry and calculus 103.

8. The senior Debating Club is having a membership drive for Juniors.

9. In addition to my english class, I'm taking british novels 107.

10. My history 212 course is a prerequisite for both sociology and government.

11. After studying latin in high school, you may find french and spanish easy to learn.

12. The Freshmen will be joining the Sophomore Rowing Club for lunch today.

13. Angie signed up for linguistics 306 at the university.

14. Should I take portuguese or french next year?

15. Donna plans to major in physics and minor in german.

16. My grandfather speaks Russian, so I plan to take russian 101 next year.

17. Is chemistry II going to be much more difficult than chemistry I?

18. The seniors signed up for trigonometry I and calculus II.

19. Our synagogue offers classes in Biblical hebrew.

20. The college is offering a new class covering Advanced Sketching.

MECHANICS

Proper Nouns, Proper Adjectives, and School Subjects

21f. Capitalize proper nouns and proper adjectives.

EXAMPLES	a **G**erman artist	**H**arriet **T**ubman
	Lamar **U**niversity	**Dr. R. F. J**amison

21g. Do not capitalize the names of school subjects, except the names of language classes or course names that contain a number.

EXAMPLES	**B**iology 301	classes in **c**hemistry and **p**hysics
	a **L**atin course	the **c**alculus teacher

EXERCISE For each of the following items, cross out any word that has an error in capitalization and correctly write the word above it. If a word or word group is already correct, write *C*.

World Trade Center
Example 1. ~~world trade center~~

1. E. b. White

2. the American Revolution

3. our dog, peaches

4. robert o'connor

5. J.C. Penney

6. reed college

7. battle of the bulge

8. memorial day

9. the holiday of purim

10. the milky way

11. the *spirit of st. louis*

12. Spingarn medal

13. the french and indian war

14. Texas commerce tower

15. the university of Iowa

16. Tomb of the unknown soldier

17. hanukkah

18. the goddess athena

19. uranus

20. Constitutional law 101

21. kentucky

22. Harry s. Truman

23. caldecott medal

24. a Hindu Holiday

25. my Geography class

MECHANICS

Titles A

21h. Capitalize titles.

(1) Capitalize a person's title when the title comes before the person's name.

Generally, a title that is used alone or following a person's name is not capitalized, especially if the title is preceded by *a* or *the*. Titles used alone in direct address, however, generally are capitalized.

EXAMPLES	**M**s. Sanchez	**S**enator Burns	**S**uperintendent Endo
	Dr. Wong	a **s**enator	Thank you, **S**enator.

(2) Capitalize a word showing a family relationship when the word is used before or in place of a person's name, unless the word follows a possessive noun or pronoun.

EXAMPLES	my **u**ncle Bert	**U**ncle Bert	your **g**randma	Yes, **G**randma.

EXERCISE A For each of the following items, cross out any word that has an error in capitalization and correctly write the word above it.

Rabbi
Example 1. ~~rabbi~~ Kanter

1. governor Ventura

2. mr. Amundsen

3. aunt Clara

4. dr. Garza

5. queen Isabella I

EXERCISE B For each of the following sentences, cross out any word that has an error in capitalization and write the correction above it.

Professor   *uncle*
Example 1. With ~~professor~~ Chang's direction, my ~~Uncle~~ José studied Buddhism.

6. Uncle Ross and aunt Fran have invited us to a family reunion.

7. Philadelphia district attorney Arlen Specter became a senator.

8. Thank you, sir, for the tape of our Class President's speech.

9. Dr. Simmons and mayor Keely are the principal speakers at the dedication ceremony.

10. His Aunt Carmelita works as an assistant to judge Rosetti.

11. What do you think, dad?

12. Her Sister and Brother are Professors at Wayne State University.

13. My Cousin Jerri sent mom, dad, and me postcards from Mackinac Island.

14. Where will the Senators be traveling today?

15. We elected Bea Sterne Captain of our intramural track team.

MECHANICS

Titles B

21h(3). Capitalize the first and last words and all important words in titles and subtitles.

Unimportant words in a title include articles: *a, an, the*; prepositions of fewer than five letters: *in, of, for,* and so forth; coordinating conjunctions: *and, but, for, nor, or, so, yet*; and the sign of the infinitive: *to*. Capitalize an article *(a, an, the)* at the beginning of a title or subtitle only if it is the first word of the official title or subtitle.

EXAMPLES *The New York Times*   *the Hays County Free Press*

Saturday Night Live   "**B**eware: **D**o **N**ot **R**ead **T**his **P**oem"

Chapter 23   *The Tragedy of Romeo and Juliet*

EXERCISE A For each of the following items, cross out any word that has an error in capitalization and correctly write the word above it.

              The Phantom   the
Example **1.** ~~the phantom~~ of ~~The~~ Opera

1. *the great gatsby*

2. *the Sound of music*

3. *newsweek*

4. chapter 17

5. the story "the most dangerous game"

EXERCISE B For each of the following sentences, cross out any word that has an error in capitalization and correctly write the word above it.

                           Digest   The   Evening Post
Example **1.** We subscribe to the *Reader's ~~digest~~* and ~~the~~ *Saturday ~~evening post~~*.

6. Read "first snow in alsace" by Richard Wilbur.

7. A reporter from the *Chicago daily news* was present to review our play's opening night.

8. Today, Jed explained his slide presentation for the operetta *the pirates of penzance*.

9. Have you read "The legend of Sleepy hollow" by Washington Irving?

10. Many of Ms. Breen's kindergarten students can recite "Peter piper."

11. Auditions for *south pacific* will begin this afternoon in the auditorium.

12. I enjoyed the movie version of *A tale of two Cities* as much as I did the novel.

13. Be sure to ask my brother about his favorite book, *early man and The Ocean*.

14. Next month, the art museum will exhibit *Water lilies* by Claude Monet.

15. After you see the musical *Forty-second street,* let me know whether you enjoyed it.

Reviewing Capitalization of Titles

21h(1). Capitalize a person's title when the title comes before the person's name.

21h(2). Capitalize a word showing a family relationship when the word is used before or in place of a person's name, unless the word follows a possessive noun or pronoun.

21h(3). Capitalize the first and last words and all important words in titles and subtitles.

EXAMPLES	**S**enator Roland Burns	**M**s. Ana Sanchez	my **u**ncle Bert
	the **c**ongresswoman	**A**unt Flora	"**N**ight and **D**ay"

EXERCISE For each of the following sentences, cross out any word that has an error in capitalization and correctly write the word above it.

Example 1. Joe's favorite ~~beatles~~ *Beatles* song is "I ~~want~~ *Want* to ~~hold your hand~~ *Hold Your Hand*."

1. We will invite dr. Rubens to discuss the painting *Whistler's mother.*

2. Last night I read Chapter 3, "why leaves change color."

3. Allow me to introduce ms. Karen Wigen.

4. Did you see the Senator's letter in today's issue of *the New York times?*

5. Arthur Franklin is a Medical Doctor.

6. My favorite short story is "A rose for Emily" by William Faulkner.

7. Yes, mother, I'll clean my room as soon as I've done my homework.

8. The newspaper said that professor Hynek was an expert in astronomical phenomena.

9. My Aunt Anne served in the Navy during the Vietnam War.

10. The general with a bad back was treated by dr. John Kim.

11. After the Civil War, general Ulysses S. Grant became President of the United States.

12. The speaker for that evening was general Colin Powell.

13. Yesterday I watched a video of an old movie, *Those magnificent men in their flying machines.*

14. The song "Blue suede shoes" was first performed by Carl Perkins.

15. The Professor wrote the equation on the chalkboard.

16. This holiday is named after Dr. Martin Luther King, jr.

17. Every episode of the old television series *The twilight zone* was introduced by Rod Serling.

18. C. S. Lewis wrote *the Chronicles Of Narnia.*

19. Please summarize the second chapter, "An unexpected party."

20. The class read the poem "Stopping by woods on a snowy evening."

Review A: **Capitalization**

EXERCISE A For each of the following sentences, cross out any word that has an error in capitalization and correctly write the word above it.

                     cousin   *Japan*

Example 1. Our ~~Cousin~~ Kichi is coming from ~~japan~~ for a visit.

1. Dora made a scale model of a greek temple and brought it to history class.

2. I think it was in, oh, about november that i got my snowboard.

3. I'm learning the stories of the constellations, and cassiopeia is my favorite.

4. Last september my family and I visited New York city.

5. A Dodge truck was parked on Vernon Avenue near Jefferson hospital.

6. Her aunt is a professor at a large university in the midwest.

7. Are you going to be in town over Labor day weekend?

8. My Grandmother used to be a doctor.

9. The Statue of liberty was a gift from the people of France.

10. after touring Yellowstone National park, we spent a week on a dude ranch in Montana.

EXERCISE B For each of the following groups of words, cross out any word that has an error in capitalization and correctly write the word above it.

                           Senator

Example 1. a bill proposed by ~~senator~~ Jennings

11. driving up one of the Boulevards to Seventh Avenue

12. the Continent of South America, bounded by two oceans

13. the Declaration Of Independence

14. pamphlets published by the U.S. Department of agriculture

15. dearest mother,

16. Ford Motor Company's new Station Wagons

17. the steep slopes of mount Everest

18. the American Author Maya Angelou

19. courses in algebra, history, and english

20. sincerely yours,

MECHANICS

Review B: **Capitalization**

EXERCISE A   For each of the following sentences, cross out any word that has an error in capitalization and correctly write the word above it.

Example 1. The address is 1308 ~~north~~ *North* Fifty-seventh ~~street~~ *Street*.

1. We drove north, past the canadian border.

2. The Grand canyon, which is in Arizona, is a spectacular sight.

3. The local paper, the *Sun times,* reviewed the chamber music concert favorably.

4. The students of Yorkville high school auditioned for roles in *South Pacific.*

5. The ancient romans used aqueducts to bring water to Rome.

6. Sacagawea, a shoshone, accompanied the Lewis and Clark expedition.

7. Uncle Aaron and aunt Jayne plan to visit in december, and i am so excited!

8. The fire station is located on Fifth avenue.

9. The last planet discovered in our solar system was pluto.

10. as participants in a special project, a group of us visited the local Traffic Court.

EXERCISE B   For each of the following groups of words, cross out any word that has an error in capitalization and correctly write the word above it.

Example 1. the ~~fourth~~ *Fourth* of July, a ~~National~~ *national* holiday

11. reading the Bill Of Rights

12. *Christina's world* by Andrew Wyeth

13. dear sirs:

14. the famous american sprinter Wilma Rudolph

15. Maika Rubin, the class President

16. published by the U.S. printing Office

17. celebrated Labor day, a national holiday

18. studied french, chemistry, and gymnastics

19. in the reception area at Riverside hospital

20. a meeting with representative Shirley Chisholm

MECHANICS

Review C: **Capitalization**

EXERCISE A For each of the following groups of words, cross out any word that has an error in capitalization and correctly write the word above it.

> *Lincoln's*   *Address*
> **Example 1.** ~~lincoln's~~ famous Gettysburg ~~address~~

1. a sandwich from burger king

2. an african nation

3. my team, the dallas cowboys

4. a south carolina city

5. oklahoma city, oklahoma

6. a winner of the heisman memorial trophy

7. a vietnamese village

8. the mayflower hotel

9. 12 state street, des moines, iowa

10. the first monday in may

EXERCISE B For each of the following sentences, cross out any word that has an error in capitalization and correctly write the word above it.

> *the*
> **Example 1.** Have you ever read Virginia Woolf's novel *To ~~The~~ Lighthouse*?

11. Turning North on Grove street, the band marched past Mandell hall.

12. I'd like to buy a painting from the hispanic artist that i met at the opening of the show.

13. Riding over here on my bike took me, Oh, about twenty minutes.

14. Fran Lewis is the Captain of the Crescentview High School debating team.

15. While on vacation in the southwest, darin sketched the artisans at work at zuni pueblo.

16. this weekend we're celebrating my Father's birthday at garner state park.

17. Venus and mercury are the planets closest to the Sun.

18. Many tourists stay at the Niagara falls hotel when visiting new york state.

19. The irish actor Liam Neeson is one of the stars of the film *The phantom menace*.

20. Our History assignment for tomorrow is to read chapter 12: "the Peloponnesian war."

MECHANICS

Proofreading Application: Directions

Good writers are generally good proofreaders. Readers tend to admire and trust writing that is error-free. Make sure that you correct all errors in grammar, usage, spelling, and punctuation in your writing. Your readers will have more confidence in your words if you have done your best to proofread carefully.

Picture this: It is a hot summer day, and you have been walking eight blocks. You are now standing under a street sign that reads "Twelfth Street." In your hand is a crumpled page of handwritten directions. The directions say, "Turn left at the twelfth street sign." What do you do? Do you turn left now? Do you continue walking for another four blocks to the twelfth street sign? The instructions could be confusing.

If the writer had capitalized *Twelfth Street,* you would know what to do. Proper capitalization makes a writer's meaning clear. Be particularly careful to use capital letters correctly whenever you write directions.

PROOFREADING ACTIVITY

Find and correct the errors in capitalization in the following directions. Use proofreading symbols such as those on page 901 of *Elements of Language* to make your corrections.

Example if you follow these directions, you will find my house.

I know that you can get to the chinese restaurant on Connor drive, so start there. Go West on Connor Drive until you get to the American legion Hall. You should pass Parker lake on the way. That's the place where we held the car wash last Valentine's day. (Do you remember how we accidentally doused ms. Webb with soapy water?)

Cross the street. A methodist Church should be on your right. Every year, my family goes to the spring carnival there, by the way. Follow Twenty-First Street past Walnut elementary school.

I hope that all this walking hasn't worn a hole in those new High Flyer Sneakers that you got last week. You're almost there. Turn left at Jackson street. We're the third house on the right. It's the one with the ugliest plastic pink flamingos in north America standing right in the middle of the yard. How embarrassing they are!

for **CHAPTER 21: CAPITAL LETTERS**   *pages 618–31*

Literary Model: Using Capital Letters in Poetry

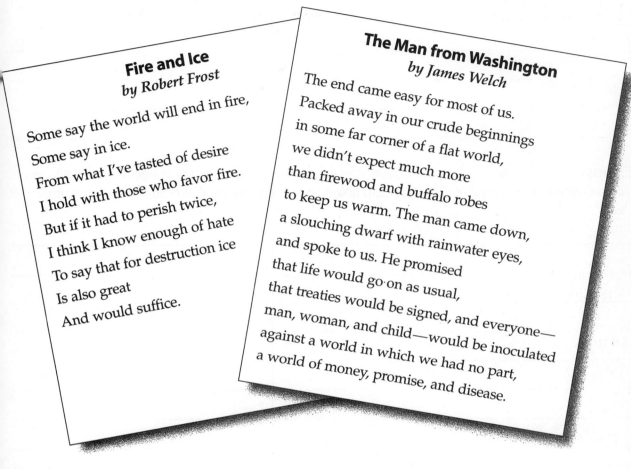

Fire and Ice
by Robert Frost

Some say the world will end in fire,
Some say in ice.
From what I've tasted of desire
I hold with those who favor fire.
But if it had to perish twice,
I think I know enough of hate
To say that for destruction ice
Is also great
And would suffice.

The Man from Washington
by James Welch

The end came easy for most of us.
Packed away in our crude beginnings
in some far corner of a flat world,
we didn't expect much more
than firewood and buffalo robes
to keep us warm. The man came down,
a slouching dwarf with rainwater eyes,
and spoke to us. He promised
that life would go·on as usual,
that treaties would be signed, and everyone—
man, woman, and child—would be inoculated
against a world in which we had no part,
a world of money, promise, and disease.

EXERCISE A

1. What rule of capitalization does Frost follow but Welch break?

_____

2. What do you think is Welch's method of deciding which words to capitalize?

_____

EXERCISE B

1. How does Frost's use of capitalization affect your reading of his poem? For instance, do the capitals draw your attention to certain words, or do they create a particular sense of style?

_____

_____

_____

_____

Literary Model (continued)

2. How does Welch's use of capitalization affect your reading of his poem?

_____

_____

_____

_____

EXERCISE C Write a poem using capitalization to emphasize certain words or images in a particular way or to create a distinct style. You may use capitalization as Frost does, as Welch does, or in some other way.

_____

_____

_____

_____

_____

_____

_____

_____

_____

_____

_____

_____

_____

_____

EXERCISE D How do you think your use of capitalization will affect a reader's understanding of your poem?

_____

_____

_____

_____

_____

Writing Application: Giving Directions

Years ago, writers could capitalize words at their discretion and often capitalized any words—verbs, common nouns, pronouns—that they wanted to bring to readers' attention, as in this 1730 couplet written by Alexander Pope in praise of the mathematician Isaac Newton.

> Nature and Nature's Laws lay hid in Night:
> God said, Let NEWTON be: And all was Light!

Today, writers capitalize only proper nouns and adjectives (and sentences' first words, of course), but the goal is similar: The capital letter draws attention to the special nature of the words.

WRITING ACTIVITY

Students at your school have planned a bike rally to raise funds for the community's food bank. Your job is to write the instructions for the bike rally. On the one hand, you need clear instructions so that all the riders make it to the rally's end. On the other hand, the directions should challenge the riders' navigational skills. In any case, capitalize all of the proper nouns and proper adjectives you use.

PREWRITING   Most prewriting can be done at a desk or in the library. For this activity, you will need to take a map, paper, and pencil with you and drive, ride, or walk the route. A compass might help, too. Take notes on the names of streets, businesses, parks, housing divisions, and other places.

WRITING   Organizing this writing assignment is easy: You must take riders from the route's beginning to its end. More challenging will be developing the right tone for this occasion and audience. Fund-raising for the food bank is a serious activity, but the bike rally itself should be fun for students. Your diction and word choice should contribute to the fun.

REVISING   After you have completed your instructions, ask a friend to check their accuracy by riding the route. Ride along with the friend so that if the directions take him or her in the wrong direction, you can locate the problem and fix it. Also ask other students, as members of your audience, to comment on the tone of the instructions and make suggestions.

PUBLISHING   Check the spelling, especially of place names, and punctuation of your instructions. Make sure that you have capitalized words such as *north* and *south* when they are part of a proper noun but not when they indicate which direction riders should travel. Distribute copies of your directions and copies of a map of the area. See which of your classmates can correctly mark the route on the map first.

EXTENDING YOUR WRITING

You may wish to develop this writing exercise further. While a bike rally is just for fun, knowing your way around your city is vital. You could develop and print a booklet to give to students who have recently moved into your school district, providing them with accurate directions to major city services, popular restaurants and stores, and school buildings such as stadiums.

Choices: Exploring End Marks, Abbreviations, Commas

The following activities challenge you to find a connection between end marks, abbreviations, and commas and the world around you. Do the activity below that suits your personality best, and then share your discoveries with your class.

PHOTOGRAPHY

Follow Your Nose

Commas are all around you. Take pictures or video footage of signs on streets, buses, sub-ways—anywhere you find commas. Then, show your pictures to your classmates. Identify correct usage and errors. Finally, post your pictures (along with corrections!) in the classroom.

MUSIC

Wanted: Musicians

How are pauses indicated in musical notation? How are notes in a series separated or joined in musical notation? You know, but your class-mates may not. Let them in on the secret. Explain what notations function as commas and as end marks in musical notation. Remember to create a handout for your classmates to keep in their notebooks.

DISCUSSION

WDEUA?

Why Does Everybody Use Acronyms? They seem to be everywhere. Sometimes a person can't even understand what is being said. "I need an ARF and a PO ASAP," said the VP. What's this lingo all about? Are we all really that pressed for time? Why is the number of acronyms increasing so fast? Research these questions, and write up a brief report. Then, share your findings with your classmates.

COMPUTER SCIENCE

Attention, Computer Experts!

Commas play important roles in computer pro-gramming. Do some research, and find out what commas do in one or more computer languages. For example, what happens when a comma is left out or put in the wrong place? Write up your findings, and share them with your classmates.

HISTORY

Calling Indiana Jones

Do a little linguistic archaeology. Find out when the practice of abbreviating began. Gather a few examples of early abbreviations, and share them with your class.

REAL LIFE

Be Prepared!

How should you address people from other countries? Find out the courtesy titles (words like *Mister*) that other cultures use. Learn how to write, abbreviate, and say them. You may want to consult language teachers at your school or foreign language speakers that you know. You could also consult a computerized dictionary that pronounces words. Complete the project by handing out a list of courtesy titles, their mean-ings, their language, and their abbreviations to your classmates.

SCIENCE

H_2O

How are abbreviations used in science? Roll out a copy of the periodic table, and expound on a few examples, pointing out their punctuation. In what other ways does science use and punc-tuate abbreviations?

ORIGINAL PROJECTS

Be Your Own Boss!

Make up your own project! Compose a collage of commas from headlines, ads, and magazines. Find strange uses of end marks, commas, and abbreviations. Then, discuss them with the class. Write and perform a dialogue between a comma and an end mark. Write a diary entry for a mark of punctuation. Dress up like a comma and be interviewed by the class. You name it; just do it! Be sure to get your teacher's approval for any project you decide to do.

End Marks

22a.	A statement (or declarative sentence) is followed by a period.
22b.	A question (or interrogative sentence) is followed by a question mark.
22c.	An exclamation (or exclamatory sentence) is followed by an exclamation point.
22d.	A command or request (or imperative sentence) is followed by either a period or an exclamation point.

STATEMENT	Yo-Yo Ma is a renowned cello player.
QUESTION	Can we get tickets for the Saturday concert?
EXCLAMATION	Wow! What a fine musician he is!
COMMAND	Please take your seats. [request]
	Stop making that noise! [strong command]

MECHANICS

EXERCISE A Add periods, question marks, and exclamation points where they are needed.

Example 1. Can you give me change for a ten?

1. Where are you going on vacation this summer

2. Otto Persky asked for a recount of the votes

3. Address this letter to your grandmother

4. She lives on Mulberry Lane, next to my aunt

5. Watch out for that truck

6. Roberto yelled for help

7. What time does the bus from Detroit arrive

8. Is that convenient for you

9. What a beautiful sunset

10. The package weighed twice as much after being wrapped

EXERCISE B In the following sentences, add end marks where they are needed.

Example 1. Discuss the role of Chinese Americans in U.S. culture.

11. Chinese Americans have made important contributions to our society

12. What a fine program Connie Chung presented

13. Maya Lin designed the Vietnam Veterans Memorial

14. Have you heard about buildings designed by the architect I. M. Pei

15. I like the East Building of the National Gallery of Art

Abbreviations A

22e. Use a period after certain abbreviations.

An *abbreviation* is a shortened form of a word or word group. Abbreviate given names only if the person is most commonly known by the abbreviated form of the name.

(1) Abbreviate social titles whether used before the full name or before the last name alone.
(2) You may abbreviate civil and military titles used before full names or before initials and last names. Spell such titles out before last names used alone.
(3) Abbreviate titles and academic degrees that follow proper names.

EXAMPLES		
J. Alfred Prufrock	**R.H.D.** Goldberg	
Ms. Markham	**Dr.** Allison Kohari	
Gov. Aleda D. Williams	**Governor** Williams	
Harvey Matthews, **M.D.**	Martin Weil, **Jr.**	

MECHANICS

EXERCISE A For each abbreviation below, add periods where necessary.

Example 1. Prof. C. S. Blyth

1. Mr Binti

2. Gen P Worthington

3. Robert James, Sr

4. Rafael Sanchez, MD

5. Dr Mary Frances

EXERCISE B For each item below, underline any words that have abbreviation errors. On the line provided, write the abbreviation correctly.

Example _____ *Jr.* _____ **1.** Randolph Emerson, <u>Junior</u>

_____ **6.** the writer WEB DuBois

_____ **7.** Sen Kassebaum

_____ **8.** Gen Carns

_____ **9.** Mister Campbell

_____ **10.** E B White

_____ **11.** Col Adam Schroeder

_____ **12.** Winton Reynolds, Sr

_____ **13.** Dr Hope Morgan

_____ **14.** Mrs Darrold Smith

_____ **15.** Jeffrey Hellmer, Medical Dr

Abbreviations B

An *acronym* is a word formed from the first (or first few) letters of a series of words. Acronyms are written without periods.

EXAMPLES   **UCLA**   University of California at Los Angeles

SPCA   Society for the Prevention of Cruelty to Animals

After spelling out the first use of the names of agencies and organizations, abbreviate these names and other things commonly known by their acronyms.

EXAMPLES   **New Hope Education and Placement Center (NHEPC)** is located downtown.

The goal of **NHEPC**'s staff is to train its students in **Common Business-Oriented Language (COBOL)** programming and then provide job placement services.

MECHANICS

EXERCISE A   For each of the following sentences, underline the words that are commonly written as acronyms and write the acronym on the line provided.

Example _USAF_ **1.** Frederick joined the <u>United States Air Force</u>.

_____ **1.** We installed a new sound card in the central processing unit.

_____ **2.** Our class has just learned about the Central Intelligence Agency.

_____ **3.** The University of New Orleans libraries are excellent.

_____ **4.** Did you buy more random-access memory for your computer?

_____ **5.** The Food and Drug Administration provided helpful statistics.

_____ **6.** My report on the North Atlantic Treaty Organization is finished.

_____ **7.** Jeanette contacted Housing and Urban Development for information on area housing.

_____ **8.** Forrest wanted to work for the Federal Bureau of Investigation.

_____ **9.** I read an interesting article about the United Nations.

_____ **10.** Courtney spoke to the class about the American Medical Association.

EXERCISE B   Consult a dictionary or a book of acronyms and abbreviations to find out what the following acronyms represent. Write the words on the line provided.

Example **1.** HTML *Hypertext Markup Language* _____

11. NAFTA _____

12. AAA _____

13. URL _____

14. MADD _____

15. SAT _____

Abbreviations C

22e. Use a period after certain abbreviations.

You may abbreviate the following kinds of words in tables, notes, bibliographies, and letter and envelope addresses: names of states and other political units, names of months and days, words in an address, and names of units of measurement. Spell out such words in regular text.

REGULAR TEXT	ABBREVIATION
Lincoln, Nebraska	Lincoln, Nebr. *or* Lincoln, NE 68502
millimeters per inch	mm per in.

Abbreviate the era designations A.D. (*anno Domini*) and B.C. (*before Christ*) and the time designations A.M. (*ante meridiem*) and P.M. (*post meridiem*).

EXAMPLES   3000 **B.C.**   **A.D.** 814   the ninth century **A.D.**   7:00 **A.M.**   1:30 **P.M.**

EXERCISE A Above each underlined item below, correctly abbreviate or spell out the underlined word or word group.

               tsp
Example 1. 1 <u>teaspoon</u> cinnamon

1. Who led the Germanic tribes during the third century <u>*anno Domini?*</u>

2. The store is located on Fifth <u>Ave.</u> in New York City.

3. Have you ever been to Minneapolis, <u>Minn.</u>?

4. Ngo and Lawanda met us at 8:30 <u>post meridiem</u> in front of the auditorium.

5. In <u>532 A.D.</u>, a monk created a system for recording dates.

6. We had always wanted to tour the coast in the San Diego, <u>Calif.</u>, area.

7. Ned ran five <u>mi.</u> today to prepare for tomorrow's benefit run.

8. First, Jacy poured three <u>pts</u> of water into a two-quart kettle.

9. 3402 Harwell Street, Austin, <u>Texas</u> 78705

10. The brochure stated, "Trains depart on the <u>hr.</u> and the half <u>hr.</u> every day."

EXERCISE B On the lines provided, write the abbreviated versions of the following word groups.

Example 1. Starkville, Mississippi   *Starkville, MS*

11. two ounces of lime juice _____

12. 107 North Bear Avenue _____

13. January 15, 1995 _____

14. Houston, Texas _____

15. 1190 before Christ _____

MECHANICS

Abbreviations Review

22e. Use a period after certain abbreviations.

EXAMPLES   Mr. Luther F. Rogers, Jr.   Valentine Ct.
               Sen. Lindy Boggs   1000 B.C.
               New Orleans, La.   12 ft 7 in.

EXERCISE   For each of the following sentences, cross out each abbreviation error and write the correct abbreviation or the entire expression above it.

Example 1. Our new family doctor is Jeanine Attaway, ~~Medical Doctor~~.
(above: M.D.)

1. The first specialized breed of dairy cattle, the Holstein, was produced in Europe around 100 before Christ.

2. The conference will be held in Tucson, Ariz.

3. Last Wed., NASA announced the launching of a new space shuttle.

4. The speed limit on several local roads was reduced to 30 m.p.h.

5. 6 ft., 3 in. (item in a table of measurements)

6. Many Roman homes built in the first few centuries *anno Domini* had elaborate courtyards.

7. Martina wrote a book report on *Out of the Silent Planet* by C S Lewis.

8. The delegates will meet in S. America for the next summit.

9. The election will take place on Mar. 14.

10. The newspaper reported that the marathon runners were exhausted after over twenty-six mi. of running.

11. Gen. Booker received the memo this morning.

12. The tourists' plane arrived in NY City.

13. Mr Granholm will build the new office building on Cedar Street.

14. The conference session on learning lasted for only one hr.

15. The gardening expert who will speak to our class is Mister Eddie Cochran.

16. The new plants grew three in. in a week.

17. Mr. Samuel Jefferson, Junior, will arrive by plane tomorrow morning.

18. The beaches of Calif. attract many tourists throughout the year.

19. The information in this computer book is nearly five yrs. out-of-date.

20. Baton Rouge, La. 70808 (address line on an envelope)

MECHANICS

Commas: Items in a Series

22f. Use commas to separate items in a series.

> **EXAMPLES** Items of folk art are often discovered in closets, attics, and barns. [words]
>
> Our exhibit has encouraged people who tell stories, who sew quilts, and who carve toys to share their talents. [clauses]

(1) If all items in a series are joined by *and, or,* or *nor,* do not use commas to separate them.

> **EXAMPLE** Diamonds **or** flowers **or** stars are good designs for a beginner.

(2) Short independent clauses may be separated by commas.

> **EXAMPLE** Plan your design, collect scraps, and seek good advice.

(3) Use commas to separate two or more adjectives preceding a noun.

> **EXAMPLE** See the loud, bright colors in her design!

EXERCISE A Insert commas where they belong in the following sentences.

Example 1. Please bring your rulers, calculators, and workbooks.

1. Do you use relish mustard and mayonnaise?

2. Uncle Hugo likes large colorful flowers in his garden.

3. Rita plays the piano writes songs and sings in a choir.

4. She gave a concert at noon signed autographs at three and visited the museum at nine.

5. The council voted to buy a firetruck to hire a police captain and to build a water tower.

6. Miami Orlando and Tampa are three Florida cities.

7. Have you noticed that Tom cleans the house cooks the meals and washes the dishes?

8. Fabian made a nutritious salad with tuna carrots beans and macaroni.

9. Are those the old ragged clothes from the attic?

10. Men women and children pay the same ticket price.

EXERCISE B Insert commas where they belong in the following paragraph.

Example [1] Old quilts, thick pottery, and wooden ware are examples of folk art.

[11] Needlework quilts and toys are parts of the new exciting exhibit. **[12]** Short interesting biographies are also provided. **[13]** Elizabeth, a girl in the 1700s, studied music spoke French and did needlework. **[14]** Her name her birthday and her school's name are sewn into a sampler. **[15]** As she sewed, Elizabeth practiced the alphabet learned to spell made up verses and showed her artistic ability.

MECHANICS

Commas with Independent Clauses

22g.   Use a comma before *and, but, for, nor, or, so,* or *yet* when it joins independent clauses.

   EXAMPLES   Marina must pass the test**,** **or** she'll have to repeat the course.
                    Somebody suggested a tutor**,** **but** she wanted to consult her teacher.

EXERCISE A   Insert commas where they are needed in the sentences below.

Example 1. The play received a poor review**,** yet it was a success.

1. We have less leisure time for we're busy with household chores.

2. Sonya carries out trash and Lionel does laundry.

3. One day she left the door open and the cat slipped out of the house.

4. We had no idea where to search nor did we have the time.

5. Did you look in the shed or did you check the neighbor's garage?

6. Jake followed the recipe yet the spaghetti was too spicy.

7. Three of us ate it but Lionel refused.

8. Jake's not a great cook but we decided not to hurt his feelings.

9. Maybe Dad will take time off or Grandma will agree to come.

10. How we appreciate Mom and how we miss her!

EXERCISE B   For each of the following sentences, add commas where necessary. If the sentence is already correct, write *C* on the line provided.

Example _____ **1.** Roberto doesn't enjoy singing**,** nor does he enjoy dancing.

_____ **11.** Joel understands French but he doesn't write it well.

_____ **12.** Kimberly will go with her family to Vermont or she will attend summer camp.

_____ **13.** Rebecca wanted to do well in her piano recital so she practiced for an hour every day.

_____ **14.** Stephen or Karl will water the plants and feed the dog while we are away.

_____ **15.** Solomon studies the Torah every night for his bar mitzvah will take place next month.

_____ **16.** Pierre enjoys science fiction films, yet he doesn't like mysteries or thrillers.

_____ **17.** Teresa wants to be a biomedical engineer so she is taking extra science classes.

_____ **18.** Will your class be working on the bulletin board or will you be decorating the gym?

_____ **19.** Kerri isn't in the math club nor is she in the chess club.

_____ **20.** Ryan and Bob joined the ensemble and both boys will be playing the violin.

MECHANICS

Commas with Nonessential Clauses and Phrases

22h. Use commas to set off nonessential subordinate clauses and nonessential participial phrases.

A *nonessential* (or *nonrestrictive*) clause or participial phrase adds information that is not necessary to the main idea in the sentence.

> **EXAMPLES** Dr. Laker**,** **who drives a yellow van,** is his advisor. [nonessential clause]
>
> My brother**,** **hoping to get a job,** requested an interview. [nonessential phrase]

When a clause or phrase is necessary to the meaning of a sentence—when it tells *which one(s)*—the clause or phrase is *essential* (or *restrictive*), and commas are not used.

> **EXAMPLES** The girl **who won third place** is my teammate. [essential clause]
>
> The jogger **wearing the red shirt** came in first! [essential phrase]

EXERCISE A Identify each underlined phrase or clause in the sentences below by writing above it *E* for *essential* or *NE* for *nonessential*. Insert commas where they are needed.

Example 1. The coconut, which is a remarkable gift of nature, grows on palm trees. *[NE]*

1. Would you like to meet some people who pick coconuts for a living?

2. The climbers all of whom wear loops around their ankles look like acrobats.

3. Who is the climber who just reached the top?

4. Isn't he the person who gave us directions?

5. Dried coconut meat which is called copra is used for many products.

6. Coconut shells once cleaned and polished are carved into bowls, cups, or spoons.

7. I would like to have some cups and bowls that are made from shells.

8. Have you seen any stands that sell those items?

9. When my meeting is over, I plan to buy a few items made from shells.

10. My family who will meet me at the airport will be pleased with the gifts.

EXERCISE B Add or delete commas as needed in the following sentences.

Example 1. Our drama teacher, whom we admire greatly, will be here soon.

11. Sri Lanka which is a country, in Southeast Asia has coconut trees.

12. What happens to the coconut fibers, that are ground up?

13. Made from the meat of the coconut candles and soap are important byproducts.

14. One of the shirts, that I bought, has buttons made from coconut shells.

15. This hat that I like, has been made from natural and dyed coconut fiber.

Commas After Introductory Elements

22i. Use commas after certain introductory elements.

(1) Use a comma to set off a mild exclamation such as *well, oh,* or *why* at the beginning of a sentence. Other introductory words such as *yes* and *no* are also set off with commas.

EXAMPLES **No,** I'm not busy tonight. **Well,** let's ask Su Ling to come along.

(2) Use a comma after an introductory participial phrase.

EXAMPLE **Jogging along her usual path,** Eloise was caught by surprise.

(3) Use a comma after two or more introductory prepositional phrases or after a long one.

EXAMPLE **At the side of the road,** she came upon a furry creature.

(4) Use a comma after an introductory adverb clause.

EXAMPLE **Whenever I go to the bank,** I stop at my aunt's office.

EXERCISE A Add commas where necessary in the following sentences.

Example 1. Before we go to the park, let's have a snack.

1. Lying on the ground Roberto admired the clouds in the sky.

2. In the corner of the room Julie found her lost earring.

3. Why I have always appreciated a good joke!

4. Even though Cynthia and Leslie were late they didn't miss the beginning of the play.

5. Toward the back of the closet Nancy noticed a bright, shiny object.

EXERCISE B Underline the introductory element in each of the following sentences. Then, add commas where necessary.

Example 1. During the course of this project, we will see many interesting things.

6. Yes I know that Alexa Canady is a neurosurgeon.

7. At the age of twenty-six she became a neurosurgeon.

8. Why what an incredible accomplishment!

9. In her junior year of college she decided to become a doctor.

10. Oh when did she decide on her specialty?

11. According to a recent interview that incident happened a few years later.

12. Planning her career Dr. Canady was sure she wanted to work with children.

13. Well isn't the branch of medicine dealing with children called *pediatrics*?

14. Yes she is a pediatric neurosurgeon.

15. After she set her goals Alexa Canady was determined to succeed.

MECHANICS

Commas with Interrupters

22j. Use commas to set off elements that interrupt the sentence.

(1) Nonessential appositives and nonessential appositive phrases should be set off with commas.

> **EXAMPLE** Dr. Okimo, **the new P.T.A. president,** asked parents to become active.

(2) Words used in direct address are set off by commas.

> **EXAMPLE** **Greta,** please hang up your jacket.

(3) Parenthetical expressions (side remarks that add information or relate ideas) are set off by commas.

> **EXAMPLE** Paulie, **on the other hand,** wanted to lead the parade.

EXERCISE A Add commas where they are needed in the following sentences.

Example 1. Your dinner, Alexandra, is getting cold.

1. The cheerleading squad not the football players will greet the visitors.

2. To tell the truth we didn't expect them until next week.

3. Althea will you introduce the speakers?

4. The new uniforms I believe will be arriving soon.

5. Please take charge of the distribution Eugene.

6. To be perfectly honest I did not like that movie at all.

7. Do you think Ted that the package will arrive today?

8. The Blanchards our new neighbors have just built a deck.

9. Nevertheless we still intend to go to the mountains this weekend.

10. I need to know by tomorrow whether you are coming to the concert Judy.

EXERCISE B Underline the appositive phrases in the following sentences, and add commas where necessary.

Example 1. We looked forward to visiting Belgium, the next stop on our tour.

11. Belgium a small country in Europe has two official languages.

12. Dutch a Germanic language is spoken by those in the northern part of Belgium.

13. The people in the southern part the Walloons speak French.

14. Some signs in Brussels the capital city are in both languages.

15. Many Belgians adults and children know more than one language.

MECHANICS

Comma Review A

22f.	Use commas to separate items in a series.
22g.	Use a comma before *and, but, for, nor, or, so,* or *yet* when it joins independent clauses.
22h.	Use commas to set off nonessential subordinate clauses and nonessential participial phrases.
22i.	Use commas after certain introductory elements.
22j.	Use commas to set off elements that interrupt the sentence.

EXAMPLES Our collection includes pop, mariachi, rhythm and blues, and hip-hop music.
Bill bathed the dog, and the cat hid under the bed.
Tim, hoping to make the swim team, practiced every day.
If you see smoke, you know there is a fire.
Harrison Ford, my favorite actor, stars in that new movie.

EXERCISE A   Add commas where they are needed in the following sentences.

Example 1. We packed jackets, a tent, cooking gear, and our food.

1. For our garden, Rob pulled weeds Gabbi planted vegetables and I added mulch.

2. The main agenda items which are listed on the chalkboard will be covered first.

3. In case you were wondering Christa will be reading the part of Juliet.

4. Ports for a modem video and sound cards and a printer are found on most computers.

5. Wow our relay team is good but would you look at the way they are running now!

6. The weather for the final day of the golf tournament was breezy mild and beautiful.

7. Should we distribute the ballots or would you prefer that we wait a little longer?

8. Gathering the bundles of magazines Ben and I prepared to visit the nursing home.

9. Neither the small black foreign sports car nor the oversized blue van was ours.

10. By the end of the year our new company Equipment Rentals expects business to double.

EXERCISE B   Add or delete commas as necessary in the following sentences.

Example 1. When Tom and Blanca, reached the top of the hill, they witnessed a beautiful sunset.

11. Searching for a new house packing our belongings and cleaning the house took a lot of time.

12. Our guide dogs carefully trained over a period of several months were ready to be placed.

13. Those two cowboys whose saddles look new have worked at the ranch for many years.

14. Over the cupboard, in the corner of the kitchen you'll find the picnic basket.

15. The students who were receiving awards, were told to come half an hour early.

Grammar, Usage, and Mechanics: Language Skills Practice

Conventional Uses of Commas

22k. Use commas in certain conventional situations.

(1) Use commas to separate items in dates and addresses.
> **EXAMPLE** Aunt Virginia was born on June 15, 1943, in France.

(2) Use a comma after the salutation of a friendly letter and after the closing of any letter.
> **EXAMPLES** Dear Magdalena,   Sincerely yours,

(3) Use commas to set off abbreviations such as *Jr., Sr.,* or *M.D.* when they follow persons' names.
> **EXAMPLE** Is Alex M. Jorgensen, Jr., here?

EXERCISE A Add commas where needed in the following letter.

Example June 5, 2001

Dear Uncle Roy

My, what an eventful month our family is having! We have good news and bad news. The good news is that Mom is now Jessie C. Hilton Ph.D. The bad news is that we're moving, for she has a new job in Kentucky. Our house is for sale now. We think it will sell quickly because the location at 1706 Madison Avenue Ames Iowa is near the schools. Our new address will be 552 Larchmont Road Louisville KY 40232. We will be in Kentucky as of July 10 2001 so please write to us there.

Your nephew

Harold

EXERCISE B Add commas where necessary in each of the following sentences.

Example 1. Composer Ludwig van Beethoven was born on December 16, 1770, in Germany.

1. The company moved its offices to Seattle Washington.

2. Uncle Leo moved to the United States on July 4 1948.

3. We learned that David Feldman Ph.D. became the company president.

4. Their first son was named Marc Divine Jr.

5. Next summer, we will visit our grandparents in Lincoln Nebraska.

6. We moved into our new home on February 23 2000.

7. The lecture on wildlife was given by Marvin Goosner Ph.D.

8. Scott McIntosh M.D. will visit our school next week.

9. These souvenirs are from Biloxi Mississippi.

10. The couple celebrated their first anniversary on June 14 1999.

MECHANICS

for **CHAPTER 22: PUNCTUATION**   page 660

Unnecessary Commas

| **22l.** | Do not use unnecessary commas. |

Have a reason for every comma and other mark of punctuation that you use. When there is no rule requiring punctuation and when the meaning of the sentence is clear without it, do not insert any punctuation mark.

    INCORRECT   My friend, Alice, lent me her skates, but now, I can't find them.

      CORRECT   My friend Alice lent me her skates, but now I can't find them.

EXERCISE A Add or delete commas as needed in the following sentences.

Example 1. Obviously, most students care about their school, yet few of them belong to the

              Booster Club.

1. Tomorrow, Hans and Sally, will present a short scene, from their skit.

2. They will use their script, costumes and props to illustrate, train travel today.

3. More people, these days it seems, are planning train trips.

4. Nowadays train fares are more affordable, than they were at one time.

5. What should people, who are in a hurry, do to reach their destination?

6. A trip by rail, of course takes longer, than one by air.

7. Moreover getting to the airport, or driving in highway traffic can be, a hassle.

8. Railroad stations are, usually in the center, of a city I believe.

9. The main station, in our city for example, is in the downtown area.

10. Therefore it is a simple matter of a convenient, bus ride to the train depot.

EXERCISE B For each of the following sentences, add or delete commas as needed.

 Example 1. At any rate, I want to celebrate my birthday with you and Tim, Mary.

11. We listened carefully to the flutes oboes and clarinets.

12. People, who drive too fast, endanger the lives of others.

13. The entire class did well on the final exam so they had a celebration dinner.

14. All of the hypotheses in fact were proven to be viable.

15. I have been looking for a book, about the life cycle of butterflies.

Comma Review B

22f.	Use commas to separate items in a series.
22g.	Use a comma before *and, but, for, nor, or, so,* or *yet* when it joins independent clauses.
22h.	Use commas to set off nonessential subordinate clauses and nonessential participial phrases.
22i.	Use commas after certain introductory elements.
22j.	Use commas to set off elements that interrupt the sentence.
22k.	Use commas in certain conventional situations.
22l.	Do not use unnecessary commas.

MECHANICS

EXERCISE A   Add commas where needed in the following sentences.

Example 1. Marco, who turns sixteen tomorrow, will soon get his driver's license.

1. Samuel will bring the food and Laura and Michael will cook.

2. I just returned from the grocery store the pharmacy and the florist.

3. Keely and Tomas who are coming from Houston will join us for dinner tonight.

4. Tonight I will finish my book make an outline for my report and type it into the computer.

5. Carrie reacting quickly caught the falling plate before it broke.

EXERCISE B   Add or delete commas as needed in the following sentences.

Example 1. The Smithsonian Institution is located in Washington, D.C.

6. This group of museums was named after James Smithson an English scientist.

7. Smithson who was a wealthy man left his fortune, to the United States of America.

8. The money was to be used for the increase, display and diffusion of knowledge.

9. On June 27 1829 Smithson died in Genoa Italy.

10. Six years were to pass however before the U.S. government was notified of his will.

11. After a great deal of debate Congress decided, to accept the gift.

12. Most of Smithson's fortune of course was in England not in the United States.

13. To use his gift Congress had to find a way, of turning English pounds into American dollars.

14. First the money was put, in the form of British gold coins.

15. These coins, were shipped to the U.S. Mint at Philadelphia Pennsylvania and recoined.

Review A: End Marks and Abbreviations

EXERCISE For each of the following sentences, add end marks where needed. Also, underline any errors in the use of abbreviations and write the correction above the error.

Example **1.** Will <u>Mister</u> Benson be our teacher next year? _(Mr. written above Mister; ? added)_

1. This organization's headquarters have been on this ave. for five years.

2. Please help Mrs Walsh with the dishes

3. Are you originally from Madison, Wisconsin

4. Rogelio Martinez, Junior, is my classmate.

5. Gen. Larson spoke briefly to the soldiers.

6. Ms Barbara Ayala teaches ballet at our school.

7. Have you met Dr Caldwell

8. We saw illustrations of structures built before 200 before Christ.

9. We visited the office of James Koenecke, Medical Doctor.

10. Have you read the biography of Gov. Long

11. The specifications indicate that the unit weighs eight lbs.

12. Would you like a tsp of sugar in your coffee, sir

13. J R Jackson will be the new mayor.

14. What a wonderful speech Sen. Brown gave

15. Have the members of the task force driven through S. Carolina

16. The poet who gave readings last week was Dennis Ellington, Senior.

17. Did you know that Dvori's family is from St. Louis, Missouri

18. The temple dated back to *anno Domini* 620.

19. Who were the earliest colonists to arrive in N. America

20. The film was shot in Portland, OR.

MECHANICS

Review B: **Commas**

EXERCISE A Add or delete commas as needed in the following sentences.

Example 1. Although millions go to the movies every week, not many people know the history
of motion pictures.

1. Thomas Alva Edison the wizard of Menlo Park played a starring role in that history.

2. He or perhaps William Dickson an assistant of Edison's invented the kinetoscope.

3. The kinetoscope was a cabinet in which fifty feet, (fifteen meters) of film revolved on spools.

4. By peering, through a peephole, in the cabinet a person could watch the pictures move.

5. The kinetoscope appeared in 1894, in New York London and Paris.

6. Using the principles of the kinetoscope European inventors developed better movie cameras
and projectors.

7. Motion pictures were screened, before a Paris audience in 1895.

8. It was the light bulb not the kinetoscope, that made Edison famous.

9. Edison's other inventions include the phonograph the mimeograph machine, and the stock
ticker.

10. This inventive genius, who had only three months of formal schooling patented more than
one thousand items.

EXERCISE B Add commas where necessary in each of the following sentences.

Example 1. Jonathan cleaned the garage, swept the patio, and raked the leaves.

11. Marcos teaches tennis and Annette teaches racquetball.

12. I bought new golf clubs last week but I have not tried them yet.

13. Dear Dad

14. We put all the cans bottles and paper products in the appropriate recycling bins.

15. Constantine and Alberto will attend the banquet yet they will not be giving speeches.

16. In the space of a minute all of our plans changed.

17. Miguel's bicycle needs new pedals so he won't be riding with us today.

18. On Wednesday July 12 2000 my little brother was born.

19. Please send all inquiries to Luther Dunster Jr. 2805 S. Lamar St. Austin TX 78704.

20. Yours sincerely

MECHANICS

Review C: **End Marks, Abbreviations, and Commas**

EXERCISE Add periods, question marks, exclamation points, and commas as needed in the following sentences.

Example 1. Since I knew many of the players, I was eager for the home team to win.

1. The holiday celebrating the birth of Dr Martin Luther King Jr fell on January 17 2000

2. Paul do you remember where we put the frying pan

3. Please forward my correspondence to 623 Lilac Ave Big Rapids MI 49307

4. Padgett our new dog is a very sweet animal

5. I have often found that reading a text backward an old proofreading technique helps a writer catch errors

6. Believe it or not we left for the fishing trip at 5:00 on a Saturday morning.

7. Yikes This salsa is hot

8. The runners crouched at their blocks the starter fired her pistol and the race began.

9. What a snug, charming house you have

10. Uncle Jim and Aunt Mimi who live in Texas sent us a puzzle for Christmas.

11. The Trojan War some scholars believe may have occurred between 1500 and 1200 B.C.

12. Alarmed at the price of a new car Mrs Alacantara bought a used car instead

13. Did you ask Joel Roger Bonnie and Stacy if they wanted to come with us

14. At the top of the snowy hill the children waited with their sleds

15. Sally in fact now goes by the title Sally Stepanek M.D.

16. The Battle of Hastings was fought I believe in the year A.D. 1066.

17. Yes I'm pretty sure that Carl and Nadja the two best debaters on the team will be going to the championship

18. Before the singer even opened her mouth the crowd gave her a standing ovation

19. Belinda arrived at last with a stack of CDs and we were able to start the party

20. Look out for that tree

MECHANICS

MECHANICS | Language in Context: Proofreading Application

Proofreading Application: Action Plan

Good writers are generally good proofreaders. Readers tend to admire and trust writing that is error-free. Make sure that you correct all errors in grammar, usage, spelling, and punctuation in your writing. Your readers will have more confidence in your words if you have done your best to proofread carefully.

Often during your school career, you will work on projects with other students. Team projects frequently require the exchange of written information. You will need to ask and answer questions, and you will need to relay lists of information. Sometimes, you will even need to give orders. For all of these messages, you will need to use end marks, abbreviations, and commas. Be a team player. Proofread carefully for correct punctuation so that your teammates can easily understand your messages.

PROOFREADING ACTIVITY

Find and correct the errors in end marks, abbreviations, and commas. Use proofreading symbols such as those on page 901 of *Elements of Language* to make your corrections.

Example 1. Could you scan Ms. Mann's photographs into the computer, Jess?

OUR RESEARCH TEAM'S ACTION PLAN

Our Question

1. What is the current status of endangered species in Texas.

Step One

2. If possible Theresa you will interview Mr Vernon our science teacher.

3. Jess contact Sen Fisher at his office in Austin Texas.

4. Carlos, search the World Wide Web, for any relevant information

5. Since Lisa's mom works at the library Lisa will search current publications.

Step Two

6. Meet at 345 W Elm Ave on Saturday March 1 at 10:00 A.M. to pool data.

Step Three

7. Theresa will draw our maps, because she is the best artist.

8. Jess, didn't you agree to do the typing.

9. Carlos, will compile current statistics

10. Depending on need Lisa will do additional research; she will also proofread the first draft.

Literary Model: Commas in a Description

Hunger stole upon me so slowly that at first I was not aware of what hunger really meant.

Hunger had always been more or less at my elbow when I played, ① but now I began to wake up

at night and find hunger standing at my bedside, ② staring at me gauntly. The hunger I had known

before this had been no grim, ③ hostile stranger; it had been a normal hunger that had made me

beg constantly for bread, ④ and when I ate a crust or two I was satisfied. But this new hunger

baffled me, ⑤ scared me, ⑥ made me angry and insistent. Whenever I begged for food now, ⑦ my

mother would pour me a cup of tea, ⑧ which would still the clamor in my stomach for a moment

or two; but a little later I would feel hunger nudging my ribs, ⑨ twisting my empty guts until they

ached. I would grow dizzy and my vision would dim. I became less active in my play, ⑩ and for the

first time in my life I had to pause and think of what was happening to me.

—from *Black Boy* by Richard Wright

EXERCISE A For each numbered comma in the above passage, write one of the following letters on the lines provided to explain why the comma is used.

a. items in a series
b. two or more adjectives before a noun
c. independent clauses joined by a coordinating conjunction

d. nonessential clause or phrase
e. introductory adverb clause

1. _____   **4.** _____   **7.** _____   **9.** _____

2. _____   **5.** _____   **8.** _____   **10.** _____

3. _____   **6.** _____

EXERCISE B How does Wright's use of commas contribute to the sound and rhythm of the passage? (Hint: Try rewriting the passage so that it contains no commas, and read it aloud. What differences do you notice?)

_____

_____

_____

for **CHAPTER 22: PUNCTUATION**　*pages 637–60*

Literary Model (continued)

EXERCISE C　Write a short paragraph describing your first memory of a particular sensation, whether pleasant or unpleasant.

_____

_____

_____

_____

_____

_____

_____

_____

_____

_____

_____

_____

_____

EXERCISE D

1. Now, rewrite two sentences of your paragraph, using commas to create a different rhythm or tone. For example, by using a comma and a coordinating conjunction, you could combine two sentences that express related thoughts, or you could use commas in a series to create an emphatic rhythm.

_____

_____

_____

_____

2. How did changing the way in which you used commas alter your sentences?

_____

_____

_____

_____

Writing Application: Script

Punctuation marks such as periods, exclamation points, question marks, and commas can easily be taken for granted. However, the function of a mark of punctuation is often crucial. For example, suppose you are Ted, and your swimming coach writes a note that says, "Ted, Ali and Diana have to swim forty laps." It makes a big difference whether the coach is addressing you or whether your name is one item in a series! Consider punctuation as a means of enhancing your writing, helping you separate your ideas, and showing the relationships between your ideas.

WRITING ACTIVITY

You have been asked by a health promotion organization to write the script for a one-minute public service announcement. The announcement is intended for teenagers who listen to commercial radio stations. The script should be a dialogue between two teenagers who are providing information and persuading listeners to adopt a certain healthful behavior. Use end marks appropriately, and include at least one example of each of the following: a comma separating items in a series, a comma joining independent clauses, a comma setting off an introductory adverb clause, a comma setting off a noun of direct address, and a comma separating items in an address. Your end marks and commas will alert the actors to use appropriate intonation and pauses.

PREWRITING Choose the healthful behavior you will promote in your public service announcement script. Research the background information you need to write a script persuading teenagers to adopt the behavior. Take notes in an organized fashion as you read relevant literature or talk to experts. Also, take notes on the two characters you will create and the tone of their speech. Then, decide whether they will both promote the healthful behavior or whether one character will try to convince a reluctant second character to adopt the behavior.

WRITING Using your notes, write a draft of your script. Keeping your audience in mind as you write is very important. Try to be the writer and a representative of the audience at the same time. Don't overload the script with facts, but do include enough of them to support what you're trying to persuade your audience to do.

REVISING Ask two classmates to rehearse your script and then perform it for you and a third classmate. Encourage them to use the intonation and expression indicated by your use of punctuation. Listen critically to their delivery of the lines, and decide whether you need to make revisions to the content or punctuation. Ask the third classmate whether the script is persuasive and how it could be improved as a public service announcement.

PUBLISHING Proofread your script carefully, paying special attention to the use of commas and end marks. Check to be sure that you have included at least one example of each use of commas specified above. Then, perform your announcement for your class.

EXTENDING YOUR WRITING

You could develop this writing exercise into an actual script for a public service announcement to be aired at a community or commercial radio station. In addition, you might collect your classmates' scripts and present them to a staff member of the local branch of a relevant health organization with the suggestion that they could be used as the basis for future public service announcements.

Choices: Exploring Semicolons and Colons

The following activities challenge you to find a connection between punctuation marks and the world around you. Do the activity below that suits your personality best, and then share your discoveries with your class.

PUBLISHING

On Safari

Go on a scavenger hunt for colons and semicolons. Look in newspapers, magazines, billboards, and other published sources to find places where a colon or a semicolon might be hiding. Then, photograph or cut them out and paste them to poster board. Be sure to note whether each colon or semicolon has been used correctly or incorrectly.

POSTER

What's Your Title?

Once you start to look around, you will notice that many titles of books and movies contain a colon. On a piece of poster board, write down at least five movie titles and at least five book titles that contain a colon. You can decorate your poster however you want, but make sure your titles are bold and easy to read. With your teacher's permission, post your list in the classroom.

DEBATE

The One and Only

Get together with two classmates, and stage an argument among a period, a semicolon, and a comma. Each one thinks that it is the best way of dividing independent clauses and that the other marks should get lost. Naturally, you'll want to stay in character. Mr. or Ms. Semicolon wouldn't use commas and conjunctions to divide independent clauses! Videotape or perform your debate for the class.

INVENTION

Make Your Mark

It's a new century! Design a new mark of punctuation for our changing times. You'll need a shape, a name, and a purpose for your mark. Begin by considering what new situations, such as e-mail, may need such a mark.

MATH AND SCIENCE

10:1

Colons are a rather all-purpose mark of punctuation, aren't they? They can identify a Bible verse just as easily as they can draw your attention to a grocery list. Besides the uses listed in your textbook, what other uses of colons can you find? Check out a scientific book, or page through a math text for starters. When you've found a few examples, fill the class in on your discoveries.

ANALYSIS

Alike and Different

Why do we bother to have both commas and semicolons? What's the difference? Think about it. Make a chart that has two columns: one labeled "Similarities" and the other labeled "Differences." Then, brainstorm ways in which commas and semicolons are alike and ways in which they are different. When you're finished, copy your chart onto poster board and show your findings to the class.

COMPUTER SCIENCE

Technical Language

How are colons and semicolons used in computer science? How do computer languages use these marks of punctuation? Choose a computer language, and give several examples of code that include semicolons and colons. Explain to the class the functions of colons and semicolons in the sample code that you chose.

Semicolons A

23a. Use a semicolon between independent clauses that are closely related in meaning if they are not joined by *and, but, for, nor, or, so,* or *yet.*

    EXAMPLE   Garth Brooks' latest CD is selling rapidly; he has become a major star.

23b. Use a semicolon between independent clauses joined by a conjunctive adverb or transitional expression.

    EXAMPLES   I've called him repeatedly; **however,** I've not been able to reach him.
                  Julio seems tired; **in fact,** he seems completely exhausted.

MECHANICS

EXERCISE Add semicolons where they are needed in the following sentences.

Example 1. The picnic is scheduled for this Saturday; however, if it rains, it will be postponed.

1. This travel book has amazing photographs I love this full-page shot of Costa Rica.

2. The students wanted a poet to teach the seminar however, none was available.

3. The scholarship letter finally arrived the whole family was ecstatic.

4. Senator Juarez is leading in the polls as a result, I think she'll win the election.

5. Kinu won't be at the party she's going to the theater with her family.

6. The auditorium will be finished in the spring meanwhile, assemblies will be in the gym.

7. New York was among the thirteen original states Ohio did not become a state until 1803.

8. My uncle spent two years in Japan while there, he learned many Japanese folk songs.

9. Thirty students signed up for the trip some of them may drop at the last minute, though.

10. There are several reasons I can't go for example, I haven't done my homework.

11. Since we live two miles from the high school, I seldom walk instead, I ride my bicycle.

12. Many activities are offered at my school among them are gymnastics and photography.

13. Cats are unique among domestic animals they retain many of the qualities of wild animals.

14. I know how to use that art software in fact, I'm using it to do my class project.

15. Carol has planned our hike carefully as a result, we can learn a lot and have a good time.

16. The play is perfectly suited for our class furthermore, it has enough parts for everyone.

17. My mother transferred to the University of Michigan in 1974 she graduated from there in 1977.

18. Roger might enjoy the book on the other hand, Faye probably will not.

19. Paolo reeled in the fish as fast as he could Carol tried to catch it in the net.

20. Maria is the fastest sprinter in her class indeed, she is the fastest sprinter I know.

Semicolons B

23c. A semicolon (rather than a comma) may be needed to separate independent clauses joined by a coordinating conjunction when the clauses contain commas.

> **CONFUSING** Bert, José, and Jette will sing, and my sister, Pat, will lead the band.
>
> **CLEAR** Bert, José, and Jette will sing; and my sister, Pat, will lead the band.

23d. Use a semicolon between items in a series if the items contain commas.

> **CONFUSING** The club officers are Kiyo Okimi, president, Lois Gould, secretary, and Jane Columbo, treasurer.
>
> **CLEAR** The club officers are Kiyo Okimi, president; Lois Gould, secretary; and Jane Columbo, treasurer.

MECHANICS

EXERCISE In the following sentences, add semicolons or replace commas with semicolons where needed.

Example 1. The coach asked only Mel, Kazuo, Cara, and Dina to practice today, but Sam, Max, and Lily will practice tomorrow.

1. In South America they visited Lima, Peru, Santiago, Chile, and La Paz, Bolivia.

2. Gloria will go with Sal, and Bob, Fred, and Tyrone will come later.

3. I've planted new parsley, chives, and dill and basil is already growing in the garden.

4. The club meets on Tuesday, May 5, Monday, June 1, and Friday, July 10.

5. The schools are in Fairfield, Connecticut, Columbus, Ohio, and Rochester, New York.

6. My father wanted to name me Charles, David, or Edward, and Franklin, George, and Henry were my mother's first choices.

7. I'll bring the plates, napkins, and beverages, and Lynn, Brian, and David can bring the sandwiches and salad.

8. Julio had thought that the corn, beans, and tomatoes would produce well this season yet, because of lack of rain, he no longer has anything growing in his garden.

9. Alfred likes to play soccer, basketball, and tennis, and football, baseball, and golf are Antonio's favorite sports.

10. Voting in runoff elections will be Tuesday, 6:00 A.M. until 7:00 P.M., Thursday, 7:00 A.M. until 7:00 P.M., and Saturday, 9:00 A.M. until 5:00 P.M.

Semicolons Review

23a. Use a semicolon between independent clauses that are closely related in meaning if they are not joined by *and, but, for, nor, or, so,* or *yet.*

   EXAMPLE   She ate her whole dinner; her sister just picked at the food.

23b. Use a semicolon between independent clauses joined by a conjunctive adverb or transitional expression.

   EXAMPLE   I decided against taking German; **instead,** I'm going to take Spanish.

23c. A semicolon (rather than a comma) may be needed to separate independent clauses joined by a coordinating conjunction when the clauses contain commas.

   EXAMPLE   Mike, Hallie, and I saw Leah and her sister; and April and Ziggie saw them, too.

23d. Use a semicolon between items in a series if the items contain commas.

   EXAMPLE   Max, the oldest; Roy, the youngest; and Cora, their sister, were all watching us.

EXERCISE   In the following sentences, add semicolons or replace commas with semicolons where needed.

Example 1. To take the test, you will need a Number 2 pencil; paper will be provided.

1. Ali has visited Toronto, Canada, Mexico City, Mexico, and Kingston, Jamaica.

2. Zora Neale Hurston is one of my favorite writers I have read several of her short stories and two of her novels.

3. Laraine's father is a traveling minister in fact, he visits a different community each month.

4. The squirrel leaped down from the branch, ran across a field, and then disappeared into the forest and, though he tried, my dog, Barks, didn't stand a chance of catching that squirrel.

5. Present at the committee meeting were Lamar, my cousin, Anita, your friend, Jerome, the new student, and Anna, my next-door neighbor.

6. Yesterday, Thad was late for class consequently, he forgot to turn in his homework.

7. Zach wrote his report on American Indians of the Northwest he also created a poster to illustrate key points of his research.

8. Denise, Scott, and Trina will go to the movies Ellis, Shani, and I will jog in the park.

9. Eva has the highest grade-point average in our class, she is this year's valedictorian.

10. I suppose you have heard of that African American literary movement it was known as the Harlem Renaissance.

Grammar, Usage, and Mechanics: Language Skills Practice

MECHANICS

Colons

23e. Use a colon to mean "note what follows."

(1) Use a colon before a list of items, especially after expressions like *the following* and *as follows.*

EXAMPLE   Please submit copies of the following documents**:** your driver's license, birth certificate, and Social Security card.

(2) Use a colon before a long, formal statement or a long quotation.

EXAMPLE   This is how I plan to begin my oral report on poetry**:** "If you want to express a complicated thought with the fewest but most memorable words, consider learning how to write a poem."

(3) Use a colon between independent clauses when the second clause explains or restates the idea of the first.

The first word of a sentence following a colon is capitalized.

EXAMPLE   Your poem is a complete success**:** It is original, and its rhythms mimic the sounds of waves!

EXERCISE   In the following sentences, add colons and capital letters where they are needed.

Example 1. Here are our choices: we can walk, take the car, or ride our bikes.

1. She has starred in the following plays *The Glass Menagerie* and *Our Town.*

2. Please stop at the store and bring home these items eggs, milk, bread, and orange juice.

3. These were the actors who tried out for the part Brad Pitt, Denzel Washington, and Wes Studi.

4. This is the last part of my letter "Thank you for accepting our invitation to discuss 'Theseus and the Minotaur.' Our mythology club is looking forward to your visit."

5. The cities I chose to write about in my report on India are as follows New Delhi, Calcutta, Bombay, and Madras.

6. The debate includes all three student government candidates Harrison, Letitia, and LaTonya.

7. The following authors were among the members of the Algonquin Round Table Dorothy Parker and Edna Ferber.

8. Yesterday, my sister's counselor suggested that she take Psychology 250, Government 201, and Algebra 301 those are the courses she needs to prepare for a college major in pre-law.

9. Walt Disney created these characters Mickey Mouse, Donald Duck, and Goofy.

10. My mother revealed to us an interesting fact she has decided to go back to college.

ELEMENTS OF LANGUAGE | Third Course

Colons in Conventional Situations

23f. Use a colon in certain conventional situations.

(1) Use a colon between the hour and the minute.

EXAMPLES 8**:**30 A.M.   11**:**25 P.M.

(2) Use a colon between the chapter and the verse in Biblical references and between titles and subtitles.

EXAMPLES *Street Smarts***:** *A Pedestrian's Guide*   Matthew 3**:**8

(3) Use a colon after the salutation of a business letter.

EXAMPLES Dear Professor Okinata**:**   To whom it may concern**:**

EXERCISE Add colons where they are needed in the following sentences.

Example 1. Have you read *Footprint in the Sand***:** *A Nomad's Life*?

1. The full title of my favorite Shakespeare play is *Hamlet Prince of Denmark.*

2. For class on Monday, be sure you have read Matthew 6 9–13.

3. Dear Sir or Madam

4. We were due at 4 00 P.M., but the traffic was bad, and it was 5 00 P.M. before we got there.

5. "The Quasar A Real Star?" is the title of my science fair project.

6. Your appointment is at 10 30, so you had better leave here at 10 15.

7. According to Exodus 20 1–26, what are the Ten Commandments?

8. You might enjoy reading *Publish and Perish Three Tales of Tenure and Terror* by James Hynes.

9. Dear Senator Simon

10. We have to get up at 4 30 in the morning to go skiing, but it's worth it.

11. Dr. Hewitt asked us to read "Chapter 5 Industrial Revolution" for tomorrow's history class.

12. "Dear Mr. Rodrigues I hope you are well," began the letter.

13. I studied last night from 6 00 P.M. until 1 30 A.M.

14. Using fifty words or fewer, paraphrase Colossians 3 12–15.

15. "Rain A Little Bit of Wonder" is the title of my haiku.

16. Dear Dr. Bainbridge

17. My sister's favorite movie is *Robin Hood Prince of Thieves.*

18. Please explain for us Paul's words in II Corinthians 9 1–15.

19. To whom it may concern

20. Hurry! It's already 7 30—we'll be late for school!

Using Colons

23e. Use a colon to mean "note what follows."

> **EXAMPLE** Please bring the following items to the test: a pencil, a notebook, and an eraser.

23f. Use a colon in certain conventional situations.

> **EXAMPLES** 6:35 P.M. *How to Meditate: A Beginner's Guide* John 3:16 Dear Ms. Fritz:

EXERCISE In the following items, add colons and capital letters where they are needed.

Example 1. Jan finished her homework: ⁵she did her math and wrote an essay.

1. Our meeting of the Foreign Language Club should begin promptly at 3 00 P.M. today.

2. Dear Sir or Madam

3. The fire marshal reviewed the drill directions exit the classroom in a single-file line; walk quickly to the closest exit; wait quietly outside for further instructions.

4. Hikers often carry the following equipment a canteen, a compass, and a sack lunch.

5. I read a great book called *Gaviotas A Village to Reinvent the World.*

6. Jill was a big winner in the swim meet she won the freestyle and the backstroke.

7. Dear Dr. Li

8. I enjoyed reading "Choice A Tribute to Dr. Martin Luther King, Jr." by Alice Walker.

9. We'll take a picnic basket to hold our lunch chicken sandwiches, lemonade, and muffins.

10. Mila must hurry, or she will miss the 10 30 express train leaving Glasgow for London.

11. This theater has nice features plush chairs, stadium seating, and a great sound system.

12. You will find a summary in the chapter called "*The Canterbury Tales* Snapshot of an Age."

13. Please turn to Luke 10 30–37, where we find the parable of the Good Samaritan.

14. Ed used an analogy he was as nervous as a long-tailed cat in a room full of rocking chairs.

15. Bring the following items to cooking class an apron, a hairnet, and a rubber spatula.

16. I gave my essay the title "Our School Cafeteria Observations of a Ninth-Grader."

17. These are the creatures my brother fears most June bugs, lizards, and opossums.

18. We agreed that we would turn off the television tonight at exactly 8 00 P.M.

19. Why do people at sporting events sometimes hold up signs that say John 3 16?

20. The architect who spoke to us was inspiring her job sounds practical and creative.

MECHANICS

Review A: Semicolons and Colons

EXERCISE   In the following sentences, add semicolons, add colons, or change commas to semicolons or colons where needed.

Example 1. The following equipment is needed for this experiment: a small beaker, a test tube, a test-tube holder, and a Bunsen burner.

1. On the science test we were asked to define the following terms *molecule, acid, base,* and *iron.*

2. Most plants need sunlight in order to grow however, there are a few kinds of plants, such as mushrooms, that can grow without any light at all.

3. The winners of the science fair were announced everyone could sense the excitement.

4. Which is the most popular breed of dog poodle, German shepherd, or pit bull terrier?

5. Our meeting will begin promptly at 7 00 P.M.

6. We hoisted the sails and set out to sea however, the changing wind pushed us east, west, and then back north toward the harbor.

7. The students were excited about the upcoming debate they had practiced for months.

8. Our itinerary includes stops in Cleveland, Ohio, Detroit, Michigan, and St. Paul, Minnesota.

9. My uncle loves to cook he has perfected his recipes for lasagna, bread, and salad.

10. The newsletter was designed by Tria, Fernando, and Chi Wan, and the articles were written by Earline, currently the only reporter on our staff.

11. Now I'll tell you my three biggest hopes for the future, to travel around the world, to graduate from college, and to make a life-sized sculpture in bronze.

12. The weather was very dry as a result, fewer flowers bloomed.

13. The text of the discussion will be I Samuel 17 20–50.

14. We did not agree with the candidates, their supporters, or their platforms but we respected the sincerity, integrity, and dedication of the speakers.

15. The curtain went up late for the play consequently, the cast must arrive earlier.

16. In our writing class, we will each create three works a poem, an essay, and a short story.

17. I wrote letters to Elvia, the editor, Marco, a reporter, and Todd, the guest editor.

18. I helped my brother Julian study for his geometry test he is smarter than he thinks he is.

19. We have three choices perform a skit, write a story, or design a collage.

20. All aboard the 10 22 express train!

Grammar, Usage, and Mechanics: Language Skills Practice

MECHANICS

Review B: **Semicolons and Colons**

EXERCISE   In the following items, add semicolons, add colons, or change commas to semicolons or colons where needed.

Example 1. The supplies we need are as follows: rubber cement, poster board, and markers.

1. We will be studying the Biblical passage Joshua 19 11–12.

2. Most of her novels take place in Iowa moreover, they focus on generations of one family.

3. At the store we bought tape, poster board, and glue we forgot to pick up markers.

4. I mailed my fees on time however, I sent the letter to the wrong address.

5. Juice four large carrots, one large apple, and one beet, and pour yourself a delicious, vitamin-packed drink.

6. The dog lay stretched across the bed the cat was curled up against the dog's belly.

7. Can you set my appointment for Monday, April 3, Wednesday, April 5, or Friday, April 7?

8. Consider the problems of filmmaking raising money, finding a cast, waiting out bad weather.

9. Daddy sang bass Mama sang tenor.

10. Ellen is talented in many ways, for example, she is skilled at acting in plays, singing at weddings, and playing on a soccer team.

11. My father's first essay was called "Freedom and Responsibility The Life of an American Teen."

12. The wind began to blow out of the southwest the ship began to move again.

13. Our families joked about a Robert Frost quote "Good fences make good neighbors."

14. The rain turned the dirt road to mud the road was impassable in a matter of minutes.

15. To whom it may concern

16. The passage that Tony read aloud was sentimental indeed, many in the audience were dabbing at their eyes.

17. The end of the movie was tragic nevertheless, the audience loved it.

18. My five-year-old brother's birthday party included several surprise guests his favorite baby sitter, one of his day-camp counselors, and our next-door neighbor's dog.

19. Mr. Martin's talk, "After the Beatles A History of Modern Pop Music," was more interesting than I thought it would be.

20. Laura did not drain the water from the hose as a result, the hose was frozen solid the next morning.

MECHANICS

Review C: Semicolons and Colons

EXERCISE   In the following items, add semicolons, add colons, capitalize letters, or change commas to semicolons or colons where needed.

Example 1. Kevin peeked at the movie screen,*the scary part was almost over.

1. Aunt Cecelia's many pets include Thor, the guppy, Max, the Siamese cat, and Cecil, the ferret.

2. Here are Tess, Fran, and Sean and Gil, Marie, and Pat will be coming later.

3. The camel rider came closer still they could not see his face.

4. Campers should bring the following a sleeping bag, warm clothing, and a canteen.

5. The train to Chattanooga leaves at 8 45 the train to Chicago leaves an hour later.

6. Dear Sir or Madam

7. When the film *Lawrence of Arabia* won seven Academy Awards in 1963, the winners included David Lean, the director, Freddie Young, the cinematographer, Anne V. Coates, the editor, and Maurice Jarre, the composer of the musical soundtrack.

8. The bus was late leaving St. Louis as a result, it will not get to its destination until 4 49 A.M.

9. The first sentence of the King James Bible, in Genesis 1 1, is one of the most famous sentences in the world "In the beginning God created the heaven and the earth."

10. It was a beautiful day the clouds opened, the birds chirped happily, and the dew sparkled.

11. While Jason was on the phone, Julia sliced the onions, washed the carrots, and started boiling the water, and Stephen cleaned the fish, measured out the spices, and minced the garlic.

12. My grandfather had several careers he was a farmer, a storekeeper, and a rodeo rider.

13. Stacy usually writes the music Roberto writes the lyrics.

14. Stevie Wonder is a talented musician he's a dynamic singer and songwriter.

15. I checked three books out of the library *The Adventures of Huckleberry Finn*, *Kidnapped*, and *The Once and Future King*.

16. Read these selections chapter three, chapter six, and chapter eight.

17. I hope Cassie can come to the party otherwise, it will be pretty dull.

18. Today's lecture is "The Temple in the Jungle The Discovery of Mayan Civilization."

19. I looked up the word in the dictionary I cannot believe I have always misused it.

20. After talking it over, we decided not to rent a video instead, we made some popcorn, started a fire in the fireplace, and read aloud to each other from *The Lord of the Rings*.

MECHANICS

for **CHAPTER 23: PUNCTUATION**   `pages 668–76`

Proofreading Application: Minutes of a Meeting

Good writers are generally good proofreaders. Readers tend to admire and trust writing that is error-free. Make sure that you correct all errors in grammar, usage, spelling, and punctuation in your writing. Your readers will have more confidence in your words if you have done your best to proofread carefully.

PROOFREADING ACTIVITY

In the following minutes of a meeting, find and correct the errors in the use of semicolons and colons. Use proofreading symbols such as those on page 901 of *Elements of Language* to make your corrections.

Example The minutes of a meeting are ⟨;⟩ notes on everything that happened.

Karen Wood opened the meeting on Wednesday, November 11. Then, Bill Nichols took roll. The minutes were read by Thomas Birch no corrections were made. Old business included: setting the date for the carnival, purchasing a plaque for Mr. Polanski, and appointing a new treasurer.

Lisa Galen proposed the following dates for the carnival, Saturday, April 10, Saturday, April 24, and Saturday, May 1. Neil Voight moved to make April 24 the date of the carnival, Kenji Chase seconded the motion, which carried unanimously.

Susan Radding moved that the club engrave the Biblical passage John 1 1 on Mr. Polanski's plaque. Some objections were voiced by: Thomas Birch, Otis Frank, and Sally Dawson; however, alternative passages could not be agreed upon, and the motion was seconded by Lee Chan and carried with one dissenting vote.

Karen Wood appointed Lee Chan treasurer, however, Lee Chan declined, and the chair appointed Neil Voight, who accepted. Sarah Mendoza moved that the meeting be adjourned so that she could call the trophy shop to order the plaque; the motion was seconded by Otis Frank. The meeting was adjourned at 4 18 P.M.; the next meeting is scheduled for Wednesday, November 18.

Literary Model: Semicolons in a Novel

> Such a bustle ensued that you might have thought a goose the rarest of all birds; a feathered phenomenon, to which a black swan was a matter of course; and in truth it was something very like it in that house. Mrs. Cratchit made the gravy (ready beforehand in a little saucepan) hissing hot; Master Peter mashed the potatoes with incredible vigor; Miss Belinda sweetened up the applesauce; Martha dusted the hot plates; Bob took Tiny Tim beside him in a tiny corner at the table; the two young Cratchits set chairs for everybody, not forgetting themselves, and mounting guard upon their posts, crammed spoons into their mouths, lest they should shriek for goose before their turn came to be helped.
>
> —from *A Christmas Carol* by Charles Dickens

EXERCISE A

1. How many sentences are in the passage? _____

2. Which semicolon breaks a rule of punctuation by joining an independent clause with a sentence fragment?

_____

EXERCISE B

1. Why do you think Dickens used numerous semicolons in this passage instead of periods?

_____

_____

_____

2. If Dickens had used periods in place of most of the semicolons, would the paragraph read differently? How? Do the semicolons reinforce the sense of "bustle"? Explain your answers.

_____

_____

_____

_____

_____

_____

Literary Model (continued)

EXERCISE C   Write a paragraph describing an occasion when you shared a meal with friends or family. Use semicolons to join some or all of the clauses.

_____

_____

_____

_____

_____

_____

_____

_____

_____

_____

_____

_____

_____

_____

_____

_____

_____

EXERCISE D

1. How did you decide where to use semicolons and where to use periods in your paragraph?

_____

_____

_____

_____

2. Read your paragraph aloud. How do the semicolons affect how the paragraph sounds? Do you read over them more quickly or more slowly than you read over periods?

_____

_____

_____

_____

Writing Application: Business Letter

On a city street, flashing lights and neon signs draw people's attention to certain details. Even when the street is busy, its yellow caution lights stand out and warn distracted drivers of hazards. Colons can function in a similar way, directing readers' attention to important sentence elements that otherwise may go unnoticed. When used effectively, colons allow writers to make sentences more interesting and emphatic.

LESS EMPHATIC   Precision is important in engineering.

MORE EMPHATIC   In engineering, one concern matters greatly: precision.

By isolating the word *precision* with a colon, the writer draws attention to it.

WRITING ACTIVITY

Pick up a copy of your favorite magazine. No matter how good it is, it could be better, and you are just the person to say how. Write a letter to the editors, complimenting them on what you like about the magazine and suggesting specific problems that they might address to improve it. Use colons to draw the busy editors' attention to the important points in your letter.

PREWRITING   Thumb through the magazine, jotting down notes about what you especially like. Then, think about what bothers you about the magazine: too many ads? not enough photographs? Perhaps you are looking for more advice from the writers. Dig deeply for what you would like to see changed. Finally, consult the magazine's inside cover for the names and address of the editors.

WRITING   Consider how you will organize your material, remembering that business letters are brief and to the point. Should you first address what you like about the magazine, or should you present the problems first? How will editors react to your chosen pattern of organization?

REVISING   Ask a friend or family member to read your letter and let you know if he or she has trouble understanding its organization or if your tone needs improvement. Make sure you have used the correct format for a business letter.

PUBLISHING   No truer test of writing exists than getting the chance to have your intended audience read what you wrote. Check your letter for spelling and punctuation. Watch especially for correctly placed colons. Finally, print out and mail your letter.

EXTENDING YOUR WRITING

You might make your letter a starting point for an essay in which you analyze the effectiveness of one printed publication. Consider addressing both design and content issues. Be sure to share your essay with the editors of whatever publication you analyze.

for **CHAPTER 24: PUNCTUATION** *pages 683–92*

Choices: Exploring Italics and Quotation Marks

The following activities challenge you to find a connection between italics and quotation marks and the world around you. Do the activity below that suits your personality best, and then share your discoveries with your class.

BUILDING BACKGROUND KNOWLEDGE

Top Forty

Take a poll of your class. What are your class-mates' forty favorite novels? Publish your list, with titles in italics, of course. Then, with your teacher's permission, post the results of your poll where everyone can read them.

TEACHING

Be a Teacher

Teach some elementary-school students how to use quotation marks. Let the young students dictate a dialogue to you. Then, show them where the quotation marks go. Third-, fourth-, and fifth-graders have loads of stories to tell.

RESEARCH

Chirp, Shout, or Mumble

Since you'll be writing some dialogue for Chapter 24, you'll need a few synonyms for *said*. Do yourself and your class a favor; make a list of these synonyms. You may want to divide the list into categories, such as volume or emotion. Then, pass out copies of your list.

WRITING

Book of Life

Do you have a favorite quotation that sums up your philosophy of life? If you do, write it down. If you don't, find one. Then, ask your classmates to do the same. Gather all the quotations, and either write or type them one quote to a page. Be sure to use proper quotation marks and end marks. If you have access to a computer, print them out in different fonts. You might also want to include a picture of each classmate on the page with his or her quote. Design a cover for your book, and bind it. With your teacher's permission, display it in the classroom.

READING AND WRITING

In the Screenwriters Guild

Playwrights and scriptwriters don't use quotation marks. How do they distinguish spoken language? Find out. Then, script a page of dialogue to serve as a model for your classmates. Share your speculations on why scripts do not use quotation marks. Also, point out how colons are used in scripts. Are there any other scriptwriting punctuation conventions you can explain to your class?

POPULAR CULTURE

We're "Open" All Night

Have you ever noticed that some people use quotation marks for emphasis rather than to indicate that someone is being quoted? Are there any signs, public notices, or even local menus you've seen that say things like *We sell "jumbo hot dogs" and "hamburgers"* or *We're "open" all day Sunday*? Have you ever noticed people using their index and middle fingers to represent quotation marks as they talk when they want to indicate that a term is meant ironically? What do you make of these and other real-world uses of quotation marks? Document some unusual uses, and share your findings with your class.

ORIGINAL PROJECTS

Break the Mold

Want to create a project of your own? Open your eyes and look around. You could write a report, give a presentation, or make a collage about what you see. Write an essay telling how you would use quotation marks and italics if you could make the rules. Better yet, show the class how you would do it. Design a T-shirt using quotation marks and italics. Come up with some other project that only you could design. Be sure to get your teacher's approval before proceeding with your plan.

Italics A

24a. Use italics (underlining) for titles and subtitles of books, periodicals, long poems, plays, films, television series, long musical works and recordings, and works of art.

EXAMPLES   *The Pearl* [book]   *Time* [periodical]

               John Brown's Body [long poem]   *Romeo and Juliet* [play]

               Fantasia [film]   *Nova* [television series]

               Both Sides Now [recording]   *The Thinker* [work of art]

MECHANICS

EXERCISE   Underline the words or word groups that should be italicized in the following sentences.

Example 1. Didn't Jeanine watch <u>Animal Trails</u>, her favorite program, yesterday?

1. A Midsummer Night's Dream will be the next Little Theater play.

2. My aunt sent me a subscription to National Geographic magazine.

3. I'm playing a selection from the opera The Magic Flute for my recital piece.

4. Tammy watches reruns of Happy Days with me sometimes.

5. We went to see Uncle Vanya, a play by Anton Chekhov.

6. How many children have watched Sesame Street since it first aired?

7. In Search of Dracula is a book about the famous fictional vampire.

8. Kirk rented the movie A Man for All Seasons.

9. We are reading Edmund Spenser's long work The Faerie Queene in my poetry class.

10. In Copenhagen, The Little Mermaid statue faces the water.

11. My little brother likes to watch the series Touched by an Angel.

12. Did you ever see the movie Toy Story?

13. My niece showed me an interesting article in Jack and Jill, a popular children's magazine.

14. The first of the Harry Potter books, Harry Potter and the Sorcerer's Stone, is my favorite.

15. Johanna Spyri wrote Heidi, a novel about a Swiss girl and her grandfather.

16. Didn't Shirley Temple star in Heidi, a movie based on the book?

17. Yes, she also starred in The Little Colonel.

18. Mom told us about Cooking for the Holidays, her favorite television program.

19. Every holiday season we watch the film It's a Wonderful Life, starring Jimmy Stewart.

20. We also read the classic book by Charles Dickens, A Christmas Carol.

Italics B

24b. Use italics (underlining) for the names of ships, trains, aircraft, and spacecraft.

EXAMPLES USS *Arizona* [ship] *Zephyr* [train]
 Graf Zeppelin [aircraft] *Discovery* [spacecraft]

24c. Use italics (underlining) for words, letters, symbols, and numerals referred to as such and for foreign words that are not yet a part of the English vocabulary.

EXAMPLES Does the *.com* in a URL ever have a capital *C*?
 The old manual typewriter was missing the *?* and *!* keys.
 Bon temps is a Cajun French expression meaning "good times."

EXERCISE Add underlining to indicate where italics are needed in the following sentences.

Example 1. The inscription was <u>carpe diem</u>, which means "seize the day" in Latin.

1. Doesn't the extra 5 in that area code make the phone number too long?

2. Pictures of Wiley Post's plane Winnie Mae were included in the advertising brochure.

3. Use the + and − notation on both sides of the parentheses to solve this equation correctly.

4. Space shuttle Columbia, welcome home; you are cleared for landing.

5. Translate goodbye into five different languages.

6. In 1819, the Savannah became the first ship to use a steam engine to cross the Atlantic.

7. In a Roman house, you might have seen the words cave canem spelled out in the tile floor.

8. My spelling of the name Aneita has an unexpected e.

9. In what year was the Pan American Clipper piloted by Clara Adams?

10. Sara's poem about the train Appalachian Breeze mentioned the railroad line's route.

11. Frequently, businesses use & instead of and to connect the names of the major owners.

12. Next summer, we will ride the riverboat the Mississippi Belle during our vacation.

13. Explain the purpose of the space station Mir, and discuss America's role in its success.

14. I never remember whether my cousin uses II or III after his name.

15. Which exhibit displayed an old land deed signed with an X in place of the person's name?

16. The Hebrew expression l'chaim means "to life!"

17. The starship in the original *Star Trek* is called the USS Enterprise.

18. Have you ever heard the old song about the train called the Orange Blossom Special?

19. Every e-mail address includes the @ symbol.

20. What does the Latin phrase Novus ordo seclorum, found on a dollar bill, mean?

MECHANICS

Italics Review

24a. Use italics (underlining) for titles and subtitles of books, periodicals, long poems, plays, films, television series, long musical works and recordings, and works of art.

24b. Use italics (underlining) for the names of ships, trains, aircraft, and spacecraft.

24c. Use italics (underlining) for words, letters, symbols, and numerals referred to as such and for foreign words that are not yet a part of the English vocabulary.

EXAMPLES			
Old Yeller	*60 Minutes*	*The Burghers of Calais*	*Voyager 1*
QEII	*Fantasia*	*Waiting for Godot*	*Newsweek*

Don't forget to put two *m*'s and one *c* in *recommend*.

EXERCISE   Add underlining to indicate where italics are needed in the following sentences.

Example 1. Ms. Bolanger explained the French term n'est-ce pas? to us.

1. We enjoyed the television show Kennedy Center Presents: The Americanos Concert.

2. Be sure to include the vowels e and i when you list frequently used letters.

3. Dad still has his copy of Great River: The Rio Grande in North American History.

4. Uncle Tim got to go on board Old Ironsides when he was in Boston.

5. Which act of The Miracle Worker do you want to help present to the class?

6. Auf Wiedersehen was one of the phrases that we learned in German I today.

7. When we visit my grandparents, we're going to ride the Hill Country Flyer, a steam train.

8. I still am confused about whether to use a : or ; between independent clauses.

9. Gayle will research whether the original version of the Odyssey used a rhyme scheme.

10. On the next line, write 649 in the box in front of your ZIP Code.

11. By next Friday, select one of the crew on the Lusitania to be the subject of your oral report.

12. Even though Jr. is part of Don's name, he does not usually include it in his signature.

13. James A. M. Whistler titled that painting No. 1: The Artist's Mother, actually.

14. Here comes the Atlantis, right on time and right on target!

15. Audie renewed his subscription to Pets: Part of the Family.

16. At the Louvre museum in Paris, we saw the Mona Lisa.

17. The Hindenburg made its intercontinental trip from Germany to New Jersey in 1936.

18. Soon my sister will be selling tickets to Fiddler on the Roof.

19. Each new flour sack label now has 323 stamped on it in bright red ink.

20. My favorite teen television show, My So-Called Life, had a very short run.

MECHANICS

Grammar, Usage, and Mechanics: Language Skills Practice

Quotation Marks A

MECHANICS

24d.	Use quotation marks to enclose a ***direct quotation***—a person's exact words.
24e.	A direct quotation generally begins with a capital letter.
24f.	When an interrupting expression divides a quoted sentence into two parts, the second part begins with a lowercase letter.
24g.	A direct quotation can be set off from the rest of a sentence by a comma, a question mark, or an exclamation point, but not by a period.
24h.	When used with quotation marks, other marks of punctuation are placed according to the following rules:

> **(1)** Commas and periods are placed inside closing quotation marks.
> **(2)** Semicolons and colons are placed outside closing quotation marks.
> **(3)** Question marks and exclamation points are placed inside the closing quotation marks if the quotation itself is a question or an exclamation; otherwise, they are placed outside.

EXERCISE In the following sentences, add quotation marks and other marks of punctuation where they are needed and draw a deletion mark (⌐) through marks of punctuation that should be deleted. Cross out any word that has an error in capitalization, and rewrite the word correctly above it.

Example 1. "I would like to welcome," said Mr. Kula, "~~Our~~ *our* guest speaker."

1. Kyung asked, should I show the guest our new gym?

2. "Please welcome Elaine Chao our principal announced.

3. He continued, "she has been serving as director of the Peace Corps".

4. At the age of six" explained Ms. Chao, "I emigrated from Taiwan.

5. I made the trip to the United States by boat" she said. "it was a long journey."

6. Simon asked, how long did it take you to learn to speak English?

7. How many volunteers Julianna asked, "Are there in the Peace Corps?"

8. "Would you tell us, please, about the countries you have visited"? asked Moise.

9. She said that the following countries had been personal "ports of call:" Nepal, Thailand, and Honduras.

10. "If you want to know more about the Peace Corps, read these articles, she added.

Quotation Marks B

24i. When you write dialogue (a conversation), begin a new paragraph every time the speaker changes.

24j. When a quoted passage consists of more than one paragraph, put quotation marks at the beginning of each paragraph and at the end of the entire passage. Do not put quotation marks after any paragraph but the last.

24k. Use single quotation marks to enclose a quotation within a quotation.

EXAMPLES   "As a child, did you play with modeling dough?" asked our teacher.

"I used it for play food," said Josefina, "when I fed my dolls. 'Don't put it in your mouth,' Mother would say. Once I tried it. She was right. Ugh!"

"Did you know, though, that astronauts have used modeling dough to hold tools in place in the weightless atmosphere of a space capsule?"

"Yes," said Josefina, "I read an article about that."

EXERCISE   In the dialogue below, place quotation marks and single quotation marks where they are needed. Place the symbol for a paragraph (¶) where each new paragraph should begin.

Example   ¶ **[1]** As Marta and I talked about holidays, she said, "At our parties you always hear the children saying, 'The piñata, the piñata!' " ¶ **[2]** "I've always wondered how piñatas are filled," I said.

[1] Olga asked, What's usually inside a piñata? **[2]** In addition to candy, replied Nina, there are little toys. **[3]** Toys! Kyoko exclaimed. That sounds like fun. **[4]** In Japan, Kyoko said, the third, fifth, and seventh birthdays are the most important. **[5]** Did I hear you correctly? Paco asked. **[6]** Did you say third, fifth, and seventh? **[7]** Yes, Kyoko replied, the children wear their best kimonos on those birthdays. **[8]** What do Russian children do on birthdays? asked Phil. **[9]** I answered, I once heard Natasha say, Somebody bakes a birthday pie. **[10]** That piece of information stuck in my mind, Phil, because I've never liked cake very much. **[11]** Ever since then I've been getting pie instead of cake for my birthdays. **[12]** Should I tell you which birthday I'm eager to celebrate? asked Helga. **[13]** I think you would say, My fifteenth, Paco guessed. **[14]** You've got it, she replied. **[15]** Then from the rest of us came the shout, Yes! in agreement.

Quotation Marks C

Use quotation marks and paragraph breaks correctly to enclose direct quotations in dialogue.

EXAMPLES   "Have you seen the new paint job on the Havana Street Bridge?" asked Kam.

"Yes, doesn't it look better," said Usha, "than when it was covered in graffiti?

"I heard that Kate is planning to cover the bridge walls with a mosaic mural," Usha continued.   "The neighborhood association is funding the project, and the sixth-graders at Dawson Elementary School are helping her."

"Wow," Kam said.   "That must be what Jerome was talking about when he said the bridge was 'an artist's canvas.'   I thought he was making a joke about the vandals who painted the graffiti."

EXERCISE   On the lines provided, correct each of the following passages, adding quotation marks where necessary. Remember to begin a new paragraph each time the speaker changes.

Example 1. What did Carla just say to you? asked Vincente. Well, said Roberto, she said, Let me know whether the computer still runs."

"What did Carla just say to you?" asked Vincente.

"Well," said Roberto, "she said, 'Let me know whether the computer still runs.'"

1. If Anya says Toodle-oo to me one more time, muttered Baxter, I'll scream. _____

_____

2. Marcus said, I hear you saw Aunt Bettina yesterday. Yes, I did, said Julia. As I came in, she said to me, Why, if it isn't my favorite niece! Wasn't that a sweet thing for her to say?

_____

_____

_____

3. Are you cooking something? said Miriam. Yes, said Todd. Why do you ask? I think I smell something burning, said Miriam. Oh no! cried Todd, dashing toward the kitchen.

_____

_____

_____

4. My television wouldn't work, said Mr. Lasalle, so I called somebody to fix it. The first thing the technician did was plug in the set. Problem solved, said the guy. Boy, did I feel silly!

_____

_____

_____

MECHANICS

Quotation Marks D

24l. Use quotation marks to enclose titles and subtitles of articles, essays, short stories, poems, songs, individual episodes of TV series, and chapters and other parts of books and periodicals.

EXAMPLES "How Wall Street Works" [article]   "On Honesty" [essay]
"The Seeing Stick" [short story]   "Opposites" [poem]
"Jailhouse Rock" [song]   "Punctuation" [chapter]
"The Trouble with Tribbles" [*Star Trek* episode]

EXERCISE A Add quotation marks where they are needed in the following sentences.

Example 1. I will read Pat Mora's poem "Now and Then, America" tonight.

1. The players on the team read the article How to Win at Soccer.

2. W. W. Jacobs's short story The Monkey's Paw is a terrifying tale.

3. Here Comes the Sun is a song recorded by the Beatles.

4. I just finished the chapter Improving Your Vocabulary.

5. Have you read Judith Viorst's poem If I Were in Charge of the World?

EXERCISE B In the following sentences, add quotation marks where they are needed.

Example 1. Our teacher asked, "Who will read 'Snow' for us today?"

6. Leah wrote an essay, What We Can Learn from Louisa.

7. Thoreau's Sky is her poem honoring Henry David Thoreau.

8. I read the mystery story A Whisper in the Dark.

9. Russell thought The Abbot's Ghost was a scarier story.

10. The song Danny Boy always makes me cry.

11. Puzzle Drawer was a monthly feature in that magazine.

12. Maybe I should call my essay One for All.

13. One of the scariest episodes of the *Twilight Zone* TV series was called It's a *Good* Life.

14. The chapter A Knife in the Dark in *The Lord of the Rings* kept me awake last night.

15. My father, my uncle, and I sang Let Me Call You Sweetheart in three-part harmony.

MECHANICS

Quotation Marks Review A

Use quotation marks and paragraph breaks correctly to enclose direct quotations in dialogue and to enclose titles and subtitles of short works.

EXAMPLES   "Nick," said Lin, "did anything unusual or interesting happen to you last night?"

"I'll say!" said Nick. "When I came home and turned on the lights, a crowd of people were waiting in the living room. They all shouted, 'Happy Birthday, Nick!'

"The evening reminded me of a scene you describe in your short story 'Party of One.'"

EXERCISE   On the lines provided, rewrite the following dialogue, adding quotation marks where necessary. Be sure to start a new paragraph each time the speaker changes.

Example   **[1]** Would you like to rent a movie tonight, Mimi? said Kazuo. **[2]** I'd love to, said Mimi. **[3]** What movie should we get?

"Would you like to rent a movie tonight, Mimi?" said Kazuo.

"I'd love to," said Mimi. "What movie should we get?"

[1] What sort of movie would you like to see? said Kazuo. **[2]** That's easy! said Mimi. **[3]** I like comedies, especially old black-and-white comedies. **[4]** Do you mean, say, Marx Brothers movies from the '30s, said Kazuo, or really old ones, like silent comedies? **[5]** Both, I guess, said Mimi. **[6]** I love the scene in *Animal Crackers* in which Groucho Marx says, One morning I shot an elephant in my pajamas. How he got in my pajamas, I don't know. **[7]** I also love the scene in *Modern Times* in which Charlie Chaplin gets caught in the gears of a giant machine. **[8]** But what about you, Kazuo? What movies do you like? **[9]** Kazuo smiled and said, I'll watch whatever you want to see. **[10]** Great! said Mimi. Let's go!

_____

_____

_____

_____

_____

_____

_____

_____

MECHANICS

Quotation Marks Review B

Use quotation marks and paragraph breaks correctly to enclose direct quotations in dialogue and to enclose titles and subtitles of short works.

EXAMPLES One of my favorite short stories is "A Rose for Emily," by William Faulkner.

"Who said, 'We have nothing to fear but fear itself'?" asked the teacher.

EXERCISE In the following sentences, add quotation marks or single quotation marks where necessary. Also, circle any incorrectly used capital and lowercase letters.

Example 1. Christopher asked, "(h)ave you ever read Rudyard Kipling's short story 'Rikki-tikki-tavi'?"

1. In today's paper is an article titled, believe it or not, Man Bites Dog.

2. Please turn to chapter nine of your history book, The Rise of the Greek City-States.

3. Jorge asked, did you enjoy the play?

4. I wonder who was the first to say The check is in the mail?

5. Many people know the song America the Beautiful; not many people know who wrote it.

6. Let's sing Row, Row, Row Your Boat, everybody!

7. After his dog died, Ronald wrote an essay titled In Memory of a Friend.

8. Do you know the poem Easter 1916?

9. I only regret that I have but one life to lose for my country: These are the last words of Nathan Hale, a hero of the American Revolution.

10. Cole Porter wrote such memorable songs as Night and Day and I Get a Kick out of You.

11. Be careful with that pottery! said Patrick.

12. "Then Mary told me, Watch out for the cat!" said Lauryn.

13. At the concert tonight, said Tranh, will the band be performing The Washington Post March?

14. The three short stories Araby, Ivy Day in the Committee Room, and The Dead appear in James Joyce's book *Dubliners*, said Mrs. Giltner.

15. The last thing my mother said to me was, What time will you be home? said Karen.

16. I hope to see Patrick tonight, said Terry, but he's got a late class.

17. Did somebody shout Fire! just now? asked Luz.

18. Madhu announced, we've finally done it!

19. I think the mayor said that light rail is "An option worth considering."

20. Michael reported, The nurse said, Matthew's arm will need a few stitches.

Review A: **Italics and Quotation Marks**

EXERCISE A The following sentences contain letters, words, and titles that should be italicized or enclosed in quotation marks. Add underlining to indicate where italics are needed, and add quotation marks where they are needed.

Example **1.** In the movie <u>Casablanca</u>, Dooley Wilson sings the song "As Time Goes By."

1. Remember to use & instead of and in the name of the law firm.

2. At the assembly the students recited Robert Frost's poem The Road Not Taken.

3. My favorite chapter in Gerald Durrell's book A Zoo in My Luggage is The Reluctant Python.

4. This issue of National Geographic has a fascinating article about the Titanic, the "unsinkable" ship that sank on its first voyage.

5. Our local newspaper, the Jersey Journal, recently ran an article titled Aiming for the Stars; it's about the space shuttle Endeavour.

6. Last night Dateline presented a report on the painting Starry Night.

7. John Campbell's science fiction story Who Goes There? was adapted into the film The Thing from Another World.

8. Shakespeare's play Hamlet has been adapted for film several times.

9. Is there anyone here who does not know the words to Itsy Bitsy Spider?

10. How many i's are in the word Hawaii?

EXERCISE B Add quotation marks and other punctuation where necessary in the following dialogue. Also, circle any incorrectly used capital or lowercase letters. Insert a paragraph symbol (¶) to indicate where each new paragraph should begin.

Example **[1]** As she watched me pack, my mother noted, "(i)t's getting late." ¶I answered, "I know. I'll be done soon."

 [11] Did you take everything on the list Kim asked. **[12]** Yes, I think so I said, looking at the list again. **[13]** it seems like an awful lot of stuff for a week's trip. **[14]** That may be Kim agreed but you'll find that you need everything. **[15]** Especially the insect repellent Mom chimed in. the bugs can be fierce at night. **[16]** I'm not sure I'm prepared for this I said doubtfully. **[17]** A whole week in the woods! Kim exclaimed. **[18]** you'll be eating your own cooking and sleeping in a tent. I don't know if you'll make it. **[19]** Nonsense! Mom cried, handing me my knapsack. you'll have a great time. **[20]** Just be sure to watch out for rattlesnakes Kim added, grinning.

MECHANICS

Review B: Italics and Quotation Marks

EXERCISE A In the following sentences, add underlining to indicate where italics are needed and add quotation marks where needed.

Example 1. Mosi asked, "How does a song become as popular as 'Stardust'?"

1. We subscribe to the Chicago Daily News, said my mother.

2. Have you ever read Edna St. Vincent Millay's poem Renascence? asked Ms. Kuznets.

3. The word millennium should be spelled with two n's, but sometimes it is mistakenly spelled with one n.

4. Shirley Jackson's best-known short story is The Lottery! exclaimed Yoshi.

5. Tonight's episode of Forbidden Planet, said Cal, is Return of the Explorers.

6. Jenny said, I thought I heard Kiki say, That controversial exhibit at the art museum opens today.

7. Tomorrow, said Mr. Kerr, we will discuss Chapter 7, Calculating Square Roots.

8. My sister's band, said Cara, is learning to play That'll Be the Day, an old Buddy Holly song.

9. I cannot find the % or the @ on this keyboard.

10. At the beginning of class, the teacher announced, Wuthering Heights is one of the books on our reading list.

EXERCISE B Add quotation marks and other punctuation where necessary in the following dialogue. Also, circle any incorrectly used capital or lowercase letters. Insert a paragraph symbol (¶) to indicate where each new paragraph should begin.

Example [1] "Where is the Yucatan located?" asked the teacher. ¶Tyler answered, "it's in southeastern Mexico, ma'am."

[11] Did your Spanish class see the movie about Mexico asked Clara as she met me in the hall.

[12] Yes, we did I replied enthusiastically. [13] How wonderful it must be to live in Mexico she exclaimed. [14] I'd never realized before that the country is so beautiful. [15] Yes, I liked the scenery in the movie I commented. [16] of course, the actors spoke very rapidly Clara went on and they used a lot of words that I didn't know. [17] could you understand them? [18] No I replied with a sigh. nor do I ever expect to be able to. [19] Have patience, my friend Clara kidded.

[20] You'll know a lot more Spanish by the time Ms. Martinez is through with you.

MECHANICS

Review C: **Italics and Quotation Marks**

EXERCISE A In the following sentences, add underlining to indicate where italics are needed and add quotation marks where they are needed.

Example 1. Don't forget that Alice Munro wrote the story "Boys and Girls"; you will need to know that on the exam.

1. Petra recalled that Marcia had said, The best painting in the show is Petra's.

2. I was moved by the article Missing Dog Returns Home in yesterday's Big Rapids Pioneer.

3. Martin shouted, Don't let the cat get out! as the kitten dashed out the door.

4. My favorite story from the anthology Great Russian Stories was Anton Chekhov's The Kiss.

5. What is the word the bird keeps repeating in Edgar Allan Poe's poem The Raven?

EXERCISE B In the following sentences, add underlining to indicate where italics are needed and add quotation marks where they are needed.

Example 1. "Oh yes, I've always been intrigued by Franz Kafka's novel The Castle!" said Rajiv.

6. I love the scene in Casablanca, said Jason, in which Humphrey Bogart says to Claude Rains, Louis, I think this is the beginning of a beautiful friendship.

7. Beware of the dog! read the sign, said Nathan.

8. How many times, asked Emilia, has Dr. McCoy on Star Trek said the line, He's dead, Jim?

9. Mr. Holmes, said Dr. Mortimer, they were the footprints of an enormous hound!

10. If I hear the song My Heart Will Go On one more time, said Dad, I'll scream.

11. Listen to what just happened to me! said Chang Ming breathlessly, as he came in the door.

12. Vernon asked, Who said, Home is the place where, when you have to go there, they have to take you in?

13. It was Robert Frost, said Tacia. It's a line from his poem The Death of the Hired Man.

14. It was Chinua Achebe who wrote the novel Things Fall Apart, said Naomi, but the line Things fall apart comes from a poem called The Second Coming by William Butler Yeats.

15. Here's something interesting, said Todd, and he pointed to the following passage from the newspaper:

The police found the stolen painting in a cave just outside of town. According to the police, the thief's footprints led into the cave, but they did not come out again. However, officers on the scene found no one in the cave.

The police cannot account for this discrepancy.

Proofreading Application: Written Interview

Good writers generally are good proofreaders. Readers tend to admire and trust writing that is error-free. Make sure that you correct all errors in grammar, usage, spelling, and punctuation in your writing. Your readers will have more confidence in your words if you have done your best to proofread carefully.

When you use a person's exact words, proofread your use of quotation marks carefully. If you don't, your readers may have difficulty figuring out who said what. Using italics or underlining correctly to distinguish titles of works such as books, plays, and periodicals is also important to avoid confusing your reader.

PROOFREADING ACTIVITY

Find and correct the errors in the use of quotation marks and italics in the following written interview. Use proofreading symbols such as those on page 901 of *Elements of Language* to make your corrections.

Example I wrote this interview for the school newspaper, ⌒"<u>Lion's Roar</u> ⌒"

"I never liked English very much, Ms. Gina Paulson, our new ninth-grade English teacher claims, "until I was in ninth grade." "That year I read the novel Summer of the Swans. Until then, I thought that stories had to be about larger-than-life events.

A bit surprised, I nod, remembering dramatic plays like Shakespeare's *Julius Caesar*. This interview is not going as I expected.

But the swan story was about an ordinary girl in an ordinary situation." Ms. Paulson continues. "I started to write my own stories about ordinary things, and English became more interesting. "I actually published one in *Plains Review*.

"What was the name of your story"? I ask.

"Paper Airplanes, she says. It's about using your imagination to solve problems.

"I see," I answer. Do you ever find that using your imagination to write a story leads you to the solution of a problem of your own?"

The talkative Ms. Paulson has nothing to say. She just smiles.

MECHANICS | Language in Context: Literary Model

Literary Model: Dialogue in Poetry

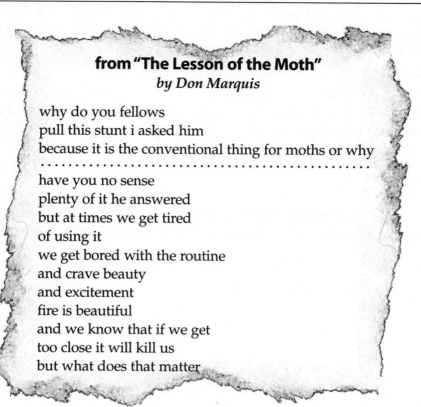

from "The Lesson of the Moth"
by Don Marquis

why do you fellows
pull this stunt i asked him
because it is the conventional thing for moths or why
· ·
have you no sense
plenty of it he answered
but at times we get tired
of using it
we get bored with the routine
and crave beauty
and excitement
fire is beautiful
and we know that if we get
too close it will kill us
but what does that matter

EXERCISE A   Rewrite the dialogue above as if it were a printed dialogue rather than a poem. Add end
marks, commas, quotation marks, and capital letters where they are needed. Begin a new paragraph
every time the speaker changes.

_____

_____

_____

_____

_____

_____

_____

EXERCISE B   Don Marquis explained this poem's lack of capitalization and punctuation by claiming that
the poem was written by a cockroach named archy. In addition to reflecting archy's typing problems,
how does the lack of punctuation and capitalization help characterize archy?

_____

_____

_____

Literary Model (continued)

EXERCISE C Write a poem that contains dialogue. First, brainstorm possible conversations that you would like to express in a poem. Then, decide whether the scenario you like best calls for standard use of quotation marks and other punctuation.

_____

_____

_____

_____

_____

_____

_____

_____

_____

_____

_____

_____

_____

EXERCISE D

1. Did you use standard punctuation in your poem? Why or why not?

_____

_____

2. If you did use standard punctuation, how would your poem be different if you had written it without standard punctuation? Would the style or meaning be different? Would readers experience the poem the same way? Explain.

_____

_____

_____

3. If you did not use standard punctuation, how does the lack of standard punctuation contribute to the style or meaning of the poem? Do you think readers will experience your poem the same way as they would if you had used standard punctuation? Explain.

_____

_____

_____

Writing Application: Dialogue

No matter how formal the writing context, writers add interest when they let readers "hear" what someone has said. An individual's choice of words tells us much that we may not learn from indirect quotations.

INDIRECT	Miguel says that he is planning to audition for the lead role in the play.
DIRECT	Miguel mused, "I'm not sure … maybe I should try out for the lead."
DIRECT	Miguel announced, "Of course, I'm auditioning—I was born to play that role!"

The indirect quotation tells us only that Miguel plans to audition, but his exact words reveal his attitude and level of confidence, too.

WRITING ACTIVITY

Often, teens need to ask adults' permission before participating in various group events—going to an amusement park or taking a camping trip, for example. Think of an upcoming event that you will need to discuss with either a parent or guardian. Write a conversation, using dialogue, in which you and the adult decide on guidelines for your participation in the event.

PREWRITING   List the details about the event as you will present them to the parent or guardian. Then, imagine questions that an adult might raise and the answers you will give. Anticipate whether the adult will be in favor of your participation; if not, brainstorm ways to persuade the adult.

WRITING   As you write the dialogue, decide what words you will use to present your case. Imagine also the words the adult might use in reply. Try to capture each speaker's attitude toward the event.

REVISING   Writers can choose from many words as they introduce quotations. Avoid overusing the verb *say*; instead, vary the verb you use to identify someone's words. Sometimes we simply say words; at other times, we insist, plead, cajole, argue, or suggest!

PUBLISHING   Check your dialogue for errors in usage, punctuation, and spelling. Make sure that you have placed end marks and commas correctly in relation to closing quotation marks and that you have begun a new paragraph each time the speaker changes. With a friend, read your dialogue in front of the class.

EXTENDING YOUR WRITING

You may wish to develop this writing exercise further. For instance, you could write an essay teaching teens how to better communicate with the important adults in their lives, inserting short dialogues to demonstrate how to keep communication lines open (and how they sometimes get shut down); or you could expand the dialogue you have written into a one-act play that focuses on relationships between teens and adults.

Choices: Exploring Apostrophes

The following activities challenge you to find a connection between apostrophes and the world around you. Do the activity below that suits your personality best, and then share your discoveries with your class.

ART

Bigger Is Better

First, outline a giant apostrophe on poster board. Then, inside the apostrophe, write as many common and uncommon contractions and plurals (those that are formed with apostrophes) as you can. Naturally, you'll want to include a few that refer to your class, the students in it, and your projects. Why not make the apostrophes red or a contrasting color?

GAMES

Brothers But Not Sisters

Compile a list of irregular plural nouns, such as *oxen.* Make it a long list. Then, have some fun! With your teacher's permission, divide the class into two teams. Then, say each singular noun aloud. The first team to give the correct irregular plural and its possessive form wins! Oh, why is the title of this project "Brothers But Not Sisters"? The irregular plural for *brother* is *brethren,* but *sisters* doesn't have an irregular plural. If that omission bothers you, make one up!

WRITING

The Challenge

Can you write a sentence that contains an apostrophe in every single word? Can anyone? You'll never know until you try. Try it! Better yet, have a contest to see who can write the longest sentence in which every word uses an apostrophe. Yes, of course, questions are allowed.

DISCUSSION

The *I's* Have It

Are there any words or types of words, such as parts of speech, that cannot be used with an apostrophe, either in a plural or a contraction? Hmmmm. With your teacher's permission, lead a class discussion. During the discussion, write example sentences on the chalkboard showing different parts of speech and the ways they take apostrophes.

BUILDING BACKGROUND KNOWLEDGE

Sioux Relatives

Compile a list of nouns that do not change forms when they are used as plurals. Then, write two sentences—one using the singular possessive and the second using the plural possessive of each noun. Alphabetize your list and print it out double spaced so that there's room for new entries. Give your classmates copies for their notebooks.

WRITING

Tongue Twister

Write a tongue twister using the words *whose* and *who's.* Increase the difficulty of your twister by using words that rhyme or almost rhyme with *who* and by using words that start with the same sound as *who.* Who knows? Your tongue twister may enter popular culture and outlive you by a century or two!

DISCUSSION

Listen Closely

Come up with a list of names that end with *s.* A book of baby names would be a good place to start. Then, for each name, decide whether the possessive of that name should be followed by just an apostrophe or by an apostrophe and an *s.* Explain your reasoning when you submit your list, item by item, for the class's approval. Expect some disagreement!

DRAMA

Center Stage

Take one particularly fine example of writing that includes dialogue containing a lot of contractions. Then, rewrite it without using contractions. Perform both versions of the dialogue (ask one or more friends to help out if more than one character is speaking). Finally, lead a discussion of what is gained or lost by changing all the contractions.

Grammar, Usage, and Mechanics: Language Skills Practice

Apostrophes A

25a. To form the possessive case of most singular nouns, add an apostrophe and an *s*.

EXAMPLES hiker's boots   baby's bottle   Mr. Moss's collection

25b. To form the possessive case of a plural noun ending in *s*, add only the apostrophe.

EXAMPLES wheels' rims   two raccoons' tracks   the Robinsons' backyard

To form the possessive case of a plural noun that does not end in *s*, add an apostrophe and *s*.

EXAMPLES mice's food   women's department   geese's migration pattern

EXERCISE A For each of the following items, change the underlined noun to the correct possessive form. Write your answers on the lines provided.

Example 1. <u>Illinois</u> motto _____*Illinois's motto*_____

1. two <u>teachers</u> cars _____

2. Mrs. <u>Rubin</u> camera _____

3. <u>Arkansas</u> capital _____

4. the <u>children</u> mittens _____

5. the <u>Sanchezes</u> horse _____

6. three <u>months</u> delay _____

7. a <u>moment</u> notice _____

8. two <u>deer</u> tracks _____

9. <u>Darnell</u> hobbies _____

10. both <u>attorneys</u> arguments _____

EXERCISE B For each of the following sentences, underline the word that requires an apostrophe, and add the apostrophe.

Example 1. It is not too soon to start clipping that <u>puppy's</u> nails.

11. George Washingtons picture is in many February ads.

12. Margos coat was torn when the sleeve got caught in the car door.

13. I believe most of these books belong to Lilas sister.

14. Three mens caps were found under the benches after the game.

15. The babies blankets are not dry yet.

MECHANICS

Apostrophes B

25c. Possessive personal pronouns do not require an apostrophe.

> **EXAMPLES** The red van is **ours**. **Its** headlight has been repaired.
>
> Which bicycle is **yours**? Why, it's parked next to **mine**!

The possessive form of *who* is *whose*, not *who's*. Similarly, do not write *it's* for *its*, or *they're* for *their*.

> **EXAMPLES** **Whose** footballs are these? **Who's** [Who is] on your team this year?

25d. Indefinite pronouns in the possessive case require an apostrophe and *s*.

> **EXAMPLES** somebody's helmet another's idea no one's fault

EXERCISE A Underline the correct word or word group in parentheses in each of the following sentences.

Example 1. They found (<u>someone's</u>, someones) playbill on the floor.

1. (They're, Their) taking Grandpa to see *Fiddler on the Roof*.

2. (It's, Its) songs are so much fun to sing.

3. Isn't that musical based on (somebodys, somebody's) stories?

4. (Whose, Who's) the author of the Tevye stories?

5. I am familiar with that author; I believe (his, his') name is Sholem Aleichem.

6. (It's, Its) not easy for me to pronounce that name.

7. Noah said he enjoyed (no ones, no one's) stories better than Aleichem's.

8. I wonder (whose, who's) book Noah read.

9. It's (our's, ours), and you are welcome to borrow it.

10. Listen, (their, they're) playing "If I Were a Rich Man"!

EXERCISE B Proofread the following sentences for errors in the use of possessive pronoun forms. Cross out any incorrect form, and write the correct word above it.

Example 1. It's the first item on ~~they're~~ *their* list.

11. Somebody's pet turtle found it's way to our swimming pool.

12. Is anybodys opinion the same as your's?

13. Whose tools have been left outside—your's or John's?

14. It's just got to be everybody elses' best chance.

15. The boy who's harmonica was stolen is a cousin of hers.

Apostrophes C

25e. Generally, in compound words, names of organizations and businesses, and words showing joint possession, only the last word is possessive in form.

COMPOUND WORD	sister-in-**law's** job
ORGANIZATION	Diabetes **Association's** letter
BUSINESS	Sleepytime **Inn's** swimming pool
JOINT POSSESSION	Cindy and **Mark's** report [but **Cindy's** and **his** report]

25f. When two or more persons possess something individually, each of their names is possessive in form.

EXAMPLE **Mr. Lee's** and **Mr. Tallchief's** classes [the classes of two different people]

MECHANICS

EXERCISE A On the line provided, rewrite each of the following items, using the possessive case.

Example 1. the game of Sue and Han-Ling *Sue and Han-Ling's game*

1. the tie that belongs to my brother-in-law _____

2. the ad printed by the Transit Group _____

3. the entrance of the Grand Hotel _____

4. the responsibility of the editor in chief _____

5. the school Tao and Phoebe attend _____

6. the grades of Yori and Manny _____

7. help given by the American Red Cross _____

8. the attorney for Diaz and Associates _____

9. the tent belonging to Cedric and you _____

10. the project of Lulu and me _____

EXERCISE B Proofread the following sentences for errors in the use of possessive forms. Cross out any incorrect form, and write the correct word above it.

Example 1. *Jean's* ~~Jean~~ and Sela's gardens are the most beautiful ones in the neighborhood.

11. The Museum's of Science and Natural History's main exhibit is about global warming.

12. Are Kevin and Carl's haircuts similar?

13. They've announced that Marguerite and his science projects tied for first place.

14. Will KMRU's fall fund-raiser be starting while KNFAs pledge drive is underway?

15. The Chihuahua's owners have Jordy and your socks, I'm afraid.

Apostrophes D

Apostrophes are often used to form the possessive case of nouns and pronouns.

SINGULAR NOUN	sparrow**'s** nest
PLURAL NOUN ENDING IN *S*	sparrow**s'** nests
POSSESSIVE PERSONAL PRONOUN	**her** nest
INDEFINITE PRONOUN	one**'s** nest
COMPOUND WORD	English sparrow**'s** nest
ORGANIZATIONS AND BUSINESSES	The Happy Sparrow**'s** menu
JOINT POSSESSION	the cardinal and sparrow**'s** birdbath
INDIVIDUAL POSSESSION	the cardinal**'s** and sparrow**'s** nests

MECHANICS

EXERCISE A On the line provided, rewrite each of the following items, using the possessive case.

Example 1. a prank of Lorenzo and Tyler *Lorenzo and Tyler's prank*

1. the overalls belonging to them _____

2. the collection of the Reform Society _____

3. the mandate of the CIA _____

4. one dog belonging to Marcy and one belonging to Sally _____

5. the duet performed by Sergio and you _____

6. the bunk bed of the twins _____

7. the state constitution of Texas _____

8. the accuracy of the guess _____

9. the habitat of the geese _____

10. the citizens of the Netherlands _____

EXERCISE B On the line provided, write the possessive form of each of the following words or word groups.

Example 1. the Mullinses *the Mullinses'*

11. flock _____ **16.** Josh _____

12. oysters _____ **17.** trout _____

13. DOT _____ **18.** islands _____

14. the Garcias _____ **19.** Han and they _____

15. Sioux _____ **20.** anyone else _____

Apostrophes E

MECHANICS

25g. Use an apostrophe to show where letters, numerals, or words have been omitted in a contraction.

EXAMPLES   they are............they're   of the clock............o'clock

                where is............where's   1998............'98

                do not............don't   should not............shouldn't

Do not confuse contractions with possessive pronouns.

CONTRACTIONS	POSSESSIVE PRONOUNS
You're late again. [You are]	Was **your** brother late?
They're moving to Toledo. [They are]	Where is **their** new home?

EXERCISE A   On the line provided, write the correct contraction for each of the following word groups.

Example 1. let us   *let's*

1. is not

2. she will

3. I am

4. they are

5. we will

6. he is

7. you are

8. does not

9. might have

10. cannot

EXERCISE B   Add apostrophes where they are missing in the following sentences.

Example 1. The lecture on the Harlem Renaissance is at two o'clock.

11. Thats an exciting period in African American history, isnt it?

12. Didnt Claude McKay's book *Home to Harlem* become a bestseller in 28?

13. Heres a photo of James Weldon Johnson and J. Rosamond Johnson.

14. Theyre the men who wrote "Lift Every Voice and Sing."

15. I guess you didnt know thats my favorite song.

Apostrophes F

In general, you should not use an apostrophe to form the plural of a noun.

EXAMPLES   **forces** [*not* force's]   **sardines** [*not* sardine's]   **Smiths** [*not* Smith's]

25h.   To prevent confusion, use an apostrophe and an *s* to form the plurals of lowercase letters, some capital letters, numerals, symbols, and some words that are referred to as words.

EXAMPLES   I have to remember to dot my *i*'s and *j*'s.
He got A's on both social studies exams.
When she writes by hand, her *8*'s sometimes look like *&*'s.
Add *and*'s, *but*'s, and *so*'s to the compound sentences.

EXERCISE A   On the line provided before each sentence, write the plural form of the underlined item or items.

Example   *n's, m's* **1.** Sometimes your *n* and *m* look alike.

_____ **1.** Your first sentence contains four *so*.

_____ **2.** Does Tamara have a hard time pronouncing *r*?

_____ **3.** Add up all the *4*.

_____ **4.** Was that popular in the *1980*?

_____ **5.** The teacher wrote *?* beside the errors.

_____ **6.** My *3* sometimes look like *8*.

_____ **7.** Add semicolons before the *and*.

_____ **8.** Has your little brother learned his *ABC*?

_____ **9.** My sister can write *X* now.

_____ **10.** Do you mix up *I* and *L*?

EXERCISE B   Proofread the following sentences for errors in the use of plural forms. Cross out any incorrect form, and write the correct word above it.

Example 1. We're planting ~~azalea's~~ ^{azaleas} and ~~camellia's~~ ^{camellias} next spring.

11. I don't know whether forty apple's will be enough for the display.

12. I think we'll find more *o*'s than *q*s in this alphabet soup.

13. Her voice-over's would have been better without so many *um*'s.

14. Did I leave the *I*s out of *I formation* and *IC 4-A*?

15. How many *11*s and *@*'s are written on that page?

for **CHAPTER 25: PUNCTUATION**   pages 707–709

Apostrophes G

25g. Use an apostrophe to show where letters, numerals, or words have been omitted in a contraction.

　EXAMPLES　she will.......she'll　　I am.......I'm　　we had.......we'd　　does not.......doesn't

25h. To prevent confusion, use an apostrophe and an *s* to form the plurals of lowercase letters, some capital letters, numerals, symbols, and some words that are referred to as words.

　EXAMPLES　Replace the *3*'s with #'s and the *5*'s with %'s.
　　　　　　　How many *o*'s should I put in *zoology*?

EXERCISE A　Underline the word or word group in parentheses that correctly completes each of the following sentences.

Example　**1.** *(They're, Their)* first choice would be to settle this peacefully.

1. Those repeated letters aren't *(s's, ss)* after all.

2. Did you buy that house in *(84, '84)*, Uncle John?

3. Please tell me *(your, you're)* not going to try to jump over that.

4. Roseanne *(didnt, didn't)* set out to be a hero, but she became one.

5. The *(lizard's, lizards)* are turning green again.

6. Well, *(whose, who's)* in charge, then, please?

7. That's enough with the *(buts, but's)*, Todd; it's time to do your homework.

8. How many *(0's, 0s)* are in a googolplex?

9. Rafiq and Caroline will surely be there by eight *(oclock, o'clock)*.

10. I made all *(A's, As)* on this quarter's science quizzes.

EXERCISE B　Fill in the blanks in the sentences below by following the instructions in parentheses.

Example　**1.** How many unneeded ___*like's*___ did he use in that speech? (Write the plural of the word *like*.)

11. We _____ the first in line, but we still got good seats. (Write the contraction for *were not*.)

12. How many _____ does she have in her first name? (Write the plural of the letter *l*.)

13. _____ time to give the team a second chance. (Write the contraction for *It is*.)

14. Do you really think _____ time to take a break? (Write the contraction of *there is*.)

15. His address ends with two _____ in a row. (Write the plural for the numeral *5*.)

ELEMENTS OF LANGUAGE | Third Course

Apostrophes H

25g. Use an apostrophe to show where letters, numerals, or words have been omitted in a contraction.

EXAMPLES He is.......He's   2002.......'02   they have.......they've   had not.......hadn't

25h. To prevent confusion, use an apostrophe and an *s* to form the plurals of lowercase letters, some capital letters, numerals, symbols, and some words that are referred to as words.

EXAMPLES All of those *Mississippi*'s should have four *s*'s and two *p*'s.
Cross out all the *7*'s.

EXERCISE A Proofread the following sentences for errors in the use of contractions and plural forms. Cross out any incorrect form, and write the correct word above it.

Example 1. ~~Whose~~ *Who's* the fellow with the parrot on his shoulder?

1. Marie said that not enough chapter's have been completed.

2. These *Mississippi*'s need dots above all four *is*.

3. Why are there !s and *Is* randomly scattered through this poem?

4. It's color is the result of a particularly embarrassing incident involving our painter's best friend.

5. Hania, can you tell the difference between these two *Us*?

6. Theres not very much of Michaels' sandwich left over, Atietie.

7. Jade had been practicing her signature, so there were *Jade*s written all over the page.

8. Are there *8*'s and 3s in that equation?

9. I really didnt think you would notice that we had moved all the hats.

10. Back in 99, I had a reliable and comfortable hatchback that I never should've sold.

EXERCISE B In each of the items below, fill in the blank with a contraction or plural word, letter, or symbol that logically completes the sentence.

Example 1. The company ___*hasn't*___ responded to our letter yet, has it?

11. I like the way that actress pronounces her _____.

12. _____ going to be the first to audition for the lead role?

13. The collie puppy _____ been trained to sit yet.

14. Do we need to add _____ before the amount on each of these price tags?

15. _____ you going to bring your notebook with you?

Review A: **Apostrophes**

EXERCISE A On the lines provided, write the singular and plural possessive forms of each of the following nouns.

	Singular Possessive	**Plural Possessive**
Example 1. Garza	*Garza's*	*Garzas'*

	Singular Possessive	**Plural Possessive**
1. teacher	_____	_____
2. freshman	_____	_____
3. hour	_____	_____
4. child	_____	_____
5. baby	_____	_____
6. brother-in-law	_____	_____
7. society	_____	_____
8. animal	_____	_____
9. church	_____	_____
10. story	_____	_____

EXERCISE B Each of the following sentences contains at least one error in the use of apostrophes. Cross out each incorrect word, and write the correct word above it.

Example 1. Whew, how many ~~nos~~ *no's* can this cranky two-year-old say in an afternoon?

11. Its too bad that Bob's plan didn't work.

12. Six boys' in Mr. Hazelton's class are on the honor roll this term.

13. Let's replace the wipers on Mark's and Nora's car.

14. Wheres Margaret's tennis racket?

15. Transition words are important in a composition, but you're paper contains too many *therefore*'s.

16. The articles appeared in this weeks papers.

17. The firefighters faces were streaked with soot, and their eyes were red from the smoke.

18. I cant go camping this weekend.

19. When Miguel brought home a report card with four As, his parents were pleased.

20. These books are your's, aren't they?

Review B: **Apostrophes**

EXERCISE A   On the lines provided, write the singular and plural possessive forms of each of the following nouns.

	Singular Possessive	**Plural Possessive**
Example 1. stowaway	*stowaway's*	*stowaways'*

	Singular Possessive	**Plural Possessive**
1. gentleman		
2. lady		
3. dollar		
4. student		
5. ox		
6. audience		
7. mouse		
8. Rodriguez		
9. planet		
10. sister-in-law		

EXERCISE B   Each of the following sentences contains at least one error in the use of possessives, plurals, or contractions. Cross out each incorrect word, and write the correct word above it.

                    he's   *year's*
Example 1. Since ~~hes~~ not a citizen yet, he can't vote in this ~~years~~ election.

11. Aren't you going on a field trip with Ms. Garcias class?

12. Call me in an hours time if you still want a ride to Kay and Bills house.

13. Please write clearly, and leave some space around you're +s and −s.

14. Im sure all the other students books are in better condition than mine.

15. If the book isnt ours, it probably belongs to Kim.

16. Whats the theme of the story Joe calls "A Dogs Tale"?

17. Try not to overuse *and*s and *but*s in you're writing.

18. Were excused from school on Election Day, arent we?

19. The basketball teams coach was proud of his award as this years best instructor.

20. We cant go swimming today because the weathers too cold.

MECHANICS

Review C: **Apostrophes**

EXERCISE A On the lines provided, write the singular and plural possessive forms of each of the following nouns.

	Singular Possessive	**Plural Possessive**
Example 1. Chen	*Chen's*	*Chens'*

	Singular Possessive	**Plural Possessive**
1. donkey		
2. newspaper		
3. Jones		
4. Tamika		
5. player		
6. photograph		
7. class		
8. Perez		
9. employee		
10. buffalo		

EXERCISE B Each of the following sentences contains at least one error in the use of possessives, plurals, or contractions. Cross out each incorrect word, and write the correct word above it.

Example 1. We all laughed as we watched ~~Rosas~~ *Rosa's* cat chase ~~it's~~ *its* tail.

11. Cynthia and Tyrone's backpacks look very similar, but their made by different companies.

12. The Murphy's live across the street from the Bernsteins.

13. Even though they are birds, ostriches dont fly.

14. Geena's and Paco's mother is Josephina, the museum curator.

15. You're undotted *is* look like *e*s.

16. The libertarians candidacy is questionable, since he's out of money.

17. Hercules feats of strength arent likely to be outdone by modern athletes.

18. The forecast calls for several days of rain, so well have to postpone the hiking trip.

19. Paris reputation for romance and beauty draws visitor's to France from all around the world.

20. Lian's earrings are made of pearl's and gold.

Proofreading Application: Newspaper Article

Good writers are generally good proofreaders. Readers tend to admire and trust writing that is error-free. Make sure that you correct all errors in grammar, usage, spelling, and punctuation in your writing. Your readers will have more confidence in your words if you have done your best to proofread carefully.

Proper use of apostrophes is especially important in informative writing, in which accurate and clear information is essential. However, when a writer uses apostrophes improperly, the meaning of information can become fuzzy and readers can become confused and frustrated. Provide accurate and clear information for your readers by proofreading your writing carefully to avoid errors in the use of apostrophes.

PROOFREADING ACTIVITY

In the following newspaper article, find the errors in the use of apostrophes and replace the incorrect words. Use proofreading symbols such as those on page 901 of *Elements of Language* to make your corrections. An item may contain more than one error.

Example The student's now have an Exploratorium!

Last Friday was opening day for the new Exploratorium for Winn Elementarys students. At two o clock, Principal Brenda Jaffe cut the big red ribbon, and dozens of third-graders streamed into the show. "The futures yours'," Ms. Jaffe told her students.

Twenty-four colorful displays lined the walls of a portable class-room devoted to the project. Jason Perez's and Celia Emerson's giant soap-bubble machine drew *oohs* and *ahs* from the pint-sized scientists. Jim Washington wasn't surprised to see the eager visitors flock to his' rainbow machine, which dazzled onlookers. Kyle Smith and Lisa White Deer's smiles drew almost as big a crowd as their magnet dis-plays, which appeared to fascinate their fan's. Another group of students clustered around the mices cage in which an energetic pair of rodents powered a tiny windmill.

Planning, funding, and completing the exhibits construction took an entire semester of the Young Scientists Saturday afternoons. Take your bow, Young Scientists'; all that work was worth it!

Grammar, Usage, and Mechanics: Language Skills Practice

Literary Model: Poetic Description

Mercutio.

O, then I see Queen Mab hath been with
   you.
She is the fairies' midwife, and she comes
In shape no bigger than an agate stone
On the forefinger of an alderman,
Drawn with a team of little atomies
Over men's noses as they lie asleep;
Her wagon spokes made of long spinners'
   legs,
The cover, of the wings of grasshoppers;
Her traces, of the smallest spider web;
Her collars, of the moonshine's wat'ry
   beams;
Her whip, of cricket's bone; the lash, of
   film;
Her wagoner, a small gray-coated gnat,
Not half so big as a round little worm
Pricked from the lazy finger of a maid;
Her chariot is an empty hazelnut,

Made by the joiner squirrel or old grub,
Time out o' mind the fairies' coachmakers.
And in this state she gallops night by night
Through lovers' brains, and then they
   dream of love;
On courtiers' knees, that dream on curt-
   sies straight;
O'er lawyers' fingers, who straight dream
   on fees;
O'er ladies' lips, who straight on kisses
   dream. . . .
Sometime she gallops o'er a courtier's nose,
And then dreams he of smelling out a
   suit;
And sometimes comes she with a tithe
   pig's tail
Tickling a parson's nose as [he] lies
   asleep,
Then dreams he of another benefice.

—from *Romeo and Juliet* by William Shakespeare
Act I, Scene 4

EXERCISE A

1. How many of the underlined words in the passage above are singular possessives? _____

2. How many are plural possessives? _____

3. How many are contractions? _____

4. Why do you think Shakespeare uses contractions instead of spelling out the words? _____

_____

_____

_____

_____

_____

Literary Model (continued)

EXERCISE B On the lines below, write a short description of an imaginary creature or person. In your description, give the being a name, explain what it looks like, and describe what fantastic powers it has. You may choose to write your description in verse, as Shakespeare did.

_____

_____

_____

_____

_____

_____

_____

_____

_____

_____

_____

_____

_____

_____

EXERCISE C

1. In what words did you use an apostrophe to show possession? _____

_____

_____

2. In what words did you use an apostrophe to form a contraction? _____

_____

_____

3. How do the contractions you used contribute to the tone of your description? If you wrote your description in verse, how do the contractions affect the meter, or poetic rhythm, of your description?

_____

_____

_____

_____

MECHANICS | Language in Context: Writing Application

Writing Application: Newspaper Article

When you were in a preschool or kindergarten class, some type of label probably served to connect you and your name with your lunchbox, book bag, and other possessions. In a way, the apostrophe serves a similar purpose: In writing, it connects an object with its owner.

WRITING ACTIVITY

For the sports section of a high school or local newspaper, write an article describing an athletic event. As you mention details such as whose free throw won the game and whose defense techniques were masterful, use at least three singular possessive nouns, two plural possessive nouns, and two indefinite pronouns in the possessive case.

PREWRITING   Either attend an athletic event, spend several minutes recalling one you attended in the past, or make up an athletic event in your head—complete with many details. Jot down phrases and complete sentences that answer the six questions crucial to any newspaper article: *Who? What? When? Where? Why?* and *How?* In addition, since all athletic events involve some kind of action, and actions are expressed by verbs, brainstorm a list of verbs you can use that are particularly descriptive and lively. If necessary, read articles from the sports section of a few newspapers to get ideas.

WRITING   Craft an opening sentence that makes your reader want to read the entire article. Use the verbs you brainstormed—or others that may pop into your head once you get in the rhythm of writing about the athletic event. If you're still not satisfied with your choice of verbs, consult a thesaurus. Remember, however, to double-check a dictionary to be sure that a word suggested by the thesaurus is appropriate for your context.

REVISING   Read your draft aloud. Listen for weak words and clichés, and replace any you find with exciting words and phrases that you use in a novel way. If your draft contains few sensory details—details observed through sight, hearing, taste, touch, or smell—consider adding some. Make the reader feel as if he or she were actually at the athletic event. Pay special attention to your use of apostrophes. Make sure you haven't confused possessive pronouns with contractions and that you used at least three singular possessive nouns, two plural possessive nouns, and two indefinite pronouns in the possessive case.

PUBLISHING   Proofread your newspaper article line by line to correct errors in spelling, grammar, and punctuation. If you have access to a computer, try designing your composition to look like an actual newspaper article. Choose a name for your publication, and write a headline for your sports story. If your class has a Web site, ask your teacher for permission to post your story online.

EXTENDING YOUR WRITING

Perhaps you could transfer what you have learned to a group of middle school students enrolled in an after-school program. You could read them your article and suggest tips for writing a successful newspaper article about an athletic event. Then, play the role of teacher as you assign them to write their own article and "coach" them during the writing process.

Choices: Exploring Punctuation

The following activities challenge you to find a connection between punctuation and the world around you. Do the activity below that suits your personality best, and then share your discoveries with your class.

1492

Do you know what happened in 1492? Of course you do. It's one of the dates that every American should know. Create a list of what you consider to be important dates in world and American history—ten or twenty should be enough. Then, write sentences for each event and put the appropriate date in parentheses. Cut out your sentences, and paste them in order on a time line.

$a(b+c)$

How are parentheses used in mathematics, especially in algebra? Find some good examples and explain them to the class. Make connections between your examples and terms that the class already knows, such as subject, predicate, complement, and clause. You may wish to transform equations into words.

:) or :(

Do you surf the Net? Internet users have some interesting uses for punctuation. Find out as much as you can about the language of the Internet. For example, what are *emoticons*? What do Internet users mean by the word *netiquette*? Then, save your classmates some embarrassment. Tell (and show) them how punctuation marks are used on the Internet.

Dashing and Daring

What exactly does the word *dash* mean? How many definitions does it have? What are the origins of the word? Find out. Then, write sentences using each definition. Make a poster using your etymology, definitions, and sentences. With your teacher's permission, hang it in plain view of your classmates.

Acronym Alert

Isn't it frustrating when you suddenly come across a group of capital letters in something you're reading, but the writer doesn't tell you what they mean? If your class hasn't already compiled a list of acronyms, such as FBI and IRS, do so now. Be sure to include the full name of each agency or organization. A telephone book is a good source for many acronyms. Write sentences using each acronym. In parentheses, spell out the full name of each acronym. Then, make a poster displaying your list and sentences. With your teacher's permission, hang your poster in the classroom.

Test Pilot

Many word-processing programs will hyphenate words automatically. However, a computer's hyphenation is seldom as good as yours. Find out how to turn on and off automatic hyphenation in a word-processing program available to you. Then, do an experiment. Turn on hyphenation, and set very wide margins. Type in a paragraph or two, and print the paragraphs out. Check the computer's hyphenation against a dictionary's. Report your findings to the class, advising them either to turn on or to turn off automatic hyphenation.

Custom-made

Create a custom-made project that suits your interests. If you like reading, find a passage that uses every mark of punctuation. If you like writing, write that passage. If you like science, investigate how science uses punctuation marks. Collect examples of dashes. Figure out a way to use a word-processing program to check that every open parenthesis has a closed parenthesis. Whatever project you choose, be sure to get your teacher's approval before you begin.

Hyphens to Divide Words

26a. Use a hyphen to divide a word at the end of a line.

> **EXAMPLES** Roberto used the wrong type of **ham-mer** to drive in the nail.
>
> Ms. De La Garza is currently **president-elect** of the Lions Club of North Kingston.
>
> The path to the western overlook was **blocked** by a fallen tree. [Do not divide a one-syllable word.]

EXERCISE Some of the numbered words in this letter are incorrectly divided. On the line provided, write the numbered word and draw vertical lines to show where it may be divided. If the word should not be divided, write *DND* after it.

Example Genealogical **[1]** disco-   *dis|cov|er|ies*

veries can be fascinating.

Dear Carly,

   I couldn't wait to write you **[1]** bec-   **[1]** _____

ause what I have to tell you is fairly **[2]** excit-   **[2]** _____

ing. Yesterday, I received a long, detailed **[3]** lett-   **[3]** _____

er from my aunt Ethyl, the one who lives **[4]** a-   **[4]** _____

lone in a tiny house on the outskirts of Pittsburgh.

Genealogy has always been her hobby. (She **[5]** pri-   **[5]** _____

des herself on having detective-like skills.) She wrote

that she's discovered that my **[6]** great-great-grand-   **[6]** _____

father (my maternal grandfather's grandfather) was

Ludwig Mueller III, the steel baron who made **[7]** yo-   **[7]** _____

ur and my birthplace of Leeds change from a **[8]** farm-   **[8]** _____

ing community to a thriving small city. To be **[9]** rel-   **[9]** _____

ated to someone famous has always been my dream,

and now it has come true.

   I hope you still plan to visit me this **[10]** summ-   **[10]** _____

er. It's only two months away, you know.

   Love,

   Cassandra

Hyphens in Compound Words

26b. Use a hyphen with compound numbers from *twenty-one* to *ninety-nine* and with fractions used as modifiers.

26c. Use a hyphen with the prefixes *ex–*, *self–*, *all–*, and *great–*; with the suffixes *–elect* and *–free;* and with all prefixes before a proper noun or proper adjective.

26d. Hyphenate a compound adjective when it precedes the noun it modifies.

EXAMPLES   **sixty-four** days   **self**-taught   **well-documented** narratives

EXERCISE   In the following sentences, place a caret (∧) to show where each compound word should be hyphenated. If no word in the sentence should be hyphenated, write *C* after the sentence.

Example 1. You should drink calcium ∧ enriched orange juice.

1. In the story, the villain dies from a self inflicted wound.

2. Bill Bradley is an ex basketball player.

3. Governor elect Rousseau was born right here in our town.

4. The Assad family left Istanbul on a bitterly cold day.

5. Have you heard that only forty two percent of the people in this area favor a bike trail?

6. The recycling bin is two thirds full.

7. Did you know that manatees have trouble hearing low frequency sounds?

8. At this location today, one hundred and three people have registered to vote.

9. Elissa is looking for an oil free moisturizing liquid.

10. The pro American position will be presented next.

11. Adelita wanted to speak to the ex governor of the state.

12. Lawrence's great uncle Peter was Speaker of the House in 1962.

13. Nine tenths of the eleventh grade students are going to college.

14. Despite the hockey team's all out effort, they still lost the game.

15. The pre Socratic philosopher Pythagoras believed that the earth revolved around the sun.

16. Mei Ling's vacation is well deserved.

17. What is a two syllable word whose second syllable rhymes with *old*?

18. That history book from 1950 is out of date.

19. As for baseball players, Kirsten's all time favorite is Mark McGwire.

20. Eric, along with Abraham and Louise, wants to look for an after school job.

Hyphen Review

26a. Use a hyphen to divide a word at the end of a line.

> **EXAMPLE** Franco is hoping to play **trom-bone** in the orchestra.

26b. Use a hyphen with compound numbers from *twenty-one* to *ninety-nine* and with fractions used as modifiers.

> **EXAMPLE** **eighty-eight** keys

26c. Use a hyphen with the prefixes *ex–, self–, all–,* and *great–;* with the suffixes *–elect* and *–free;* and with all prefixes before a proper noun or proper adjective.

> **EXAMPLE** **all-**encompassing

26d. Hyphenate a compound adjective when it precedes the noun it modifies.

> **EXAMPLE** a **world-renowned** author

EXERCISE In the following paragraph, some hyphens are missing and others are used incorrectly. Cross out the word(s) that involve an error in hyphenation and write the correction above it.

Example [1] Do you consider Martin Ochoa a ~~self made~~ *self-made* man?

[1] By the time Martin Ochoa was in the tenth grade, he had already dec-ided that he wanted to be a politician. [2] He made an all out effort when he ran for the student senate of his high school; he won ninety one percent of the vote. [3] His campaign motto was "Self governing students are the wave of the future." [4] Of course, the school administration did not always agree completely with his ph ilosophy. [5] In fact, Martin had to tone down his well intentioned rhetoric quite a bit, thus learning his first lesson in compromise. [6] Years later, he told an ex-princip-al of his school that throughout his political career this lesson had proved invaluab-le. [7] During Martin's senior year, when he was president elect of the student senate, he devised a volunteer program. [8] It eventually became a model that was a-dopted by more than two-thirds of the city's middle schools and high schools. [9] By mid November of that year, Martin, with his seemingly-endless supply of charisma, had recruited over eighty students to do volunteer work in the community. [10] Martin majored in political science at the state university, gradua-ting with honors, and worked for four years for his state representative before launching into politics himself.

MECHANICS

Parentheses

26e. Use parentheses to enclose material that is added to a sentence but is not considered to be of major importance.

> **EXAMPLES**   Orion **(**my favorite constellation**)** was a mighty hunter in Greek mythology.
>
> Gold Mountain's history is one of change. **(**See the time line on page 3.**)**

EXERCISE A   In the following sentences, insert parentheses to set off parenthetical elements.

Example 1. Our state representative *(*a so-called "man of the people"*)* does not confer with his constituents enough to satisfy me.

1. I didn't realize that Judy Blume author of *Superfudge* has written novels for adults.

2. Did you know that Harlingen it's my hometown is named after the town of the same name in the Netherlands?

3. Fill in each circle on the answer sheet completely use a number 2 pencil only.

4. The Chilean poet Pablo Neruda winner of the 1971 Nobel Prize for literature was often referred to as the "poet of enslaved humanity."

5. I plan to send this calendar we bought it at a Mexican restaurant to our friends in Wisconsin.

EXERCISE B   In the following sentences, insert parentheses to set off parenthetical elements. If a sentence is correct, write *C* at the end.

Example 1. Kylene *(*I've known her for seven years*)* loves to write poems.

6. For the poetry competition, Kylene she's my best friend decided to write a tanka poem.

7. Japanese tankas they date to the seventh century have five unrhymed lines and a total of thirty-one syllables.

8. As tankas should, Kylene's poem produces strong feelings on the part of the reader.

9. She was inspired by the tankas of Ono Komachi a ninth-century poet.

10. Kylene was also impressed by the fact that Komachi supposedly one of the most beautiful women of her time was highly renowned during a period of Japanese history when women dominated society and literature.

Grammar, Usage, and Mechanics: Language Skills Practice

MECHANICS

Dashes

26f. Use a dash to indicate an abrupt break in thought or speech or an unfinished statement or question.

> **EXAMPLES**   I simply cannot understand—Gerald, are you listening to me?—why the O'Tooles refuse to trim those trees.
>
> "How can I help you when I don't know—" the nurse broke off when she saw the anguish on the child's face.

26g. Use a dash to indicate *namely, that is,* or *in other words* or to otherwise introduce an explanation.

> **EXAMPLE**   Irene is perfect for the part—the subtle yet powerful energy she exudes will transform the entire production.

EXERCISE   In the following sentences, insert carets (∧) where dashes are appropriate.

Example 1. Can you guess why Rhode Island's most common nickname ∧ though it is unofficial ∧ is Little Rhody?

1. Ms. Tan, Amelia's mom, has decided to pursue a degree in a field she finds fascinating micro-biology.

2. Most voters I'm sure you'll agree with me want to be represented by someone to whom they can relate.

3. The work of a volcanologist that is, someone who studies volcanoes is anything but dull.

4. Tabitha had finally realized her mistake she had depended too heavily upon someone other than herself.

5. That artist obviously is enchanted by clouds cumulus clouds, to be exact.

6. "Why can't" Rubén began, then faltered.

7. Every time Monica goes with us well, maybe just *most* of the time we all end up arguing.

8. My grandma's neighbor the one on the nearest corner has three fig trees and two pear trees in his tiny yard.

9. Jean-Pierre's father he speaks at least four languages fluently does business consulting work around the world.

10. "Do you do you really expect me to believe that excuse?" Lauren's mother demanded.

MECHANICS

Parentheses and Dashes

26e. Use parentheses to enclose material that is added to a sentence but is not considered to be of major importance.

26f. Use a dash to indicate an abrupt break in thought or speech or an unfinished statement or question.

26g. Use a dash to indicate *namely, that is,* or *in other words* or to otherwise introduce an explanation.

EXERCISE In the following sentences, parentheses and dashes are missing. Insert parentheses where appropriate. Insert carets (∧) to show where dashes are appropriate.

Example 1. Occasionally, people (including good friends) need to be corrected.

1. Yesterday, Kelley he's definitely one of a kind made the statement that women had no part in the early development of computer languages.

2. I found this hard to believe, considering according to my mother and aunts how many women work in the field of computer languages today.

3. My skepticism and curiosity they're both trademarks of mine prompted me to research the issue.

4. In no time, I'd learned about Grace Murray Hopper 1906–1992.

5. This American Navy officer and mathematician helped to develop COBOL a programming language for the UNIVAC, the first commercial electronic computer.

6. Several years earlier in 1952, she had devised the first compiler, which is a program that translates instructions in English to a computer language.

7. She retired from the Navy at the age of 80 when most people are putting their feet up only to begin serving as a senior consultant for a major computer manufacturer.

8. During her long lifetime 86 years! she frequently must have been amazed by technological advances.

9. The next day I supplied Kelley gently, of course with the information about Hopper.

10. I hope that in the future though I have my doubts he will check out the facts before he gives his opinion.

MECHANICS

Ellipsis Points

26h. Use ellipsis points (. . .) to mark omissions from quoted materials and pauses in a written passage.

EXAMPLE "Peter Piper picked a peck of pickled peppers **. . . .** [H]ow many pecks of pickled peppers did Peter Piper pick?"

EXERCISE Read the paragraph below. Then, follow the instructions for the items after the paragraph.

[1] Archaeologists already knew that ancient ruins existed near the Italian city of Pisa (famous for its leaning tower). [2] Therefore, when construction began on a junction for the Italian state railway at Pisa, the archaeologists decided to do some excavating. [3] By fall of 1999, the archaeological team had turned up sixteen ships! [4] The ships dated from the third century B.C. to the sixth century A.D. [5] The shortest was 23 feet long, the longest nearly 100 feet. [6] In addition, the archaeologists unearthed cargoes of fruit and olives still in storage jars. [7] Probably the most emotional discovery was that of the skeletons of a man (possibly a sailor) and a dog near one of the cargo ships.

Example 1. Rewrite the first sentence, omitting the words *(famous for its leaning tower)*.

Archaeologists already knew that ancient ruins existed near the Italian city of Pisa. . . .

1. Rewrite the first sentence, omitting the words *the Italian city of.*

_____

_____

2. Rewrite the second sentence, omitting *on a junction for the Italian state railway.*

_____

_____

3. Rewrite the third and fifth sentences, omitting the fourth sentence.

_____

_____

4. Rewrite the fifth and sixth sentences, omitting the words *In addition.*

_____

_____

5. Rewrite the seventh sentence, omitting the words *(possibly a sailor).*

_____

Brackets

26i. Use brackets to enclose an explanation within quoted or parenthetical material.

EXAMPLES The audience was moved when the speaker said, "Without him [his brother] , I wouldn't be here today." [The words are enclosed in brackets to show that they have been inserted into the quotation and are not the words of the speaker.]

The concept of supply and demand is crucial to one's understanding of economics. (See Chapter 2 [especially Section 1] .) [The words are enclosed in brackets because they are within parenthetical material.]

EXERCISE In the following sentences, insert brackets where they are needed.

Example 1. "This [Kahlil Gibran's *The Prophet*] should be required reading for every person over fourteen years of age," Mr. Brock-Jones was quoted as saying.

1. Lisette's speech contained the following remark: "I accept this medal Comal College Student of the Year with the acknowledgment of the support of my family, friends, and teachers."

2. The actor remarked, none too humbly, "When I deliver my character's famous speech Act I Scene 3, the audience weeps."

3. If you read the quotation from the Navy captain (see the article entitled "Life Down Under" page 4, column 5), you will have a better understanding of life on a submarine.

4. At one point in the interview, the singer responded, "When I'm home London, England, I occasionally give free concerts."

5. As part of the preparation for your trip, you will find it immensely helpful to read about the local customs (the "When in Rome . . ." section of Chapter 2 pages 18–20).

6. The mayor-elect then commented, "It is imperative that we make this the proposed loop around the city a priority of this administration."

7. The winner answered my question about the best type of racing bicycle with "There's no doubt that mine a twenty-seven speed Italian bicycle is the best."

8. To get to the Connellys' farm, you go down Arrowhead Road (between Route 10 the turnoff is north of Evinston and Route 52).

9. "Do you happen to know the year that Tony Dorsett was awarded it the Heisman Trophy?" Luella asked.

10. Please turn to the statistics on world population (see page 46 Chart C) before continuing.

MECHANICS

Review A: **Hyphens**

EXERCISE   For each of the following words, rewrite the word on the line provided and draw a vertical line or lines to indicate where the word may be divided at the end of a line. If a word should not be divided, write *do not divide*.

Example 1. accepted _____ *ac|cept|ed* _____

1. salt-free _____

2. pavement _____

3. caught _____

4. along _____

5. racing _____

6. unlike _____

7. nail-biter _____

8. postdate _____

9. antebellum _____

10. porridge _____

11. eighth _____

12. elect _____

13. mid-June _____

14. scary _____

15. hammer _____

16. viewed _____

17. lady-in-waiting _____

18. written _____

19. usage _____

20. preheat _____

MECHANICS

Review B: Hyphens, Dashes, and Parentheses

EXERCISE Rewrite each of the following sentences to add the hyphens, dashes, or parentheses that are needed.

Example 1. Although Catherine the Great 1729–1796 expressed her opposition to serfdom, she actually caused its expansion in eighteenth century Russia. *Although Catherine the Great (1729–1796) expressed her opposition to serfdom, she actually caused its expansion in eighteenth-century Russia.*

1. The cartoon on the editorial page did you see it? pokes fun at both candidates. _____
_____

2. Does Coach Mata Ray Mata, not Tony Mata choose the all star team? _____
_____

3. Carl Martin spent several years 1991–1997 with the Peace Corps in sub Saharan Africa. _____
_____

4. "But but we weren't making any noise," Enrico stammered. _____
_____

5. There are only twenty one days I can't believe it before the end of school. _____
_____

6. My cousin Winkie her real name is Ann is going to stay with us next week. _____
_____

7. Is Susie's mom self employed? _____
_____

8. Jane Reagan she's in my gym class is a top notch skier. _____
_____

9. "What I started to tell you oh, never mind," said Rodrigo. _____
_____

10. In mid August Rafe stepped off the train in New Orleans birthplace of the blues. _____
_____

Review C: Hyphens, Dashes, Parentheses, Ellipsis Points, and Brackets

EXERCISE   Rewrite each of the following sentences to add any hyphens, dashes, parentheses, ellipsis points, and brackets that are needed.

Example 1. The anti dumping tariffs are discussed later in this chapter see pages 101–104.

> *The anti-dumping tariffs are discussed later in this chapter (see pages 101–104).*

1. "I I'm ready to tell you everything," the witness said hesitatingly to the attorney. _____

2. Forty two percent or is it forty four percent? of the votes have been counted. _____

3. According to Mr. O'Rourke my history teacher, self reliance is worth cultivating. _____

4. "Are you trying to tell me" Sean stopped when he saw the look on Mara's face. _____

5. In his speech, the president elect of the Rotary Club said, "We the club's members will do all we can to help Robstown." _____

6. One fourth cup of solution is needed. (See page 328 Appendix B for a conversion chart.) _____

7. I find that decade the so called Roaring Twenties the most fascinating of all. _____

8. Rufino Tamayo 1899–1991 was inspired in part by pre Columbian art. _____

9. "Well, I can't I can't really say whether it's a well written story or not," the man hedged. _____

10. "The award Employee of the Month goes to Trish Rubinstein," the manager announced. _____

Proofreading Application: Advertising Flier

Good writers are generally good proofreaders. Readers tend to admire and trust writing that is error-free. Make sure that you correct all errors in grammar, usage, spelling, and punctuation in your writing. Your readers will have more confidence in your words if you have done your best to proofread carefully.

Fliers are one of the most inexpensive ways of advertising. In a single page, a flier can give the public a great deal of information about an event or service. When you write a flier, pay particular attention to proofreading for correct use of the punctuation marks you have studied in this chapter. Give special attention to parentheses and brackets. If you leave out one half of a pair, many of your readers will be lost because they won't understand you.

PROOFREADING ACTIVITY

In the following flier, find the errors in the use of hyphens, dashes, parentheses, brackets, and ellipsis points and correct them. Use proofreading symbols such as those on page 901 of *Elements of Language* to make your corrections.

Example Joel's business—he takes care of pets—is doing quite well.

> ### Joel's Pet Sitting Service
>
> ### 546 Fifty seventh Street
>
> *Your pets—dogs, cats, birds, ponies, iguanas, and tropical fish*
>
> *are our specialty!*
>
> **Our business is pet sitting, but we don't just sit!**
>
> We offer feeding, walking, washing elephants require an extra
>
> charge), and tender loving care.
>
> Even exotic pets (we once cared for a boa constrictor (her name
>
> was Nancy) are no problem for us! Your beloved pet won't suffer a
>
> moment's discomfort or loneliness when we are on the job!
>
> ### Call 555 5442   555 4455 after 4:00 P.M.
>
> *Three-quarters of our customers use our services more than once!*
>
> The following is a testimony from Mrs. Rhonda Peal, one of our
>
> loyal customers:
>
> *"My three dogs and two cats love Joel. He has been my pet sitter*
>
> *many times . . . and I have found him to be dependable and kind."*

Literary Model: Dashes in a Story

The stranger looked at me again—still cocking his eye, as if he were expressly taking aim at me with his invisible gun—and said, 'He's a likely young parcel of bones that. What is it you call him?'

'Pip,' said Joe.

'Christened Pip?'

'No, not christened Pip.'

'Surname Pip?'

'No,' said Joe, 'it's a kind of family name what he gave himself when an infant, and is called by.'

'Son of yours?'

'Well,' said Joe, meditatively—not, of course, that it could be in anywise necessary to consider about it, but because it was the way at the Jolly Bargemen to seem to consider deeply about everything that was discussed over pipes; 'well—no. No, he ain't.'

'Nevvy?' said the strange man.

'Well,' said Joe, with the same appearance of profound cogitation, 'he is not—no, not to deceive you, he is *not*—my nevvy.'

'What the Blue Blazes is he?' asked the stranger. Which appeared to me to be an inquiry of unnecessary strength.

—from *Great Expectations* by Charles Dickens

EXERCISE A   In the excerpt above, circle four places where Dickens uses dashes to indicate abrupt breaks in thought or to introduce an explanation. Hint: Two dashes used to set off one element count as a single use.

EXERCISE B

1. What do the dashes in Joe's speech indicate about how he talks and feels in this situation?

_____

_____

_____

_____

2. What do the dashes in the narration indicate about the way the narrator (Pip) talks and how he feels describing this scene?

_____

_____

_____

_____

Literary Model (continued)

EXERCISE C Think about a time when a friend or family member introduced you to someone you didn't know—for example, on the first day of school or at a family gathering. If the meeting was unexpected or the person you were being introduced to kept asking questions, the situation may have been a little uncomfortable. Write a short dialogue portraying such a scene, whether it's an actual event or one that you imagine. Use dashes to indicate abrupt breaks in thought or to mean *namely* or *that is.*

_____

_____

_____

_____

_____

_____

_____

_____

_____

_____

_____

_____

_____

_____

EXERCISE D

1. How did you use dashes to indicate how you felt while you were being introduced?

_____

_____

_____

_____

2. How did you use dashes to indicate how the person introducing you and the stranger you were being introduced to felt?

_____

_____

_____

_____

for **CHAPTER 26: PUNCTUATION** *pages 716–26*

Writing Application: Reports

Each element of punctuation has specific functions that help you make your writing as clear as possible. Some elements help your reader understand the relationships among the words and ideas you are trying to get across. For example, when you write "My great-aunt Roberta (she's 78 years young) is an amazing storyteller," your reader realizes that the information in parentheses is less important than your great-aunt's storytelling abilities. Other elements of punctuation are like road signs in that they provide specific information. Ellipsis points, for instance, can indicate that something has been omitted from quoted materials.

WRITING ACTIVITY

Mentally walk yourself through a typical day. Pause whenever you visualize yourself using an ordinary object. At the end of your mental stroll, choose one of the ordinary objects you imagined and use it as the topic of a short report. In no more than three paragraphs, describe how the object came into existence and, if applicable, how its function has changed over time. Use at least three of the five elements of punctuation (hyphens, dashes, parentheses, brackets, and ellipsis points) discussed in this chapter.

PREWRITING You'll need to locate and read information about the object in reference sources. To read with a purpose, apply the following techniques: Don't start off by reading from the first page of the reference source. Look for key words in the index, study the table of contents, and skim text to check headings, charts, and illustrations. When you find information on your topic, slow down and read every word. Take notes on main ideas and specific details. Don't copy every word into your notes; use your own words instead. However, you may want to use one or two direct quotations in your report. Be sure you keep track of the sources that contain relevant information.

WRITING Use your notes to write a draft. Spend extra time on your opening sentence; a well-crafted opening sentence will entice your reader to continue. Clearly connect and arrange the ideas in chronological order. In addition, use transitional words and phrases to show how the ideas are connected.

REVISING Set your draft aside for a while before you begin final revisions. When you read the report again, ask yourself whether you could improve it by including quoted material from one of your sources. If so, use ellipsis points correctly if you decide to omit parts of the material. Be sure that you have used at least three of the five elements of punctuation mentioned above.

PUBLISHING Proofread your report for errors in spelling, grammar, and punctuation. In particular, ask yourself whether every sentence is a complete sentence, whether the tense and form of each verb are correct, and whether the report is free of errors in subject-verb and pronoun-antecedent agreement. Double-check your use of hyphens, dashes, parentheses, brackets, and ellipsis points for correctness and clarity. With your teacher's permission, post your report on the class bulletin board or Web page.

EXTENDING YOUR WRITING

Collect your classmates' reports. Create an anthology titled *Extraordinary Histories of Ordinary Objects*. Exchange anthologies with other classes or donate yours to the school library.

Choices: **Exploring Spelling**

The following activities challenge you to find a connection between spelling and the world around you. Do the activity below that suits your personality best, and then share your discoveries with your class.

LINGUISTICS

Pore, Poor, and *Pour*

The homonyms that you see in your textbook are not the only ones in English. What are some of the other homonyms that can often be confused? Make an alphabetized list of at least ten of these word pairs and their definitions. Be sure to make copies to hand out to your classmates.

GEOGRAPHY

From Arabia to India to England

Show the class how American English has borrowed words from every continent in the world. Copy or sketch a good-sized world map. Then, trace the path of ten words as they entered the English language.

RESEARCH

Swahili or Cherokee?

When English-language speakers hear a good word, they remember it. Oh, sometimes they change the pronunciation a bit or fiddle with the spelling, but pretty soon the word is listed in an English dictionary. Investigate your own roots. What words did your ancestors contribute to the English language? Feel free to make more than one list if you have a multicultural background! Make a note of the dictionary or book where you found the origin of each word.

INVENTION

Phydough

What! You can't pronounce this title? It's *Fido.* It's just spelled by different rules. Because English has borrowed so many words from other languages, spelling can be confusing. Take advantage of the situation! Invent new ways to spell a few words. Your inventions *must* follow an acknowledged pattern of spelling.

HISTORY

The Mystery Man

Who was William Caxton, and what did he have to do with spelling? Do a little research, and find out. Then, give a short speech or write a few pages explaining his relationship to spelling rules.

REAL LIFE

Bakers and Forrests

How did we get last names, anyway? We didn't always have them, so where did they come from? What circumstances or events made them seem necessary? Fill your classmates in on the story. While you're at it, find out what your own last name means and a few other surnames, too.

DISCUSSION

Move Over, Webster

You've been reading and writing for a lot of years now. You probably have a few of your own opinions about spelling. What are they? Discuss them with a group of friends. Listen to their ideas, too. Then, together, come up with your own new and improved spelling guide for the English language.

REAL-LIFE EXAMPLES

Candid Camera

If you've got a camera, some film, and a sense of humor, here's the project for you! Go on a photo scavenger hunt for misspelled signs. Unfortunately for English but fortunately for you, you'll find them everywhere, especially on vehicles sporting hand-painted messages and on business marquees. Of course, some of these misspellings are intentional. Go ahead and snap them, too. They'll help fill up the scrapbook you make for the class to peruse.

Good Spelling Habits

27a. To learn the spelling of a word, pronounce it, study it, and write it.

(1) Pronounce words carefully. Mispronunciation can lead to misspelling.
(2) Use a dictionary. Whenever you find that you have misspelled a word, look it up.
(3) Spell by syllables. A *syllable* is a word part that is pronounced as one uninterrupted sound.

EXAMPLES	**One Syllable**	**Two Syllables**	**Three Syllables**	**Four Syllables**
	though	luck·y	min·i·mum	her·biv·o·rous
	stairs	re·gion	e·lev·en	cou·ra·geous·ly

EXERCISE A Divide each of the following words by drawing vertical lines between syllables.

Example 1. car|pen|ter

1. straighten

2. triangle

3. invisible

4. probably

5. necessary

6. realize

7. literature

8. adventure

9. crawling

10. previous

EXERCISE B On the line provided, write each word syllable-by-syllable. Draw a vertical line between syllables. Check a dictionary if you are unsure of a word's division.

Example 1. furious _____ fu | ri |ous _____

11. separate _____

12. eighty _____

13. mutual _____

14. honest _____

15. persuade _____

16. frustration _____

17. statistics _____

18. creative _____

19. official _____

20. temporary _____

MECHANICS

Spelling Rules: *ie* and *ei*

27b. Write *ie* when the sound is long *e*, except after *c*.

EXAMPLES	gr**ie**f	f**ie**ld	rec**ei**ve	c**ei**ling
EXCEPTIONS	**ei**ther	l**ei**sure	n**ei**ther	s**ei**ze

27c. Write *ei* when the sound is not long *e*.

EXAMPLES	for**ei**gn	h**ei**r	v**ei**l	w**ei**gh
EXCEPTIONS	w**ei**rd	fr**ie**nd	misch**ie**f	kerch**ie**f

These two rules apply only when the *i* and the *e* are in the same syllable.

EXAMPLES   p**i•e•**ty   sc**i•**ence

EXERCISE A   Underline the correctly spelled word in each of the following pairs.

Example 1. <u>ceiling</u>, cieling

1. feind, fiend
2. reveiw, review
3. deceive, decieve
4. niether, neither
5. heifer, hiefer

6. soceity, society
7. height, hieght
8. cheif, chief
9. vareity, variety
10. freight, frieght

EXERCISE B   Above each underlined word in the following sentences, rewrite the word, spelling it correctly. If a word is already spelled correctly, write *C* above it.

Example 1. If you study hard, I <u>beleive</u> *believe* you will pass your math test.

11. For several years my cousin was a <u>nieghbor</u> of Tiger Woods.
12. For one <u>breif</u> moment, I thought I had won a million dollars.
13. You will <u>receive</u> a ticket if you drive over the speed limit.
14. If I have any <u>liesure</u> time, I want to read Alex Haley's last book.
15. Hatim decided to paint the walls <u>biege</u> and the woodwork white.
16. Passports are required for travel in <u>foriegn</u> countries.
17. The turtle's hard shell <u>shields</u> it from harm.
18. Bianca isn't <u>concieted</u>, but she knows how talented she is.
19. During what years did Queen Victoria <u>riegn</u> in Great Britain?
20. Screech owls make the <u>wierdest</u> sounds I've ever heard!

Spelling Rules: *-cede, -ceed,* and *-sede*

27d. Only one English word ends in *–sede: supersede.* Only three words end in *–ceed: exceed, proceed,* and *succeed.* Almost all other words with this sound end in *–cede.*

EXAMPLES ac**cede**   inter**cede**   re**cede**

EXERCISE A Underline the correctly spelled word in each of the following pairs.

Example 1. <u>supersede</u>, supercede

1. proceed, procede

2. conceed, concede

3. seceed, secede

4. preceed, precede

5. acceed, accede

EXERCISE B Above each underlined word in the following sentences, rewrite the word, spelling it correctly. If a word is already spelled correctly, write *C* above it.

Example 1. If you <u>*exceed*</u> your curfew, you will be grounded.

6. In which year did Hanukkah <u>precede</u> Christmas by only a few days?

7. The committee will <u>acceed</u> to Malcolm's being the next project leader.

8. Anibal watched the tide slowly <u>recede</u> from the Greek seashore.

9. By this time next week, Jaleh will <u>succede</u> in finishing her term paper.

10. Should a primary source <u>anteceed</u> a secondary source in a bibliography?

11. Because of the odd circumstances, Nadie agreed to <u>intercede</u> for me.

12. Explain the order in which those states would <u>seceed</u> from the Union.

13. Vanko will <u>procede</u> to show us the chemical reaction for today's lab.

14. Do not <u>excede</u> the amount of time you have in class to complete the test.

15. Tehya said, "<u>*Retroceed*</u> is another word for *retract* or *retrograde.*"

MECHANICS

Adding Prefixes

| **27e.** | When a prefix is added to a word, the spelling of the original word itself remains the same. |

EXAMPLES mis + spell = mis**spell**   im + movable = im**movable**

EXERCISE A Spell each of the following words, adding the prefix that is given.

Example 1. under + estimate = _underestimate_

1. inter + twine = _____

2. a + blaze = _____

3. mid + field = _____

4. de + classify = _____

5. im + mortal = _____

6. mal + function = _____

7. in + secure = _____

8. centi + meter = _____

9. un + necessary = _____

10. bio + sphere = _____

EXERCISE B On the line provided in each of the following sentences, spell the word in parentheses, adding the prefix that is given.

Example 1. Red tape marks the ___*irregular*___ spots on these sale items. (*ir + regular*)

11. Eva decided to _____ her old sofa. (*re + upholster*)

12. Someone wrote this tag so fast that it is _____. (*un + readable*)

13. In the _____ event that you return that, be sure to keep the receipt. (*un + likely*)

14. The customer was so thrilled by the sale that he _____. (*over + bought*)

15. Although we found many great deals, Dad was _____ with the bill. (*dis + pleased*)

16. How far is ten miles in _____? (*kilo + meters*)

17. The current was faster _____ than by the banks. (*mid + stream*)

18. A _____ lawn mower is often as good as a new one. (*re + conditioned*)

19. The _____ in the steel made it weak. (*im + purities*)

20. The spy _____ the coded message. (*un + scrambled*)

MECHANICS

Adding Suffixes A

| **27f.** | When the suffix *–ness* or *–ly* is added to a word, the spelling of the original word itself remains the same.

> **EXAMPLES** sad + ness = **sad**ness   solid + ly = **solid**ly
>
> **EXCEPTIONS** 1. Words ending in *y* usually change the *y* to *i* before *–ness* and *–ly*:
> easy + ly = **easi**ly.
> 2. However, most one-syllable adjectives ending in *y* follow Rule 27f:
> wry + ly = **wry**ly.
> 3. *True, due,* and *whole* drop the final *e* before *–ly*: true + ly = **tru**ly.

MECHANICS

EXERCISE A Spell each of the following words, adding the suffix that is given.

Example 1. clever + ness = ___*cleverness*___

1. silky + ness = _____

2. kind + ly = _____

3. tacky + ness = _____

4. stubborn + ness = _____

5. quick + ly = _____

6. shy + ly = _____

7. bossy + ness = _____

8. personal + ly = _____

9. entire + ly = _____

10. wordy + ness = _____

EXERCISE B On the line provided in each of the following sentences, spell the word in parentheses, adding the suffix that is given.

Example 1. Humor is ___*definitely*___ an important link among Native Americans in the United States. (*definite + ly*)

11. Ceremonies, traditions, seasons, and foods may bear no _____ among the various Indian tribes in the United States. (*like + ness*)

12. However, many share a history of life on reservations where food and especially water might not always be _____ available. (*ready + ly*)

13. Water-truck jewelry by Clarence Lee shows _____ to detail, down to wheels that turn. (*faithful + ness*).

14. Lee will often include a dog in his jewelry, its ears _____ blowing in the wind as the truck rolls along. (*floppy + ly*)

15. His popular goat pin capitalizes on a goat's _____ to eat anything, which in this case includes a football, a wrench, and a bag of beans. (*willing + ness*)

ELEMENTS OF LANGUAGE | Third Course

Adding Suffixes B

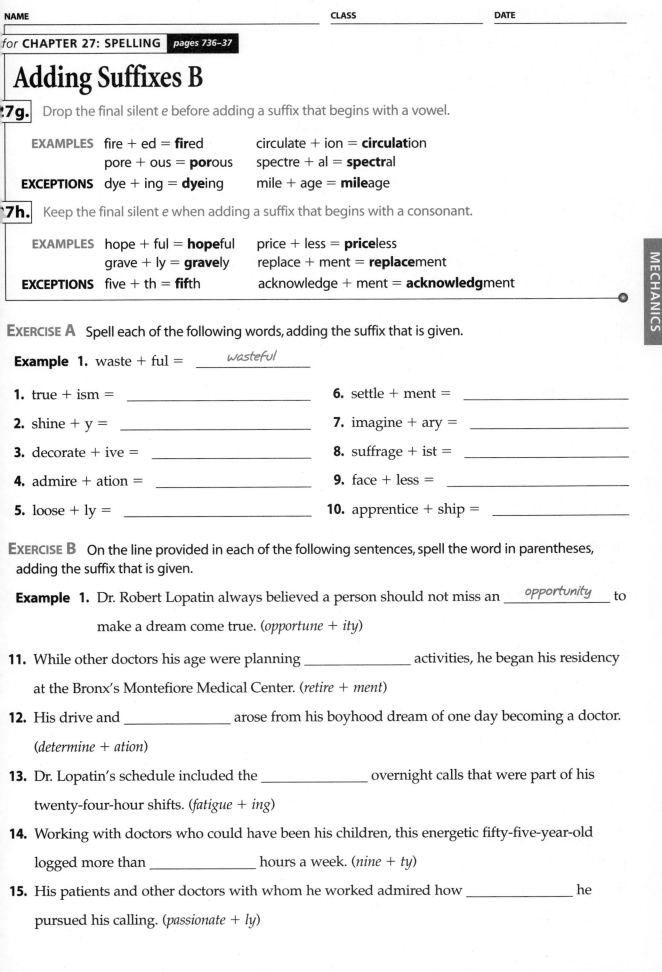

27g. Drop the final silent *e* before adding a suffix that begins with a vowel.

EXAMPLES	fire + ed = **fir**ed	circulate + ion = **circulat**ion
	pore + ous = **por**ous	spectre + al = **spectr**al
EXCEPTIONS	dye + ing = **dye**ing	mile + age = **mile**age

27h. Keep the final silent *e* when adding a suffix that begins with a consonant.

EXAMPLES	hope + ful = **hope**ful	price + less = **price**less
	grave + ly = **grave**ly	replace + ment = **replace**ment
EXCEPTIONS	five + th = **fif**th	acknowledge + ment = **acknowledg**ment

EXERCISE A Spell each of the following words, adding the suffix that is given.

Example 1. waste + ful = _____*wasteful*_____

1. true + ism = _____

2. shine + y = _____

3. decorate + ive = _____

4. admire + ation = _____

5. loose + ly = _____

6. settle + ment = _____

7. imagine + ary = _____

8. suffrage + ist = _____

9. face + less = _____

10. apprentice + ship = _____

EXERCISE B On the line provided in each of the following sentences, spell the word in parentheses, adding the suffix that is given.

Example 1. Dr. Robert Lopatin always believed a person should not miss an ____*opportunity*____ to make a dream come true. (*opportune + ity*)

11. While other doctors his age were planning _____ activities, he began his residency at the Bronx's Montefiore Medical Center. (*retire + ment*)

12. His drive and _____ arose from his boyhood dream of one day becoming a doctor. (*determine + ation*)

13. Dr. Lopatin's schedule included the _____ overnight calls that were part of his twenty-four-hour shifts. (*fatigue + ing*)

14. Working with doctors who could have been his children, this energetic fifty-five-year-old logged more than _____ hours a week. (*nine + ty*)

15. His patients and other doctors with whom he worked admired how _____ he pursued his calling. (*passionate + ly*)

Adding Suffixes C

| **27i.** | When a word ends in *y* preceded by a consonant, change the *y* to *i* before any suffix except one beginning with *i*. |

EXAMPLES   bury + al = bur**i**al   economy + cal = econom**i**cal
                happy + ness = happ**i**ness   ferry + ing = ferr**y**ing

| **27j.** | When a word ends in *y* preceded by a vowel, simply add the suffix. |

EXAMPLES   obey + ed = obe**y**ed   convey + ing = conve**y**ing
                joy + ful = jo**y**ful   employ + ment = emplo**y**ment
EXCEPTIONS   inlay + ed = inla**id**   underpay + ed = underpa**id**

EXERCISE A Spell each of the following words, adding the suffix that is given.

Example 1. day + ly = _____*daily*_____

1. pay + ment = _____   **6.** harmony + ous = _____

2. lovely + ness = _____   **7.** ordinary + ly = _____

3. plenty + ful = _____   **8.** boy + hood = _____

4. lavatory + es = _____   **9.** qualify + ing = _____

5. repay + ed = _____   **10.** funny + ness = _____

EXERCISE B On the line provided in each of the following sentences, spell the word in parentheses, adding the suffix that is given.

Example 1. Australia was known as Terra Incognita by the _____*earliest*_____ groups that searched for this, the sixth continent. (*early + est*)

11. *Discovery: The Quest for the Great South Land,* by Miriam Estensen, tells of the many searches, often _____ difficult, for the island. (*extraordinary + ly*)

12. Her book spans two millennia of ship captains and _____, kings and pirates, mapmakers and merchants, seeking adventure, mystery, and wealth. (*castaway + s*)

13. She began reading and _____ accounts by Australia's explorers as the result of a trip with her husband through Torres Strait. (*verify + ing*)

14. Estensen begins her tale with the plate tectonics, _____ specimens, and wild myths that made Australia a "fabled" land for so many centuries. (*zoology + cal*)

15. She assesses the Greek, Indian, Chinese, Dutch, and Portuguese claims to be the first to bring the _____ of this land to the rest of the world. (*reality + es*)

            ELEMENTS OF LANGUAGE | Third Course

MECHANICS

Doubling Final Consonants

27k. When a word ends in a consonant, double the final consonant before a suffix that begins with a vowel only if the word has only one syllable or is accented on the last syllable *and* ends in a *single* consonant preceded by a *single* vowel. Otherwise, simply add the suffix.

EXAMPLES spin + ing = spi**nn**ing   refer + ed = refe**rr**ed
track + ing = trac**k**ing   profit + able = profi**t**able

EXERCISE A Spell each of the following words, adding the suffix that is given.

Example 1. occur + ence = _____*occurrence*_____

1. suit + able = _____

2. control + ing = _____

3. hot + er = _____

4. account + ing = _____

5. plan + ing = _____

6. omit + ed = _____

7. regret + able = _____

8. design + er = _____

9. begin + ing = _____

10. finish + ed = _____

EXERCISE B On the line provided in each of the following sentences, spell the word in parentheses, adding the suffix that is given.

Example 1. Harlem's Apollo Theater _____*opened*_____ in 1913. (*open + ed*)

11. The Apollo was first known as the Hurtig and Seaman Theater but was later _____ the Apollo Theater. (*call + ed*)

12. My parents remember _____ in the audience on amateur night. (*sit + ing*)

13. They recall _____ for a new singer named Aretha Franklin. (*clap + ing*)

14. They _____ that they never saw Duke Ellington perform. (*regret + ed*)

15. Today we are _____ the theater's comedy and music performances. (*applaud + ing*)

MECHANICS

Adding Suffixes Review

27f. When the suffix –*ness* or –*ly* is added to a word, the spelling of the original word itself remains the same.

27g. Drop the final silent *e* before adding a suffix that begins with a vowel.

27h. Keep the final silent *e* when adding a suffix that begins with a consonant.

27i. When a word ends in *y* preceded by a consonant, change the *y* to *i* before any suffix except one beginning with *i*.

27j. When a word ends in *y* preceded by a vowel, simply add the suffix.

27k. When a word ends in a consonant, double the final consonant before a suffix that begins with a vowel only if the word has only one syllable or is accented on the last syllable *and* ends in a *single* consonant preceded by a *single* vowel. Otherwise, simply add the suffix.

EXAMPLES	good + ness = **good**ness	happy + est = **happi**est
	motive + ation = **motiv**ation	boy + ish = **boy**ish
	care + ful = **care**ful	hop + ing = **hopp**ing

EXERCISE A Spell each of the following words, adding the suffix that is given.

Example 1. pity + ful = _____*pitiful*_____

1. dark + ness = _____

2. leave + ing = _____

3. assay + er = _____

4. scary + er = _____

5. hope + less = _____

6. promote + ion = _____

7. tune + ful = _____

8. glad + ly = _____

9. hungry + est = _____

10. step + ing = _____

EXERCISE B On the line provided in each of the following sentences, spell the word in parentheses, adding the suffix that is given.

Example 1. Who were you ___*smiling*___ at from the back of the room? (*smile + ing*)

11. The catcher dropped the ball, and the runner slid _____ home for the winning run. (*safe + ly*)

12. Marc Antony said that Brutus was _____ than any other Roman. (*noble + er*)

13. Will the band be _____ any of the Wallflowers' songs? (*play + ing*)

14. As Kerry and her coach _____ her attack, she knew it would be one of her toughest matches of the tournament. (*plan + ed*)

15. The teacher's _____ of Scott's proposed topic sent him scrambling to the library to find a new one. (*deny + al*)

Forming Plurals of Nouns A

27l. To form the plurals of most English nouns, simply add *s*.

EXAMPLES friend—friend**s**   mongoose—mongoose**s**   Jill—Jill**s**

27m. To form the plurals of other nouns, follow these rules.

(1) If the noun ends in *s, x, z, ch,* or *sh,* add *es*.

EXAMPLES loss—loss**es**   box—box**es**   Gomez—Gomez**es**
watch—watch**es**   crush—crush**es**

(2) If the noun ends in *y* preceded by a consonant, change the *y* to *i* and add *es*. For the plurals of proper nouns ending in *y*, simply add *s*.

EXAMPLES pony—pon**ies**   fly—fl**ies**   country—countr**ies**
ninety—ninet**ies**   Dewey—Dewey**s**   Grigsby—Grigsby**s**

EXERCISE A On the line provided, write the plural for each of the following words.

Example 1. testimony ___*testimonies*___

1. distributor _____

2. charity _____

3. Lydia _____

4. hatbox _____

5. porch _____

6. eyelash _____

7. vertebrate _____

8. fizz _____

9. MacLeish _____

10. monitor _____

EXERCISE B Above each of the underlined words in the following sentences, write the plural of the word.

Example 1. One of the *artists* artist who assisted the *sculptors* sculptor at Mt. Rushmore National Memorial is also known for his work on the Crazy Horse Memorial.

11. Korczak Ziolkowski, usually just called Korczak *[CORE-jahk]*, acquired construction and other skill by working at a variety of job with his foster father in the Boston area.

12. His study of other artists' works resulted in several portraits and statue that paid tribute to people who had helped him and whom he admired.

13. Lakota chief Henry Standing Bear of the Sioux Indian asked Korczak to create the memorial, which Korczak did after making sketch and then a scale model of Crazy Horse.

14. The construction method mixed several blasting technique to be able to clear huge chunks of granite and form the sculpture.

15. After fifty year, Korczak Ziolkowski's sculpture of Crazy Horse is taking shape at a granite mountain in South Dakota's Black Hill area.

Forming Plurals of Nouns B

27m. To form the plurals of certain nouns, follow these rules.

(3) For some nouns ending in *f* or *fe*, add *s*. For other nouns ending in *f* or *fe*, change the *f* to *v* and add *s* or *es*.

    EXAMPLES   tariff—tarif**fs**   safe—safe**s**   Rolf—Rolf**s**
                   leaf—lea**ves**   life—li**ves**

(4) If the noun ends in *o* preceded by a vowel, add *s*.

    EXAMPLES   cacao—cacao**s**   presidio—presidio**s**

(5) If the noun ends in *o* preceded by a consonant, add *es*.

Some common nouns ending in *o* preceded by a consonant (especially musical terms) and proper nouns form the plural by adding only *s*.

    EXAMPLES   embargo—embargo**es**   torpedo—torpedo**es**
  EXCEPTIONS motto—motto**s** or motto**es** piano—piano**s** Castillo—Castillo**s**

EXERCISE A Write the plural for each of the following words on the line provided.

Example 1. knife _____*knives*_____

1. wharf _____ **6.** avocado _____

2. duo _____ **7.** tornado _____

3. calf _____ **8.** sheaf _____

4. Romero _____ **9.** contralto _____

5. belief _____ **10.** potato _____

EXERCISE B For each underlined word in the following sentences, write the plural above the word.

Example 1. Mina wishes there were more ZeZe Macedo *(Macedos)* who could be hero *(heroes)* and models of comic performance for other Brazilian actors.

11. The two Julio in our class began to research Web sites with the best pictures of leaf.

12. "A better life for all" might be one of the motto describing the efforts of Julius Nyerere, Tanzania's first president, to span the gulf of tribal differences and unify Africa.

13. How many calf are born each year to buffalo?

14. In a photo-portrait of Raisa and Mikhail Gorbachev among Anya's memento, Raisa is wearing one of the scarf Anya had always thought most flattering.

15. In many North American zoo, Sumatran tiger cubs spend much of their life playing.

Forming Plurals of Nouns C

| **27m.** | To form the plurals of certain nouns, follow these rules.

(6) The plurals of some nouns are formed in irregular ways.

    EXAMPLES goose—**geese**   mouse—**mice**   woman—**women**

(7) Some nouns have the same form in both the singular and the plural.

    EXAMPLES species   Chinese   moose   trout

EXERCISE A Write the plural for each of the following words on the line provided.

Example 1. Sioux _____*Sioux*_____

1. child _____

2. mouse _____

3. deer _____

4. salmon _____

5. fowl _____

6. foot _____

7. scissors _____

8. man _____

9. aircraft _____

10. Javanese _____

EXERCISE B For each underlined word in the following sentences, write the plural above the word.

Example 1. Several of those <u>woman</u> collect hand-painted figurines. *(women)*

11. Which players in recent years' <u>World Series</u> had never been in the playoffs before?

12. Scientists may one day know why some kinds of <u>goose</u> migrate and others don't.

13. What type of dwellings did the <u>Iroquois</u> construct in their villages?

14. Forty <u>ox</u> had filled the barn and a good part of the feeding pen outside it.

15. Wesley climbed inside both models of <u>spacecraft</u> on display at the museum.

16. How many <u>child</u> are on the playground?

17. Fourteen <u>sheep</u> were missing in the morning after the storm.

18. I caught two <u>trout</u> from that stream yesterday.

19. Several of my <u>tooth</u> are loose, doctor.

20. Many <u>Sioux</u> fought in the Battle of the Little Bighorn.

MECHANICS

Forming Plurals of Nouns Review

| **27l.** | To form the plurals of most English nouns, simply add *s*. |

| **27m.** | To form the plurals of other nouns, follow these rules. |

(1) If the noun ends in *s, x, z, ch,* or *sh,* add *es*.
(2) If the noun ends in *y* preceded by a consonant, change the *y* to *i* and add *es*. For plurals of proper nouns ending in *y,* simply add *s*.
(3) For some nouns ending in *f* or *fe,* add *s*. For other nouns ending in *f* or *fe,* change the *f* to *v* and add *s* or *es*.
(4) If the noun ends in *o* preceded by a vowel, add *s*.
(5) If the noun ends in *o* preceded by a consonant, add *es*.
(6) The plurals of some nouns are formed in irregular ways.
(7) Some nouns have the same form in both the singular and the plural.

EXERCISE   For each underlined word in the following sentences, write the plural above the word.

Example   1. Did you see any <u>mouse</u> *(mice)* running around the <u>studio</u> *(studios)*?

1. <u>Echo</u> of bleating <u>sheep</u> filled the valley in the early morning.

2. Have you read <u>story</u> of how the various <u>circus</u> became established?

3. The <u>soprano</u> were trying out for the leading <u>role</u> in the Japanese opera.

4. Next, we will present the <u>trophy</u> to the top three <u>child</u> in the best-costume category.

5. Jumping to their <u>foot</u>, the startled campers ran off as three <u>moose</u> approached the camp.

6. The miner watched flocks of <u>goose</u> flying south as he loaded his <u>supply</u> into the wagon.

7. Would you please put those <u>handkerchief</u> and <u>scarf</u> in the top drawer of the bureau?

8. <u>Crew</u> checked <u>radio</u> in both spacecraft before ground control decided which to send up.

9. Last night, we visited the <u>Smith</u> and heard Armand tell about the <u>life</u> of Irish people today.

10. A jeweler repaired the <u>catch</u> on the bracelets with Baltic <u>topaz</u> in their settings.

ELEMENTS OF LANGUAGE | Third Course

MECHANICS

Compound Nouns

27m. To form the plurals of certain nouns, follow these rules.

(8) For most compound nouns, form the plural of only the last word in the compound.

EXAMPLES background   standby   sea horse
background**s**   standby**s**   sea horse**s**

(9) For compound nouns in which one of the words is modified by the other word or words, form the plural of the word modified.

EXAMPLES attorney general   blackberry   whistle-blower
attorney**s** general   blackberr**ies**   whistle-blower**s**

MECHANICS

EXERCISE A Write the plural for each of the following words on the line provided.

Example 1. stepchild _____*stepchildren*_____

1. bedspread _____

2. sweat shirt _____

3. two-year-old _____

4. wristwatch _____

5. goldfish _____

6. runner-up _____

7. waterfall _____

8. notary public _____

9. brother-in-law _____

10. stomachache _____

EXERCISE B For each underlined word in the following sentences, write the plural above the word.

Example 1. How many <u>center fielder</u> *center fielders* will be named to the regional <u>hall of fame</u> *halls of fame*?

11. <u>Grasshopper</u> did not take long to eat their way across the field of <u>buttercup</u> and grasses.

12. Why did the fairy <u>godmother</u> wave their magic wands at both of the castle's <u>drawbridge</u>?

13. Our <u>great-great-grandmother</u> had given those necklaces as <u>heirloom</u> to their daughters.

14. <u>Bank note</u> found in the walls of three <u>boardinghouse</u> dated back to the Civil War.

15. The <u>mayor-elect</u> from four cities attended the session on the use of existing <u>railroad</u>.

Grammar, Usage, and Mechanics: Language Skills Practice

Latin and Greek Loan Words

27m(10). Some nouns borrowed from Latin and Greek form the plural as in the original language. A few Latin and Greek loan words have two correct plural forms.

EXAMPLES	amoeba	radius	stratum	phenomenon	oasis
	amoeba**e**	rad**ii**	strat**a**	phenomen**a**	oas**es**
	or amoeba**s**	*or* radius**es**	*or* stratum**s**		

EXERCISE A Write the plural for each of the following words on the line provided. You may use a dictionary if necessary.

Example 1. cherub _____*cherubim*_____

1. datum _____

2. octopus _____

3. bacterium _____

4. ellipsis _____

5. antenna _____

6. curriculum _____

7. nucleus _____

8. synthesis _____

9. maximum _____

10. vortex _____

EXERCISE B For each underlined word in the following sentences, write the plural above the word.

Example 1. Where might the various types of *auroras or aurorae* aurora be visible?

11. Those particular phenomenon have not yet been fully analyzed.

12. Refer to the appendix for references on authors, titles, and literary terms.

13. Please present the criterion for creating a new greenbelt on the east side of town.

14. Cactus from the local nursery have grown well in Lana's garden this summer.

15. Parenthesis, always used in pairs, set off explanatory information in a sentence.

MECHANICS

Numerals, Letters, Symbols, and Words Used as Words

27m(11). To form the plurals of numerals, most capital letters, symbols, and words used as words, add either an *s* or an apostrophe and an *s*.

To prevent confusion, always use an apostrophe and an *s* to form the plurals of lowercase letters, certain capital letters, and some words used as words.

EXAMPLE The extra ***7's*** (or ***7s***), ***R's*** (or ***Rs***), and ***a's*** in that address made it incorrect.

EXERCISE A Write the plural for each of the following numerals, letters, symbols, or words used as words.

Example 1. & _____&'s_____

1. *A* _____

2. 1400 _____

3. *5* _____

4. *and* _____

5. *uh-oh* _____

6. # _____

7. *S* _____

8. *if* _____

9. $ _____

10. ! _____

EXERCISE B For each underlined item in the following sentences, write the plural above the item.

Example 1. How many <u>and</u> and <u>so</u> are in this paragraph?
         and's   *so's*

11. Who are your favorite actors from movies of the '<u>40</u> and '<u>50</u>?

12. Asad corrected the Web site address by deleting the extra <u>@</u> and all of the <u>$</u> from it.

13. Emma did not spend much time on <u>*hello*</u> or <u>*goodbye*</u> since she saw us every week.

14. Jaime was ill during so much of last semester that he received <u>*I*</u>, which stand for *incomplete*, instead of <u>*F*</u>.

15. Calculate the sum of three <u>6</u> and two <u>8</u>.

Spelling Numbers

MECHANICS

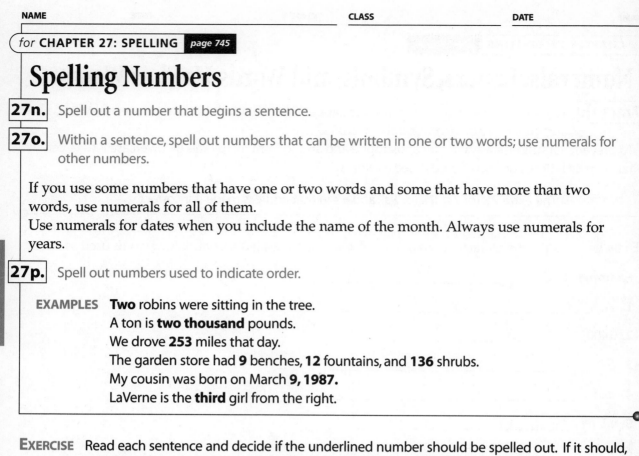

| **27n.** | Spell out a number that begins a sentence. |

| **27o.** | Within a sentence, spell out numbers that can be written in one or two words; use numerals for other numbers. |

If you use some numbers that have one or two words and some that have more than two words, use numerals for all of them.

Use numerals for dates when you include the name of the month. Always use numerals for years.

| **27p.** | Spell out numbers used to indicate order. |

EXAMPLES **Two** robins were sitting in the tree.
A ton is **two thousand** pounds.
We drove **253** miles that day.
The garden store had **9** benches, **12** fountains, and **136** shrubs.
My cousin was born on March **9, 1987.**
LaVerne is the **third** girl from the right.

EXERCISE Read each sentence and decide if the underlined number should be spelled out. If it should, write the spelled-out form above it. If the number is already correct, write *C* above it.

Example 1. The year <u>2000</u> was a census year in the United States.

1. The <u>1st</u> U.S. census was taken in 1790.

2. <u>8</u> years later, the Naturalization Act was passed.

3. Within <u>100</u> years, the Statue of Liberty was erected.

4. In the decade before <u>1900</u>, many immigrants arrived in the United States.

5. More than <u>12,000,000</u> came through Ellis Island in New York.

6. However, in <u>1921</u> Congress set a ceiling on the United States' long-standing open immigration policy.

7. <u>2</u> important immigration laws are the Refugee Act of 1980 and the Reform Act of 1986.

8. In my school, there are more than <u>236</u> students who were born in another country.

9. The U.S. Bureau of the Census was established in <u>1902</u>.

10. Most countries conduct a census every five or <u>10</u> years.

Words Often Confused A

Review the Words Often Confused covered on pages 746–48 of your textbook for information on the correct spelling and usage of the following words:

advice, advise   *all together, altogether*   *capital, capitol*
affect, effect   *altar, alter*   *choose, chose*
all ready, already   *brake, break*   *coarse, course*
all right

EXERCISE   Underline the words in parentheses that correctly complete the sentences.

Example 1. A lawyer can (*advice*, *advise*) you of your rights.

1. Everyone congratulated Terri for successfully completing the obstacle (*coarse*, *course*).

2. Some students have (*all ready*, *already*) finished their research.

3. Are you going to the free concert in front of the (*capital*, *capitol*) tonight?

4. Stop turning the knob as soon as you feel resistance; otherwise, you will (*brake*, *break*) it.

5. If you (*altar*, *alter*) the configuration, you will void the warranty.

6. Did the teacher tell you it was (*all right*, *allright*) to report on that topic?

7. The school nurse will (*advice*, *advise*) us on keeping our first-aid skills current.

8. If our teams work (*all together*, *altogether*), we should be able to raise even more money.

9. There is much discussion about whether the full moon (*affects*, *effects*) human behavior.

10. The Cleveland Spiders (*choose*, *chose*) to change their name to the Cleveland Indians to honor

Louis Sockalexis, the first American Indian professional baseball player.

11. Jason's pen pal lives in the (*capital*, *capitol*) city of Guatemala.

12. Misty is researching the (*affects*, *effects*) of listening to different types of music while studying.

13. Everyone must (*choose*, *chose*) his or her own path in life.

14. Mark carefully checked the (*brakes*, *breaks*) on his bike before he left on his trip.

15. If you are (*all ready*, *already*), gentlemen, we may begin practice.

16. Suddenly, everyone in school had (*advice*, *advise*) for Chris before she went to the state finals.

17. The director told the actors that they were using (*all together*, *altogether*) too many pauses.

18. The next step is to sand the table with (*coarse*, *course*) sandpaper.

19. What (*affect*, *effect*) will the new high school have on the district rivalries?

20. As the couple reached the (*altar*, *alter*), the guests fell silent.

Words Often Confused B

Review the Words Often Confused covered on pages 749–50 of your textbook for information on the correct spelling and usage of the following words:

complement, compliment	*councilor, counselor*
consul, council, counsel	*desert (n.), desert (v.), dessert*

EXERCISE Underline the word in parentheses that correctly completes the sentence.

Example 1. What a (*complement*, <u>*compliment*</u>) for your classmates to select you as Person of the Year!

1. The guide pointed to a man and said that he was the Italian (*counsel, consul*).

2. After the war ended, visitors discovered a soldier who had refused to (*desert, dessert*) his post.

3. After the meeting, one (*councilor, counselor*) volunteered to write up the committee's report.

4. I think that fresh fruit would (*complement, compliment*) the dinner nicely.

5. For (*desert, dessert*) the waiter brought us strawberry yogurt.

6. I asked the guidance (*councilor, counselor*) to help me choose courses for next semester.

7. In many states, an arts (*council, consul*) meets to determine who should receive money.

8. Any traveler who crosses the (*dessert, desert*) should carry extra water.

9. Catherine received many (*complements, compliments*) on her singing.

10. On Saturday soccer player Mia Hamm will visit our school to (*council, counsel*) students who are considering sports careers.

11. What sort of (*desert, dessert*) should I make for the party?

12. The film is a good (*complement, compliment*) to the book.

13. The Japanese (*consul, council*) left his gloves at the embassy.

14. Do you have an appointment to see the career (*counselor, councilor*)?

15. Las Vegas, Nevada, is surrounded by (*desert, dessert*).

16. The (*council, counsel*) will vote this afternoon on your proposal.

17. What sort of (*council, counsel*) would you offer young writers, Ms. Morrison?

18. Do not (*desert, dessert*) your post, Sergeant.

19. Allow me to (*complement, compliment*) you on your hat, Mr. Ozu.

20. All city (*councilors, counselors*) serve for two years.

MECHANICS

Words Often Confused C

Review the Words Often Confused covered on pages 750–52 of your textbook for information on the correct spelling and usage of the following words:

formally, formerly	*lead (n.), led, lead (v.)*	*passed, past*
hear, here	*loose, lose*	*peace, piece*
its, it's	*moral, morale*	

EXERCISE Underline the word in parentheses that correctly completes the sentence.

Example 1. Dad asked who found the (*peace, <u>piece</u>*) of driftwood.

1. Elia's father had (*lead, led*) us on a tour of the older part of town.

2. I was careful not to (*loose, lose*) the name of the restaurant that Elia recommended.

3. It was (*formally, formerly*) called Hunan Palace, but now it is the Canton Kitchen.

4. She said it was well known for (*its, it's*) terrific service, as well as the wonderful food.

5. We had almost walked (*passed, past*) it before we saw the sign.

6. After spending the afternoon at the noisy market, we enjoyed the (*peace, piece*) inside the restaurant.

7. When we started to look at the menus, Sarah took the (*lead, led*).

8. Yes, you can order bird's-nest soup (*hear, here*).

9. A good meal can do wonders for the (*moral, morale*) of a group of tired visitors.

10. Since all the food was in the center of the table, no one (*passed, past*) around dishes.

11. If you have never used chopsticks before, it is easy to (*loose, lose*) your grip.

12. When you place your chopsticks across your bowl, (*its, it's*) a sign that you're finished.

13. The fortune in Sarah's cookie was the same as the (*moral, morale*) of the fable she had read.

14. I wore very (*loose, lose*) clothes because I knew that I would eat many different foods.

15. Some of the other diners were dressed (*formally, formerly*), but others were more casual.

16. Each food is chosen for (*its, it's*) taste, texture, and color.

17. The sounds that you (*hear, here*) are the bustling kitchen staff preparing orders.

18. For dessert you may take one (*peace, piece*) of orange and one of apple.

19. While Jenny was trying to compute the tip on a napkin, the (*lead, led*) in her pencil broke.

20. During the week we spent with Elia, we drove (*passed, past*) the restaurant several more times.

MECHANICS

Words Often Confused D

Review the Words Often Confused covered on pages 753–54 of your textbook for information on the correct spelling and usage of the following words:

plain, plane	*shone, shown*	*than, then*
principal, principle	*stationary, stationery*	*their, there, they're*
quiet, quite		

EXERCISE A Underline the word in parentheses that correctly completes the sentence.

Example **1.** Were (*plains*, <u>*planes*</u>) or helicopters named for the designer Sikorsky?

1. The letter was written on very elegant (*stationary, stationery*).

2. Each freshman was (*shone, shown*) around the building by a senior.

3. The crowd was eerily (*quiet, quite*) while the last free throws were taken.

4. Since I already have the theater tickets, we can meet (*their, there*) just before eight.

5. Suddenly, the beam of a flashlight (*shone, shown*) through the window.

6. I'm training my dogs, since (*they're, their*) going to grow to be very large.

7. If you hand me that (*plain, plane*), I'll shave the edge of the door.

8. Mrs. Jefferson asked the school (*principle, principal*) to introduce her to the staff.

9. Cary Grant, Tony Curtis, and Beverly Sills all changed (*their, there*) names.

10. It is very important to remain (*stationary, stationery*) while observing wildlife.

EXERCISE B Draw a line through each incorrect word in the following paragraph, and write the correction above it.

Example **[1]** How do I decide which author I like best if ~~their~~ *they're* all fascinating?

[11] Dorothy Sayers, John Dos Passos, and Vladimir Nabokov are known for they're writing. **[12]** Yet each author had more then one talent. **[13]** Sayers studied medieval times and held strong religious principals. **[14]** Dos Passos drove an ambulance in World War I, than later sailed the Bahamas with Ernest Hemingway. **[15]** In numerous articles he published, it was plane that Nabokov had studied butterflies.

MECHANICS

Words Often Confused E

Review the Words Often Confused covered on pages 755–56 of your textbook for information on the correct spelling and usage of the following words:

threw, through	*weak, week*	*who's, whose*
to, too, two	*weather, whether*	*your, you're*
waist, waste		

EXERCISE Underline the word in parentheses that correctly completes the sentence.

Example 1. (*Your*, <u>*You're*</u>) surprised that I knew that Notah Begay won a PGA golf tournament in 1999.

1. The (*whether, weather*) in the Caribbean does not change as dramatically as it does here.

2. Don't throw out that (*waist, waste*) paper; it may be useful for someone else.

3. We walked (*threw, through*) the old part of the city, which is now a historic zone.

4. If you want (*to, too, two*) work on the play, you must attend the audition.

5. The waitress asked (*weather, whether*) you want the soup or the salad.

6. They had to make reservations to visit the caves, since the tour can't take (*to, too, two*) many people at once.

7. Did you turn in (*your, you're*) permission slip on time?

8. My legs feel very (*week, weak*) after a whole afternoon of skiing.

9. After you go (*threw, through*) that intersection, take the next left turn.

10. Send in the next (*to, too, two*) contestants.

11. Will the (*weather, whether*) be nice enough for us to have the carnival outside?

12. The rainbow trout glided effortlessly (*threw, through*) the water.

13. Secure the safety line firmly around your (*waist, waste*).

14. Manuel went to the park and (*threw, through*) a ball for his dog to fetch.

15. Have you heard (*who's, whose*) headlining the concert?

16. Let's have the study session at (*your, you're*) house this time.

17. This menu has (*to, too, two*) many delicious choices!

18. (*Who's, Whose*) jacket is this lying on the floor?

19. When are you going (*to, too, two*) the gym?

20. For the next (*week, weak*), we'll be studying *Romeo and Juliet*.

MECHANICS

Review A: **Spelling Rules**

MECHANICS

EXERCISE In each of the groups of words below, underline the misspelled word. On the line provided, write the word correctly.

Example _____*slyness*_____ **1.** naturally, happiness, infinitely, <u>sliness</u>

_____ **1.** height, believe, recieve, achieve

_____ **2.** sieze, neither, relief, reign

_____ **3.** usually, hopeing, amusement, immortal

_____ **4.** reccommend, truly, admiration, unnecessary

_____ **5.** women, tomatos, cupfuls, rodeos

_____ **6.** definitly, comparable, transformed, dining

_____ **7.** largely, grayest, terrifiing, determination

_____ **8.** continous, advantageous, becoming, ridiculous

_____ **9.** comparison, useage, advertisement, saying

_____ **10.** controlled, denial, exciting, swimer

_____ **11.** lovely, meanness, developement, courageous

_____ **12.** arguement, perspiration, occurrence, parallel

_____ **13.** flying, shining, ninty, safety

_____ **14.** proceed, pursuit, preceed, immense

_____ **15.** safely, unusual, ilegal, receipt

_____ **16.** weight, receed, overrule, lateness

_____ **17.** foxs, tongues, ditches, giraffes

_____ **18.** *a*s, leaves, *3*s, stories

_____ **19.** donkeys, copies, photoes, theories

_____ **20.** selves, thiefs, radios, churches

Review B: Words Often Confused

EXERCISE A In each of the groups of phrases below, underline the misspelled word. On the line provided, write the word (or words, if the correct spelling requires more than one word) correctly.

Example _____*shown*_____ **1.** tinted stationery, had <u>shone</u> us the way, as quiet as a library

_____ **1.** too much sugar, their are two ways, better than mine

_____ **2.** don't chose this one, it's certainly hers, the last week of school

_____ **3.** high moral principals, affected her deeply, the capital city

_____ **4.** a coarse sand, are you allright, effected many changes

_____ **5.** of course not, all ready finished, all right to begin

EXERCISE B Underline the words in parentheses that will correctly complete each of the following sentences.

Example 1. Rosa was too (*week*, <u>*weak*</u>) to move after she had (<u>*led*</u>, *lead*) her team to victory.

6. Congratulations! I (*hear*, *here*) that the editor of the school magazine was (*all together*, *altogether*) impressed with the story that you wrote.

7. (*Their*, *There*, *They're*) were not many passengers on the bus because it was still (*to*, *too*, *two*) early for the evening rush hour.

8. Grace (*threw*, *through*) the ball so hard that it zipped (*passed*, *past*) me before I saw it.

9. You'll (*brake*, *break*) those test tubes if (*your*, *you're*) not careful.

10. The (*councilor*, *counselor*) (*lead*, *led*) his campers down the narrow trail.

11. It is a (*waist*, *waste*) of time to give Tiffany (*advice*, *advise*); she never follows it.

12. The members of the city (*council*, *counsel*) have gone (*threw*, *through*) the proposed budget and have cut out several items.

13. The refreshments committee will have to (*altar*, *alter*) (*its*, *it's*) plans in order to feed thirty extra people.

14. The study hall was (*quiet*, *quite*) when the (*principal*, *principle*) came in.

15. (*Who's*, *Whose*) bicycle is lying (*hear*, *here*) in the driveway?

Grammar, Usage, and Mechanics: Language Skills Practice

MECHANICS

Review C: Spelling Rules and Words Often Confused

EXERCISE A In each of the groups of words below, underline the misspelled word. On the line provided, write the word correctly.

Example _____perches_____ **1.** retrocede, <u>perchs</u>, illogical, oxen

_____ **1.** definitely, nineth, copies, wolves

_____ **2.** awesome, leadder, precedes, either

_____ **3.** monkeys, stories, potatos, radios

_____ **4.** speechs, science, guidance, useful

_____ **5.** precede, ticklish, playful, procede

_____ **6.** mispell, leisure, supersede, readily

_____ **7.** careful, dryly, usually, hopless

_____ **8.** confidential, sheild, ceiling, easily

_____ **9.** chief, geese, seize, sombreroes

_____ **10.** decieve, niece, receipt, height

EXERCISE B In each of the groups of phrases below, underline the misspelled word. On the line provided, write the word (or words, if the correct spelling requires more than one word) correctly.

Example _____moral_____ **1.** hear the bells, <u>morale</u> of the story, the French consul

_____ **11.** sing all together, take my advise, the capital city

_____ **12.** already to leave, choose a book, too big

_____ **13.** take my counsel, feel all right, brake the plate

_____ **14.** formerly from New York, of coarse, a lead pencil

_____ **15.** wandering in the dessert, lose a game, they're here

_____ **16.** colored stationary, too bad, Carmen led the way

_____ **17.** a quiet dog, the stars shone, walk passed the school

_____ **18.** can't here you, fair weather, the story's moral

_____ **19.** I feel weak, fly a plain, the foreign consul

_____ **20.** there books, follow your principles, more than that

MECHANICS

Review D: Spelling Rules and Words Often Confused

EXERCISE A In each of the groups of words below, underline the misspelled word. On the line provided, write the word correctly.

Example _____*bathing*_____ **1.** judgment, moderately, parables, <u>batheing</u>

_____ **1.** connection, <u>allys</u>, imaginary, glorious

_____ **2.** largely, dining, cafeterias, <u>skys</u>

_____ **3.** loading, <u>loveing</u>, leaving, going

_____ **4.** dimest, preferring, copied, finally

_____ **5.** believing, drying, <u>regreting</u>, denying

_____ **6.** loaves, <u>halfs</u>, ladies, teeth

_____ **7.** accidentally, reddish, reliable, <u>exceled</u>

_____ **8.** knowledgeable, relieve, tracable, argument

_____ **9.** leanness, <u>happyly</u>, development, pavement

_____ **10.** daily, saving, cleanliness, <u>aweful</u>

EXERCISE B Underline the words in parentheses that correctly complete each of the following sentences.

Example 1. We took many pictures as we drove (*threw*, <u>*through*</u>) the cactus-filled (*dessert*, <u>*desert*</u>).

11. I believe the guidance (*councilor*, *counselor*) is paying you a (*complement*, *compliment*).

12. We had to (*alter*, *altar*) our picnic plans when it rained for a whole (*week*, *weak*).

13. If you drive (*threw*, *through*) town on (*your*, *you're*) way home, please stop in.

14. Whichever game you (*choose*, *chose*), be sure not to (*waist*, *waste*) your money.

15. It's (*to*, *too*) bad you didn't (*here*, *hear*) the lecture.

16. I'm not sure (*who's*, *whose*) directions we're following, but we've gone (*past*, *passed*) that

building three times.

17. I ran out of (*plain*, *plane*) (*stationary*, *stationery*) after writing all those letters.

18. Our (*principal*, *principle*) goal is to bring (*peace*, *piece*) to the region.

19. Steve's shoelaces are (*loose*, *lose*) (*all ready*, *already*).

20. I (*advise*, *advice*) you to choose the red shoes rather (*than*, *then*) the blue ones.

MECHANICS

for **CHAPTER 27: SPELLING** | pages 731–56 |

Proofreading Application: Poster

Good writers are generally good proofreaders. Readers tend to admire and trust writing that is error-free. Make sure that you correct all errors in grammar, usage, spelling, and punctuation in your writing. Your readers will have more confidence in your words if you have done your best to proofread carefully.

Using correct spelling is especially important in writing that will be put before the public. No matter what you are writing, every minute that you spend running a spellchecker, consulting a dictionary, and proofreading your paper adds to your credibility.

PROOFREADING ACTIVITY

In the following poster, find the errors in spelling and correct them using the proofreading symbols in the chart on page 901 of *Elements of Language* to replace incorrect words.

Example Do you like writing?

Come to our 1st meeting!

Franklin Junior High Writers Club

Meet the principle contributor to the popular book *Writing Made Easy*.

Mr. Daniel Gillette is an experienced writer who has published articles in numerous magazines. He will be lecturing on journals and giving advise to beginning writers. Mr. Gillette's lecture will be followed by punch and desert.

Refreshments will be free too everyone attending.

Meet us right here in Room Two hundred fifty-seven at 6:30 P.M. on Friday, November 1!

See Your Name in Print!

We will be publishing our own magazine, which is named *Cameo Appearrances*. 15 poems and stories have already been excepted for the inaugural edition.

Send submissions to Lance Ward. (Photoes and drawings will also be considered.)

for **CHAPTER 27: SPELLING** pages 731–56

Literary Model: Play

Quince. *Is all our company here?*
Bottom. *You were best to call them <u>generally</u>, man by man, according to the scrip.*
Quince. *Here is the scroll of every man's name, which thought fit, through all Athens, to play in our interlude before the duke and duchess, on his wedding day at night.*

Bottom. *Let me play the lion, too. I will roar that I will do any man's heart good to hear me. I will roar, that I will make the duke say, "Let him roar again, let him roar again."*
Quince. *An you should do it too terribly, you would fright the duchess and the ladies, that they would shriek; and that were enough to hang us all.*
All. *That would hang us, every mother's son.*
Bottom. *I grant you, friends, if you should fright the ladies out of their wits, they would have no more discretion buy to hang us: but I will <u>aggravate</u> my voice so that I will roar you as gently as any sucking dove; I will roar you as 'twere any nightingale.*

Bottom. *We will meet; and there we may rehearse most <u>obscenely</u> and courageously. Take pains; be perfit: adieu.*

Bottom. *Masters, you ought to consider with yourselves. To bring in—God shield us!— a lion among ladies is a dreadful thing. For there is not a more fearful wild fowl than your lion living; and we ought to look to't.*
Snout. *Therefore another prologue must tell he is not a lion.*

Bottom. *Nay, you must name his name, and half his face must be seen through the lion's neck, and he himself must speak through, saying thus, or to the same <u>defect</u>— "Ladies"—or, "Fair ladies—I would wish you"—or, "I would request you"—or, "I would entreat you—not to fear, not to tremble: my life for yours. If you think I come hither as a lion, it were pity of my life. No, I am no such thing. I am a man as other men are."*

—from *A Midsummer Night's Dream* by William Shakespeare
(act 1, scene 2 and act 3, scene 1)

EXERCISE A As you can see from the preceding examples, Bottom often confuses words that sound alike or have related meanings. Judging from the context of each underlined word, choose the word that Bottom meant to say.

exaggerate   seemly   genuinely   serenely

effect   individually   affect   moderate

1. generally _____

2. aggravate _____

3. obscenely _____

4. defect _____

Literary Model (continued)

EXERCISE B How does Shakespeare characterize Bottom by having him confuse words?

_____

_____

EXERCISE C Write a short skit in which three students make plans to perform together in a school talent show. One student tries to take charge of the performance by using fancy words but ends up using the wrong ones. Use the **Words Often Confused** list in your textbook to help you find examples of words this would-be director might (mis)use.

_____

_____

_____

_____

_____

_____

_____

_____

_____

_____

_____

_____

_____

_____

EXERCISE D

1. What words did the student in your skit confuse for each other?

_____

_____

2. How did the confusion of these words affect the meaning of what he or she was trying to say?

_____

_____

_____

Writing Application: Business Letter

When the language is English, learning to spell correctly is no easy task. Unlike some languages in which a relatively simple sound-to-letter correspondence exists, English has an impressive number of words whose spelling seems to scorn any set of logical rules—take *though* and *scissors* and *rhythm* as examples. Rules that can help you improve your spelling do exist. You can also progress toward mastery by simply memorizing the spelling of the most commonly misspelled words.

It may not be quite as important to spell every word accurately when you're writing in a journal that only you will see, or when you're taking notes whose content will be revised and proofread several times before it appears in a finished document. However, anything you write that will be read by others should be free of spelling errors—including, of course, letters to potential employers in which first impressions are crucial.

WRITING ACTIVITY

You are seeking an internship at a real or imaginary company or business. Write a letter to the person in charge of interns. Discuss the type of position you would like and why you would be a good candidate, including your relevant academic and work experience. Use at least five words from the spelling lists and at least five words from the lists of words that are often confused.

PREWRITING   Decide the type of internship you will request in your letter. Brainstorm to create a list of qualifications. Think about your interests, hobbies, and other leisure-time activities, as well as academic coursework and previous jobs. Then, brainstorm a list of ways that your serving as an intern could benefit the company. Order the items in each list from most to least significant, from the perspective of the person who hires interns.

WRITING   Begin your letter by clearly explaining your purpose and the type of internship you are seeking. Then, using your notes, write one paragraph about your qualifications and another paragraph that addresses how the company will benefit from your internship. Conclude by thanking the person for his or her time and by requesting an interview.

REVISING   Read your draft to determine whether you have expressed yourself clearly, succinctly, and in standard formal English. Ask yourself if there are other qualifications you have or ways the company will benefit that you could include in the letter. You may want to have an adult look at your draft to see whether you have successfully promoted yourself. Be sure that you have used at least five words from the spelling lists and at least five words from the lists of words that are often confused.

PUBLISHING   Try proofreading your letter beginning with the bottom line and moving to the top. This will help you concentrate on locating errors in spelling, grammar, and punctuation rather than on the content. In class, form job-search committees and read through a selection of letters of application. Finally, conduct mock interviews to find the best candidate for the job.

EXTENDING YOUR WRITING

Add this letter to the anthology you are maintaining of your best writing. You may want to refer to this letter in the future when you really are seeking employment or an internship.

COMMON ERRORS | Language in Context: Choices

Choices: Learning More About Common Errors

The following activities challenge you to find a connection between common errors and the world around you. Do the activity below that suits your personality best, and then share your discoveries with your class.

DRAMA

A Comedy of Errors

Now that you've heard the whole sad story of English errors, you've probably noticed that errors are sometimes funny. Have you also noticed that certain errors can be used for characterization? For instance, sentence fragments can characterize a scatterbrained person—someone who never finishes a thought. For this activity, write a comedy sketch. Include at least one character who makes as many language errors as possible. For contrast, have at least one character who never makes an error. Plan your sketch so that everyone is friends in the end. Then, perform your sketch for the class.

DISCUSSION

Why, Oh, Why?

The name of this chapter is "Correcting Common Errors." The errors that appear in it certainly are common. Why do these errors appear so frequently, even among the best writers? Under what circumstances might some of these errors be considered artistic or at least acceptable? Cut strips out of a big sheet of paper. Each strip should be large enough for one sentence written with a marker. Then, have everyone write down one reason for each error. Collect the strips, and use them as a springboard for discussion.

WRITING

Taking Stock

Write a letter to your teacher that tells him or her how this class has helped you understand English better. Identify the specific areas that are no longer a problem for you as well as the things that particularly interested you. It would be nice if you took special care proofreading this document.

DISCUSSION

Cold Feet

Like it or not, almost any kind of success in life requires at least a minimal ability to speak and write well. Yet, there are some people who just plain have cold feet when it comes to writing or speaking to people they don't know. Lead your class in a discussion about the feelings that make people nervous about writing or speaking. Also, discuss the feelings that enable other people to do so with ease. Then, brainstorm ways to overcome any obstacles to successful communication.

SURVEY

Pet Peeves

Although few people are experts at usage and mechanics, just about everybody has an opinion about what the worst type of error is. For some it's spelling, for others it's sentence fragments, and for others it's incorrect pronoun references. Do you have a pet peeve? Take a survey of your classmates and teachers. Ask your parents, neighbors, and relatives, too. After collecting your data, look for patterns. Do many people abhor a certain type of error? Write up your findings, and share them with your class.

RESEARCH

Past, Present, Future

Already, there are computer programs that can understand what you say and type it for you! Do you think these programs will become popular? Will most computers of the future be programmed for voice recognition? Do some research on voice-recognition programs to find out what functions they can perform today, and present your findings to your class.

Sentence Fragments and Run-on Sentences A

EXERCISE On the line before each item, identify each of the following word groups by writing *F* for *sentence fragment*, *R* for *run-on sentence*, or *S* for *complete sentence*.

Example _____F_____ **1.** On Tuesday, after we went to the performance at the theater.

_____ **1.** Never have I seen so many drummers in one place at the same time!

_____ **2.** We have finished reading the Declaration of Independence we will start studying the Bill of Rights next week.

_____ **3.** The crystal clear river that runs through our town.

_____ **4.** The boys, terrified by the strange noises but afraid to turn on their flashlights.

_____ **5.** My family seldom eats strawberries my brothers are allergic to them.

_____ **6.** As the woman walked down the dusty street, balancing a huge basket on her head.

_____ **7.** Did you tell me that you had already read this book?

_____ **8.** If we hurry, we'll be on time, don't forget the tickets!

_____ **9.** Despite a lack of evidence, Ned still believed that Matt had broken the window.

_____ **10.** We'll put away the clean clothes and straighten the living room, then we'll vacuum the rug.

_____ **11.** This homework is just too frustrating; I think I'll take a walk and come back to it later.

_____ **12.** The farmhouse, its roof caved in and its windows broken, will be restored.

_____ **13.** Does anyone have Samantha's new phone number, I think she moved last week?

_____ **14.** The paintings in the gallery, with their bright colors and bold brush strokes.

_____ **15.** Your uncle is certainly a talented magician, has he been practicing for many years?

_____ **16.** His card tricks, which are especially difficult to perform, both clever and amazing.

_____ **17.** Whenever we get up late, rush around the house, and are tardy to school.

_____ **18.** I did not know that newborn giraffes were so big, that one is taller than I am!

_____ **19.** Do you remember when the squirrels got into our attic last fall?

_____ **20.** Put the bread in the oven, set the timer for forty minutes, and left the room.

COMMON ERRORS

Sentence Fragments and Run-on Sentences B

EXERCISES   On the line before each item, identify each word group in the following paragraph as a sentence fragment (F), a run-on sentence (R), or a complete sentence (S).

Example ___R___ **[1]** Time is a relatively new human concept before people began farming, they had no need to keep track of passing days.

___F___ **[2]** Watching day turn into night and winter turn into spring.

_____ **[1]** Humans first developed calendars in the early river-valley civilizations these river valleys were the Nile, Tigris and Euphrates, Indus, and Huang He. _____ **[2]** Farmers had to know when to plant crops, sometimes the farmers even needed to predict the arrival of yearly floods. _____ **[3]** Most early calendars based on lunar months, the amount of time between each full moon. _____ **[4]** A problem with using lunar months is that the calendar would fall short of a full year, each year the months would come earlier until the calendar would no longer be useful.

_____ **[5]** Many cultures solving the problem by adding extra days to the calendar. _____ **[6]** Feasts and holidays, for example, on the five extra days of the ancient Egyptian calendar.

_____ **[7]** Since the popularity of the Chinese rulers of the Shang dynasty depended on the accuracy of their astronomers' calendar, the astronomers were very important. _____ **[8]** The astronomers also predicted eclipses of the moon with great skill an error of twenty-four hours caused outrage and alarm. _____ **[9]** Today, official atomic clocks measuring the vibrations of electrons in cesium atoms. _____ **[10]** These atomic clocks are so precise that they have to be adjusted to make up for the slowing in the earth's rotation scientists occasionally have to add leap seconds on New Year's Eve!

COMMON ERRORS

Subject-Verb Agreement A

EXERCISE A In each of the following sentences, underline the form of the verb in parentheses that agrees with its subject.

Example 1. Either Matt or Mark (*has, have*) an uncle who is an astronaut.

1. One of these apples (*taste, tastes*) better than the other one.

2. Every student in the school (*has, have*) the opportunity to use the library.

3. Neither Malika nor Aline (*think, thinks*) that is the correct answer.

4. This set of colored pencils (*include, includes*) both magenta and turquoise.

5. Whenever my sister and I (*give, gives*) a party, we do all the cooking.

6. Those shrubs and this tree (*have, has*) grown a lot in the past year.

7. (*Does, Do*) the colors in this fabric go with the paint color we chose?

8. All of the fruit in the market (*look, looks*) good this month.

9. Everyone liked the Caesar salad, but none of the tiny spinach quiches (*was, were*) eaten.

10. (*Is, Are*) 7:00 P.M. or 8:00 P.M. the correct time?

EXERCISE B In each of the following sentences, cross out any verb that does not agree with its subject and write the correct form of the verb above the incorrect form. If the sentence is already correct, write *C* after it.

Example 1. Either a raccoon or an opossum ~~have~~ been getting into our garbage can at night.

has

11. Marilyn, in addition to Sandy and Juan, want to help decorate the gym.

12. Not a single one of the choir members was late for rehearsal on Wednesday.

13. The city park or the one by the lake are good for picnics.

14. Haven't either Kim or Lana called yet?

15. If the class raise some money, the tickets for the dance will be less expensive.

16. The tuba players in the band was not happy about the long parade route.

17. Jack, together with Karen, Ed, and Tricia, were working in the biology lab.

18. In that family, neither the mother nor the children eat enough vegetables or fruit.

19. Magnets and electricity is the next topic we'll be studying in science.

20. Either my father or my younger brothers sorts the recycling, but I carry it to the curb.

COMMON ERRORS

Subject-Verb Agreement B

EXERCISE A For each of the following sentences, decide whether the underlined verb agrees in number with its subject. If the verb form is incorrect, cross it out and write the correct form above it. If the verb form is correct, write *C* above it.

Example 1. Each of us ~~have~~ *has* a different set of skills and talents.

1. The ice on the streets this morning <u>is</u> treacherous.

2. He sometimes <u>take</u> a short nap after school, especially if he stayed up late the night before.

3. Neither James nor Cam <u>play</u> in the school orchestra.

4. <u>Have</u> either of them joined any clubs this year?

5. Both my father and his brother, my uncle Ted, <u>tries</u> to run at least ten miles every week.

6. <u>Do</u> Hannah and her friends need a ride to the rehearsal?

7. Meredith, along with Carol and Bill, <u>have</u> signed up for tennis lessons.

8. Those sections of the newspaper <u>is</u> not particularly interesting to me.

9. Mr. Gonzalez and Ms. King <u>were</u> my favorite teachers last year.

10. In addition to Nick, Daniel, and Simon, who else <u>want</u> extra time on this project?

EXERCISE B In each of the following sentences, cross out any verb that does not agree with its subject, and write the correct form of the verb above the incorrect form. If the sentence is correct, write *C* after it.

Example 1. The club president is concerned because no one ever ~~arrive~~ *arrives* on time for the meetings.

11. Ninety-five percent of the students has chosen classes for next year.

12. What will you do when the baseball season start?

13. Several of the members have conflicting meetings on Tuesday and Thursday.

14. Either Ms. Eldridge's class or the members of the drama group is responsible for publicity.

15. The lawyers will wait in the hall until the jury come back into the courtroom.

16. The main attraction at the carnival are the rides.

17. She couldn't trim the bushes because the clippers was too dull.

18. We might be late for the game unless someone know an alternate route to the stadium.

19. One hundred dollars are too high a price for most students to pay.

20. Do everyone in the club know the schedule of the meetings?

ELEMENTS OF LANGUAGE | Third Course

Pronoun-Antecedent Agreement A

EXERCISE A In each of the following sentences, circle the antecedent of the pronoun or pronouns in parentheses. Then, underline the choice in parentheses that agrees with the antecedent.

Example 1. Every (student) should concentrate on (*their, his or her*) own work.

1. One of the players on my team has injured (*their, his*) knee.

2. The Camera Club meets tomorrow to discuss (*their, its*) field trip.

3. In (*their, its*) early years, the United States tried different forms of government.

4. The class was delighted when the turtle poked (*its, her*) beak through the eggshell.

5. Anyone can meet us at the restaurant if (*they, he or she*) is interested.

6. Nora, Janet, and Phyllis were sure that (*she, they*) did well on the essay test.

7. Either California or Texas claims (*it, they*) is the largest state in the continental United States.

8. Neither Joan nor Fiona allowed (*herself, themselves*) enough time to finish the experiment.

9. Sal and Juan, together with Josh, will represent (*his, their*) school at the meet.

10. My dad and his brothers treated (*themselves, himself*) to a nice dinner.

EXERCISE B In each of the following sentences, cross out any pronoun that does not agree with its antecedent. Then, write the correct pronoun above the incorrect one. If a sentence is already correct, write *C* after it.

Example 1. The United States made Yellowstone ~~their~~ *its* first national park.

11. Some Indonesian islands are well known for its spices.

12. One of Pablo Picasso's paintings, *Guernica,* is admired for their powerful message.

13. Kathryn and Michael liked the taste of the pasta he or she had made together.

14. I paid a lot for those pants, but I don't like to wear it anymore.

15. *Peter and the Wolf,* a composition by Sergey Prokofiev, uses music to tell its story.

16. The Nelson twins, Harriet and Matilda, are known for her long red hair.

17. According to Irish folklore, leprechauns will reveal the location of treasure to his captors.

18. *Carpe diem* is one of the most famous Latin proverbs; their translation is "Seize the day."

19. Could you tell me Nicole's address so that I can take her the book?

20. If Byron and Blake go to the tryouts together, he can encourage and support each other.

COMMON ERRORS

Pronoun-Antecedent Agreement B

EXERCISE In each of the following sentences, circle the antecedent of the pronoun or pronouns in parentheses. Then, underline the choice in parentheses that agrees with the antecedent.

Example 1. I don't particularly enjoy standardized (tests) but I do well on (*them*, *it*).

1. I know that garlic, tomatoes, and oregano are on the list of ingredients, but what else is on (*them*, *it*)?

2. Each of the cats has to have (*their*, *its*) own food bowl.

3. Chad, one of Jeremy's brothers, will bring (*their*, *his*) basketball to the practice.

4. I think that most of the eggs have hatched; could you count (*it*, *them*) once more?

5. The team displays (*their*, *its*) trophies in the case outside the gym.

6. Does everyone in the class, including Mike and Raymond, know that (*his or her*, *their*) paper is due on Tuesday?

7. Your change will be four dollars and seventy-nine cents; do you want (*them*, *it*) now?

8. Both Maxine and Lisa think (*their*, *her*) history teacher is the best in the school.

9. I can't stay awake for the news; (*they*, *it*) will come on too late.

10. Neither Tara nor Melissa forgot (*their*, *her*) homework this time.

11. One of those trees still has (*their*, *its*) leaves.

12. Not all of the children have remembered to bring (*his or her*, *their*) jackets.

13. The audience rose from (*their*, *its*) seats and applauded wildly.

14. Both of these books belong to Jeremiah; please take (*them*, *it*) to him.

15. When the bell rang, the students rushed from (*his or her*, *their*) classroom.

16. Katrina and Al are excited about learning German; neither of (*them*, *him or her*) minds going to the language lab.

17. We need to buy another car because the one we have is on (*our*, *its*) last legs.

18. Anyone who wants to help collect newspapers for recycling should write (*his or her*, *their*) name on this list.

19. Both of the mother elephants tended (*its*, *their*) newborn calves.

20. In order to increase productivity, the manager of the two restaurants must find a way to make (*her*, *their*) employees more committed.

Verb Forms A

EXERCISE A In each of the following sentences, underline the correct form of the verb in parentheses.

Example 1. Has Noel ever (*rode, ridden*) a horse before?

1. I heard he (*broke, breaked*) his collarbone when he fell off a horse last year.

2. She (*teared, tore*) her jacket when she climbed over the fence.

3. Have all the geese (*flown, flew*) south already?

4. Before he (*writed, wrote*) the essay, he made a detailed outline and organized his notes.

5. We (*thought, thinked*) the car was finally fixed, but we were mistaken.

6. I asked him if he had (*spoke, spoken*) to his grandfather recently.

7. When I was ten, my father and I (*build, built*) a treehouse in the backyard.

8. I (*drawed, drew*) the plan, and he bought the supplies.

9. All the leaves have (*fell, fallen*) off the trees, and the branches are bare.

10. The story of my family's immigration has been (*telled, told*) for generations.

EXERCISE B On the line provided, write the correct past or past participle form of the verb in italics.

Example 1. *teach*   My father, who is an excellent cook, has _____*taught*_____ cooking classes for

many years.

11. *eat*   Most people these days have _____ a variety of foods.

12. *try*   I have always _____ new foods offered to me.

13. *choose* Just yesterday I _____ to put jicama in my salad.

14. *drink* Have you ever _____ coconut milk?

15. *raise* Last week, Emilio _____ his hand when our teacher asked who had ever

had sushi.

16. *enjoy* He says he has _____ sashimi, too.

17. *bring* Sara has _____ falafel for lunch.

18. *know* Who would have _____ it would taste so good?

19. *take*   She _____ tabouli to the Food Fest last year, and it was quite a hit!

20. *begin* Meals are more fun for me now that I have _____ to explore new dishes.

Verb Forms B

EXERCISE A   In the following paragraph, cross out each incorrect verb form and write the correct form above it. If all the verbs in a sentence are correct, write *C* above the sentence.

Example   [1] Railroads in the United States ~~begun~~ *began* with a few horse-powered lines in the 1800s.

[1] After the introduction of steam-powered locomotives in the 1820s and 1830s, railroad companies lay more track and the number of railroads in the United States growed rapidly. [2] In 1850, Congress give federal lands to the states to develop railroads. [3] The federal government thought railroads would attract settlers to unpopulated areas. [4] Railroad companies that got lands from the states kept some of the land for development and selled the rest to pay for construction. [5] In return for the land, the railroads carried soldiers, supplies, and mail at reduced rates. [6] After the Civil War, iron and steel rail bridges were builded across major rivers like the Mississippi, the Missouri, and the Ohio. [7] In 1869, the Union Pacific and the Central Pacific tracks meeted at Promontory, Utah, finally completing a transcontinental rail line. [8] The Union Pacific had lain track westward from Nebraska, and the Central Pacific start from Sacramento, California. [9] Officials from the two companies droved in the last spike, connecting the tracks. [10] By the end of the nineteenth century, the United States have five transcontinental lines.

EXERCISE B   On the line provided, write the correct past or past participle form of the verb in italics.

Example 1. *grow*   Makelo and Kirby are proud of the vegetables they _____*grew*_____.

11. *dig*   They _____ deeply into the soil and added plenty of compost.

12. *choose*   They _____ vegetables that would grow easily in their part of the country.

13. *get*   Makelo _____ out the tools while Kirby read the seed packages.

14. *become*   When the first plants came up, the boys _____ really excited.

15. *spend*   They _____ hours in the garden each week, weeding and watering.

16. *freeze*   A late ice storm _____ some of their seedlings.

17. *lose*   When the weather turned hot, they _____ some plants.

18. *seek*   All through the summer, they _____ advice from other gardeners.

19. *teach*   One neighbor _____ them how to stake up their tomato plants.

20. *eat*   When the first tomatoes ripened, Kirby _____ them right off the vine.

Pronoun Forms A

EXERCISE A In the following sentences, underline the correct form of the pronoun in parentheses.

Example 1. Please introduce the new students (*who, whom*) you invited to the party to the rest of the guests.

1. Tamika's sisters and (*she, her*) are excelling in their computer class.

2. Their teacher has taught (*they, them*) and the other students some interesting programs.

3. It was (*he, him*) who showed them how to detect a computer virus.

4. Mr. Gonzales wrote a few simple steps to help (*they, them*) understand.

5. My friends and (*I, me*) are looking forward to learning more about computers.

6. Next year, Tamika will help teach (*we, us*) newcomers the basics of programming.

7. The new students, Paul, Mia, and (*I, me*), have already started our research.

8. To (*we, us*), the important thing is to get started and begin experimenting.

9. Among the three of (*we, us*), only Paul has his own Web page.

10. Do you know many people (*who, whom*) are interested in computers?

EXERCISE B In each of the following sentences, cross out any incorrect pronoun and write the correct pronoun above it.

Example 1. She and ~~me~~ are the only students who have finished the assigned novel.

11. Do you know whom is responsible for returning the slide projector?

12. Mr. Johnson showed her and he the pictures of his family.

13. She and Kim are going to the carnival this weekend with my parents and I.

14. As soon as we arrived at the campsite, us new campers set up our tent.

15. I will meet Terry and they outside the front door of the school.

16. The girl who dropped her necklace behind the bleachers in the gymnasium is her.

17. To who should we address our sympathy letter?

18. Hand me the chessboard, please; I want to challenge he to a game.

19. The neighbor waved to Shari and I as we rode by on our bikes.

20. The fastest runners in our class are him and her.

COMMON ERRORS

Pronoun Forms B

EXERCISE In each of the following sentences, underline the correct pronoun or pronouns in parentheses. Then, identify the use of the pronoun by writing above it *S* for *subject*, *PN* for *predicate nominative*, *DO* for *direct object*, *IO* for *indirect object*, *OP* for *object of a preposition*, or *A* for *appositive*.

Example 1. Our classmates, (*he, him*) and Mary, tied for first place in the tournament. [A above *he*]

1. (*Who, Whom*) could be ringing the doorbell at this hour of night?

2. Hey, give (*we, us*) boys a turn on the rope swing!

3. Three of the coaches in the school, Mr. Nichols, Ms. Knight, and (*she, her*), attended the national conference.

4. I am sure you have met (*he, him*) before.

5. The winner of the sportsmanship award was (*she, her*).

6. When Craig tripped, he fell on top of (*they, them*).

7. Nelson showed Kim and (*I, me*) how to use that software program.

8. If you can call (*he, him*) and his sister tonight, I will call the rest of the group tomorrow.

9. Did either Eduardo or (*he, him*) borrow my bicycle lock yesterday?

10. The superintendent invited the student representatives—Kelly, Marjorie, and (*he, him*)—to the next board meeting.

11. What Elvis and (*I, me*) have in common is our last name.

12. When we caught up with Caitlin and Phil, we bicycled alongside (*they, them*) for a mile.

13. Are (*them, they*) the neighbors who moved here from Philadelphia last month?

14. (*Him, He*) and Brandon play in the same league, but on different teams.

15. Did you leave detailed instructions for Emma and (*she, her*)?

16. George Washington, Thomas Jefferson, and Abraham Lincoln are presidents (*who, whom*) everyone in my class admires.

17. The one person you most admire is (*who, whom*)?

18. Pass Eli or (*me, I*) the ball next.

19. Just between you and (*me, I*), I thought Ted should have won a prize.

20. The winner had to have been either (*she, her*) or her sister Martina.

COMMON ERRORS

Clear Pronoun Reference A

EXERCISE   On the lines provided, rewrite each sentence to correct all inexact or unclear pronoun references.

Example 1. Rosalia asked Christina questions about the sports she plans to play.

Rosalia asked Christina questions about the sports Christina plans to play.

1. Christina thinks rock climbing and cave exploring are both fun, but she likes it better. _____

_____

2. Rock climbing requires many safety precautions, which Christina emphasized. _____

_____

3. Before Christina and Rosalia begin a climb, she inspects their equipment. _____

_____

4. Amanda asked Carla about the book she had just read. _____

_____

5. This car is smaller than that one. Do you like it better? _____

_____

6. Most of my friends like to swim, which is why I spend so much time at the pool. _____

_____

7. Ned said it really makes him happy when he learns something new. _____

_____

8. The farmer and his brother plowed the field that he had cleared the week before. _____

_____

9. On the weather report last night, they said a hurricane is forming near Bermuda. _____

_____

10. Mrs. Niemann bought several paintings from John; she said he should study it in school. ____

_____

COMMON ERRORS

Clear Pronoun Reference B

EXERCISE On the lines provided, rewrite each sentence to correct all inexact or unclear pronoun references.

Example 1. Nell waved to her sister when she got off the plane. *When her sister got off the plane, Nell waved to her.*

1. According to the program I saw last night, they say that gerbils are easy to raise. _____

_____

2. Fiona is studying French and German, and she says it's fairly difficult. _____

_____

3. Rafiq told Bill that he had stepped on a piece of gum. _____

_____

4. In my mother's family, they like to play cards. _____

_____

5. Tad reminded Carlos that he had an appointment. _____

_____

6. Melissa forgot to invite Clara, which is why she is so upset. _____

_____

7. They walked with their friends in the park so that they would not get lost. _____

_____

8. In the documentary, it said that the volcano had erupted twice in the last ten years. _____

_____

9. My father made an appointment with the doctor after his vacation. _____

_____

10. I am always running late, which is why I never go anywhere without my watch. _____

_____

COMMON ERRORS

Comparative and Superlative Forms A

EXERCISE A In each of the following sentences, underline the correct form of the adjective or adverb in parentheses.

Example 1. My cousins are triplets, but Anita is the (older, <u>oldest</u>) of the three.

1. Which of your two brothers finished the book (quicker, more quickly)?

2. The exhibit has some pieces of the (ancientest, most ancient) pottery ever found.

3. Do you think silk is (more warm, warmer) than wool?

4. My neighbor's yard has (manier, more) trees than ours.

5. Unfortunately, I read the instructions (less carefully, the least carefully) than I should have.

6. He is the (more skillful, most skillful) of the three acrobats we saw last night.

7. Are you sure you're feeling (weller, better) than you did yesterday?

8. Some new students are (interesteder, more interested) than others in learning about school clubs.

9. I can't decide whether I like choir or band (best, better).

10. At the talent show, Juan told some (funniest, funnier) jokes than Rodney.

EXERCISE B In each of the following sentences, cross out any double comparisons or other errors in the use of comparative and superlative forms of modifiers. Then, write the correct form above the error.

Example 1. One of the ~~most highest~~ and ~~barrenest~~ regions in the world is Tibet.
                              highest   *most barren*

11. No area of the world has mountains as higher as the Himalayas.

12. Of all the Himalayan peaks, Mount Everest is higher.

13. Everest had never been climbed to its summit more earlier than 1953.

14. Probably no other summit is most coveted by mountaineers.

15. The air at the top of the Himalayas is much more thinner than the air at sea level.

16. Many mountaineers use bottled oxygen to breathe most easily on the peaks.

17. There are arguments for and against oxygen, so it's hard to say which is the best choice.

18. Near Tibet, in western China, is also one of the lower points in the region, the Turfan Depression, which sinks to 505 feet below sea level.

19. It's hard to imagine a contrast in elevation more greater than that between Mount Everest and the Turfan Depression.

20. What are the most highest and lowest points in the region in which you live?

Comparative and Superlative Forms B

EXERCISE On the lines provided, write the appropriate form of the adjective or adverb given in italics.

Example 1. *well* Did your team play _____*better*_____ in this game than in the last one?

1. *late* The movie ended _____ than I thought it would.

2. *good* These peaches are the _____ I've eaten all year.

3. *much* We spent _____ time at the beach this summer than we did last summer.

4. *bad* I was sure it was the _____ essay I had ever written.

5. *early* Jake left for school _____ than Camila.

6. *graceful* Tomás is certainly one of the _____ dancers in the group.

7. *slowly* No train moved _____ than the one that departed from Platform 2.

8. *happy* Marcus felt _____ in the morning than he did the previous evening.

9. *loudly* The choir director instructed us to sing that part _____ than we had during our first performance.

10. *important* The first and _____ step in solving this problem is to read carefully.

11. *gentle* That dog may look mean, but it is _____ than a lamb.

12. *decisive* I believe his first move was the _____ move in the game.

13. *incredible* None of the stories were _____ than the one José told us.

14. *fortunate* Some days, I admit, I have to remind myself that I am _____ than a lot of people.

15. *recent* Which weather report is the _____?

16. *powerful* Lying on the banks of the lake, Charles was overcome by a _____ feeling of joy than he had ever had.

17. *reasonable* Which of these six numbers do you think is the _____ estimate?

18. *pretty* Of the two landscapes, I think this one is _____.

19. *frozen* I don't know which feels _____, my nose or my feet.

20. *nice* She was the _____ substitute we've had this year.

Double Negatives

EXERCISE In each of the following sentences, cross out the double negative and write the correct form above it.

Nobody had

Example 1. ~~Nobody hadn't~~ thought of that solution to the problem before.

1. Unfortunately, there isn't no way I can finish my paper and watch that program tonight.

2. The rain is so heavy that you can't barely see the building next door.

3. I haven't heard nothing about the class field trip.

4. Haven't you never seen that kind of painting on your visits to the museum?

5. He promised not to tease his little sister no more.

6. This model kit didn't have no instructions in the box.

7. There aren't no seats left in the whole theater.

8. You can't never say I didn't warn you!

9. She couldn't hardly depend on Mina to keep her secret.

10. Don't never pick none of those flowers again!

11. My teacher doesn't accept no excuses for late homework.

12. If the store doesn't have no more coats on sale, why is the advertisement still running in the newspaper?

13. Neither warmth nor food nor dry clothes nor nothing else was as important as reaching the summit.

14. Why didn't no one think about that problem earlier?

15. Wasn't nobody willing to demonstrate the experiment for the class?

16. My baby brother declared that he doesn't like applesauce or bananas no more.

17. The rehearsal ran so late last night that I didn't have no time to fix my bike.

18. If you ask me, that really isn't none of your business!

19. The old house was so creepy we didn't hardly dare to set a foot inside.

20. The people who run the food bank don't turn no one away.

Misplaced Modifiers

EXERCISE On the lines provided, rewrite each of the following sentences to correct the misplaced modifier. You may need to rearrange or add words to make the meaning of a sentence clear.

Example 1. Exhausted from the long climb, food and rest revived the hikers. _____

Food and rest revived the hikers, who were exhausted from the long climb.

1. Walking slowly, the car waited for the dog to cross the road. _____

_____

2. Perched on a high branch, the boy spotted the escaped canary. _____

_____

3. The girl grew up to become an astronaut, who had long dreamed of flying to the moon. _____

_____

4. My brother took the letter to the post office that had to be mailed by Friday. _____

_____

5. Tangled in the branches of a tree, the little boy left the park without his kite. _____

_____

6. In China, Lien told us many people ride bicycles to work. _____

_____

7. Miriam found the error looking over her program one more time. _____

_____

8. I heard about the concert in honor of Cesar Chavez in the park. _____

_____

9. Once considered omens, we now know what comets really are. _____

_____

10. Performing a difficult stunt on his skateboard, the crowd cheered Michael on. _____

_____

COMMON ERRORS

Dangling Modifiers

EXERCISE   On the lines provided, rewrite each of the following sentences to correct the dangling modifi-er. You may need to rearrange or add words to make the meaning of a sentence clear.

Example 1. While climbing the cliff, a rock slide started. *A rock slide started while we were climbing the cliff.*

1. Walking through the streets, the sounds of the parade filled my ears. _____

   _____

2. While calling Felicity on the phone, the doorbell rang. _____

   _____

3. Engaging in polite conversation, the words *please* and *thank you* are often used. _____

   _____

4. When on vacation at Yosemite National Park, a bear ate all my food. _____

   _____

5. To learn a new skill, practice and effort are usually necessary. _____

   _____

6. Turning right at the second stoplight, my house is on the left side of the street. _____

   _____

7. Before taking a test, a good night's sleep can help. _____

   _____

8. Weary but proud of our work, the storage shed was cleaned out. _____

   _____

9. After reading all the information about the summer programs, the decision was easy to make.

   _____

10. Arriving late for the dinner party, the table had already been cleared. _____

   _____

COMMON ERRORS

Misplaced and Dangling Modifiers

EXERCISE On the lines provided, rewrite each of the following sentences to correct the misplaced and dangling modifiers. You may need to rearrange or add words to make the meaning of a sentence clear.

Example 1. Visiting England, the old buildings at Oxford University were very impressive.

When we visited England, we were very impressed by the old buildings at Oxford University.

1. While running for a touchdown, the crowd went wild. _____

_____

2. Meredith's aunt takes care of her neighbor's baby, who is a pediatric nurse. _____

_____

3. After a long walk, Sunday evening was perfect for a family cookout. _____

_____

4. Studying the topographic map, the trail was not difficult to follow. _____

_____

5. Underneath a rock in the garden, Jamie examined the bug he had discovered. _____

_____

6. To learn your lines in the play, rehearsing with a friend is good practice. _____

_____

7. Singing and clapping, the hay wagon full of children rolled down the road. _____

_____

8. While making my lunch for school, the weather report came on the radio. _____

_____

9. Please put the rest of the soup in the refrigerator you made for dinner. _____

_____

10. Into the backpack, the boy put the sandwich he had owned since third grade. _____

_____

COMMON ERRORS

for **CHAPTER 28: CORRECTING COMMON ERRORS**   *pages 595–611*

Standard Usage A

EXERCISE A   For each of the following sentences, decide whether the underlined word or words are correct according to standard, formal English usage. Draw a line through any word that should be corrected or deleted, and write the correct usage above it. If the usage is already correct, write *C* above it.

Example 1. The <u>reason</u> for the decision is ~~because~~ *that* we didn't have funding.

1. We <u>ought not to of</u> left all the lights on.

2. I think this new package contains <u>less</u> crackers than the other package.

3. A good night's sleep can have a positive <u>effect</u> on one's concentration and attitude.

4. On that block is the hospital <u>where</u> I was born <u>at</u>.

5. <u>Can</u> I leave the room to wash my hands, please?

6. After an hour, they found <u>theirselves</u> in an unfamiliar part of the city.

7. This lemonade is a little too sweet, but it's still <u>kind of</u> good.

8. Sam and Dave, <u>which</u> are old friends of mine, now live in Tucson, Arizona.

9. The twins asked <u>they're</u> father for a ride.

10. Two witnesses saw the accident <u>what</u> happened in front of the bank.

EXERCISE B   On the lines provided, rewrite each of the following sentences, correcting any errors in standard, formal English usage.

Example 1. Didn't you use to live on Filbert Avenue? *Didn't you used to live on Filbert Avenue?*

11. Your new clothes are laying on the bed. _____

_____

12. We scraped some paint off of the woodwork when we moved the furniture. _____

_____

13. Neville looks like he's been staying up too late again. _____

_____

14. If she had of known you needed a ride, she would have been here. _____

_____

15. I've looked everywhere, but that wallet ain't nowheres to be found. _____

_____

COMMON ERRORS

Standard Usage B

EXERCISE A   For each of the following sentences, decide whether the underlined word or words are correct according to standard, formal English usage. Draw a line through any word that should be corrected or deleted, and write the correct usage above it. If the usage is already correct, write *C* above it.

Example 1. You won't be able to memorize this poem ~~without~~ *unless* you're willing to study.

1. These <u>kind</u> of oranges are not particularly sweet or juicy.

2. When my twin sister and I were six, my mother <u>learned</u> us to tie our shoes.

3. Just <u>sit</u> the groceries down on the table, please.

4. Tranh decided he <u>must of</u> lost his keys when he leaned over the rail.

5. For this project, we'll need the usual supplies: paper, pencils, rulers, <u>and etc.</u>

6. <u>My aunt she</u> lives in a suburb of Minneapolis.

7. The chipmunk <u>that</u> was sitting on a park bench eating a chocolate chip cookie made me laugh.

8. I read <u>where</u> the mayor will be speaking at our school.

9. He intended to divide the chores <u>between</u> the three of us boys.

10. The child didn't look as though he felt too <u>good</u>.

EXERCISE B   On the lines provided, rewrite each of the following sentences, correcting any errors in standard, formal English usage.

Example 1. My teacher he don't accept no excuses for late papers.   *My teacher doesn't accept* _____ *any excuses for late papers.* _____

11. Beside my aunt, few people try and eat banana peels. _____

_____

12. They're less mosquitoes around this here lake then their use to be. _____

_____

13. For this here hike, bring plenty of food, water, and etc. _____

_____

14. We always do like the rangers say and extinguish all campfires. _____

_____

15. In them days, my uncle was suppose to milk the cows before school. _____

_____

COMMON ERRORS

Capitalization A

EXERCISE In each of the following sentences, circle any letter that should be capitalized.

Example 1. Ⓦas Ⓦilliam the Ⓒonqueror at the Ⓑattle of Ⓗastings?

1. elena quintanilla and her grandmother, sra. vasconcelos, recently opened a bakery.

2. nora was able to identify all the countries in south america and africa except for paraguay.

3. the u.s. capitol building and the washington monument are in washington, d.c.

4. uncle pat, who is a physical therapist, shares an office with arianna wexler, m.d.

5. next year, mattie's sister sondra is going to the university of virginia in charlottesville.

6. on a clear, dark night, i can identify the constellations orion and cassiopeia.

7. judge matthews told me that the two lawyers are actually good friends.

8. how many pages of chapter 17 does mr. kazen expect us to read tonight?

9. does your aunt read *the new york times, the wall street journal*, or both newspapers?

10. if you have a few extra days, i recommend that you also tour the headquarters of the fbi; the library of congress; and arlington national cemetery, where you can see the tomb of the unknown soldier and the grave of president kennedy.

11. my grandfather tried to join the navy when he was only seventeen.

12. the civilian conservation corps cleared these trails and built these cabins during the great depression.

13. we stopped at the convenience store next to tan's cleaners on forty-fifth street.

14. on saturday, we went shopping at the midtown mall; then we watched a movie on tv.

15. the parakeets, budgie and bridget, belong to my sister louisa.

16. in many cities, you can dial 911 to reach the police, the fire department, or an emergency medical service.

17. we have studied the myths and gods of ancient greece; soon we will read homer's *iliad*.

18. michael held up the shoe and asked aaron, "were you looking for this?"

19. t. s. eliot (1888–1965) was born an american but became a british subject in 1927.

20. the soldiers rewarded for their bravery included two lieutenants and colonel simmons.

COMMON ERRORS

Capitalization B

EXERCISE In each of the following sentences, circle any letter that should be capitalized and draw a slash (/) through any letter that is capitalized but should not be.

Example 1. (n)igel enjoys stories about *T*he *L*egendary (k)ing Arthur of (b)ritain and his *K*nights.

1. The Capital city of el Salvador is san salvador.

2. I have read *The hobbit,* by J.R.R. Tolkien, but I haven't read *The Lord of The Rings* Trilogy.

3. My Aunt Sara used to live on west Seventy-Sixth Street in New York city, very near central park and the American museum of natural history.

4. Take the north Abbott Avenue Exit, turn left, or north, and go three blocks until you see the sign for the Athena greek restaurant.

5. Were the roman gods jupiter and juno the same as the greek gods zeus and hera?

6. the rio Grande, which many people associate with texas, actually begins in colorado.

7. New hampshire, vermont, and maine are three of the new England States.

8. The Winner will face the republican nominee on the First Tuesday in November.

9. last winter, my Family went skiing on muleshoe mountain.

10. Thursday night, after we'd eaten Thanksgiving Dinner, we went to a movie at the state theater.

11. "Nancy and Nora," my Aunt Ann told me, "Are actually cousins, not sisters."

12. Jan's newest video game, *Sonic The Hedgehog,* is fun to play.

13. I saw a silent film, *the mark of Zorro,* starring Douglas Fairbanks as zorro.

14. at my school, we can take spanish, french, german, or latin.

15. the letter I found in my Great-Grandmother's papers began, "my dearest mimi."

16. If you like stories about horses, you really must read *black beauty,* by anna sewell.

17. In american history class, we read Lincoln's Gettysburg address, which begins, "four score and seven years ago."

18. Many people call any tissue by the brand name kleenex.

19. The holidays for Lincoln's birthday and Washington's birthday were combined into a single holiday called presidents' day.

20. our team's name is the farham falcons.

Commas A

EXERCISE In each of the following sentences, insert any missing commas.

Example 1. You will need cinnamon, allspice, nutmeg, and ginger for these spice cookies.

1. Ms. Fuller could I use the office telephone to call my parents please?

2. No thank you I don't need a ride to practice tomorrow.

3. We can drop you off at the corner and you can catch the four o'clock bus.

4. Each night before she goes to bed Anita brushes her hair.

5. My choir performances are on Thursday Friday and Saturday evenings.

6. My twin baby brothers were born on January 1 2001 very early in the morning.

7. The flood the worst in over thirty years caused millions of dollars in damage.

8. When my grandfather was young and lived on the farm he had to walk five miles to school.

9. At the end of the second block go right and look for a white house with a purple door.

10. Do you like pizza with a thin crisp crust or do you prefer a thick chewy crust?

11. I was planning to sleep late on Saturday but my parents had other plans.

12. If you will bring the groceries in from the car I will put them away.

13. She served the cake to her grandmother her aunt and uncle and the two little boys her brother had invited to the party.

14. My brother Jim who was trying to climb the fence fell down and hurt his knee.

15. On a cold January night nothing is as nice as a cup of hot cocoa.

16. Unfortunately two of the rats that used to live in that cage Mitch and Twitch escaped.

17. My mother who has a gift for languages speaks fluent Arabic Italian and German in addition to English.

18. Your homework and your chores of course must be finished before you go to Samantha's house.

19. Ms. Filson the concert band director has scheduled three rehearsals next week.

20. According to an article in the newspaper yesterday's temperature was 102 degrees.

Commas B

EXERCISE In each of the following sentences, insert any missing commas and circle any unnecessary commas.

Example 1. John, who recently transferred to our school, has already joined⊘the Drama Club, the French Club, and the track team.

1. On March 16 2002, Merilee—in addition to Sal Frank and Demetrius—will represent the school, in the debate competition.

2. No matter what else happens today I'll be there to pick you, and your brother, up so please be waiting near the front door.

3. The dog's "crime" according to our neighbor was that it buried three bones, in the flower bed.

4. If tomorrow is windy we will fly a kite.

5. "Farrah" her mother answered sleepily "it's eleven o'clock it's a school night and no I don't think you should order a pizza right now."

6. Winston my brother's friend told us, his family would be moving to Ames Iowa.

7. The eggs that we put in the incubator, began to hatch on Wednesday May 12 2002.

8. The constant blaring sound of the faulty car alarm annoyed everyone who lived on the street.

9. Displayed, on the shelves the trophies looked impressive.

10. Why I don't think I've ever seen a cat like that before but I'm really not sure.

11. If you can't find the instructions call me when you get home, from school today.

12. Eli not Sam has Ms. King the same teacher my brother Aaron had.

13. On the contrary she enjoys carrots, and celery, but she does not care for cucumbers.

14. My favorite song "As Time Goes By" was written for the movie, *Casablanca*.

15. Miguel could you Ming and Nathan please stay after class for a few minutes?

16. Christine's aunt's name is Anna not Ann.

17. Students I'd like you to welcome our guest speaker Dr. Mays who is a pediatrician.

18. The woman who was walking on the trail by the river, was once our governor by the way.

19. My family's ferrets Willy and Wolfgang, like to exercise but they prefer to sleep.

20. Please address the letter to 479 Arendt Avenue Suite 710 Providence RI 02906.

ELEMENTS OF LANGUAGE | Third Course

Semicolons and Colons

EXERCISE   In each of the following sentences, insert any missing semicolons and colons.

Example 1. My grandmother's recipe for biscuits is easily made in the following way. Sift the flour, baking powder, and salt together, add the cream to the dry ingredients, stir the mixture well, and roll out the dough.

1. My sister and I have very different schedules this year as a consequence, we hardly ever walk home together.

2. In the junk drawer in our kitchen, I found the following items three pairs of chopsticks, which I've never used pliers, which are broken and the keys to the car.

3. First, I went to the library next, I located some information and took notes and then, I wrote the outline and first draft.

4. One of my twin brothers was born at 1152 P.M., but the other was not born until 1215 A.M. the next morning that's why they have different birthdays.

5. John had a long list of chores to do on Saturday wash the car, mow the lawn, and give the dog a bath.

6. The guinea pigs are not allowed to have broccoli or cabbage on the other hand, any of the following items are fine carrots, celery, apples, spinach, cucumbers, and parsley.

7. Our team has games on Saturday, March 25 Friday, March 31 and Saturday, April 8.

8. Please put these items on your shopping list milk, vitamins, sandwich bread, sliced turkey, and orange juice.

9. You must be at the designated bus stops on time buses will leave promptly at the following times 330, 345, 400, 415, and 500 P.M.

10. This year, in addition to English, math, and history, my schedule includes the following classes Spanish II, earth science, and band.

COMMON ERRORS

Quotation Marks and Other Punctuation A

EXERCISE   On the lines provided, rewrite each of the following sentences, inserting quotation marks, commas, and end marks where necessary. Also, make any necessary changes in capitalization.

Example 1. Does anyone Sam asked know the words to The Star-Spangled Banner

"Does anyone," Sam asked, "know the words to 'The Star-Spangled Banner'?"

1. My favorite part of the movie Karen said was the surprise ending _____

_____

2. Natalie, Sherman asked did Celia speak to you yet _____

_____

3. She runs fast, Natalie replied she can always beat me. _____

_____

4. One of the lines is On the eighteenth of April in '75 said Paul. _____

_____

5. The sign says abierto, which means open said Miguel. _____

_____

6. Peter told Cam, the swim meet has been postponed a week _____

_____

7. Did you hear, Micah asked Celie that I won the raffle _____

_____

8. That's great news! Ruth said. the weather will be perfect. _____

_____

9. At my house, we're not allowed to say Yuck! about any food, said Tim _____

_____

10. Which chapter is better, Planting Flowers or Garden Care _____

_____

Quotation Marks and Other Punctuation B

EXERCISE A   For each of the following sentences, add single and double quotation marks where necessary.

Example 1. "I have memorized 'Macavity: the Mystery Cat,' by T. S. Eliot," Teresa said.

1. Is Oklahoma! from the musical *Oklahoma!* also the state song of Oklahoma?

2. I left a message on Mother's voice mail, Jane said, but I forgot to ask her about lunch.

3. Did Tonya say, Let's leave early? Sean asked.

4. Mason stared at the old house. I wonder who lives there, he said.

5. Leatha said, Mary told me, Martha was not a bit upset when she didn't win first place.

EXERCISE B   For each of the following sentences, add underlining to any words that should be italicized, and insert hyphens, dashes, and parentheses where necessary. Use a caret (∧) to show where a dash should be inserted.

Example 1. I was able to find the reference works I needed∧an unabridged dictionary and

several handbooks for writers∧at the public library.

6. If one fourth five out of twenty of the class has the flu, what percent will be out?

7. Is vacuum a word derived from Latin the only English word that has two u's in a row?

8. We knew as soon as we saw her although we had never met her in person that the woman in

the wild orange and purple hat must be Dad's great aunt Clarissa.

9. He is, well, a "guitar picking, blues singing, church going" kind of man.

10. Sandra read the book Raindrops and Teardrops.

Apostrophes

EXERCISE In each of the following sentences, insert apostrophes where necessary.

Example 1. Carmen's uncle's bicycle is in the shop; one of its wheel rims was bent when he ran into the curb.

1. We wouldve arrived in Chicago much sooner, but four hours delay at the Atlanta airport caused us to miss our connection.

2. This afternoons meeting will be brief; well discuss next weeks dance.

3. William should catch a ride with Daniel and Nicks father.

4. The Ashes cats names are Tinker and Bella; theyre treated like members of the family.

5. In my opinion, youve overused !s in your writing.

6. The performance begins promptly at eight o clock; please dont be late or youll have to stand at the back of the theater until intermission.

7. From 95 until the end of 98, my family lived in San Diego at my aunts house.

8. Last summers heat wave was extraordinary; some of Uncle Teds crops died.

9. Im going to shop around before I buy a jacket; Id like to get my moneys worth.

10. Did you hear that someones gold earrings were found in the restaurant?

11. My parents store closed in 1990.

12. This sleeves cuff is frayed and the collars too tight.

13. Whats the name of the man whose sons car was involved in the accident?

14. After a long days hike, well reach the river, where well set up camp and get a good nights rest.

15. Tesss canaries cage needs cleaning; I hope shell do that right after school.

16. Each players moves were carefully planned; neither disturbed the others composure.

17. Whos interested in seeing the two o clock show?

18. Isnt Doriss van large enough to carry everyones equipment?

19. The Camera Clubs posters inspired six new students to attend its meeting.

20. Lenas aquarium has a pump and filter to supply her fishs oxygen needs.

Punctuation Review

EXERCISE In the following letter, add necessary end marks, commas, semicolons, colons, apostrophes, hyphens, dashes, parentheses, and quotation marks. Underline any words that should be italicized.

Example [1] The game was scheduled for 7:00; however, it was postponed because of the rain.

[1] 302 B East Twenty third Avenue

[2] Dry Lake CA 93546

[3] May 3 2001

[4] Action Photo Magazine

    3201 Fleet Street

    Winston CO 80308

[5] Dear Sir or Madam

    [6] Ive been a reader and an admirer of your magazine ever since I received my first camera in 1996 I believe on my tenth birthday [7] When I saw the title of your contest Super Action Sports Shots I knew I had to enter [8] Please find enclosed the following items the required entry form two slides of my entry one glossy print and a statement of authenticity

    [9] As you can see from the print the picture I am submitting has all the elements for which Action Photo Magazine is known bright colors a balanced composition and most importantly action [10] The photographs subject a bicycle and its rider flying upside down through the air is Im sure you will agree eye catching [11] Im happy to inform you that my brother his name is Eli and he is only nine received only slight bruises upon landing however I cannot say the same for the bicycle [12] The people in the lower left hand corner of the photograph were never in any danger I assure you [13] Isnt it an amazing picture

    [14] This was a spur of the moment shot Im thankful I had my camera ready [15] My brother was riding too fast and simply did not see the dip in the trail [16] How I wish Id been able to capture the expression on his face as he and his bike became airborne [17] The one good result of this incident in addition to a great photograph of course is that my brother really understands the importance of a helmet [18] Better safe than sorry is now his motto

    [19] Thank you for considering my entry and for making Action Photo Magazine the worlds best photography magazine

[20] Sincerely

Cynthia Humphries

Spelling A

EXERCISE A   In each of the following sentences, two words are underlined. If an underlined word is misspelled, write the word correctly above the misspelled word. Write *C* above the correctly spelled underlined words.

> *conceded*
> **Example 1.** At the end of her interview with the police officer, the girl conceeded that she had
>   *C*
>   been driving too fast.

1. I sometimes baby-sit for our neighbor, whose children can be quite mischievous.

2. A good night's sleep before a big game is absolutely essential for me to sucede.

3. I received two separate forms for the foriegn language club.

4. The announcment is that Mrs. Goldstein has planned a class trip to the Greek art exhibit.

5. I admire Nelson Mandela's determination to act on his believes.

6. Dad read a business article about how to acheive success.

7. We would truly enjoy eating some of your prize tomatos.

8. I have neither the desire nor the courage for a weird sport like bungee jumping.

9. Occasionally, the government offices are closed on that day.

10. Ricardo finally payed all of his bills.

EXERCISE B   In each of the following sentences, cross out any misspelled word and write the word correctly above the misspelled word.

> *likeness*   *really*
> **Example 1.** His ~~likness~~ to his grandfather wasn't ~~realy~~ apparent.

11. The soprano's soloes were excelent.

12. Although he came in 3rd, he knew he had tryed his very best.

13. Autumn, when the leafs begin to change color, is becomeing my favorite season.

14. Have you past the thorough physical exam required to join the baseball team?

15. My teacher takes off 5 points for each mispelled word.

16. Watching the whether forecast is a senseible thing to do.

17. When the floodwaters receed, we'll return the ponys to thier stalls.

18. I think we can all agree that the heros in the play behaved irationally.

19. If these analysis are correct, we can expect erratic weather patterns for the next few years.

20. Megan's neice had the flu; she had to forfiet the match.

Spelling B

EXERCISE A In each of the following sentences, cross out any misspelled word and write the word correctly above it.

Example 1. After the children finished ~~dying~~ *dyeing* the eggs, they left them on the table to dry.

1. What does "Mind you're *p*s and *q*s" mean?

2. He was satisfyed with the grade he'd gotten on the test, but he knew he should have spent more time prepareing and studying.

3. I watched as the feild mouse escaped from the clutchs of the hawk.

4. Her behavior was more than mischeivous; I would call it decietful.

5. These datas are incomplete; we'd better run the experiment one more time.

6. My great-uncle, who served in two wars during the twentyeth century, lived to be ninty-nine years old.

7. The celloes are still not comeing in at the right time.

8. Although we weighed the baby twice, we did not beleive the result.

9. My neice asked if the hotel would accommodate us.

10. The amount of homework we have is usually managable, but occasionally we have too much.

EXERCISE B On the lines provided, write the plural form of each of the following words.

Example 1. alley _____*alleys*_____

11. hoof _____
12. phenomenon _____
13. brother-in-law _____
14. thief _____
15. deer _____
16. Kelly _____
17. technicality _____
18. tax _____
19. ally _____
20. cargo _____

21. quiz _____
22. ox _____
23. success _____
24. crisis _____
25. *B* _____
26. ten-year-old _____
27. Balinese _____
28. fly _____
29. index _____
30. *and* _____

COMMON ERRORS

Words Often Confused

EXERCISE A In each of the following sentences, underline the correct word or words in parentheses.

Example 1. The Texas (*capitol*, *capital*) is on Congress Avenue in Austin; (*it's*, *its*) dome is

magnificent.

1. I just bought these skates, and one of them is (*all ready*, *already*) broken.

2. To raise (*capital*, *capitol*) a business may seek investors or, of (*course*, *coarse*), issue stock.

3. The best (*advice*, *advise*) I can give you is to get good legal (*counsel*, *council*).

4. She was (*formally*, *formerly*) employed at a large accounting firm, but now she is (*quiet*, *quite*)

happy working for herself.

5. The (*led*, *lead*) in these pencils has a tendency to (*brake*, *break*).

6. Some novels (*effect*, *affect*) me more (*then*, *than*) others do.

7. The (*course*, *coarse*) gravel beneath our bare feet felt (*all together*, *altogether*) unpleasant.

8. When he (*past*, *passed*) me, I saw that he had (*altered*, *altared*) his appearance.

9. Don't (*lose*, *loose*) (*you're*, *your*) ticket!

10. As she grew (*weak*, *week*), her (*moral*, *morale*) plummeted.

EXERCISE B In each of the following sentences, cross out any incorrect word and write the correct word above it. If all the words in a sentence are correct, write *C* after the sentence.

Example 1. The tourists had an appointment to meet with their nation's ~~counsel.~~ *consul*

11. After many years have past, the affects of sun on you're skin become apparent.

12. A peace of the screen on the door is lose.

13. The principal reason the company ran that ad was to attract attention.

14. He has been riding a stationery bicycle at the advise of his doctor.

15. Remembering my manners, I formerly introduced my friends to my grandmother.

16. The plane truth is that I don't want to go hiking in the dessert.

17. You want to reach the bottom of that hill in one piece; check your breaks carefully.

18. What kind of vegetable will best compliment this fish?

19. There sure they're first-aid course will be quite useful.

20. After the party, we through away the paper tablecloths.

Spelling and Words Often Confused

EXERCISE In the following memorandum, cross out each misspelled or misused word and write the correct spelling or word above the incorrect word.

Example [1] One of the ~~nineth~~ *ninth*-grade homerooms has ~~all ready~~ *already* delivered ~~it's~~ *its* recommendations to

the main office.

[1] February seventeenth, 2002

[2] To: Dr. Jasmine Ringgold, Principle

[3] From: Mr. Nielson's class, room three hundred fifty–two

[4] Subject: Improveing the cafeteria situation

[5] We are writing to let you know that the situation in the cafeteria is becomeing all together

unbearable. [6] As you know, most nineth-graders eat during the first lunch period. [7] By the

time we go threw the serving line, we have about ten minutes to eat. [8] In addition, the cafeteria

is quiet crowded; there simpley aren't enough seats to accommodate everyone at one time.

[9] Finally, the cafeteria is so noisey that we can hardly here announcements or eat our lunchs in

piece.

[10] Of coarse, we know your aware of these problems, and we are responding to your request

for suggestions. [11] First, to alleviate the overcrowding, allow the freshman class to eat in the

courtyard, as we were formally permited to do. [12] Second, set up too serveing lines. [13] We

waist most of our all ready breif lunch period waiting in line. [14] Its difficult to eat lunch in the

little time left. [15] Last, soothing music in the cafeteria might have an affect on the noise levels.

[16] Everyone needs a brake during a busy day. [17] We beleive these changes would improve

student moral and make cafeteria service more efficient and convenient.

[18] Other class's have similar problems during there lunch periods, two. [19] Therefore, we

have made a copy of this advise for the student counsel, which will consider the problem at it's

next meeting.

[20] Thank you for the opportunity to share our ideas for improving the school.

COMMON ERRORS

Review A: **Usage**

EXERCISE A Most of the following sentences contain an error in subject-verb or pronoun-antecedent agreement. Cross out any incorrect verb or pronoun form and write the correct form above it. If a sentence is correct, write *C* after it.

Example 1. Each of the members of the girls' volleyball team ~~have~~ brought money for ~~their~~ *her* uniform. *has*

1. Neither Randall nor Mike remembered to bring their toothbrush.

2. Most of Borneo, the third-largest island in the world, is covered by jungle and rain forest.

3. Most of the aluminum and steel cans was sorted for the recycling drive.

4. That statue is one of my grandmother's treasures; please dust her carefully.

5. This new chess set was a present from my father, who gave them to me for my birthday.

EXERCISE B On the lines provided, rewrite each of the following sentences, correcting any errors in the use of modifiers. You may need to rearrange or add words to make the meaning of a sentence clear.

Example 1. Flying through the moonlit sky, we saw a huge owl last night. *Last night, we saw a huge owl flying through the moonlit sky.*

6. Of all the movies I've ever seen, I believe I enjoyed that one more. _____

_____

7. The girl sat on a log near the fire, who had fallen into the pond. _____

_____

8. Lying on our backs under the old oak tree, the sun set behind the hill. _____

_____

9. We repaired the fence with a new board that was broken and sagging. _____

_____

10. Geography was probably my most hardest subject last year. _____

_____

Review B: Mechanics

EXERCISE On the lines provided, rewrite each of the following sentences, using capitalization and punctuation where needed and correcting any misspelled or incorrect words. Underline words that should be italicized.

Example 1. philomena wants to buy a basic cookbook I recomended *Joy of cooking* to her

Philomena wants to buy a basic cookbook; I recommended Joy of Cooking to her.

1. no said Tyrone my little brother I dont want to take a nap _____

_____

2. the magicians nephew is my favorite book in the series the chronicles of narnia by c s lewis __

_____

3. watch out yelled simon that bicyclist didnt yeild the right of way at that intersection _____

_____

4. Ive heard that music somewhere before was it used in the soundtrack of a movie _____

_____

5. what a detailed map marcys sister has drawn _____

_____

6. They try to get up at 630 A.M. every morning but their still late to school sometimes _____

_____

7. My uncles phil and dave they are my mothers brothers own a landscaping service _____

_____

8. Unfortunatly the actors and actresss costumes wont be finished until tomorrow _____

_____

9. I beleive one of our nieghbors sons will be at home when the delivery truck arrives _____

_____

10. Sarah began in conclusion ladies and gentlemen er I seem to have lost my place _____

_____

Review C: **Usage and Mechanics**

EXERCISE In the following letter, most of the punctuation and capitalization has been omitted. In addition, the writer has made errors in usage and spelling. Add appropriate punctuation marks, and circle any letters that should be capitalized. Cross out any errors in usage or spelling, and write the correction above the word.

Example [1] "David," my father began, "don't you think it's about time you wrote ⓖrandma Ⓢnyder a letter?"

[1] november 11 2001

[2] dear grandma

[3] I know i havent writen in quiet a few months but life have been very busy and hectic [4] this year my coarses are much more difficulter than it was last year [5] Im taking the following biology I which also has a separate lab period geometry english spanish II and pe [6] for my electives Ive chose choir and keyboard skills [7] I have so much homework that I dont hardly have no free time [8] Im not really complainning do I sound like I am because most of the subject Im taking is interesting to me [9] In addition I still play baseball and take guitar lessons too days a week as you can see its kind of a full schedule

[10] how have you been [11] did nicky ever have its puppys [12] did uncle charlie fix that gate for you I apologize again for driveing the tractor threw it or do it still have a lose hinge [13] next summer I promise ill be more careful

[14] I miss those big breakfasts you use to fix for me eggs oatmeal milk and juice [15] my eating habits has improved since I come home I dont skip breakfast no more [16] As mom always says the car wont run without gas in the tank

[17] Oops I almost forgot to thank you for the sweater you knit me for my birthday [18] Its beautiful and it fits more better then the one I buyed at the store

[19] I have to be in bed by 1030 P.M. so ill sign off now

[20] love from your most youngest grandson

Dave

Proofreading Application: Letter

Good writers are generally good proofreaders. Readers tend to admire and trust writing that is error-free. Make sure that you correct all errors in grammar, usage, spelling, and punctuation in your writing. Your readers will have more confidence in your words if you have done your best to proofread carefully.

Errors are stumbling blocks to your reader. They make writing hard to understand. Avoiding errors is especially important when you are writing to a person who may not have a full command of the English language. Letters to children or to people who are learning English should be especially clear and easy to understand. Be courteous; proofread these letters very carefully.

PROOFREADING ACTIVITY

In the following letter to a nonnative speaker of English, find the common errors in usage and mechanics and correct them using the proofreading symbols such as those on page 901 of *Elements of Language.* You may need to rewrite some sentences. If a numbered item is correct, write *C* above it.

Example **[1]** Dear Gretchen:

---

  [1] Hi! I'm Wendy. Me and my family are so happy that you are coming to stay with us. **[2]** I'll tell you a little about our home. **[3]** You'll be sharing a room with my sister Tara and I. **[4]** Don't worry; its a big yellow room, and there's plenty of space for everyone. **[5]** You're bed is right by a window, so you can see the street. **[6]** The school that you will be attending. Only five blocks from our house, so we will walk to school together in the morning. **[7]** We have a black and white dog named Patches, our cat is named Peanut. **[8]** They are very freindly and like everyone. **[9]** Well, actually Peanut likes everyone accept Uncle Ed. **[10]** Write to us soon, and tell us when you will arrive so that we can meet you at the airport! Everyone can't hardly wait to see you!.

Sincerely,

Wendy Days

Grammar, Usage, and Mechanics: Language Skills Practice   **407**

Literary Model: Sentence Fragments in a Description

> The black stove, stoked with coal and firewood, glows like a lighted pumpkin. Eggbeaters whirl, spoons spin round in bowls of butter and sugar, vanilla sweetens the air, ginger spices it; melting, nose-tingling odors saturate the kitchen, suffuse the house, drift out to the world on puffs of chimney smoke. In four days the work is done. Thirty-one cakes, dampened with whiskey, bask on window sills and shelves.
>
> Who are they for?
>
> Friends. Not necessarily neighbor friends: Indeed, the larger share are intended for persons we've met maybe once, perhaps not at all. People who've struck our fancy. Like President Roosevelt. Like the Reverend and Mrs. J. C. Lucey, Baptist missionaries to Borneo who lectured here last winter. Or the little knife grinder who comes through town twice a year. . . . Or the Young Wistons, a California couple whose car one afternoon broke down outside the house and who spent a pleasant hour chatting with us on the porch (young Mr. Wiston snapped our picture, the only one we've ever had taken). Is it because my friend is shy with everyone *except* strangers that these strangers, and merest acquaintances, seem to us our truest friends? I think yes. Also, the scrapbooks we keep of thank-you's on White House stationery, time-to-time communications from California and Borneo, the knife grinder's penny postcards, make us feel connected to eventful worlds beyond the kitchen with its views of a sky that stops.
>
> —from "A Christmas Memory" by Truman Capote

EXERCISE A   Truman Capote's description of the people to whom Buddy (the narrator) and his friend send Christmas fruitcakes is written mostly in sentence fragments. In the passage above, underline all the sentence fragments.

EXERCISE B

1. Why do you think Capote uses sentence fragments rather than complete sentences in this passage?

_____

_____

2. If the passage were rewritten to include only complete sentences, how would it sound different?

_____

_____

Literary Model (continued)

EXERCISE C   Write a brief description of your own or an imaginary character's preparations for a holiday or celebration. Experiment with using sentence fragments in your description.

_____

_____

_____

_____

_____

_____

_____

_____

_____

_____

_____

EXERCISE D

1. Look back over your passage. What sentence fragments did you use?

_____

_____

_____

_____

_____

2. How did the sentence fragments you used affect the tone, voice, and style of the description?

_____

_____

_____

_____

_____

for **CHAPTER 28: CORRECTING COMMON ERRORS** | *pages 320–756*

Writing Application: Pamphlet

Good writers do not capitalize words arbitrarily. They capitalize them as an indication to the reader that they are referring to a title; starting a new sentence; or referring to a specific person, place, or thing. In some cases, whether a word is capitalized or not changes the meaning of a sentence. Compare these sentences:

Spend some time at hot springs before leaving Arkansas.

Spend some time at Hot Springs before leaving Arkansas.

WRITING ACTIVITY

Have you ever heard people lamenting that the only time they visit places of interest in their own town or city is when they're taking out-of-town guests there? Many of us are more familiar with the special attractions and areas of a city five hundred miles away than with those close to our own backyard. You've decided to get to know your town or city much better so that you'll be the perfect guide the next time your relatives come to visit. You're going to take a real or imaginary tour through parts of your town or city and jot down notes about your route and what you see. Then, you'll use these notes to create a pamphlet about your discoveries that your future visitors can enjoy. Since you'll be mentioning the names of buildings, sites, and perhaps historical figures, remember to capitalize all proper nouns and titles as needed.

PREWRITING Decide how you will arrange your ideas. You may prefer to think in spatial terms—for example, beginning with places of interest in the southern part of the city and ending with places in the northern part. Alternatively, you may want to use a logical order, according to which you might categorize outdoor places, historical places, and special places for children. In addition to the arrangement of ideas, determine the tone you will adopt. The tone you use will influence your choice of words and sentence structure.

WRITING Using your notes and keeping in mind the arrangement of ideas and tone you have chosen, begin your draft. Write freely while still expressing your ideas clearly. Enhance your draft by adding sensory details that will bring to life for your reader each place of interest you're describing. As you write, visualize how the text will appear in the pamphlet.

REVISING Have a classmate read your draft of the pamphlet text. Ask him or her to imagine being an out-of-town visitor and to answer this question: Would these descriptions, intended for a pamphlet, make you want to visit these places of interest? Encourage your classmate to give you suggestions about how to further enliven the writing.

PUBLISHING As you proofread your draft, pay special attention to capitalization. Consult a dictionary if you're not sure whether to capitalize a word. Since your pamphlet is intended for people unfamiliar with the places you've mentioned, carefully check the spelling of the place names. You may choose to add pictures to your pamphlet. Make copies of the final product and pass them out to the class.

EXTENDING YOUR WRITING

Perhaps you could create a pamphlet using the text you've written and graphics generated by a software program. You could then collect your classmates' pamphlets and present them to the local chamber of commerce.